D1551319

KURBSKY'S
HISTORY OF IVAN IV

PRINCE
A. M. KURBSKY'S
HISTORY OF
IVAN IV

EDITED WITH

A TRANSLATION AND NOTES

BY

J. L. I. FENNELL, M.A., Ph.D.

Fellow of University College, Oxford

CAMBRIDGE

AT THE UNIVERSITY PRESS

1965

CAMBRIDGE UNIVERSITY PRESS
Cambridge, New York, Melbourne, Madrid, Cape Town, Singapore, São Paulo, Delhi

Cambridge University Press
The Edinburgh Building, Cambridge CB2 8RU, UK

Published in the United States of America by Cambridge University Press, New York

www.cambridge.org
Information on this title: www.cambridge.org/9780521055017

First published 1965
This digitally printed version 2008

A catalogue record for this publication is available from the British Library

ISBN 978-0-521-05501-7 hardback
ISBN 978-0-521-08842-8 paperback

CONTENTS

INTRODUCTION

The *History of the Grand Prince of Moscow* by Prince Andrey Mikhaylovich Kurbsky, which describes events in the reign of Ivan IV from 1533 to the early 1570's, is the first attempt at a historical monograph in Russian. It was probably written in, or completed by, the summer of 1573,[1] nine years after Kurbsky had deserted from Muscovy to Poland–Lithuania. Yet in spite of this considerable time-lag, many of the details of the first thirty years of Ivan's life still remained fresh in Kurbsky's memory and he was able to give a vivid and at times revealing picture of the first half of the tsar's reign. The period of repression—from 1564 to 1573—is, of course, described from hearsay, and, as might be expected, is in places repetitive and unimaginative (see, for instance, the hackneyed descriptions of the moral virtues of most of the tsar's victims).

As a historical source, Kurbsky's *History* must be treated with extreme caution. Firstly, it is essential to bear in mind Kurbsky's probable purpose in writing the work—namely to blacken the character of the tsar in the eyes of his Polish–Lithuanian and Russian readers (perhaps even to damage his chances as candidate for the Polish throne in 1573), posthumously to immortalize those "martyrs" who had suffered at the hands of the "tormentor", and to glorify and exonerate the two figureheads of the fifties, Adashev and Sil'vestr, whom he looked upon, albeit erroneously, as his ideological partisans, if only

---

[1] Such is the opinion of the Soviet historian, A. A. Zimin (A. A. Zimin, *Kogda Kurbsky napisal*). Convincing as Zimin's views are, it must be pointed out that Kurbsky mentions two incidents which occurred *after* 1573 (Khabarov's execution, 1581, and Archbishop Leonid's execution, 1575, see below, pp. 211, 247). It should also be borne in mind that there is a striking similarity between Kurbsky's last three letters to Ivan, all written after 1578, and certain passages in the *History*. While it is possible that Kurbsky quoted from his *History* five or six years later, it would seem more probable that the letters and those passages of the *History* which are similar were written more or less at the same time.

because the tsar had previously lumped them together with Kurbsky and the boyars.[1] Secondly, it must be remembered that Kurbsky himself was not the best informed of historians. In the first half of his life his career, to judge from the only sources to mention him (the *razryady* and the chronicles), was confined to the army. The offspring of a junior branch of the appanage princes of Yaroslavl', he appears to have been almost exclusively engaged in military affairs from the first mention of him as a minor commander in 1550 to 1564 when he defected. If he enjoyed any popularity or influence at court, it was only due to a tenuous relationship on his mother's side with the tsaritsa Anastasia. We have no indication (apart from Kurbsky's own assurances) that he was *persona grata* with the tsar or that he had anything to do with the political administration of the State during the years of the great reforms (the 1550's), the heyday of his posthumously glorified heroes, Adashev and Sil'vestr. True he was appointed boyar in 1556, in other words he was made a member of the Boyar Council, the body of advisers whom the tsar consulted, in theory at least, on matters of home and foreign policy. But shortly after this the Livonian war began, and from 1558 to 1564 we find him again on almost permanent active service, fighting Livonians and Lithuanians and away from the intrigues of the Muscovite court.

And yet for all Kurbsky's tendentiousness, for all his unreliability as a witness, for all his probable ignorance of affairs of state, his *History* is of capital importance to the modern historian. Firstly, it gives us a strangely true and sober picture of the age which often serves as a corrective to the more sensational descriptions given by foreigners, such as Taube, Kruse and Schlichting. Even though the writing may at times appear hackneyed and unsubtle—especially in the delineation of character—nevertheless Kurbsky's *History* impresses the reader with its immediacy. It is the work of a contemporary, of a true

---

[1] It is interesting to note that Kurbsky himself made no mention of either Adashev or Sil'vestr in his first and second letters to Ivan. It is only in his last three letters (written 1578 and 1579) and in his *History* that Kurbsky took up the cudgels on behalf of the "blessed Sil'vestr" and the "angelic Adashev", after Ivan in his two letters to Kurbsky had virtually portrayed them as the ringleaders of the aristocratic opposition.

Muscovite: Kurbsky's Muscovy is Muscovy described by a Muscovite. Secondly, it provides the modern historian with a large amount of factual detail, particularly as regards the lists of Ivan's political victims: indeed much of his information can often be used as an additional check to other sources and in many cases it fills in useful gaps in our knowledge. Thirdly, Kurbsky's *History* is invaluable for the light it throws on certain episodes in Ivan's reign of which Kurbsky had expert knowledge, such as the capture of Kazan' and the Livonian war, or on individuals whom Kurbsky knew personally, such as Feodorit the Enlightener of the Lapps. But above all the *History* is important as a document written by a representative of the boyar aristocracy, an opponent of autocracy, a conservative with a hankering after a return to the good old days of "appanage freedom". Indeed one might say that the historian today can learn most from the very tendentiousness of the work. Even when distorting facts, Kurbsky sheds light on his viewpoint and on the viewpoint of that section of the community he professed to represent—the conservative opposition to the tsar.

In spite of the importance of the work, no edition has been undertaken since 1914 when the Imperial Archaeographical Committee edited the main bulk of Kurbsky's writings in Volume XXXI of the Russian Historical Library (*RIB*). Before this, the only complete edition of the *History* was undertaken by N. G. Ustryalov (three editions: 1833, 1842 and 1868). No translation of the *History* into English (or into any other language, as far as I know) has ever been published before. The present edition is designed as a companion volume to the *Correspondence between Prince A. M. Kurbsky and Tsar Ivan IV of Russia 1564–1579* (C.U.P., 1955).

I have based the Russian text entirely on that of the 1914 edition of Kurbsky's works (*RIB*, vol. XXXI), in which four MSS., all of the late seventeenth century, were used for the *History*. Variants in the critical apparatus of this book are only given when the basic text (Ar.) is clearly at fault or where I have considered other readings of importance for the understanding of the text (for abbreviations in the critical apparatus, see below, p. xi). The orthography has been modernized (i.e.

ѣ replaced by *e*, *i* by *u*, θ by *ф*, and final ъ omitted; *й* has been substituted for *u*, where necessary, to conform to modern usage).

As for the question of transliteration, I have used the "British" system of latinization advocated by the *Slavonic and East European Review* (see W. K. Matthews, *The Latinisation of Cyrillic Characters, SEER,* vol. xxx, no. 75 (June 1952), pp. 531–49); I have made one or two minor exceptions to this system: (i) *e* and *ё* are always transliterated *e* (thus *Elena*, and not *Yelena*); (ii) the endings -*ый* and -*uй* are always rendered by -*y* (*Kurbsky, posluzhny,* etc.); (iii) the "soft sign", the letter ь, is rendered by an apostrophe (*Yaroslavl'*); (iv) in the spelling of feminine names ending in -*iya*, the spelling -*ia* has been used throughout (*Solomonia, Maria*). As for place-names, where two or more versions of a particular place exist, I have kept as close as possible to Kurbsky's usage (e.g. Derpt, rather than Russian Yur'ev or Estonian Tartu), indicating in brackets the other versions where I consider it helpful or necessary.

There are two glossaries at the end of the book—one of Russian words which are borrowed from foreign languages, mainly Polish, and which are not, for the most part, to be found in Sreznevsky's dictionary; the other of common words of Russian, Tatar, Polish or Greek origin which have been used for convenience in the translation or the footnotes.

In conclusion I would like to thank the Syndics of the Cambridge University Press for their assistance in the publication of this book and those of my colleagues in this country who have helped me with various problems, especially Dr G. L. Lewis, Professor B. O. Unbegaun and Mr J. S. G. Simmons of Oxford University, and Dr L. Lewitter and Dr T. Armstrong of Cambridge University.

J. L. I. F.

OXFORD
1963

LIST OF ABBREVIATIONS

I. ABBREVIATIONS OF COPIES OF TEXT USED IN CRITICAL APPARATUS OF THIS EDITION

Ar.   Rukopis' Tsentral'nogo Gosudarstvennogo arkhiva drevnikh aktov v Moskve, fond No. 181, delo No. 60.

Patr.   Rukopis' Gosudarstvennogo istoricheskogo muzeya, (Sinodal'noy (Patriarshey) biblioteki), No. 136.

Pog.   Rukopis' Rukopisnogo otdela Gosudarstvennoy publichnoy biblioteki imeni M. E. Saltykova-Shchedrina, Pogodinskoe Sobranie, No. 1494.

T.   Sobranie N. S. Tikhonravova, No. 636.

II. ABBREVIATIONS OF WORKS CITED

(for full details see List of Works cited, pp. 302–4)

Chteniya   *Chteniya v imperatorskom obschchestve istorii i drevnosti.*

Correspondence   Fennell. *Correspondence between Prince A. M. Kurbsky and Tsar Ivan IV of Russia.*

DRK   *Drevneyshaya Razryadnaya Kniga.*

DRV   *Drevnyaya rossiyskaya vivliofika.*

IZ   *Istoricheskie zapiski.*

NL   *Novgorodskie letopisi.*

Ocherki   Smirnov. *Ocherki politicheskoy istorii Russkogo gosudarstva 30–50-x godov XVI v.*

PG   Migne. *Patrologiae cursus completus.*

PL   *Pskovskie letopisi.*

PSRL   *Polnoe sobranie russkikh letopisey.*

RIB   *Russkaya istoricheskaya biblioteka.*

RMC   Herberstein. *Rerum Moscoviticarum Commentarii.*

SEER   *Slavonic and East European Review.*

Sinodik   Veselovsky. *Sinodik opal'nykh tsarya Ivana.*

TODRL   *Trudy otdela drevnerusskoy literatury.*

VP   Bazilevich. *Vneshnyaya politika Russkogo tsentralizovannogo gosudarstva.*

HISTORY OF THE
GRAND PRINCE OF MOSCOW

I

История о великом князе Московском, еже слышахом у достоверных, и еже видехом очима нашима, сие сокращенне вмещаючи, елико возмогох, написах прилежнаго ради стужания от многих.[a]

Много крат ото многих светлых мужей вопрошаем бых, с великим стужанием: "Откуды сия приключишася, так прежде доброму и нарочитому царю, многажды за отечество и о здравии своем не радяшу, и в военных[b] вещах, сопротив врагов креста Христова, труды тяжкие, и беды, и безчисленные поты претерпевающу, и прежде от всех добрую славу имущему?" И многажды умолчах со воздыханием и слезами, не восходех отвещати; последи же, частых ради вопрошений, принужден бых нечто рещи отчасти о случаех, приключьшихъся таковых, и отвещах им: аще бы из начала и по ряду рех, много бы о том писати, яко в предобрый Русских князей род всеял диявол злые нравы, наипаче же женами их злыми и чародейцами, яко и во Израильтеских царех, паче же которых поимовали от иноплеменников. Но сия вся оставя, нечто изреку о том самом настоящем.

Яко глаголют многие премудрые: "доброму началу и конец бывает добр"; такожде и сопротив: злое злым скончавается; а наипаче, от самовластнаго человеческаго естества, злым произволением и по всему сопротивным[c] противу Божиих заповедей дерзати. Князь великий Василий Московский ко многим злым и сопротив закона Божия делом своим и сие приложил (иже и писати, и исчитати,

---

[a] Pog. heading omitted in Ar.   [b] Patr., Pog., T. воинн이х: Ar.
[c] T. супротивных: Ar.

---

[1] An undisguised reference to Sofia Palaeologa and Elena Glinsky, wives of Ivan III and Vasily III respectively. Sofia (the grandmother of Ivan IV) was niece of the last Emperor of the East, Constantine XI, and was brought up in Rome. Elena Glinsky, the mother of Ivan IV, was a Lithuanian. As

I

*The History of the Grand Prince of Moscow. That which we
have heard from trustworthy people and that which we have seen
with our eyes I have written down, pertinaciously importuned by
many, abridging it in as far as I was able.*

Many times by many illustrious men I have been asked with
great importunity: "how did these things happen to the tsar
who was formerly so good and distinguished, who many times
for the sake of his fatherland has had no care for his own health
and who in war against the enemies of the cross of Christ suffers
grievous labour and woes and countless toil, and who formerly
enjoyed good renown from all?" And many times I remained
silent, sighing and weeping, for I did not wish to answer. But
afterwards, because of the frequent questions, I was compelled
to say at least something about such occurrences as have
happened, and I answered them: if I were to speak from the
beginning and [to narrate all things] in turn, there would be
too much to write—about how the devil sowed evil habits
among that most excellent clan of Russian princes especially
by means of their evil and sorcerous wives, just as among the
kings of Israel—above all those wives whom they took in
marriage from foreigners.[1] But leaving aside all these things, I
will say something about the present itself.[2]

As many wise men say: "a good beginning has a good end
as well". So too is the opposite true: evil ends with evil—
especially the evil of free human nature defying the commandments of God with evil and altogether hostile intent. Grand
Prince Vasily of Moscow to his many evil deeds committed
against the law of God added this too (the writing and enu-

for Sofia's "sorcery", Kurbsky's accusation, repeated below (see pp. 256–7),
may have originated in the report of one of the chroniclers who stated that
in 1497, after a conspiracy against Ivan III's grandson, Dmitry Ivanovich,
had been brought to light, it was discovered that "women were coming to
her [Sofia] with poisonous herbs". (*PSRL* VI, p. 279; XII, p. 263.)

[2] Or perhaps "about the present prince himself", i.e. Ivan IV.

3 1-2

краткости ради книжицы сея, не вместно, а еже достоит воспомянути, зело вкратце напишем по силе): живши со женою своею первою, Соломаниею, двадесять и шесть лет, остриг ея во мнишество, не хотящу и немыслящу ей о том, и заточил в далечайш монастырь, от Москвы больши двусот миль, в земли Каргапольский лежащь, и затворити казал ребро свое в темницу, зело нужную и уныния исполъненую, сиречь жену, ему Богом данную, святую и неповинную. И понял себе Елену, дщерь Глинского, аще и возбраняющу ему сего беззакония многим святым и преподобным, не токмо мнихом, но и сигклитом его; от нихже един Васьян, пустынник, сродник ему сущь по матери своей, а по отце внук княжати Литовского, Патрикиев, и оставя мирскую славу, в пустыню вселился, и так жестоко и свято житие препровожал во мнишестве, подобне великому и славному древнему Антонию. Да не зазрит[a] кто дерзостне рещи,—

[a] Т. зазрите: Ar.

---

[1] In November 1525 Vasily had his first wife, Solomonia Yur'evna (*née* Saburov) tonsured, "because of the malady of her childlessness" (*PSRL* VIII, p. 271; XIII, p. 45). The chronicler of Pskov explains Vasily's action by his fear of the chaos which would ensue should he die childless and be succeeded by one of his incompetent brothers (*PL* I, p. 103). Vasily had been married to Solomonia 20 years, not 26.

According to the Vologdo–Permsky Chronicle, Solomonia was tonsured in the Rozhdestvensky convent in Moscow and was then sent to the Pokrovsky convent in Suzdal' (*PSRL* XXVI, p. 313). She died there in 1542. Her monastic name was Sofia. According to Herberstein (*RMC*, vol. I, p. 50), she was tonsured in the Pokrovsky convent in Suzdal'. Kurbsky is not the only source to mention Kargopol'; in the sixteenth-century *Postnikovsky letopisets* there is an entry under 1525 which describes how Solomonia, after being tonsured in the Rozhdestvensky convent was sent to Kargopol', where Vasily ordered "a cell to be built in the forest surrounded by wooden palings". She remained there for five years and was then transferred to Suzdal' (see M. N. Tikhomirov, *Zapis'*, p. 279). The convent was probably the Uspensky convent; here Agrippina Fedorovna Chelyadnin, sister of Grand Princess Elena's lover, Ivan Telepnev-Obolensky, and governess of Ivan IV, was made to take the veil by the Shuyskys when they took control of the government in 1538 (*PSRL* XIII, p. 123).

The Russian mile is the equivalent of seven versts, or just under seven and a half kilometres.

4

merating of all these things have not been included in order
that this little book may be kept short; but that which is worthy
of remembrance I will write to the best of my ability and with
great brevity): having lived twenty-six years with his first wife
Solomonia, he made her take the monastic tonsure, though she
neither desired it nor even thought about it, and imprisoned
her in a most distant monastery in the district of Kargopol',
more than two hundred miles from Moscow; and he ordered
his rib, that is to say his holy and innocent wife given to him
by God, to be shut in a dire gloom-filled dungeon.[1] And he
took in marriage Elena, the daughter of Glinsky, even though
this lawless deed was forbidden by many holy and reverend
men, not only monks, but also his counsellors,[2] of whom one,
Vassian, the hermit, being his kinsman on his mother's side,
and on his father's side—the grandson of the Lithuanian prince
Patriky, abandoned the glory of the world and took up his
abode in a hermitage and thus led a harsh and holy life in
monkhood like unto the great and glorious Antony of old.[3] Let

[2] For the word сиглит, see *Correspondence*, p. 9, note 7.
Metropolitan Daniil married Vasily to Elena Glinsky in January 1526
(*PSRL* xiii, p. 45).
[3] Vasily Patrikeev (Vassian, after his tonsure) was in fact the *great-
grandson* of Patriky Narimuntovich, the Lithuanian prince who entered the
service of Vasily I in 1408. His grandmother Maria was Vasily II's sister
and Ivan III's aunt (his mother Evdokia Vladimirovna Khovrin was not
related to the grand princely family). After a distinguished career in the
service of Ivan III, Vasily Patrikeev fell from favour in 1499 together with
his father Ivan Yur'evich, his brother Ivan Mynin Patrikeev and his
brother-in-law Semen Ivanovich Ryapolovsky. The reasons for his disgrace
are not known; "treason" is mentioned by one source. It may be that all
four were involved in the dynastic crisis of 1497-9. Ryapolovsky was
executed, but the three Patrikeevs, thanks to the intervention of the senior
clergy, were spared. Vasily/Vassian was sent to the monastery of St Kirill in
Beloozero; he was later allowed to move to the hermitage of Nil Sorsky, and
eventually to the Simonov monastery in Moscow where he evidently lived
until his trial in 1531.
That Vassian Patrikeev openly rebuked Vasily III may be questioned.
Kurbsky was probably influenced by a description of the second marriage
of Vasily III written by one Païsy of the Ferapontov monastery (*Chteniya*,
1847, No. 8), who states that Vassian, when consulted by Vasily III on the
possibility of a divorce, protested against the illegality of such action and
that as a result he was put on trial together with Maksim the Greek. Vassian

Иоанну Крестителю ревностию уподобился; бо и оный о законопреступном браку царю возбранял, беззаконие творящу. Он в Моисейском, сей же во Евангельском беззаконовал. От мирских сигклитов возбранял ему Семен, реченный Курбский, с роду княжат Смоленских и Ярославских, о немже и о святом жительстве его не токмо тамо Русская земля ведома,ᵃ но и Герберштен, нарочитый муж, цесарский и великий посол, на Москве был и уведал, и в кронице своей свидетельствует, юже Латинским языком, в Медиоламе, в славном граде, будучи, написал.

Он же, предреченный Василий, великий, паче же в прегордости и в лютости, князь, не токмо их не послушал, так великих и нарочитых мужей, но оного блаженнаго Васьяна, по плоти сродника своего, изымав, заточити повелел, и связана святаго мужа, аки злодея, в прегорчайшую темницу, к подобным себе в злости презлых Осифляном, в монастырь их отослал и скорою смертию уморити повелел. Они же, яко лютости его скорые послушницы и во всех злых потаковницы, паче же еще и подражатели, умориша его

ᵃ Той Герберштен приходил два крата к Москве, послом великим от славнаго цесаря христианскаго, Карлуса, о великих делех, или паче, постановляющи мир вечный между царствы христианскими, и вооружающи их и подвизающи сопротив поганом; и аще муж был искусный в шляхетных науках и делех, но в вараварских языцех (глубоких ради их и жестоких обычаев) не возмог сего достохвальнаго дела до конца исправити: in margin of Ar., Pog.; in text of Patr., T.

was clearly not arrested in 1525 nor did he fall from favour until 1531 when he was tried shortly after the second trial of Maksim. Maksim was first put on trial in the beginning of 1525, some ten months before the tonsure of Solomonia.

"Antony" refers to St Antony the Great, the founder of monachism.

The word княжа (pl. княжата), which in sixteenth-century Russian meant "son of a prince" (cf. дети боярские), is used indiscriminately by Kurbsky for "prince". Cf. Polish książę, pl. książęta.

¹ A strange use of the present passive participle ведомый, "known", "well-known".

² A marginal note reads as follows: "This Herberstein came twice to Moscow as great ambassador from the glorious Christian emperor Charles,

no one condemn me for saying boldly—he was like unto John the Baptist in zeal; for the latter too reproved the law-breaking king for his unlawful marriage. He [Herod] transgressed the law of Moses, but this one [Vasily] the law of the Gospel. Of his lay counsellors he was rebuked by Semen Kurbsky, from the kin of the princes of Smolensk and Yaroslavl', about whom and about whose holy way of life not only is the Russian land aware,[1] but also Herberstein, that eminent man, the great ambassador of the emperor, who was in Moscow and learned about it and bears witness to it in his chronicle, which he wrote in the Latin tongue when he was in the glorious city of Milan.[2]

But he, the aforesaid Vasily, the great (especially in pride and ferocity) prince, not only did not listen to them, such great and distinguished men, but he seized that blessed Vassian, his blood-relative, and ordered him to be imprisoned, and having bound the holy man he sent him away like an evil-doer to the direst prison—to those most wicked Josephians, his equals in evil—to their monastery, and he ordered him to be put swiftly to death. And they, quick to obey him in ferocity, to connive at all evil deeds and, still more, to imitate him, killed him in a

concerning matters of great importance, or rather in order to draw up [lit. 'drawing up'] a permanent peace between the Christian kingdoms and to arm them and urge them on against the heathens; and although he was a man skilled in noble arts and affairs he was unable among the barbarian peoples, because of their infernal and cruel practices, to carry this praiseworthy matter to the end."

Baron Sigismund von Herberstein (1486–1566), the distinguished ambassador in the service of the emperor, twice visited Moscow (1517, 1527) on diplomatic missions. His *Rerum Moscoviticarum Commentarii*, a detailed and valuable description of Muscovy during the rule of Vasily III, appeared in Vienna in 1549. Not one of the known editions of his work, however, which could have been available to Kurbsky was printed in Milan.

Herberstein describes the scene of Solomonia's tonsure with considerable pathos; he concludes his description with an uncorroborated report to the effect that Solomonia gave birth to a son shortly after her tonsure. He also describes the ascetic way of life of Semen Kurbsky, the brother of Andrey Kurbsky's grandfather. Semen Kurbsky's main claim to fame, apart from his protest at Vasily's divorce, was his leadership of the great expedition to the northern Ural district (Yugra) in 1499–1500, which he described in some detail to Herberstein. See *PSRL* viii, p. 237; K. V. Bazilevich, *VP*, pp. 403–6; Herberstein, *RMC*, vol. ii, pp. 34, 43.

вскоре. И других святых мужей, овых заточил на смерть, от нихъже един, Максим философ, о немъже напреди повем; а других погубити повелел, ихже имена зде оставлю. А князя Семена ото очей своих отогнал, даже до смерти его. Тогда зачалъся нынешний Иоанн наш, и родилася,[a] в законопреступлению и во сладострастию, лютость, яко рече Иоанн Златоустый в слове о жене злой, емуж начало: днесь нам Иоанново преподобие и Иродова лютость егда возвещалась, смутились и внутренные, сердца вострепетали, зрак помрачился, разум притупился, слух скутался, и протчее. И аще святые великие учители ужасалися, пишуще от мучителей на святых дерзаемые, кольми паче нам грешным подобает ужасатися, таковую трагедию возвещати! Но послушание вьсе преодолевает, паче же стужения, або докучания ради вашего частого. Но и сие к тому злому началу еще возмогло, понеже остался отца своего зело млад, аки дву лет; по немногих летех, и мати ему умре; потом питаша его велицые гордые паны, по их языку боярове, его на свою и детей своих беду, ретящеся друг пред другом, ласкающе и угождающе ему во всяком наслаждению и сладострастию.

[a] Patr., T. родих: Ar. родился: Pog.

---

[1] Vassian Patrikeev was arrested and put on trial in 1531. He was accused of tampering with sacred literature, blasphemy, heresy and probably other things as well (the account of his trial which has survived breaks off in the middle). Evidently Metropolitan Daniil and the senior clergy found him guilty, for he was sent to the monastery of Volokolamsk. He was still alive in 1532 as Vasily III wrote to the abbot in that year with instructions for his custody. He died some time before 1545. See V. Zhmakin, *MD*, p. 250.

The monastery founded by Joseph of Volokolamsk was frequently used during the sixteenth century as a jail for political and religious offenders. Kurbsky's abhorrence of the "Josephians", however, was due to his interpretation of their—or, more specifically, their founder's—philosophy and political views, that particular brand of militant monasticism which he associated with support of autocracy and opposition to the conservative aristocracy.

[2] In Kurbsky's *Novy Margarit*, a compilation consisting mainly of translations of the works of St John Chrysostom and made between 1572 and 1576, there is a section entitled На усекновение святаго Иоана Крестителя,

8

short time.[1] And as for other holy men, some he imprisoned until death (one of these was Maksim the philosopher, about whom I will relate further on); others, whose names I will not mention here, he ordered to be destroyed. And Prince Semen [Kurbsky] he banished, even until his death.

At that time our present Ioann [Ivan] was conceived and ferocity was born in transgression and concupiscence, as John Chrysostom said in his sermon about the evil woman, which begins: "Today, when the virtues of John and the ferocity of Herod were announced to us, our innermost parts were disturbed, our hearts trembled, our vision was dimmed, our mind was blunted, our hearing was dulled",[2] and so forth. And if the great holy teachers were aghast, writing of acts brazenly committed by torturers against the saints, how much more befitting is it for us sinners to be aghast, telling of such tragedy! But obedience overcomes all things, especially in view of your frequent importunity or entreaties. But this too added still further to that evil beginning: he lost his father while very young—when about two years old.[3] After a few years his mother died too; then great proud *pans* (or boyars, in their tongue) brought him up—to their own misfortune and to the misfortune of their children—quarrelling with each other, flattering him and pleasing him in every enjoyment and lust.[4]

где глаголется о злой жене, беседа. This section does in fact correspond, except for the first sentence, to the spurious sermon on the beheading of St John the Baptist (see Migne, *PG*, vol. 59, cols. 485–90), but has very little in common with the passage quoted here by Kurbsky. See F. Liewehr, *Kurbskij's "Novyj Margarit"*, pp. 81–2.

[3] Ivan IV was born on 25 August 1530. Vasily III died on 21 September 1533. Ivan was therefore three at his father's death.

[4] Elena died on 3 April 1538. Shortly afterwards her lover, Telepnev-Obolensky, was arrested. Power was seized by the two Shuysky brothers, Ivan and Vasily Vasil'evich, who released Ivan Fedorovich Bel'sky and Andrey Mikhaylovich Shuysky from prison (they had been arrested by Elena). In October 1538, however, the Shuyskys arrested I. F. Bel'sky, and in the following year removed his supporter Metropolitan Daniil. In 1540 the tables were turned. I. F. Bel'sky was released from prison and "ruled" until January 1542, when Ivan Shuysky again ousted him. For details of the "Time of Troubles" following Elena's death, see *Correspondence*, pp. 73 *sq*.

Егда же начал приходити в возраст, аки лет в дванадесять, и впредь что творил, умолчю иные и иные, обаче же
возвещу сие. Начал первие безсловесных крови проливати,
с стремнин высоких мечюще их, а по их языку с крылец,
або с теремов, тако же и иные многие неподобные дела
творити, являющи хотящее быти немилосердое произволение в себе, яко Соломон глаголет (мудрый, рече, милует
души скотов своих, тако ж и безумный биет их нещадно);
а пестуном ласкающим, попущающе сие и хваляще, на свое
горшее отрока учаще. Егда же уже приходяще к пятому-
надесять лету и вящей, тогда начал человеков ураняти. И
собравши четы юных около себя детей и сродных оных предреченных сигклитов, по стогнам и по торжищам начал на
конех с ними ездити и всенародных человеков, мужей и
жен, бити и грабити, скачюще и бегающе всюду неблагочинне. И воистину, дела разбойнические самые творяше,[a] и
иные злые исполняше, ихже не токмо глаголати излишно,
но и срамно; ласкателем же всем таковое на свою беду
восхваляющим: "О, храбр, глаголюще, будет сей царь и
мужествен!" Егда же прииде к седьмомунадесять лету,
тогда теже прегордые сигклитове начаша подущати[b] его и
мстити им свои недружбы, един против другаго; и первие
убиша мужа пресильнаго, зело храбраго стратига и велико-
родного, иже был с роду княжат Литовских, единоколенен
кролеви Польскому Ягайлу, имянем князь Иван Бельский,
иже не токмо быв мужествен, но и в разуме мног и в священных писаниих в некоторых искусен.

По мале же времени, он же сам повелел убити такожде
благородное едино княжа, имянем Андрея Шуйского, с
роду княжат Суждальских. Потом, аки по двух летех,

---

[a] Pog. творяще: Ar.   [b] Pog., T. порущати: Ar.

---

[1] Or "when he came to the age of about twelve".

[2] Evidently a condescending attempt by Kurbsky to enlighten his ignorant Russian readers by giving as an alternative to the Church Slavonic
стремнины the vernacular крыльца and теремы.

[3] Lit. "showing the merciless will which is going to be...".

[4] Prov. xii. 10, the second half of which reads: "but the mercies of the
wicked are cruel".

But as for what he used to do when he came of age, at about twelve or later,[1] I will be silent on most things; however this I will relate. At first he began to spill the blood of dumb creatures, hurling them from lofty places (in their language: from porches or from the top stories of houses[2]) and to do many other unbefitting things as well, betraying in himself the future merciless will;[3] for, as Solomon says: "a wise man regardeth the life of his beasts; likewise the foolish man beats them unsparingly".[4] But while his tutors flattered him by allowing this and praising him, they taught the child to their own detriment. And when he came to his fifteenth year, he began to harm people. Gathering around him groups of youths and relatives of those above-mentioned counsellors, he rode with them on horseback through the squares and market-places and beat and robbed the common people, men and women, indecorously galloping and racing everywhere. And in truth he committed real acts of brigandage and performed other evil deeds which it is not only unbefitting to relate, but shameful too; and all his flatterers would praise such behaviour, to their own detriment, saying: "O, brave and manly will this tsar be!" But when he came to his seventeenth year, then those same arrogant counsellors began to urge him on and through him to avenge their hostilities, one against the other. And first of all they killed a most powerful man, a very brave general and a man of great stock, who came from the kin of the princes of Lithuania, of the same family as King Jagiello of Poland, Prince Ivan Bel'sky by name, who was not only manly, but was great in intellect and versed in the holy scriptures.[5]

And after a short time he himself ordered a certain noble prince by the name of Andrey Shuysky, from the kin of the princes of Suzdal', to be put to death.[6] Then, after about two

[5] According to the chronicles Ivan Fedorovich Bel'sky was seized in January 1542 (when Ivan was eleven, not seventeen) by a council of boyars "without the knowledge of the grand prince". He was imprisoned in Beloozero and, again without the knowledge of the grand prince, put to death (*PSRL* XIII, pp. 140–1). Bel'sky was the great-great-grandson of Grand Prince Ol'gerd of Lithuania, the father of Jagiello.

[6] Andrey Mikhaylovich Shuysky, the leader of the Shuysky faction, was imprisoned by Elena in 1533 for organizing the rebellion of Yury, the

убил трех великородных мужей: единаго, ближняго сродника своего, рожденнаго с сестры отца его, князя Иоанна Кубенского, яже был у отца его великим земским маршалком; а был родом княжат Смоленских и Ярославских, и муж зело разумный и тихий, в совершенных уже летех; и вкупе побиени с ним предреченные мужие, Феодор и Василий Воронцовы, родом от Немецка языка, а с племени княжат Решских. И тогда же убиен Феодор, глаголемый Невежа, зацный и богатый землянин. А мало пред тем, аки за два лета, удавлен от него князя Богдана сын Трубецкого, в пятинадесяти летех младенец, Михаил имянем, с роду княжат Литовских; и потом, помятамися,[a] того ж лета убиени от него благородные княжата: князь Иоанн Дорогобужский, с роду великих княжат Тверских, и Феодор, единочадый сын князя Иоанна, глаголемаго Овчины, с роду княжат Торуских и Оболенских, яко ягнцы неповинно

[a] Т. помятались: Аг.

---

brother of Vasily III, immediately after the latter's death. Previously he had attempted to "depart" (i.e. to transfer his allegiance) from Vasily to Yury, but without success. He was released after Elena's death in 1538. In 1540, during the short rule of the Bel'skys, he was made governor of Pskov; he returned to power with his second cousin Ivan Vasil'evich Shuysky, after the coup of January 1542 (see *Correspondence*, pp. 76–9). In September 1543 he tried to get rid of Ivan IV's favourite, F. S. Vorontsov. Vorontsov was beaten and arrested, but was saved from death by Metropolitan Makary. It was probably at the latter's instigation that in December 1543 Shuysky was handed over to the keepers of the royal hounds, who murdered him.

[1] Prince Ivan Ivanovich Kubensky (like Kurbsky, a descendant of Fedor Rostislavich, prince of Yaroslavl' and Smolensk) played a leading role in the political intrigues during Ivan IV's minority. He had been given the senior administrative post of *dvoretsky Bol'shogo dvora* by Vasily III (the position of *marshalok zemsky* ascribed to him by Kurbsky was a rank in the Lithuanian administration), a post which he held till his death. After the failure of the conspiracy of Mikhail Glinsky in 1534 he became a member of the Regency Council. Until 1538 he appears to have been on the side of the Shuyskys, but after the fall of the Bel'skys (October 1538) he appears to have turned against the Shuyskys and sided with I. F. Bel'sky, whom he helped to attain power in 1540. In January 1542, however, he was again on the side of the Shuyskys, helping I. V. Shuysky regain control. In September 1543 he

years, he killed three men of great stock: one, a near kinsman, born of the sister of his father, Prince Ioann Kubensky, who had been the great marshal of the land at his father's court; and he was of the kin of the princes of Smolensk and Yaroslavl' and a man of great wisdom and gentleness, already of mature years;[1] and together with him were killed the above-mentioned [sic] men, Fedor and Vasily Vorontsov, born of German stock from the kin of the imperial princes.[2] And then Fedor Nevezha was killed, a distinguished and rich landowner.[3] And shortly before this, about two years earlier, the son of Prince Bogdan Trubetskoy was executed by him, an infant of fifteen years, Mikhail by name, from the kin of the princes of Lithuania. And then, I recall, in the same year the following noble princes were killed by him: Prince Ioann Dorogobuzhsky, from the kin of the grand princes of Tver', and Fedor Ovchina, the only son of Prince Ioann, from the kin of the princes of Torusa and Obolensk, slaughtered in their innocence like lambs, with the

attempted, together with A. M. Shuysky and others, to eliminate Voron-tsov. He was disgraced and arrested in December 1544 on vague charges of treason, but was released six months later. In October 1545 he was disgraced a second time (together with Vorontsov), but the *opala* was removed in December 1545. He was eventually beheaded in July 1546.
The strange vicissitudes of his political career are not easy to explain. I. I. Smirnov considers that his numerous *volte-face* were motivated by his desire to retain his high position and political power in the state (I. I. Smirnov, *Ocherki*, pp. 104 *sq.*). His father, Ivan Semenovich, had married the daughter of Prince Andrey the Elder, Ivan III's brother. Ivan Ivanovich was therefore a second cousin of Ivan IV on his mother's side.
[2] After the fall of the Shuyskys in 1543 (see above, p. 11, note 6) Fedor Semenovich Vorontsov enjoyed considerable power at court and influence over Ivan. In October 1545, however, he was temporarily disgraced together with I. I. Kubensky (see above, p. 12, note 1) "for wrong deeds" (за неправду). In the following year he, Ivan Kubensky and Vasily Mikhaylovich Vorontsov were arrested and executed for alleged complicity in the revolt of fifty Novgorod musketeers (*PSRL* xiii, pp. 448–9). According-ing to a legend the founder of the Vorontsov family was one Prince Shimon Afrikanovich who came to Yaroslav in Kiev from Norway in 1027. Решский is derived from *Reich*.
[3] It is not known who Fedor Nevezha was and when or why he was executed. The chroniclers mention a Fedor Nevezhin who was connected with Russo-Astrakhan' diplomatic relations in 1541 and 1542 (*PSRL* xiii, pp. 137, 142–3).

заколены, еще в самом наусии. Потом, егда начал всякими безчисленными злостьми превосходити, тогда Господь, усмиряющий[a] лютость его, посетил град великий Москву презельным огнем, и так явственне гнев свой навел, аще бы по ряду писати, могла бы повесть целая быти, або книжица; а пред тем, еще во младости его, безчисленными плененьми варварскими, ово от царя Перекопскаго, ово от Татар Нагайских, сиречь Заволских, а наипаче и горши всех, от царя Казанского, сильнаго и можнаго мучителя христианского, (яже подо властию своею имел шесть языков различных), имиже безчисленное и неисповедимое пленение и кровопролитие учинял, так, иже уже было все пусто за осьмнадесять миль до Московского места. Тако же и от Перекопского, або от Крымского царя, и от Нагай вся Резанская земля, аже по самую Оку реку, спустошена; а внутрь человекоугодником, со царем младым, пустошащим и воюющим нещадно отечество. Тогда ж случилось, после того предреченнаго пожару, презельного и воистинну зело страшного, о немъже никто же сумнитця рещи явственный гнев Божий — а что ж тогда бысть?

Бысть возмущение велико всему народу, яко и самому царю утещи от града со своим двором его; и в том возмущению убиен вой[b] его князь Юрий Глинский от всего народа, и дом его весь разграблен; другий[c] же вой его, князь Михаил Глинский, которой был всему злому начальник, утече, и другие человекоугодницы сущие с ним раз-

a Patr. усмиряюща: Ar.   b Т. убиен от вои: Ar.   c Т. другие: Ar.

---

[1] Kurbsky's chronology is at fault here. Although this is the only reference to the execution of Mikhail Bogdanovich Trubetskoy, the others, Ivan Ivanovich Dorogobuzhsky and Fedor Ovchinin-Obolensky, the son of Elena's lover Ivan Telepnev-Obolensky, were executed in January 1547 (*PSRL* xxii, p. 526). The execution of Dorogobuzhsky may have been linked with the removal of Kubensky and Vorontsov in the previous year, as I. P. Chelyadnin-Fedorov, an influential adherent of Kubensky and Vorontsov who was exiled in 1546, was Dorogobuzhsky's stepfather. The Trubetskoys were the descendants of Dmitry of Bryansk, son of Grand Prince Ol'gerd of Lithuania.

first down of manhood still on their cheeks.[1] After that, when he began to surpass himself in all kinds of countless evil deeds, the Lord tempered his ferocity by visiting the great city of Moscow with an exceedingly large fire and thus manifestly inflicted His wrath—if one were to write about it all in turn, there could be a whole story or a small book;[2] but before this, while he was still in his youth, [God visited the land] with countless barbarian conquests, now by the khan [lit. "tsar"] of Perekop,[3] now by the Nogay Tartars, that is to say those from beyond the Volga; but more and worse than all, by the khan of Kazan', the strong and powerful tormenter of Christians, who in his power held six different tribes,[4] by means of which he brought about countless and ineffable conquests and bloodshed so that everything was barren for eighteen miles before the town of Moscow; and also the whole land of Ryazan', right up to the very Oka river, was laid waste by the khan of Perekop, or Crimea, and by the Nogays;[5] while within the country the men-pleasers, together with the young tsar, laid waste and mercilessly ravaged the fatherland. And then occurred, after that above-mentioned exceedingly large and in truth most terrible fire, in which no one will hesitate to discern the manifest wrath of God—but what occurred then?

There was a great tumult of all the people, so that the tsar himself had to run away from the town with his court; and in that tumult his uncle[6] Prince Yury Glinsky was killed by the common people and all his house was plundered; and his other uncle[6] Prince Mikhail Glinsky, who was the author of all evil, ran away, and other men-pleasers who were with him dis-

[2] For the great fire of 1547, see *Correspondence*, pp. 80–3.

[3] I.e. the Crimean Tatars. The isthmus of Perekop joins the Crimea to the mainland.

[4] For a list of these, see below, p. 73.

[5] Between 1535 and 1545 Muscovy was subjected to frequent Tatar raids both on her southern and on her eastern borders. The Tatar danger during the tsar's minority is mentioned by Ivan in his first letter to Kurbsky. See *Correspondence*, pp. 70–1.

[6] вой is clearly a scribe's error for вуй (cf. Polish *wuj*, "maternal uncle") which in fact is found in certain late copies of the text. See N. Ustryalov, *Skazaniya*, p. 7.

15

бегошася. И в то время дивне неяко Бог руку помощи подал отдохнути земле християнской, образом сим. Тогда убо, тогда, глаголю, прииде к нему един муж, презвитер чином, имянем Селиверстр, пришлец от Новаграда Великого, претяще ему от Бога священными писаньми и срозе заклинающе его страшным Божиим имянем; еще к тому, и чюдеса и аки бы явление от Бога поведающе ему (не вем, аще истинные, або так ужасновение пущающе, буйства его ради, и для детских неистовых его нравов, умыслил был собе сие; яко многажды и отцы повелевают слугам детей ужасати мечтательными страхи, и от излишных игор презлых сверстников, сице, и сеᵃ мню блаженный малую грозу присовокупляетᵇ благокознению, еюже великое зло целити умыслил).ᶜ Яко и врачеве делают, по неволе, согнившие гагрины стружуще и режуще железом, або дикое мясо, возрастающее на ране, обрезающе аж до живаго мяса; сему негли подобно, и он блаженный, льстец истинный, умыслил; яко и последовало дело: иже душу его от прокаженных ран исцелил и очистил был, и развращенный ум исправил, тем и овым наставляюще на стезю правую. С ним же соединяетсяᵈ во общение един

ᵃ Patr., T. сице и не: Ar., Pog.   ᵇ Pog., Patr. присовокупляю: Ar.
ᶜ Patr., Pog., T. No bracket in Ar.   ᵈ T. соединятся: Ar.

---

¹ After the fall of Kubensky and Vorontsov the Glinskys, notably the two brothers (Yury and Mikhail) and the mother (Anna) of Elena Glinsky, rose to power. They remained in authority, however, only for a short time. Two days after the most disastrous of a whole series of fires in Moscow (21 June 1547) Ivan and several senior boyars conferred with Metropolitan Makary at an emergency meeting of the Boyar Council. At this meeting Ivan's confessor, Fedor Barmin, and certain boyars, in an effort to rid the State of the Glinskys, accused them of responsibility for the fire. On 26 June Yury Vasil'evich Glinsky was handed over to the "common people" (черные люди) by the boyars and murdered, after which the mob took vengeance on Yury's followers. Three days later the mob, in full military equipment according to one account, came to Vorob'evo outside Moscow where Ivan was staying and demanded that Anna and Mikhail Glinsky, whom they believed Ivan was hiding, be handed over to them. Although the rebellion was quelled successfully, the events of June 1547 marked the end of the influence of the Glinskys. For Ivan's version of the fire and rebellion of 1547, see *Correspondence*, pp. 80–3.

persed.[1] And at that time in a somewhat wondrous way God stretched out the hand of help, [allowing] the Christian land to rest, in this manner: at that time, at that time, I say, there came to him a man, a priest by rank, by name Sil'vestr, a new-comer from Novgorod the Great, divinely rebuking him with holy scriptures and sternly conjuring him in the terrible name of God; and furthermore telling him of miracles and apparitions sent as it were by God (I do not know if they were true or if he devised them for himself in order to scare him because of his folly and his childish unbridled ways; just as fathers often order their servants to scare their children with imaginary horrors and [to turn them] from the senseless games of their wicked playfellows, so too did this blessed man, I think, add to his well-meaning cunning[2] a little threat, with which he planned to heal a great evil). For physicians do this in case of need, scraping and cutting the putrid gangrene with a knife, or cutting away the raw flesh which grows on the wound even as far as the live flesh.[3] And perhaps in a similar way to this did that blessed man, the true deceiver,[4] plan; for so it followed: he healed and purified his soul from leprous sores and rectified his depraved mind, in this way[5] guiding him to the right path.[6]

[2] An approximate rendering of the oxymoron благокознение, which appears to have been invented by Kurbsky. He uses it again (to describe Sil'vestr) in his third letter to Ivan. See *Correspondence*, p. 202.

[3] This sentence is repeated almost word for word in Kurbsky's third letter to Ivan. See *Correspondence*, pp. 202–3.

[4] The point of this oxymoron is presumably that Sil'vestr was obliged to deceive for the sake of truth and goodness.

[5] Lit. "by this and by that". A possible alternative rendering is: "in all matters".

[6] For the origins and background of Sil'vestr, see *Correspondence*, p. 24, n. 6. Very little is known about his position and authority in the government. The description of him as "all-powerful" given by the tendentious and anti-Sil'vestr *Tsarstvennaya Kniga* (*PSRL* xiii, p. 524) must be treated with reserve; so too must the effusive praise of Kurbsky who identifies Sil'vestr and Adashev with the reactionary opposition of the boyars (probably as a result of Sil'vestr's uncompromising refusal to swear allegiance to Ivan's infant son in 1553). No more reliable, of course, is the bitter denunciation of him by Ivan, who, when later convinced of his "treachery" in 1553 and of his hostility to his wife Anastasia, accused him of depriving him of all authority, of forming conspiracies and of plotting "to see all the Russian land under

благородный тогда юноша, ко доброму и полезному общему, имянем Алексей Адашев; цареви ж той Алексей в то время зело любим был и согласен, и был он общей вещи зело полезен, и отчасти, в некоторых нравех, ангелом подобен. И аще бы вся по ряду изъявил о нем, воистинну вере не подобно было бы пред грубыми и мирскими человеки. И аще же возрим, яко благодать Святаго Духа верных в Новом Завете украшает, не по делом нашим, но по преизобильности щедрот Христа нашего, иже не токмо не дивно будет, но и[a] удобно, понеже и крови своей Сотворитель всяческих не жаловал за нас излияти. Но, прекратив сие, до предреченных паки возвратимся.

Что же сие мужие два творят полезное земле оной, спустошенной уже воистинну и зело бедне сокрушеной? Приклони же уже уши и слушай со прилежанием! Сие творят, сие делают: главную доброту начинают — утверждают царя, и якого царя? царя юнаго, и во злострастиах и в самовольствии без отца воспитаннаго, и преизлище прелютаго, и крови уже напившися всякие, не токмо всех животных, но и человеческия. Паче же, и согласных его на зло прежде бывших, овых отделяют от него (яже быша зело люты), овых же уздают и воздержат страхом Бога живаго. И что ж еще по сем придают? Наказуют опасне благочестию; молитвам же прилежным ко Богу, и постом, и воздержанию внимати со прилежанием завещавает оный презвитер, и отгоняет от него оных предреченных прелютейших зверей (сиречь ласкателей и человек угодников, над нихъже ничто же может быти поветреннейшаго во царстве), и отсылает и отделяет от него всяку нечистоту и

[a] Т. ино: Ar.

his feet" (see *Correspondence*, both letters of Ivan to Kurbsky). It would appear that Sil'vestr was in fact a close political adviser of Ivan from 1547 until his banishment in 1560—or at any rate until the tsar's illness in 1553 —and that he acted rather as the young tsar's agent than as the "usurper" of his power.

[1] For details concerning Aleksey Adashev, see *Correspondence*, p. 85, n. 8. His career was in many ways similar to that of Sil'vestr, but was marked by

At that time a noble youth, Aleksey Adashev by name, joined him in association for the common good and prosperity; now this Aleksey at that time enjoyed the favours of the tsar and was in concord with him, and he served the common weal most beneficially, and in part—in some of his ways—he was like unto the angels.[1] And if I were to declare everything about him in turn it would indeed be incredible to uncouth men and to laics. And if we behold how the grace of the Holy Spirit bedecks the faithful in the New Testament, not according to our deeds but according to the superabundance of the bountiful mercies of our Christ, not only will it not be wondrous but it will be simple [to comprehend], for the Creator of all things did not shrink from shedding His blood for us. But let us stop this and return to what we were saying before.

What good do these two men do to that land which had indeed been laid waste and most sorely shattered? Incline your ears and listen with diligence! This they create, this they do: they begin their main good deed—they strengthen the tsar. And what kind of tsar? A young tsar brought up fatherless in evil passions[2] and self-will, and most excessively vicious, having already drunk his fill of every kind of blood, not only of all animals but also of men. And furthermore, as for those who had formerly approved of his evil ways, some (who were exceedingly vicious) they separate from him, others they bridle and restrain by the fear of the living God. And what still further do they do after this? With care they instruct him in piety; that priest enjoins him diligently to give heed to assiduous prayers to God, to fasting and to restraint, and he drives away from him those above-mentioned vicious beasts (that is to say the flatterers and men-pleasers, than whom nothing can be more pestilential in the tsardom), and he removes and separates from

an even swifter rise to fame from comparatively humble origins. The period of his political activity was from 1547 to 1560, during most of which time he clearly enjoyed the confidence of the tsar and carried out a striking number of important governmental functions.

[2] The usual meaning of злострастие, according to Sreznevsky, is "suffering", "misery", "distress" (Greek κακοπάθεια). The meaning here, however, is clearly *evil* passions (cf. сладострастие). See I. I. Sreznevsky, *Materialy*, vol. I, col. 1005.

скверну, прежде ему приключшуюся от сатоны; и подвижет па то и присовокупляет себе в помощь архиерея оного великого града, и к тому всех предобрых и преподобных мужей, презвитерством почтенных; и вожбужают царя к покаянию, и исчистив сосуд его внутренний, яко подобает, ко Богу приводят, и святых, непорочных Христа нашего тайн сподобляют, и в сицевую высоту онаго, прежде бывшаго окаянного, возводят, яко и многим окрестным языком дивитися обращению его и благочестию.

И к тому еще и сие прилогают: собирают к нему советников, мужей разумных и совершенных, во старости мастите сущих, благочестием и страхом Божиим украшенных; других же, аще и во среднем веку, тако же предобрых и храбрых, и тех и онех в военных и в земских вещах по всему искусных; и сице ему их в приязнь и в дружбу усвояют, яко без их совету ничесоже устроити или мыслити. Воистинну по премудрому Соломану глаголющему: царь, рече, добрыми советники, яко град претвердыми столпы утвержен, и паки: любяй, рече, совет, хранит свою душу, а не любяй его, совсем изчеснет; понеже, яко безсловесным есть, належит чувством по естеству управлятися, сице всем словесным советом и разсуждением. И нарицались тогда оные советницы у него избранная рада; воистинну по делом и наречение имели, понеж все избранное и нарочитое советы своими производили, сиречь суд праведный, нелицеприятен, яко богатому, тако и убогому, еже бывает во

Lit. "he urges him to this and joins him to himself". A reference to Makary (Metropolitan of Moscow from 1542 to 1563), one of the leading statesmen in the government, who appears to have wielded considerable political influence during the last part of the forties and throughout the fifties of the sixteenth century.

[2] Proverbs xxv. 28.   [3] Proverbs xv. 32.

[4] The expression "Select Council" (избранная рада) is only used by Kurbsky and is part-Polish in origin, the word *Rada* being Polish for Duma or Council. Other sources make no mention of it.

Historians have been divided in their opinions of the composition and functions of the so-called Council, some seeing in it the Boyar Duma (Боярская дума) or the Privy Council (Ближняя дума); others, merely a private côterie of favourites gathered around Sil'vestr and Adashev.

0

him all kind of uncleanliness and filth with which he was formerly beset by Satan. And he induces the prelate of that great city to join him and help him,[1] as well as all good and virtuous men dignified with priesthood; and they stir the tsar to repentance, and having purified his inner vessel, as is befitting, they lead him to God and they make him worthy of the holy and immaculate mysteries of our Christ, and to such a height they lead him who was formerly accursed that even many of the surrounding peoples are amazed at his conversion and piety.

And to all this they add this too: they gather around him advisers, men of understanding and perfection, of venerable old age, adorned with piety and the fear of God; and others too who even though of middle age are also excellent and brave —and all of these are wholly skilled in military affairs and affairs of the country [i.e. administration]; and they draw them close to him in amity and friendship, so that without their advice nothing is undertaken or planned. In truth, according to the wise Solomon who says: "a ruler with good counsellors is like a city strengthened with towers"[2] and again: "he that loves counsel preserves his own soul, but he that does not love it perishes altogether".[3] For just as it is fitting for animals to be governed according to their nature by feeling, so is it fitting for all humans to be governed by counsel and by reason. And at that time those counsellors of his were named the Select Council;[4] in truth according to their deeds they had this name, for by their counsel they produced all that was select and distinguished, that is to say true impartial justice, both for rich and for poor, such as is best in the tsardom. And furthermore

That during the period 1547–1560 Ivan IV ruled principally with the aid of a Privy Council consisting of his closest advisers seems indisputable in the light of available information.

The reforms carried out at this time, presumably by the tsar and his intimate advisers, undoubtedly favoured the rising class of the service nobility (*dvoryanstvo*) and impeded the interests of the aristocracy (*boyarstvo*). Paradoxically, however, Kurbsky on the one hand can find no fault with Sil'vestr and Adashev and their associates; Ivan, on the other hand, in retrospect can say no good word for "Sil'vestr...and his evil counsellors" (see *Correspondence*, pp. 85 *sq.*) from whom he categorically disassociates himself.

царстве наилепшее; и к тому воевод, искусных и храбрых мужей, сопротив врагов избирают, и стратилатские чины устрояют, яко над езными, так и над пешими; и аще кто явитца мужественным в битвах и окровил руку в крови вражии, сего дарованьми почитано, яко движными вещи, так и недвижными. Некоторые же от них, искуснейшие, того ради и на вышние степени возводились. А парозитов, или тунеядцов, сиречь подобедов или товарищей[a] трапезам, яже блазенством или шутками питаются и кормы хают, не токмо тогда не дарованно, но и отгоняемо, вкупе и скомрахи и со иными, прелукавыми и презлыми, таковыми роды; но токмо на мужество человеков подвизаемо и на храбрость, всякими роды даров или мздовоздаяньми, кождому по достоянию.

[a] T. творяще: Ar.

---

[1] The word стратилатский is borrowed from the Greek στρατηλάτης. See *Correspondence*, p. 234, n. 2.

[2] Note the Polish construction in this and later sentences—past passive participle, neuter singular (почитано), governing an object in the accusative (сего). Cf. *Correspondence*, p. 209, n. 7. The passage in question clearly refers to the distribution of fiefs (*pomest'ya*)

they chose commanders, skilled and brave men, to fight against the enemies and they arranged who should be in command both of the cavalry and of the infantry regiments.[1] And should anyone show himself to be courageous in battle and stain his hands with the blood of the enemy, he would be honoured with gifts, both movable and immovable.[2] And because of this certain of them, the most skilled, were elevated to higher ranks. But the parasites or sycophants, that is to say the fawners or comrades of the table,[3] who are fed for their buffoonery or jests and sneer at the food, not only were not awarded at that time, but they were even chased away together with the *skomorokhi*[4] and other such kinds of people, most cunning and most evil; but men were urged on only to manly and brave deeds by all kinds of gifts or rewards, each one according to his deserts.

among service men as a reward for good service on campaigns. When deciding on the extent of the award, reports by their previous commanding officers were taken into consideration. See Smirnov, *Ocherki*, p. 434, n. 42.

[3] For the expression товарищи трапезам(-ы), see *Correspondence*, p. 8. As for подобеды, I have conjectured "fawners", although the meaning is obscure.

[4] The *skomorokhi* were professional buffoons, actors, musicians, wandering entertainers. They were frequently attacked by the Church in Russia, mainly on grounds of obscenity.

II

И абие, за помощию Божиею, сопротив сопостатов возмогоша воинство християнское. И против яких сопостатов? так великого и грознаго Измаильтескаго языка, от негож некогда и вселенная трепетала, и не токмо трепетала, но и спустошена была; и не против единого царя ополчашеся, но абие против трех великих и сильных, сиречь, сопротив Перекопского царя, и Казанского, и сопротив княжат Нагайских. И за благодатию и помощию Христа Бога нашего, абие от того времяни, всем трем возражаше нахождение, частыми преодоленьми преодолеваху и преславными победами украшахуся, о нихъже по ряду писати сия краткая повесть не вместит; но вкратце рекши: по толику спустошению Русские земли бе от них, не по толику, но множайше пределы христианские разширишася за малые лета: идеже были прежде, в пустошенных краех Руских, зимовища Татарские, тамо грады и места сооружишася; и не токмо кони Руских сынов во Азии с текущих рек напишася, с Танаиса[a] и Куалы и з прочих, но и грады тамо поставишася.

Видев же таковые неизреченны Божия шедроты, так вскоре бываемыя, и сам царь, возревновав ревностию, начал против врагов сам ополчатися, своею главою, и собирати себе воинство[b] множайшее и храбрейшее, не хотяше покою наслажатися, в прекрасных полатах за-

[a] Танаис по Римски, а по Руску Дон, яже Европу делит со Асиею, яко космографи описуют в землемерительной книзе. Куала же Исмаилтским языком глаголется, а Словенски Медведица: in margin of Ar., T.

[b] Pog., T. воинству: Ar.

---

[1] I.e. the Mohammedans, or, more specifically, Tatars. See *Correspondence*, p. 13, n. 4.
[2] I.e. the Crimea. See above, p. 15, n. 3.
[3] The word град, город (cf. Polish *gród*) seems to be used by Kurbsky to

II

And straightway, with the help of God, the Christian army prevailed against the enemies. And against which enemies? The great and awesome Ishmaelite race,[1] before which the whole universe once trembled—and not only did the universe tremble, but it was even laid waste by them. And not against one khan only did they take up arms but straightway against three great and powerful khans—to wit against the khan of Perekop,[2] against the khan of Kazan' and against the Nogay princes. And with the grace and help of Christ our God from that time forward they drove off invasion by all three, won frequent conquests and bedecked themselves with most glorious victories; indeed were I to relate all of them in turn, this short tale would not suffice to contain them. To put it briefly: during a few years the boundaries of our Christian land were expanded not only to the extent of the devastation which the Russian land had suffered from them, but to a far greater degree; for where previously, in the devastated Russian districts, there had been Tatar winter-quarters, there fortresses and towns[3] were built. And not only did the horses of the sons of Russia drink from the flowing rivers in Asia, from the Tanais and the Kuala[4] and others, but even fortresses were built there.

Now having seen such ineffable bountiful mercies of God which came to pass so quickly, the tsar himself, burning with zeal, began in person to take up arms against his enemies and to gather around him a most numerous and brave army, for he did not wish to enjoy quiet, to stay shut up in fine chambers,

denote a fortified place, a citadel, as well as a town, whereas место (cf. Polish *miasto*) is used for a town.

[4] A marginal note reads as follows: "Tanais in Roman, but in Russian Don, which divides Europe from Asia, so the cosmographers write in their geographical book. Kuala is called thus in the Ishmaelite tongue, but in Slavonic it is the Medveditsa."

What is meant by the Kuala, itself not a Turco-Mongol word, is not known. Ustryalov hazards "Kayala", the unidentified river which is mentioned in the *Slovo o polku Igoreve* and the *Slovo Sofoniya* (*Zadonschchina*) and on which Igor's battle with the Polovtsy took place in 1185.

творяся, пребывати, яко есть нынешним западным царем обычай (все целыя нощи истребляти, над карты седяще и над протчими бесовскими бреднями); но подвигся многажды сам, не щадячи здравия своего, на сопротивнаго и горшаго своего супостата, царя Казанского, единова в лютую зиму; аще и не взял места оного главнаго, сиречь Казани града, и со тщетою немалою атоиде, но всяко не сокрушилось ему сердце и воинство его храброе, укрепляющу Богу оными советники его. И размотрив тамо положения места, паки по лете едином¹ или дву, град тамо превеликий, зело прекрасен, абие поставити повелел на реце Свияге, от Волги за четверть мили, а от великого Казанского места аки миль пять. Так близу приближился.²

И того ж лета выправя дела великие стенобитные рекою Волгою, а сам сухим путем хотяще абие поити. И прииде ему весть, иже царь Перекопский с великими силами на него идет, возбраняюще хождение ему на Казань; он же, аще и войско великое прежде, града поставления ради, послал, тако же и при делах множество воинов, но обаче, того ради, на Казань хождение на мало время отложил. И еще, аки бе с большою частью войска, иде сопротив предреченнаго оного врага Христова, и сам стал на Оке реке, ожидающе его ко сражению брани, во едином месте; а другие войска разложил по другим градом, яже лежат при той же реце, и выведыватися повелел о нем, бо не ведомо еще было, на которое место итти мел. Он же егда услышал: великий князь стоит с войском против его, готов над надежду его (бо певне споведался, иже уже на Казань пошел), тогда возвратился и облег место великое, мурованное, Тулу, аки во штинадесяти милех от места Коломны, идеже царь християнский лежал с войском, ждуще его; а нас тогда

---

¹ Perhaps a corruption of единою.

² The first Kazan' campaign in which Ivan personally took part was in the winter of 1547–8 (*PSRL* xiii, pp. 457–8). It was quite unsuccessful, as was the second, which took place in the winter of the following year and to which Kurbsky here refers. According to the chronicle (*PSRL* xiii, pp. 460–1), the campaign failed because of the unexpectedly severe weather

26

as is the habit of the western rulers of today (spending whole nights sitting at cards and other devilish follies); but many a time he himself took the field, not sparing his health, against his bitterest enemy, the khan of Kazan'—and once[1] during a fierce winter; and although he did not take that main town, that is to say the city of Kazan', and although he withdrew with no small loss, nevertheless his heart and his brave soldiery were not shattered, for God strengthened him by means of those counsellors. And having inspected the situation of the city, after a year or two he ordered a mighty fair fortress to be built forthwith on the river Sviyaga, a quarter of a mile from the Volga and about five miles from the great city of Kazan'. And so he drew nigh.[2]

And in that same year he sent off the great siege artillery by the river Volga and was himself about to set off by land. And news came to him that the khan of Perekop was moving against him with great forces in order to prevent him marching against Kazan'. But although Ivan had already sent a large army to build the fortress and although there was a large number of troops with the artillery, none the less because of this he postponed his march against Kazan' for a little time. And then, as he had with him a large part of the army, he set off again against that afore-mentioned enemy of Christ, and stopped on the river Oka in a certain town, expecting him to join battle; and the other forces he distributed throughout other fortresses which lie on that same river, and ordered that information be sought about the enemy, for it was not yet known against which town he intended to march. Now when the khan heard that the grand prince was standing opposite him with his army, ready beyond expectation (for he had certainly reckoned that he had already set off against Kazan'), he returned and besieged the great stone town of Tula about sixteen miles from Kolomna where the Christian tsar lay waiting for him with his army;

conditions. It was clear that Kazan' could not be taken without greater preparations and smaller supply lines. Consequently in the spring of 1551 the Russians built the fortress of Sviyazhsk (near the influx of the Sviyaga river into the Volga), which served as a garrison, a supply depot and a base for future attacks on Kazan'.

послал со другими о нем выведыватися, и земли от взгонов бронити; и было с нами тогда войска аки пятьнадесять тысящей. Мы ж, преплавясъ[a] чрез великую Оку[b] реку со многим потщанием, того дня зело скоро устремишася, и преехаша аки тринадесять миль, и положишася к нощи на едином потоце, близу стражи царя Перекопского, от града же Тулы за пол-2 мили, под нимъже сам царь стояше. Стража же Татарская утече ко царю, и поведа ему о множестве войска християнского, и мняще, иже сам князь великий прииде со всем своим войском; и тое нощи царь Татарский от града утече, аки миль осмь, в поле дикое, за три реки препроводившеся, и дела некоторые и кули потопил, и порогов[c] и верблюдов отбеже, и войско в войне оставил (бо три дни хотяще воевати, а два же дни точию под градом стоял, а против третьяго дня побежал).[d]

На утро ж[e] мы, воставши рано, поидохом ко граду и положихомся с войском, идеже шатры его стояли. Войска ж Татарского аки третина, або вяще, остала была в загонех, и шли ко граду, надеящеся царя их стояща. Егда ж разсмотриша и уведаша о нас, ополчишася противу нас. Мы ж абие срозившеся с ними,[f] и пребывала битва аки на пол-2 годины; потом помог Бог нам, християном, над бусурманы, и толико избиша их, яко[g] зело мало осталось[h] их, едва весть в орду возвратилася. На той то битве и сам аз тяшкие раны на телеси отнесох, яко на главе, так и на других составех.

[a] Patr., T. приплавясь: Ar.   [b] Patr., Pog. ону: Ar.   [c] Ar. порохов: Patr., Pog., T.   [d] T. No brackets in Ar.   [e] Patr., Pog. на троу ж: Ar.   [f] Patr., Pog., T. с нами: Ar.   [g] Pog. яко omitted in Ar.   [h] Pog. осталось omitted in Ar.

---

[1] Either a corruption of пороков, "siege guns"; or perhaps порохов (found in some copies), "powder".

[2] Kurbsky's account of the attack on Tula corresponds fairly closely with the chronicle account (see *PSRL* XIII, pp. 188–90, 486–8). According to the latter on 21 June 1552 Ivan was informed at his headquarters in Kolomna that the Crimean Tatars were marching on Tula. He immediately sent three detachments there—Petr Mikhaylovich Shchenyatev and Kurbsky from Kashira, Ivan Ivanovich Pronsky and Dmitry Ivanovich Khilkov

and Ivan sent us and others to get information about the khan and to protect the land from raiding parties; and we had with us at that time about fifteen thousand troops. And having crossed the great Oka river with much speed, we hastened very quickly on that same day and covered about thirteen miles and by night took up our positions by a stream, near the outpost of the khan of Perekop, one and a half miles from the town of Tula at the walls of which the khan himself stood. But the Tatar outpost ran off to the khan and told him of the great size of the Christian army, thinking that the grand prince himself had come with all his troops; and that night the Tatar khan fled from the town about eight miles into the open steppe, crossing three rivers. And he sank some pieces of artillery and cannon-balls and he abandoned both siege guns[1] and camels and he left his army to fight (for he had intended to campaign for three days; for two days only he had stood near the town and on the third day he had run away).

And in the morning, having risen early, we went to the city and took up our positions with our army where his tents stood. Now about one-third or more of the Tatar army had remained behind as raiding parties, and they marched towards the town, hoping to find their khan standing there. But when they saw and learned about us, they drew up in battle order against us. And we straightway joined battle with them and the fight lasted for about one and a half hours; then God helped us Christians against the Mussulmans and we slaughtered so many of them that very few remained and the news only just got back to the Horde. In that battle I myself suffered grievous bodily wounds, both in my head and in other parts of my body.[2]

from Rostislavl' and Mikhail Ivanovich Vorotynsky from Kolychevo (near Serpukhov). When he heard from Grigory Temkin, the commander of Tula, that the attack on Tula by 7000 Tatars and "Turkish janissaries" was the spearhead of an invasion led by Khan Devlet Girey, Ivan moved to Kashira *en route* for Tula. However, when the Tulans sighted the Russian relief army in the distance they emerged from the city and drove the Tatars off. When Kurbsky's force arrived they had only Tatar rearguard elements to deal with. The expedition of the Crimean Tatars had been originally undertaken, so prisoners informed the Russians, because Devlet Girey had heard that Ivan and his army were in the Kazan' area.

Ivan, in his first letter to Kurbsky, accuses the latter of failing to catch up

Егда же возвратихомся ко цареви нашему, со пресветлым одолением, он же тогда повелел опочивати оному утружденному войску аки 8 дней. И по осми днях, сам поиде с воинством х Казани, на место великое, глаголемое Муром, еже лежит от поля уже х краине, х Казанским пределом, и оттуду, чрез поле дикое, аки месяц шел ко оному предреченному новому граду, поставленному на Свияге, идеже воинство его ждало с великими делы и со многими запасы, яже приплыша Волгою, рекою великою. А нас тогда послал, со тремянадесять тысящей люду, чрез Резанскую землю и потом чрез Мещерскую, идеже есть Мордовский язык. Потом препроводясь, аки за три дни, Мордовские лесы, изидохом на великое дикое поле и идохом от него по правой руце, аки в пяти днях конем езду; понеже мы заслониша его тем войском, еже с нами шло, от Заволских Татар (бояшебося он, да не приидут на него безвесно те княжата Нагайские); и аки бы по пяти неделях, со гладом и с нуждою многою, доидохом Суры реки великие, на устья Борыша речки, идеже и он в том же дни с войски великими прииде. И того дни хлеба сухаго наядохомся со многою сладостию и благодарением, ово зело дорогаго купующе, ово позычающе от сродных, и приятель и другов; бо нам его было не стало аки бы на десять дней, и Господь Бог препитал нас и войско, ово рыбами, ово иными зверьми, бо в пустых тех полях зело много в реках рыб.

Егда же преплавишася Суру реку, тогда и Черемиса Горняя, а по их Чуваша зовомые, язык особливый, начаша встречати по пяти сот и по тысеще их, аки бы радующеся цареву пришествию (понеже в их земле поставлен он предреченный град на Свияге). И от тое реки шли есмя войском 8 дней, полями дикими и дубровами, негде же и лесами; а сел со живущими зело мало, понеже у них села при великих

---

with the Tatars owing to a feast with Temkin: "you went to our *voevoda*, Prince Grigory Temkin, to eat and drink, and having eaten you went after them; and they got away from you unscathed". See *Correspondence*, pp. 138–9.

Now when we returned to our tsar with a brilliant victory, he ordered that our wearied army rest for about eight days. And after eight days he himself set off with the army towards Kazan', to that great city called Murom, which lies on the border of the steppe-land, near the frontiers of the territory of Kazan'; and from there he marched over the steppe for about a month to that above-mentioned new fortress built on the Sviyaga where the troops awaited him with the large guns and much stores which had sailed down the great river Volga. And at that time he sent us with thirteen thousand men through the land of Ryazan' and then through the land of Meshchera where the Mordvinian people dwell.[1] Then having crossed the Mordvinian forests in about three days, we came out on to the great steppe and marched from it on the right hand side, about five days ride on horseback; for with the army accompanying us we were shielding Ivan from the Tatars from beyond the Volga (he was afraid lest the Nogay princes should attack him without warning). And after about five weeks of hunger and dire distress we arrived at the river Sura at the mouth of the little river Barysh, and he arrived there too on the same day with the main army. And on that day we ate our fill of dry bread with much relish and thanksgiving, buying some at a very dear price, borrowing some from our fellows, both friends and comrades. For we had had none for about nine days, and the Lord God fed us and the army now with fishes, now with other animals, for in those barren steppes there are very many fishes in the rivers.

Now when they had crossed the river Sura, the Hill Cheremisians,[2] called in their tongue the Chuvashians, a foreign people, began to meet them in groups of five hundred and a thousand, evidently rejoicing in the arrival of the tsar (for that above-mentioned fortress on the Sviyaga had been built in their land). And from that river we marched with the army for eight days, over the steppe and through woods and sometimes through forests—there are very few inhabited villages there, for

---

[1] In other words, Kurbsky sailed down the Oka through Pereyaslavl'-Ryazansky and Kasimov, formerly known as Gorodets-Meshchersky.

[2] For the Hill Cheremisians, see below, p. 39, n. 5.

крепостях ставлены и незримы, аще и поблизку ходящим. И ту уже нам привожено и, по странам ездя, добывано купити хлеба и скотов. Аще и зело дорого плачено, но нам было, яко изнемоглым от гладу, благодарно; (а малвазии и любимых трунков з марцыпаны¹ тамо не воспоминай! Черемисский же хлеб сладостнейший, паче драгоценных колачей, обретеся), и наипаче же сего ради, иже подвизахомся за отечество правовернаго христианства, сопротив врагов креста Христова, паче же вкупе со царем своим; сие было всего благодарнейши и радостнейши, и не чюлось ни единые нужды, друг пред другом к добрым подвигом ретящеся; наипаче же сам Господь Бог помогал нам.

Егда же приидохом близу новопоставленного града, воистину зело прекрасного, тогда выехаша во стретение царя гетмани² они, яко градский, так которые и з делы приидоше, с немалыми вои, по чину благочинне устроени полки имущи; с ними же конного войска тысящ аки пятьнадесять изыдоша во стретение, тако ж и пеших множество много; к тому и гуфов оных варварских, новопокорившихся царю, немало, аки четыре тысячи; их же обитания и села близу града онаго быша (яже, хотяще и не хотяще, покоришася). И бысть там радость не мала о здравию пришествия царева со множествы воев, тако же и о победе преже реченной, яже на Крымскаго пса одержахом (бо зело трепетахом о прихождению и помощи его Казани), и о поставлению града оного превеликого. И тамо х тому приехали есмо, воистину, яко в свои домы от того долгова и зело нужнаго пути, понеже привезено нам множество, от домов наших Волгою, мала не кождому, в великих в галиях запасу; тако же и купцов безчисленное множество, с различными живностьми и со многими иными товары, приплыша, идеже бяше всего достаток, чего бы душа восхотела (точию нечистоты тамо купить не обрящешь). И опочинув тамо войско аки три дни, начаша великую реку Волгу превозитися; и превезошася все войско аки за два дни.

---

¹ Lit. "marzipan", "marchpane".   ² I.e. commanders.

their villages are built hard by great strongholds and are invisible even to those who go near. But now [food] was brought to us there and while we travelled through various districts we were able to get bread and cattle by buying them. Even though we had to pay very dearly for them, still we were thankful, as we were faint from hunger; (but as for Malmsey wine and favourite drinks with almond cakes[1]..., you can forget them there! Still, Cheremisian bread was found to be even tastier than costly buns). And the fact that we were fighting for our Orthodox Christian fatherland against the enemies of the Cross of Christ and were together with our tsar was the most gratifying and joyful of all; and we felt no distress at all, vying with one another in good deeds; and especially the Lord God Himself helped us.

Now after we had come near the newly built fortress—in truth it is very fine—the *hetmans*,[2] both the commander of the fortress and those who had come with the artillery, came out to meet the tsar with many soldiers, having their regiments drawn up in good array. And with them about fifteen thousand cavalry came out to meet the tsar as well as a great multitude of infantry; furthermore there were many of those barbarian detachments which had recently submitted to the tsar, some four thousand of them, whose dwellings and villages were near the fortress—and they had submitted both willingly and un-willingly. And there was great rejoicing there for the safe arrival of the tsar with his multitude of soldiers, as well as for the previously mentioned victory which we had won over the Crimean dog (for we had trembled greatly lest he should come and aid Kazan') and for the founding of that great fortress. And what is more, it was really like coming to our own homes after that long and very arduous journey, for many things had been brought along the Volga from our homes—almost for each man—in great store galleys; and also countless numbers of merchants with various victuals and many other goods had sailed there; and there was an abundance of all the heart could wish for (only unclean food you would not find to buy there). And when the army had rested there for about three days, they began to cross the great river Volga; and the whole army crossed in about two days.

И на третей же день двигнушася в путь, и преидохом четыре мили, аки за 3 дни, бо тамо не мало рек, еже впадают в Волгу; препровожашеся чрез мосты и гати, которые были пред нами показили Казанцы. И на четвертый день изыдохом сопротив града Казанского, на великие, и пространные, и гладкие, зело веселые луги, и положишася все войско подле реки Волги; а лугов оных до места аки миля зело велика,¹ бо стоит он град и место не на Волзе, но река под ним, Казань реченная, от неяж и наречен. И положение его на великой горе, а наипаче от приходу Волги сице зритца,² а от Нагайские страны, от Камы реки, от реченного Арского поля, равно приити к нему. Опочинувши же аки день един, паки дела некоторые с кораблей выложены, яже пред полки хождаше. На другий же день рано, по Божиих литоргиях, воздвижеся войско от станов, со царем своим, и развивши хоругви христианские, со многим благочинием и устроением полков, поидоша ко граду сопостатов. Град же видехом аки пуст стоящ, иже а ни человек, а ни глас человечь ни един отнюд слышашеся в нем, яко многим неискусным радоватися о сем и глаголати, яко избегоша царь и все воинство в лесы, от страха великого войска.

Егда ж приидохом³ близу места Казанского, яже в великой крепости лежит, с востоку от него идет Казань река, а з западу Булак речка, зело тиновата и непроходима, под самое место течет и впадает под уголную вежу в Казань реку;⁴ а течет из езера, Кабана глаголемаго, не малого, которое езеро кончится аки полверсты от места; и як преправитися тую нужную речку, тогда между озером и местом лежит с Арскаго поля гора зело прикрая и ко восхождению нужная. А от тое реки, около места, ров копан, зело

---

¹ Or perhaps, "there is a good mile [*from*] those meadows to the town".

² Presumably the meaning of the elliptical от приходу Волги, literally: "from the arrival of the Volga".

³ Literally "But when...". There is, however, no main verb corresponding to the temporal subordinate clause "when we came close".

⁴ In fact the Kazanka river flows westward and north of Kazan'; the Bulak flows into and under the town from the south.

And on the third day we set off and covered four miles in about three days, for there are many rivers there which flow into the Volga; and we crossed over bridges and brushwood paths, which the people of Kazan' had destroyed before us. And on the fourth day we emerged opposite the city of Kazan' on to great broad, smooth and exceedingly merry meadows, and the whole army took up positions alongside the river Volga. Now there is a good mile of those meadows stretching to the town,[1] for the fortress and the city are not on the Volga, but a river called Kazan' runs by it from which it gets its name. And it is situated on a great hill and thus it can be seen especially well by one coming from the direction of the Volga;[2] and from the Nogay side [i.e. from the south], from the river Kama, and from the so-called Arsky plain the approach is level. And after we had rested for about a day, some more artillery pieces were unloaded from the boats which had gone before the troops. Now on the next day in the morning, after Divine Liturgies had been sung, the army moved from its camp together with the tsar, and with the Christian banners unfurled and the regiments drawn up in good array they marched towards the city of the foe. And we saw the citadel standing as it were empty, for not a single man was to be seen, nor a single voice to be heard in it, so that many inexperienced men rejoiced and said that the khan and all his soldiers had fled into the forests in fear of the great army.

And then[3] we came close to the city of Kazan', which lies in a great strong position; on the east of it flows the Kazan' river and on the west the little Bulak river,[4] which is very muddy and impassable and which flows under the town itself and falls into the river Kazan' by a corner tower; it flows from a large lake called Kaban, which ends about half a verst from the town. And on the other side of[5] that difficult little river there lies between the lake and the town on the side of Arsky plain[6] a hill which is very steep[7] and difficult to ascend. And from that river around the town there is a very deeply dug moat, which

[5] Lit. "when we had crossed".
[6] See below, p. 44, n. 1.
[7] Lit. "unpleasant". Cf. Polish *przykry*.

глубокий, аж до езерка, реченнаго Поганаго, еже лежит подле самую Казань реку; а от Казани реки гора так высока, иже оком возрити прикро; на ней же град стоит и полаты царские и мечиты, зело высокие, мурованные, идеже их умершие царие клалися; числом, памятамися, пять их. Егда же начаша обступати место оное бусурманское, и войско христианское повеленно итти трема полком, чрез предреченную речку Булак; егда же первие препроводился,[a] направя мостки чрез нее, предний полк, а тамо обыкли его звати яртаул, в немже бе войска избраннаго, аки седмь тысящей, а над ними стратилаты два, княжа Пронский Юрей и княжа Феодор Львов, с роду княжат Ярославских, юноши зело храбрые, и прииде им итти с нуждою прямо на оную гору, на Арское поле, между места и Кабана, пред-реченного озера, от врат градцких аки два стреляния лучных; другий же великий полк начаша только препро-важатися чрез оную реку по мостом, — царь же Казанский выпустил войска конского из места, аки пять тысящ, а пеших от десяти тысещь, на первый предреченный полк, конные Тотаровя с копьи, а пешие со стрелами. И абие удариша посреди полка христианского, аки в полгоры оные, и прерваша его, дондеже поправишася оные стратилатове, бо уже аки со двема тысящами и вяще взошли были на оную гору. И сразишася с ними крепце, и бысть сеча не мала между ими. Потом поспешишася другие стратилати с пешими нашими ручными стрельцы и сопроша бусурма-нов, яко конных, так и пеших, и гониша их биюще аже до самых врат градских, и около десять и живых поимаша. В той же час, вкупе во сражение оное, и стрельбу огненную со града изъявиша, яко со веж высоких, так и с стены

---

[a] Pog., T. препровадная: Ar., Patr.

---

[1] See above, p. 35, n. 7.
[2] Lit. "when... the advance regiment had crossed".
[3] *Yartaul* (or more correctly, *yortawul* or *yortaghul*) is a Turco-Mongol word meaning "raiding party" rather than "advance guard".
[4] According to the *razryady*, "in the *yartauly*" were Prince Yury Ivanovich

runs even as far as the little lake called Poganoe which lies beside the Kazan' river itself. From the Kazan' river the hill is so high that it is hard[1] to look up at it with the eye. On it stands the fortress and the khan's palace and the mosques; these are very tall, built of stone, and their dead khans used to be laid there—there are five of them in number, I recall.

Now at the beginning of the siege of that Mussulman town the Christian army was ordered to cross the above-mentioned little river, the Bulak, in three regiments. The first to cross, having thrown bridges over it, was the advance guard[2]—in that country they are wont to call it the *yartaul*;[3] it had in it select troops, about seven thousand, and in command of them were two generals, Princes Yury Pronsky and Fedor L'vov, exceedingly brave young men from the kin of the princes of Yaroslavl';[4] and they had to go with great difficulty right on to that hill, to Arsky plain, between the city and the above-mentioned Lake Kaban, about two arrow-flights from the gates of the city. The second regiment had only begun to cross the river by bridges when the khan of Kazan' sent out his cavalry from the city, about five thousand strong, and infantry, about ten thousand strong, against the first regiment which I have just mentioned —the Tatar cavalry had spears and the infantry arrows. And straightway they struck at the middle of the Christian regiment, which was about half-way up the hill, and they held it up until the two generals turned back, for they had already gone up the hill with about two thousand or more men. And they fought fiercely with them and there was a great battle between them. Then other generals hurried up with our foot musketeers and they drove away the Mussulmans, both cavalry and infantry, and chased them fighting even to the very gates of the fortress, and they captured about ten men alive.[5] And at that moment, at the same time as the battle was going on, they opened fire from the city, both from the high towers and from the town

Pronsky-Shemyakin and Prince Fedor Ivanovich (L'vov) Troekurov". See *DRK*, pp. 155, 156.

[5] The first skirmish is reported in the chronicle as having taken place on 25 August 1552. The general who came to the aid of the Advance Guard was Prince Dmitry Ivanovich Khilkov. See *PSRL* XIII, p. 205.

меские, на войско христианское стреляюще; но ничто же, за Божиею благодатию, тщеты сотвориша.

И абие в той день обступихом место и град бусурманский полки христианскими и отняхом ото всех стран пути и проезды ко граду: не возмогли они никако же ни из града, ни во град преходити. Тоже стратилатове, а по их воеводы полков, передовый полк, который ходит у них за яртаулом, прииде на Арское поле, и еще другий полк, в немъже бе царь Шигалей, и другие великие стратилатове залегоша тамо пути, яже от Нагайские страны ко граду лежат.

Мне же тогда, со другим моим товарыщем, правый рог, а по их правая рука, поручена была устрояти, аще ми и во младых летех сущу, бо еще мне было тогда лет аки двадесят и четыре от рождения; но всяко, за благодатию Христа моего, приидох к тому достоинству не туне, но по степенем[a] военным взыдох. И было в нашем полку вящей, нежели дванадесят тысящей, и пеших стрельцов и казаков аки шесть тысящей. И повелено нам итить за Казань реку; и прострошася войско полка нашего аж до Казани реки, яже выше града, а другий конец до мосту, яже по Галицкой дороге, и до тое же реки, яже ниже града; и залегохом пути ото всея Луговыя Черемисы, яже ко граду лежат. И случилося нам стояти на месте в равнине, на лугу, между великими блаты; граду же с нашей стороны на превеликой горе стоящу, и сего ради зело нам, паче всех, нужно было от огненныя стрельбы со града, а ззади с лесов от частаго наезжания Черемискаго. Другия же полки сташа между

_____

[a] T. по стенем: Ar., Patr., Pog.

_____

[1] During campaigns the Russian army was divided into five regiments or corps (полки): the Great Regiment (большой полк), the Right Hand (правая рука), the Left Hand (левая рука), the Leading Regiment (передовой полк) and the Guard (or Reserve) Regiment (сторожевой полк). On this occasion there was also an Advance Regiment, or Advance Guard (предний полк, яртаул).

[2] Shah Ali, a former puppet khan of Kazan', was nominally in command of the Great Regiment during the 1552 campaign. See *DRK*, p. 156.

walls, shooting at the Christian army. But thanks to the grace of God they did no damage.

And straightway on that day we surrounded the Mussulman city and fortress with Christian regiments and we cut off on all sides the paths and passages to the town: they could in no way come out of the town or go into the town. Then the generals (or in their language: the *voevody* of the regiments) and the Leading Regiment,[1] which with them marches behind the *yartaul*, came on to Arsky plain, and yet another regiment, in which was Khan Shah Ali,[2] and other great generals lay astride the ways which run from the Nogay side to the city.

Now at that time I and another comrade of mine were entrusted with the command of the Right Wing (or, in their language, the Right Hand),[3] although I was of tender years (for at that time I was still only about twenty-four years old); but nevertheless, thanks to the grace of my Christ, I achieved this rank not without reason, but I ascended by military degrees.[4] And in our regiment there were more than twelve thousand men, and about six thousand foot archers and Cossacks. And we were ordered to cross the Kazan' river; and the troops of our regiment stretched out right as far as that part of the Kazan' river which is above the fortress, and on the other side as far as the bridge on the Galich road and as far as that part of the river which is below the fortress; and we lay astride the approach routes leading towards the town from the entire district of the Meadow Cheremisians.[5] And we had to stand on a level place, in a meadow, between great bogs, the fortress opposite us being on a very high hill—for this reason we suffered more than all the others from firing from the fortress and in the rear from frequent Cheremisian raids from the forests. The other

[3] At the time of the Kazan' campaign Kurbsky was second in command of the Right Hand under Prince Petr Mikhaylovich Shchenyatev. See *DRK*, pp. 151, 156; *PSRL* xiii, pp. 207, 486.

[4] This seems to have been Kurbsky's first senior appointment. In 1550 he was *voevoda* of Pronsk, evidently a minor post. See *DRK*, p. 147.

[5] The "Meadow Cheremisians" (or Mari, Merians) inhabited an area west of Kazan' and north of the Volga (the "Low" or "Meadow" bank of the Volga being the left bank); the "Hill Cheremisians" lived south of the river, on the "Hill" bank.

Булаком и Казанию, об сю страну от Волги. Сам же царь с вальным гуфом, або со множеством воев, стал от Казани, аки за версту, або мало больши от града, с приходу своего от Волги, на месте на погористом. И сицевым чином месты и грады бусурманския облегоша. Царь же Казанский затворися во граде, со тремадесять тысящей избранных своих воинов и со всеми карачи духовными их и мирскими и з двором своим; а другую половину войска оставил вне града на лесех, тако же и те люди, яже Нагайский улубий прислал на помощь ему, а было их аки две тысящи и колько сот. И по трех днях начаша близу места шанцы ставити. Того бусурманы зело возбраниша, ово биюще со града, ово, вытекающе, вручь секошася, и падаху с обою стран множество люду, но обаче вяще бусурманов, нежели християн; и сего ради знак Божия милосердия являшеся християном, и дух храбрости нашим прискоряшеся.

Егда же добре и крепце заточиша шанцы, и стрельцы с[a] стратилати их закопашася в землю, аки уже безстрашны от стрельбы меские и от вытечек мняшеся, тогда привлекоша великие дела, и средние и огненные, близу града и места, имиже вверх стреляют; а памятамись, всех было аки полтораста и великих и средних, за всеми шанцами, ото всех стран града и места поставлены; а и мнейшие было по полторы сажени; окроме того были польные многие, около царских шатров. Егда же начаша бити со всех стран по стенам града, и уже очистиша стрелбу великую на граде, сиречь не даша им стреляти с великих дел на войско християнское, точию гаковничныя и ручничния не могоша отняти, еюже много тщеты делали войску християнскому в людех и конех.

[a] Pog. c omitted in Ar.

---

[1] Cf. Polish *walny huf*. Probably here = the Great Regiment.

[2] The word *karach*, a fairly common Tatar name in the sixteenth and seventeenth centuries, evidently designated a rank, such as beg or emir, as well.

[3] *Uluby*—probably a corruption of *ulus* or *ulush*, "nation", "tribe", "people".

regiments took up their positions between the Bulak and the Kazan' on this side [i.e. east] of the Volga. The tsar himself with the main force,[1] with a large number of soldiers, stood in a hilly place about a verst or a little more from the citadel of Kazan', having come from the Volga. And in such array they beleaguered the Mussulman city and fortress. Now the khan of Kazan' shut himself up in the city with his thirty thousand picked warriors and with all their spiritual and secular *karachi*[2] and with his bodyguard. And he left the other half of his army outside the fortress in the forests as well as those men whom the Nogay people[3] had sent to help him—of the latter there were about two thousand and several hundred. And after three days the Russians began to dig trenches near the town. This was fiercely contested by the Mussulmans, who now fought from the citadel, now ran out and fought hand to hand. And on both sides a great number of people fell, but more Mussulmans than Christians; and thus did the sign of God's mercy appear to the Christians, and the spirit of bravery was increased in our men.

Now when they had well and truly set the trenches in order and when the soldiers and their commanders had dug themselves into the earth, thinking themselves to be safe from the firing from the city and from sorties, then they dragged up to near the fortress and the town the large and the medium guns with which they fire upwards;[4] I remember that in all there were about one hundred and fifty large and medium guns behind all the trenches, placed on all sides of the fortress and town. And the smallest distance between them was one and a half *sazhen'*.[5] And apart from that there were many field guns near the tsar's tents. Now when they began to fire from all directions at the walls of the fortress, they had already silenced the large guns in the citadel, that is to say they did not allow the enemy to shoot from their heavy pieces at the Christian army; they were unable to silence only the arquebuses and muskets, with which the Tatars caused much damage to the Christian army in men and horses.

[4] I.e. mortars.
[5] Presumably the meaning of this elliptical sentence. A *sazhen'* is 2·134 metres, about seven feet.

И еще к тому тогда иную хитрость изобрете царь Казанский против нас. Яковую же? Молю, повеждь ми. Исте таковую. Но слухай прилежне, раздрочены воине! Ибо уложил он таковой совет со своими, с тем войском, ихъже оставил вне града на лесех, и положил с ними таковое знамение, а по их языку ясак: и егда изнесут на высокую вежу, або иногда на град, на высочайшее месце, хоруговь их, зело великую бусурманскую, и начнут ею махать, тогда, глаголю, — понеже далося нам знати, — ударят со всех стран с лесов, зело грозно и прутко, во устроению полков, бусурманы на полки християнские; а от града во все врата вытекали в тот же час на наши шанцы, и так зело жестоце и храбре натекали, яко и вере не подобно. И единова изыдоша сами карачи з двором царевым, а с ними аки десять тысящей войска, на те шанцы, идеже быша дела великие заточены, и так сотвориша сечу злую и жестокую бусурманы на християн, уже всех наших далеко от дел отогнали были; и, за помощию Божиею, приспеша шляхта Муромского повету; бо негде ту близ станы их были, и межи Русскими та шляхта зело храбры и мужественны мужие сущии, стародавныи в родех Руских. Тогда абие взопроша карачей со всеми силами их, аже принудишася от них подати тыл; а они аж до врат[a] меских секоша, биюще их, и не так множество посекоша, яко во вратех подавишася, тесноты ради; множество же и живых поимаше. В той же час и на другие врата вытекаше, но не так крепце бишася.

И воистину, на всякий день, аки три недели, тое беды было, яко и брашна нам оного зело нужнаго не дали приимати многожды. Но сице нам Бог помогал, ово храбре, за помощию Божиею, сражахуся с ними, пешие с пешими, от

[a] Patr., Pog., T. врать: Ar.

---

[1] *Yasak* usually means "tribute (in furs)" in Russian. It has an additional meaning of "order" or "command".

[2] The Polish word *szlachta* in the sixteenth century was the equivalent of the East Russian *dvoryanstvo* or *deti boyarskie*—in other words, the minor

And the khan of Kazan' at that time devised yet another piece of cunning against us. Of what kind? Tell me, I beseech you. Of such a kind, in truth. But listen attentively, O weary warrior! He arranged the following plan with the troops which he had left outside the fortress in the forests, and arranged this signal (or, in their tongue, *yasak*[1]): when they brought out their huge Mussulman banner on to a high tower—or sometimes on to the highest point on the citadel—and began to wave it, then, I say (for we got to know of this) the Mussulmans were to strike in battle array on all sides from the forests, most formidably and swiftly, against the Christian regiments. And at that very moment they ran out of the citadel through all the gates and attacked our trenches, and so fiercely and boldly did they attack that it is not believable. And at the same time the *karachi* themselves came out with the khan's bodyguard, and with them about ten thousand troops, to attack those trenches where the large guns had been placed; and so the Mussulmans fought a bloody, fierce battle with the Christians and drove all our men far away from the guns. And thanks to the help of God, the *szlachta*[2] from the district of Murom arrived there, for their camp was somewhere near at hand; and even among the Russians the men of this *szlachta* were exceedingly brave and valiant, and of ancient Russian stock. Then straightway they drove back the *karachi* and all their forces, so that the enemy were even forced by them to turn their backs. And they drove them back fighting as far as the gates of the city, but they did not kill a great number of them as they were crushed in the gates owing to their narrowness; but they captured many alive. And at the same time the Tatars made sorties through[3] other gates as well, but the fighting was not so fierce.

And indeed every day for about three weeks we suffered, because many a time they did not give us the opportunity to eat even the most essential food. But thus did God aid us: with the help of God our men fought bravely with the enemy, foot-

service nobility, the lesser gentry as opposed to the *pans* and the boyars, the aristocracy. In this context the word probably means little more than "detachment".

[3] на другие врата is probably in error for в другие врата.

43

града изходящими, конники же с конники, с леса наезжающими; а к тому и дела великия, яже суть з железными кулями, обращающе от града, стреляюще на те полки бусурманские, яже отовне града, с лесов, наезжали. А горее всех было от их наезжания тем христианским полком, яже стояли на Арском поле, яко и нам, з Галицкие дороги, яже суть от Луговые Черемисы. А которое стояло войско наше под градом, за Булаком, на которой стране и царь наш стоял, от Волги, те ото внешняго нахождения бусурманского в покою пребывали; точию из града частые вытечки имели, яко же ближайшие стояли под стенами града при делех. А кто бы поведал, яковую нам тщету в людех и в конех делали, которые слуги наши добывали травы, ездяще на кони наши, они[a] ротмистры, стрегуще с полки своими, не могуще везде обраняти их, злохитроства ради бусурманского и наглаго, внезапнаго, пруткаго их наезжания, — воистино и пишучи, не исписал бы по ряду, колько бито их и поранено.

Видев же царь Казанский, яко уже изнемогло было зело войско християнское, ноипаче тое, яже близу стень меских, пришанцовався, лежало, ово от частых вытечок и наезжания их с лесов, ово от скудости пищи — бе зело уже драго куповано всякие брашна; войску, за неиспокоем, яко рехом, не дано и сухаго хлеба наястися, а к тому мало не все нощи пребывах без сна, храняще дел паче же живота и чести своей, — егда же, яко рех, уразумел сие яко царь их, так и вне града бусурманские воеводове утружения войска нашего, тогда тем сильнее и частейше отовнее наезжали и из града исходили. Царь же наш со всеми сигклиты и стратилаты вниде в совет о сем, и совет в конец добр, благодати ради Божии, произведе: разделити повелел войско

[a] Т. аки: Ar.

---

[1] Arsky plain (lit. "field") lay to the north of Kazan'. It was named after the town of Arsk, or Arsky Gorod, fifty-six versts distant from Kazan'.

[2] A complicated sentence as it stands, and probably corrupt. I have read которые as некоторые, and они (var. аки) as ани (cf. Polish *ani*).

[3] Lit. "entered into council".

soldiers against foot-soldiers coming from the fortress, horsemen against horsemen attacking from the forest. And what is more, they even trained the large guns—those with the iron cannon-balls—away from the fortress, firing on those Mussulman regiments who were attacking outside the fortress, from the forests. But the worst to suffer from their attacks were those Christian regiments, such as ours, which were standing on Arsky plain,[1] for we were attacked by the Meadow Cheremisians along the Galich road. But those troops of ours which stood beneath the fortress beyond the Bulak river, on the side where our tsar stood, [east] of the Volga, were untroubled by Mussulman attacks from outside; only from the fortress were they subjected to frequent sorties, for they stood closest to the walls of the fortress by the guns. And who could tell of what damage the enemy inflicted upon us in men and horses? While some of our servants, riding on our horses, were foraging for hay, not even the cavalry commanders who were guarding them with their troops were able to afford them protection on all sides[2] because of the evil cunning of the Mussulmans and because of their sudden, unexpected swift raids—indeed, were I to write about it [in detail], I would not be able to enumerate how many of them were killed and wounded.

Now when the khan of Kazan' saw that the Christian army was already exhausted, especially that part of it which lay entrenched near the city walls, both because of the frequent sorties and their attacks from the forests and because of the shortage of food—for all victuals were bought at an extremely high price; the army, as I have said, was not given the opportunity to eat its fill even of dry bread because of the enemy's harassing tactics; and, what is more, almost every night I remained without sleep, guarding the guns more than my life and my honour—now when, as I have said, both the khan and the Mussulman generals outside the town realized the dire condition of our army, they attacked from outside and sallied forth from the fortress all the more strongly and frequently. But our tsar with all his advisers and generals discussed this matter in council.[3] And their council, which, by the grace of God, was extremely good, decided as follows: it ordered that

все на двое; аки половину его под градом при делях оставя, части ж не малой здравия своего стрещи повелел, при шатрех своих; а тридесят тысящей конников, устроя и розделив на полки по чину рыцерскому, и поставя над кождом полком по два, негде и по три стратилатов, храбрых, в богатырских вещах свидетельствованных; тако же и пеших, аки пятьнадесять тысящей, изведе стрельцов и казаков, и тако ж разделиша на гуфы по устроениям стратилатьским, поставя надо всеми ими гетмана великого, княжа Суздальского Александра, нареченнаго Горбатого, мужа зело разумнаго и статечнаго и в военных вещах свидетельствованного.[a] И повелел ждати, закрыв все войско христианское за горами; егда же изыдут бусурманы с лесов, по обычаю своему, тогда повеленно сразитися с ними.

Во утрие же, аки на третии године дня, изыдоша на великое поле, глаголемое Арское, от лесов полки бусурманские, и первие удариша на родмистров, яже на стражех в полцех стояще, коим было заповедано уступити им, уклоняющеся, аже[b] до шанцов; они же уповающе, аки боящеся християне побегоша, гнаша за ними.[c] Егда же втиснуша их уже в обоз, тогда начаша под шанцами круги водити и герцовати, стреляюще из луков, по подобию частости дождя; овы же, во устроению мнозем, по малу полки грядуще, конные и пешие, аки уже християн пожрети хотяще. Тогда убо, тогда, глаголю, изыдоша абие гетман с войском християнским, тако же во устроению мнозем, и приближишася со тщанием ко сражению. Видевше же бусурманы, и рады бы назад к лесу, но не возмогоша, уже бо далеко отъехали от него на поле; но обаче, хотяще и нехотяще, дали битву и крепце сразишася со первыми полки. Егда же надспел великий полк, в немже сам бяше гетман, такоже

[a] Patr., Pog. свидетельствованных: Ar. [b] Patr., Pog., T. яже: Ar. [c] T. нами: Ar.

---

[1] Prince Aleksandr Borisovich Gorbaty, a descendant of the princes of Suzdal', was made a boyar in 1544 and took part in the Kazan' campaign

the whole army be divided into two; about half were left by the guns beneath the citadel, while a considerable part were ordered to stay by their tents and keep out of danger; thirty thousand horsemen were arranged and divided into regiments according to cavalry array, and over each regiment were placed two, sometimes even three, generals, who were brave and tested in deeds of valour; and also the infantry, both archers and cossacks, were led away, some fifteen thousand strong, and were divided into regiments according to the dispositions of the commanders, and a great *hetman* was placed over them all, Aleksandr Gorbaty, prince of Suzdal',[1] a very wise and reliable man, experienced in military matters. And he ordered them to wait, having concealed all the Christian troops behind the hills; when the Mussulmans emerged from the forests according to their custom, they were ordered to fight them.

Now on the next day, at about the third hour, the Mussulman regiments came out from the forests on to the great plain called Arsky and first they attacked the cavalry commanders who were standing on guard with their regiments and who had been instructed to yield to them and to retreat as far as the trenches. And the Tatars, hoping that the Christians had fled in fear, chased after them. And when they had driven them back as far as their base, they began to circle around by the trenches and fight, shooting from their bows after the fashion of a heavy rainstorm. And some of them in full battle array little by little advanced on our troops, both cavalry and infantry, wishing, as it were, to swallow up the Christians. Then, however, then, I say, the *hetman* came out straightway with the Christian army, also in full battle array, and with haste they approached the fighting. But when the Mussulmans saw them, they would have been glad to go back to the forest, but they were not able to do so, for they had already gone far from it on to the plain; but nevertheless, whether they wanted to or not, they joined battle and fought fiercely with the first regiments. And when the Great Regiment, in which the *hetman* himself was, arrived and when the infantry regiments ap-

of 1549. He was appointed the first governor (*namestnik*) of Kazan' after the capture of the city. For his subsequent fate, see below, pp. 184–5.

и пешие полки приближашася, обходяще их, ноипаче от лесу, тогда абие в бегство обратишася все полки их; християнское же воинство гониша за ними, биюще их, и яко на пол-2 мили трупия бусурманского множество лежаше, и к тому аки тысячю живых поимаша. Тогда, за Божиею помощию, таковую пресветлую победу християне над бусурманы одержаша.

Егда же приведоша живых вязней оных ко царю нашему, тогда повелел, пред шанцы выведши, привязати их х колью, да во граде сущих своих молят и напоминают, да подадут Казанское место цареви християнскому; тако же и наши ездяше, напоминали их, обещевающе им живот и свободу, яко тем вязнем, так и сущим во граде, от царя нашего. Они же, сих словес выслухав тихо, абие начаша стреляти с стен града, не так по наших, яко по своих, глаголюще: "Лутче, рече, увидим вас мертвых от рук наших бусурманских, нежели бы посекли вас кгауры необрезанные!" И иные словеса отрыгающе хульные, с яростию многою, яко и всем нам дивитися зряще.

И по сем, аки по трех днех, повелел царь наш итти тому княжати Александру Суздальскому[a] с тем же войском на засеку, яже были бусурманы сооружили стену, между великими блаты, на горе единой, аки две мили от места, идеже паки, по разбежанию оном, собрашася множество их, и умыслиша оттуду, аки из града единаго выезжаючи, паки ударяти на войско християнское. И к тому еще, ко оному предреченному гетману придано другаго гетмана, а по их великого воеводу, со полки его, именем князя Семена Микулинского, с роду великих княжат Тверских, мужа зело храбраго и в богатырских вещах искуснаго; и дано им повеление таково: аще им бы Бог помогл оную стену проломити, да идут всем войском аж до Арского города, который лежит от Казани дванадесять миль великих. Егда же при-

[a] Pog., T. суздаскому: Ar.

---

[1] Prince Semen Ivanovich Mikulinsky-Punkov had a distinguished military career before the last Kazan' campaign. The youngest son of

proached, outflanking them particularly on the side of the forest, then straightway all the Tatar regiments turned to flight. And the Christian army chased after them, fighting them, and for one and a half miles a great number of Mussulman corpses lay scattered; furthermore they captured about a thousand alive. And so with God's help the Christians won a brilliant victory over the Mussulmans.

And when they brought the prisoners whom they had captured alive to our tsar, he ordered them to be led out in front of the trenches and be bound to stakes, so that they might beg and warn their comrades within the fortress to hand over the city of Kazan' to the Christian tsar. And our men rode on horseback and warned them, promising in the name of the tsar life and freedom, both for the prisoners and for those in the fortress. But having listened to these words in silence, the Tatars began to shoot from the walls of the fortress, not so much on our men as on their own men, saying: "We would rather see you killed by our Mussulman hands than slaughtered by the uncircumcised Giaours!" And other blasphemous words they belched forth with much fury so that all of us who were watching were amazed.

And about three days after this our tsar ordered Prince Aleksandr Suzdal'sky, with the same force, to go against the abattis—a wall which the Mussulmans had erected on a hill between the great swamps, about two miles from the city; for after they had dispersed, they had gathered there in large numbers and they planned to attack the Christian army from there, sallying forth as it were from a fortress. Furthermore, to that above-mentioned *hetman* was attached another *hetman*, or in their language, great *voevoda*, with his troops, Prince Semen Mikulinsky, from the kin of the grand princes of Tver', a man of great bravery and skilled in deeds of valour.[1] And they were given the following order: should God help them to break through that wall, they were to go with all their army as far as Arsky Gorod, which lies twelve great miles from Kazan'. Now

Grand Prince Mikhail Aleksandrovich of Tver' (d. 1399), Fedor, was appanage prince of Mikulin in the district of Tver'. S. I. Mikulinsky was descended from him.

идоша ко оной стене, опрошася бусурманы и начаша бранитися крепце, аки на две годины биющеся; потом, за Божиею помощию, одолеша их наши, яко огненною стрельбою, так ручною, и побегоша бусурманы; наши жь гонили их. Егда же препроводишася все войско великое за оную стену, и оттуду цареви нашему с сеунчем[1] послали; и тамо наше воинство об нощь пребыло и обретоша в шатрех и в станех бусурманских не мало корыстей; и приидоша, аки за два дни, до онаго[a] предреченнаго града Арского и обретоша его пуст покинен, от страха бо избежаша из него все, страха ради, в далечайшие лесы. И плениша тамо в земли оной аки 10 дней, понеже в земле той поля великие, и зело преизобильные и гобзующе на всякие плоды; тако же и дворы княжат их и вельможей зело прекрасны и воистину удивлению[b] достойни, и села часты; хлебов же всяких такое там множество, воистину вере ко исповеданию неподобно: аки бы на подобие множества звезд небесных; тако же и скотов различных стад бесчисленныя множества, и корыстей драгоценных, наипаче от различных зверей, в той земли бывающих; бо тамо родятся куны дорогие, и белки и протчие зверие ко одеждам и ко ядению потребны; а мало за тем далей соболей множество, такожде и медов: не вем, где бы под солнцем[c] больши было. И по десятих днех, со бесчисленными корыстьми и со множеством плену бусурманских жен и детей, возвратишася к нам здраво, тако же и своих древле заведеных многих от бусурман свободиша от многолетныя работы. И бысть тогда в воинстве християнском велия радость и благодарение к Богу воспевали, и так было таней в войску нашем всякие живности, иже краву куповано за десять денег Московских[2], а вола великого за десять аспр.

[a] Patr., Pog., T. до наго: Ar.   [b] Patr., Pog., T. удоблению: Ar.
[c] Pog. селцом: Ar. сонцем: Patr.

---

[1] Сеунч—a Tatar word of obscure origin usually denoting a message.
[2] A Moscow *den'ga* was half a copeck, or a sixth of an *altyn*. An *aspr* was

when they arrived at that wall, the Mussulmans stood firm and began strongly to resist, fighting for about two hours. Then with God's help our troops overcame them with musketry and archery, and the Mussulmans fled while our troops chased them. And when all the great army had crossed that wall they sent information from there to our tsar by messenger.[1] Our men spent the night there and they found much booty in the tents and in the camps of the Mussulmans. And in about two days they came to the town of Arsk which I have mentioned and they found it empty and abandoned, for all had fled in fear from it into the most distant forests. And they ravaged the land for about ten days, for in that land there are great plains, which are most fertile and which abound in all kinds of fruits; also the courts of their princes and magnates are extremely fine and indeed amazing, and the villages are frequent. As for grain, there are so many different kinds that it would indeed be hard to believe, were one to tell of them all—it would be like the multitude of the stars in the sky. There are, too, countless herds of different kinds of cattle and there is valuable profit to be had especially from the various wild beasts which are in that land; for costly martens breed there and squirrels and other animals which can be used for clothing and for food. Furthermore there are a great number of sables and also many kinds of honey—I know not where beneath the sun there are more. And after ten days they returned safely to us with incalculable booty and with a multitude of captive Mussulman wives and children; and also they freed from long-lasting slavery many of their countrymen, who had long ago been captured by the Mussulmans. And at that time there was great rejoicing in the Christian army and we sang our thanks to God, and in our army all forms of livestock were cheaper—one could buy a cow for ten Moscow *den'gi* and a large ox for ten squirrel skins.[2]

used by the Poles to denote a squirrel skin, which in Muscovy was still used as a monetary unit in the mid sixteenth century, being approximately the equivalent of three *den'gi*.

The capture of Arsky Gorod, which took place in September 1552, is described in greater detail in *PSRL* xiii, pp. 210–11.

Скоро по возвращению онаго войска потом, аки по четырех днях, собралося Черемисы Луговыя не мало, и ударили на наши станы задние, з[a] Галицкие дороги, и не мало стад коней наших отграмили. Мы же абие послали в погоню за ними трех ротмистров, и за ними других посылочные полки во устроению, засады ради; и угонено их в трех, або в четырех милах, и овых избиша, других живых поимаша.

А естьли бы писал по ряду, яко тамо под градом на кождый день деялось, того бы целая книга была. Но вкратце сице воспомянути достоит, яко они[b] на войско христианское чары творили и великую плювию наводили: яко скоро по облежанию града, яко солнце начнет восходити, взыдут на град, всем нам зрящим, ово пристаревшися их мужи, ово бабы, и начнут вопияти сатанинские словеса, машуще одеждами своими на войско наше и вертящеся неблагочинне. Тогда абие востанет ветр и сочинятся облаки, аще бы и день ясен зело начинался, и будет такий дождь, и сухие места в блат обратятся и мокроты исполнятся; и сие точию было над войском, а по сторонам несть, не точию по естеству аера случишася. Видевше же сие, абие советоваше цареви послати по древо спасенное до Москвы, яже во крест вделано, который всегда при царском венце лежит. И сбегано, за Божиею помощию, зело скоро, водою до Новаграда Нижнего, аки в три, або четыре дни, Вяцкими, зело скоро плавающими кораблецы, а от Новаграда аж до Москвы прудкошественными подводами. Егда же привезен честный крест, в немъже частка вделана спасеннаго древа, на немже Господь наш Исус Христос плотию страдал за человеки, тогда прозвитеры соборне, со церемониями християнскими, обхождения творяху, и по обычаю церковному освятиша им воды, и силою животворящаго креста абие от того часа ищезоша и без вести быша чары оные поганские.

И в то же время у них подкопом воду отнято, за 2, або

Soon after the return of that army, some four days later, a large number of Meadow Cheremisians gathered together and attacked our rear camps from the Galich road and drove off many of our herds of horses. And straightway we sent three cavalry commanders to chase them, and after them we sent other flying detachments in battle array in order to ambush them. And they pursued them for three or four miles, and some they killed and others they captured alive.

If I were to enumerate all the things that happened every day near the fortress, it would result in a whole book. But it is worth briefly recalling how the Tatars worked magic against the Christian army and brought on great rains. Soon after the investment of the fortress, when the sun began to rise, both very old men and women would come out on to the citadel in full view of us and would shout out satanic words, waving their clothes at our army and turning round in an indecorous manner. Then straightway the wind would rise and clouds would be made even if the day had started very clearly, and there would be such rain as to turn the dry places into swamps and fill them with moisture. And this would only happen directly over our army, and not outside it—and it did not occur according to the nature of the air.[1] And seeing this the tsar's counsellors advised him to send to Moscow for the wood of the Saviour inserted into the Cross which always lies by the tsar's crown. And with God's help the journey was made extremely quickly—by water to Nizhny Novgorod in about three or four days, on very swift small Vyatka sailing-boats, and from Novgorod as far as Moscow by fast-moving carriages. Now when they brought the holy Cross into which had been inserted the piece of the Saviour's wood on which our Lord Jesus Christ suffered in the flesh for man, then all the priests together went in procession around the whole army, performing the Christian rites, and according to the custom of the Church sanctified the water with it. And thanks to the power of the life-giving Cross straightway from that hour onwards all trace of the pagan magic disappeared.

And at that same time the enemy's water was cut off by

[1] In other words, it was not a natural phenomenon.

за три недели до взятья; бо ся тамо под вежу великую и под тайники подкопано, откуду они на весь град воду брали, и порохов подставлено, аки двадесять бочек великих: башню и вырвало. И к тому у нас вежу, над обычай великую и высокую, за две недели уроблено потаемне, за полмили от града, и единыя нощи близу рва мескаго поставлено и на нея взношенно стрельбы десять дел и пятьдесят гаковниц; и зело великую шкоту в месте и во граде на всяк день чинено с нее; бо до взятья градскаго побито люду бусурманского военного,[a] кроме жен и детей, близу десяти тысящей со всех стран, и з дел и на вытечках их, ис тое то вежи. А яко ее ставлено, и яковым обычаем и иные различные стенобитные хитрости творено, сие оставляю, краткости ради и истории, бо широце в летописной Руской книзе о том писано. Толико о взятии града мало воспомянем, елико можем вспамятати, вкратце опишем. Понеже не токмо Бог разум и дар духа храбрости тогда подавал, но явления некоторыя достойным и чистыя[b] совести мужем, в нощных видениях, изъявил о взятию града бусурманского, к сему подвижуще воинство, яко мню, отомщающе безчисленное и многолетное разлияния крови християнские, а оставльшихся еще тамо живых избавляюще от многолетные работы.

Егда же, по скончанию седми недель от облежения града, заповедано нам, еще во дни, утренной зари ждати до востока солнца, и повелено готовлятися со всех стран ко штурму, и дано таково знамение: егда взорвут стену порохи, яже в подкопе; бо было в другий раз подкопано и засажено 48 бочек пороху под стеною мескою; и большую половину войска пешого ко штурму послано; аки же третина войска

---

[a] Pog. воеинного: Ar.   [b] Patr., Pog., T. частыя: Ar.

---

[1] For a more detailed description of the cutting of the town's water supply, see *PSRL* xiii, pp. 210, 505–6. According to these two sources the date was 4 September and the number of barrels of powder eleven.

undermining, two or three weeks before the capture of the city. The great tower and the secret passages were undermined in the place from where water was taken for the whole town, and about twenty large barrels of powder were placed beneath it, and the tower was blown up.[1] And we too had a tower, extraordinarily large and tall, which was secretly built in two weeks half a mile from the town. And one night it was placed near the moat of the city and on to it were raised ten artillery pieces and fifty muskets; and great damage was caused by it every day both in the town and in the fortress, for up to the capture of the city nigh on ten thousand Mussulman soldiers all told, apart from women and children, were killed from that tower, both by the guns and as a result of the raids carried out from it. As for how it was placed in position and in what way various other cunning battering devices were made, I forbear to relate for the sake of the brevity of my story, for in the Russian chronicle book[2] this has been written about at length. We will only recall a little about the taking of the town and will describe it in short, in so far as we can remember it. Not only did God grant understanding and the gift of the spirit of bravery, but also He manifested by night to men of merit and of clear conscience certain visions of the taking of the Mussulman town, urging the army on to this and, I think, avenging the incalculable and long-lasting shedding of Christian blood and freeing those Christians who still remained there alive from their longlasting slavery.

Now when seven weeks had elapsed from the investment of the city, we were told while it was still daylight to wait for dawn at the rising of the sun on the following day, and we were ordered to prepare for an assault on all sides. And the following signal was given: [we were to attack] when the wall was blown up by the powder which was in the underground passage, for the city wall had been undermined a second time and fortyeight barrels of powder had been placed beneath it. More than half of the infantry were sent to storm the town, while about a

[2] A reference, evidently, to the *Tsarstvennaya Kniga*, in which a detailed description of the erection and application of the tower is given. See *PSRL* XIII, pp. 507–8.

всего, або мало больши, на полю осташася, паче же стрегуща здравия царева. Мы же, по повеленному, рано к сему уготовавшеся, аки за две годины еще до зори, бо аз тогды послан был к нижайшим вратом, с верху Казани реки, приступати, а со мною было дванадесять тысещей войска. Ото всех же четырех стран тако же устроено пресильных[a] и храбрых мужей, некоторых и з большими почты. Царь же сие Казанские и сенаты его уведали о сем, и так же на нас уготовались, яко же и мы на них.

Пред самым же солничным восходом, або мало что уже нача солнцу являтися, взорвало подкоп: войско же християнское абие ударело со всех стран на место и град, по повелению цареву. Да свидетельствует кождый о себе; аз же, что пред очима тогда имех и делах, повем истину вкратце. Разрядих войско мое дванадесять тысещей под устроением стратилатов; потекохом ко грацким стенам и к той великой башни, яже пред враты стояла на горе. Егда же еще быхом подалече от стен, не из единыя ручницы, або стрелою, на нас стрелено; егда уже близу быхом, тогда первие много огненный бой на нас пущен с стен и з башен; тогда стрел густость такая, яко частость дожда, тогда камения множество безчисленное, яко и воздуха не видети! Егда же близу стену подбихомся с великою нуждою и бедою, тогда вары кипящими начаша на нас лити и целыми бревны метати. Всяко же Божия помощь помогаше нам тем, еже храбрость и крепость и запамятания смерти дароваше, и воистинну с поощрением сердца и с радостию бишася з бусурманы за православное християнство; и аки бы за полгодины отбиша их от окон стрелами и ручницами. А к тому и дела из за шанцов наших помогаше нам, стреляюще на них; бо они явственно уже стояще на башне оной великой и на стенах града, не хранящеся, яко прежде, но крепце с нами, и обличне и вручь, бьющесь. И абие могли бы их избити, но много нас ко штурму приидоша, а мало под стены градные приидоша: некоторые возвращающеся, множество лежаще и творящеся побиты и ранены.

[a] Т. присылных: Аг.

third of the whole army, or a little more, remained on the plain, guarding the life of the tsar. But we, according to the orders given to us, prepared for the attack early—about two hours before dawn: I had been sent to assault the lower gates from upstream on the Kazan' river, and I had with me twelve thousand troops. On all four sides mighty and valiant men were drawn up, some of them with large detachments. When the khan of Kazan' and his counsellors learned about this, they too prepared against us as we had against them.

Just before the rising of the sun, or a little after it had begun to appear, the underground passage exploded and the Christian army immediately attacked the town and the fortress on all sides, according to the order of the tsar. Let each man tell of his own deeds; I will briefly and truthfully narrate what I had before my own eyes at that time and what I did. I allocated my twelve thousand troops to their various commanders and we ran up to the walls of the fortress, to that great tower which stood on a hill in front of the gates. When we were still quite far off from the walls, we were not fired at from a single musket or bow; but when we got near, then for the first time fire was directed on us from the walls and from the towers. The arrows fell so thickly that they were like heavy rain, and so incalculably great was the number of stones that the sky could not be seen! And when we had fought our way up to the wall with great difficulty and suffering, they began to pour boiling water on us and to hurl whole beams at us. None the less God helped us by giving us bravery and strength and forgetfulness of death, and in truth with cheerful heart and with joy we fought the Mussulmans for Orthodox Christianity; and within about half an hour we drove them away from the embrasures with arrows and musket fire. Furthermore, the guns from behind our trenches helped us, firing at them; for they now stood openly at that great tower and on the walls of the fortress, not concealing themselves as before, but fighting fiercely with us, face to face and hand to hand. And we might straightway have killed them all, but, although many of us took part in the assault, few came right up to the walls of the fortress: some went back and many lay on the ground pretending to be killed or wounded.

За тем Бог поможе нам! Первый брат мой родный на стену града взыде по лествице, и другии воини храбрые с ним; а овые, секущесь и колющесь з бусурманы, в окна оные великие башни влезже, а из башни сметавшись во врата великие градные; бусурманы же абие тыл подаша, стены градные оставив, побегоша на великую гору, ко двору цареву, бо бе зело крепок, между полат и мечетей каменных, оплотом великим обточен. Мы же за ними ко двору цареву, аще и удружденны во збройах, а многие храбрые мужие на телесах раны уже имуще, и зело нас мало осталося биющихся с ними. А войско наше, яже было остало,[a] вне града, яко увидели, иже мы уже во граде, а Татаровя с стен побегоша, все во град ринулося: и лежащая, глаголемыя раненые,[b] воскочиша и творящия сна мертвыя возкресоша. И со всех не токмо те, но и с станов, и кашавары, и яже были у конех оставлены,[c] и друзии, яже и с куплею приехаша, все збегошася во град, не ратного ради дела, но на корысть многую; бо то место воистинну полно было дражайших корыстей, златом, и сребром, и камением драгоценным, и собольми кипело и другими великими богатствы. Татаровя же запрошася с нашу страну на цареве дворе, а дольную часть места покинули, елико их могло утещи; а другую сторону, яже с Арского поля, откуду подкоп взорвало, царь Казанский з двором своим уступя, аки в половину места, застоновился на Тезицком рве, по нашему на купецком, биющесь крепце со християны; бо того места две части, аки на равнине, на горе стоят; а третия часть зело удольна, аки в пропасти; а поперег, аки в половицу места, от стены Булака аж до дольные части места,[d] ров не малый. А место оно не мало, мало что от Виленского мнейше.

И бысть сее предреченныя битвы аки на четыре годины и

<hr />

[a] T. оттамо: Ar.   [b] Patr., Pog., T.   раненых: Ar.   [c] Patr., T. уставлены: Ar.   [d] Patr., Pog., T. место: Ar.

<hr />

[1] Kurbsky had two brothers, Roman and Ivan. Roman was with him at the time of the siege of Kazan'.

After this God helped us! My own brother[1] was the first to mount the fortress wall by ladder, and there were other brave soldiers with him. And some, cutting and thrusting at the Mussulmans, climbed into the embrasures of the great tower and from the tower they rushed to the great gates of the fortress; and straightway the Mussulmans turned their backs, and leaving the fortress walls, ran to the great hill, to the court of the khan, for it was in a very strong position between stone palaces and mosques, surrounded by a great barrier. And we followed them to the khan's court, although we were encumbered by our armour and although many brave men amongst us had already suffered wounds and there remained very few of us fighting them. And when those of our troops who had remained outside the fortress saw that we were already in it and that the Tatars had fled from the walls, they all rushed into the fortress; and those who called themselves wounded and were lying on the ground jumped up, and those who feigned the sleep of death rose from the dead. And everyone on all sides—not only those whom I have mentioned, but men from the camps, and cooks, and those who had been left with the horses, and others who had come with the merchandise—all ran together into the fortress, not for military reasons, but in order to get at the vast booty there. For the city was indeed full of the most valuable spoils, both gold and silver and precious stones, and it teemed with sables and other great riches. Now the Tatars on our side of the town barricaded themselves in the khan's court, and as many as could run away abandoned the lower half of the town; and on the other side, on the side of Arsky plain—the side from which the underground passages had been blown up—the khan of Kazan', withdrawing with his bodyguard to about half-way through the town, stopped at Tezitsky Ditch (in our tongue: Merchants' Ditch), fighting fiercely with the Christians; for two-thirds of the town stands on a hill, as it were on a plain, while the other third is low-lying, as it were in a gulf; and across, cutting the town roughly in half, from the Bulak wall to the lower part of the city, there runs a large ditch. The town is large, a little smaller than Vilna.

This battle I have just mentioned—the scaling of the walls

вящей, памятамись, ото всех стран добывания на стены и во граде сечно. И як видевше бусурманы, иже християнского войска мало оставает, — мало не все на корысти падоша: мнози, яко глаголют, по два крат и по три в станы отхождаху с корыстьми и паки возвращахуся, храбрии же воини безпрестани бьющесь, — видевше же сие бусурманы, иже утрудишася уже воины храбрые, и начаша крепце налегати, ополчающесь на них. Корыстовники же оные предреченные, егда увидели, что наши по нужде уступают по малу, бранящесь бусурманом, в таковое абие бегство вдашася, яко и во врата многие не попали; но множайшие и с корыстьми чрез стену метались, а иные и корысти повергоша, только вопиюще: секут! секут! Но, за благодатию Божиею, храбрым сердцем не сокрушили; бо и с нашу сторону зело было тяжко от належания бусурманов: в то время, отнележе во град внидоша и изыдоша, в моем полку девяносто и осмь храбрых мужей убито, кроме́ раненых; но обаче, благодати ради Божии, устояхом на нашей стороне сопротив их неподвижны. Со оныя же предреченныя страны мало что поступиша, яко рекохом, великого ради множества належания их. И даша о собе ведати цареви нашему и всем советником, окрест его в тот час бывшим, яко и самому ему зрящу бегство из града оных предреченных бегунов: и зело ему не токмо лице изменяшесь, но и сердце сокрушися, уповая, иже все войско уже християнское бусурманы из града изгнаша. Видевше же сицевое, мудрые и искусные сигклитове его повелеша херуговь великую християнскую близу врад градцких, нареченных Царских, подвинути, и самого царя, хотяща и не хотяща, за бразды коня взяв, близ хоругови поставиша — понеже были нецыи, между синглицы оными, мужие веку еще отцов наших, состаревшиеся в добродетелях и во всяких искуствах ратных. — Полку же царскому великому, в котором было вяще, нежели двадесять тысещей воинов избранных, абие повелено соити с коней, аки половине; такожде[a] не токмо детем своим и сродным повелеша,

[a] Т. тамо же: Аг.

and the fighting in the fortress—lasted for about four hours or more, I recall. And when the Mussulmans saw that few of the Christian troops remained—for practically all of them fell on to the spoil, and many, so they say, went back two or three times to the camps with loot and returned again, while the brave soldiers fought on without ceasing—when the Mussulmans saw that these brave soldiers were exhausted, they began to press strongly and to attack them. Now when the looters I have mentioned saw that our troops, while resisting the Mussulmans, were of necessity retreating little by little, they immediately took to flight in such a way that many of them were unable to get through the gates; but a great number rushed over the wall with their loot, while others even threw away their loot crying: "They are killing! They are killing!" But thanks to the grace of God the brave of heart were not stricken. In our sector many suffered sorely from the attack of the Mussulmans—for from the time we entered the fortress to the time we left it ninety-eight brave men in my regiment were killed, to say nothing of the wounded. However, thanks to the grace of God, we on our side held our ground against them. But in the other sector which I have mentioned above they barely moved owing, as I have said, to the great pressure of the enemy. And they sent word about their position to our tsar and to all his counsellors who were with him at that time—the tsar himself was watching the flight of those above-mentioned runaways. And not only did the tsar's face change, but his heart was stricken, for he had hoped that all the Christian troops had already driven the Mussulmans from the fortress. And when his wise and skilled counsellors saw what was going on, they ordered the great Christian banner to be raised near the gates of the fortress called the Royal gates, and, taking his horse by the bridle, they placed the tsar himself, whether he liked it or not, near the banner—for amongst those counsellors were some men of the generation of our fathers, men mature in virtues and in all kinds of military skills. And about half of the tsar's Great Regiment, in which there were more than twenty thousand picked men, were ordered forthwith to dismount. And also the counsellors not only ordered their children and relatives to dis-

но и самих[a] их половина, сшедше с коней, потекоша во град, на помощь утружденым оным воином.

Егда же приидоша во град внезапу так много воинства свежего, в пресветлые зброи оболченнаго, абие царь Казанский со всем воинством начаша уступовати назад, обаче броняшеся крепце; наши же по них неотступъно крепцей находяще, секущеся с ними. Егда уже погнаша их аж до мечетей, яже близу царева двора стоят, абие изыдоша во сретение наших абазы их, сеиты, молвы, пред великим бискупом их, а по их с великим анарыи, або амиром, имянем Кулшериф-молвою, и сразишась с нашими так крепце, аж до единаго избиша их. Царь же со всеми остатними затворился во дворе своем, нача бранитися крепце, аки еще на полторы годины биющеся. Егда же видев, яко не возможе уже помощи собе, тогда на едину сторону отобраша жен и детей своих, в прекрасных и в преиспещренных одеждах, околько десять тысещей, и сташа на единой стране великого предреченного двора царева, уповающе, иж прельстятся войско християнское на красоту их и живити их будут. Сами же Татаровя со царем их отобрашесь во един угол и умыслиша не датися живым в руки, точию бы царя живаго соблюсти; и поидоша от царева двора на дольную[b] сторону места к нижайшим вратом, идеже аз сопротив их у царева двора стоях, и не остало уже было со мною полутороста воинов, а их еще было о десять тысещей; обаче, тесноты ради улицы, бронились есмя им, отходяще и опирающеся, крепце. Наше же войско великое з горы оные да потиснуша их зело, паче же задний конец Татарского полку, секуще и бьюще; тогда едва с великою нуждою, за Божиею помощию, изыдохом из врат градцких. Наши же с великие горы крепце належаще, тиснуша их, нам же об ону страну стоящим, во вратех биющеся, не пущающе их из града; уже бо нам на помощь два полка християнские приспеша. Им же так тиснушася

a

[a] Patr., Pog. сами: Ar.   [b] Patr., Pog. дальную: Ar.

[1] *Abaz* is presumably a corruption of *hafiz*, one who knows the Koran by heart. *Seyyid*: a descendant of the Prophet; *molla*: priest, or judge. The meaning and origin of *anary* are not known.

mount, but half of them did so too, and they ran into the fortress to help the exhausted soldiers.

Now when so many fresh troops clad in brilliant armour suddenly came into the fortress, the khan of Kazan' straightway began to retreat with all his forces, though strongly defending himself, while our men attacked them and fought them relentlessly and fiercely. When they had driven them as far as the mosques which are near the khan's court, their *abazes*, *seyyids* and *mollas* in front of their great bishop (or in their language, great *anary* or *emir*) who was called Molla Kul-Sherif,[1] came out straightway to meet our men, and they fought with our troops so fiercely that they [the Russians] killed them all to a man. Now the khan shut himself up in his court with all his remaining troops and began to resist strongly, fighting for about another hour and a half. And when they saw that they could no longer help themselves, they took to one side their wives and their children clad in their fair multicoloured garments, some ten thousands in number, and they stood on one side of the khan's great court hoping that the Christian troops would be seduced by their beauty and would spare their lives. The Tatars themselves withdrew with their khan to one corner and planned not to surrender themselves alive, so as to protect the life of the khan alone; and they went from the khan's court to the lower part of the town, towards the lower gates; and I stood opposite them as they left the khan's court,[2] and I had not even a hundred and fifty men left, whereas they were about ten thousand strong. But owing to the narrowness of the street we resisted them fiercely, both withdrawing and holding our ground. And our great force [came down] from that hill and pressed them strongly, especially the rear section of the Tatar troops, slashing and striking them; at that time with God's help we came out from the fortress gates with great difficulty. Now our troops from the high hill attacked fiercely and pressed them, fighting in the gates, while we stood on the other side; but they did not let them out of the fortress, for already two Christian regiments had come to our help. And the Tatars

[2] Presumably the meaning of this elliptical clause, which, translated literally, reads: "where I stood opposite them by the khan's court".

63

неволею, великого ради належания з горы, иже с вежею высокою равно, яже надо врты бяше, полно трупия их лежаше; средним же и задним людем аж по людем своим идуще на град и на вежу. Егда же возведоша царя своего на вежу, тогда начаша вопияти, просяще малого времяни на розмову; мы же, мало утишився, послушавше прошения их. Они же абие сице реша, глаголюще: "Поки, рече, а юрт[a] стояше и место главное, идеже престол царев был, потыя ж до смерти броняху же за царя а отечество; а ныне царя вам отдаем здрава: ведете его ко царю своему. А остаток[b] нас исходим на широкое поле испити с вами последнюю чашу." И отдаша нам царя своего со единым корачом, што наибольшим их, и со двема имилдеши.[c] Царю их было имя бусурманское Идигер, а князю оному Зениеш. И отдав нам царя здрава, по нас абие стрелами, а мы по них. И не поидоша на нас во врата, но абие поидоша с стены просто чрез Казань реку, и хотяше пробитися, прямо против моего стану, на шанцы теми дирами, идеже шесть дел великих стояло.

И абие по них ударено иза всех тех дел. Они же воздвигошася оттуду и поидоша налево вниз, водле Казань реку, берегом, аки три перестрелы лучных, и по конец шанец наших; тамо сташа и начаша лехчитися и метати у себя зброи и розувати себя, ко бредению реки, еще бо бе их остал полк, аки шесть тысещей, або мало мнейше. Мы же видевши сие, мало нас нечто добыша собе коней от своих станов за реку, и так, седши на свои кони, устремишася скоро сопротив их и заступиша им путь, имже хотяху поити. И обретоша еще их не[d] пришедших чрез реку, и собрашася нас сопротив их мало что больши дву сот коней,

[a] юрт исмаилтеским языком обыче нарицатися царство само в себе стояще: in margin of Patr. and Pog.   [b] Patr. отостаток: Ar.
[c] мамичи яже бывают питаеми единем сосцом с царским отрочатем: in margin of Ar.   [d] Patr., Pog. на: Ar.

---

[1] A marginal note reads as follows: "in the Ishmaelite tongue a kingdom standing by itself is usually called a *yurt*".

were so sorely pressed because of the great attack from the hill that the place level with the high tower which stood above the gates was piled up with their corpses, and those in the middle and in the rear clambered up to the citadel and the tower over the bodies of their own men. But when they brought their khan up on to the tower, they began to cry out, begging for a little time in which to parley. And we quietened down a little and hearkened to their request. And straightway they spoke as follows, saying: "As long as our *yurt*[1] stood and the main city in which is the throne of our khan, so long have we defended unto death both khan and fatherland. But now we hand over to you our khan alive: lead him to your tsar. And the remainder of us are going out on to the open plain to drink with you the last cup."[2] And they handed over their khan to us with a certain *karach*, who was the most important of them, and with two *imeldeshi*.[3] And their khan's Mussulman name was Ediger and the prince's, Zeniesh. And having handed over their khan to us alive, they straightway began to fire arrows at us, and we at them. And they did not attack us in the gates but went straight from the walls across the Kazan' river; they wanted to fight their way through—right opposite my camp—to the trenches by the pits in which the six large guns stood.

And immediately they were fired on by all guns, and they moved from there and went down to the left along the bank of the Kazan' river, about three bow-shots away, as far as the end of our trenches. There they stopped and began to dress their wounds and to cast off their armour and remove their footwear so as to be able to ford the river, for a whole regiment of them still remained, about six thousand or a little less. Now when we saw this, a few of us got our horses from the camps on the other side of the river, and, having mounted them, galloped off against them and blocked the path along which they were about to go. And we caught them before they had crossed the river. There were a little more than two hundred of us who

[2] "To drink the cup (of death)" was a favourite battle image in medieval Russian military tales.

[3] A marginal note opposite the word "*imeldeshi*" reads: "nurse-children who are fed from the same breast as the royal infants".

бо зело скоро сия случишася, понеже что остало войска сколько, об ону сторону места, при царе было, паче же мало не все во граде уже. Абие жь они, предбредши реку (бо мелка была в том месцу, по их сщастью), зжидатися начаша на самом брегу, ополчающесь, готови суще ко сражению, с различными броньми, паче же мало не все со стрелами, и уже на тетивах луков стрелы имуще. И абие начаша мало от берегу подвигатись, учиня чело не малое, а за ними всем идущим, вкупе, зело густо и долго, аки два стрелния не малые лучных, по примете. Християнского ж войска множество бесчисленное на стене града, тако же с палат царьских[a] зрящим, а помощи нам, стремнины[b] для великия и зело прикрые горы, никако же возмогоша подати.

Мы же, отпустя их мало что от брегу, бо еще самому концу остатному из реки не явившуся, тогда удариша на них, хотяще их прервати и устроеные полки их расторгнути. Молюся, да не возмнит мя хто безумна, сам себя хваляща! Правду воистинну глаголю, и дарованна духа храбрости, от Бога данна ми, не таю; к тому и коня зело быстра и добра имех. И всех первие вразихся во весь полк он бусурманский, и памятаю то, иже, секущеся, три разы в них конь мой оперся; и в четвертый раз зело ранен повалился в средине их со мною, и уже от великих ран не памятуя вяще. Очъхнувжеся уже потом, аки по мале године, видех, аки над мертвецом, плачющим и рыдающим, двема слугом моим надо мною стоящим, и другим двема воином царским. Аз же видех себя обнаженна лежаща, многими ранами учащенна, а живот цел, понеже на мне збройка была праотеческая, зело крепка; паче же благодать Христа моего так благоволила, иже ангелом своим заповедал сохранити мя[c] недостойнаго во всех путех. Последи же, потом уже, уведах, иже те все благородные, ихъже уже собралося было

[a] Т. царским: Ar.   [b] Т. стреминны: Ar.   [c] Т. ся: Ar.

[1] The obscure phrase по примете has been omitted from the translation. It occurs again below (see p. 80), where the meaning may be "at a target".

had gathered on horseback against them, for all this had happened very quickly and a few of the remnants of our troops were on the other side of the town with the tsar, while nearly all of them were in the citadel. And the Tatars crossed the river (fortunately for them it was shallow at that place) and immediately began to prepare for us on the bank itself, drawing themselves up and getting themselves ready for battle with various types of armour; furthermore, nearly all of them were armed with arrows, having their arrows ready on their bowstrings. And they began to withdraw from the bank, covering a broad front, and all followed after them together, densely and for a long time, for a distance of about two long bow-shots.[1] But the countless multitude of Christian troops on the walls of the fortress, as well as those who were watching from the khan's palace, were unable to give us any help owing to the extremely steep and difficult nature of the hill.

Now when we had let them go a short way from the bank—the very last troops of their rearguard had not yet come out of the river—we attacked them, intending to cut them off and to throw their battle array into disorder. I pray that no one should think me mad for praising myself! Indeed I tell the truth and do not conceal the gift of the spirit of bravery bestowed upon me by God; what is more, I had an extremely swift and excellent horse. Before all others I struck my way into the middle of that Mussulman army, and I recall how thrice my horse jibbed while I was fighting and how the fourth time it fell, badly wounded, in their midst; and I recall how I lost consciousness as a result of my great wounds. And when I came to, just about an hour later, I saw two servants of mine and two other soldiers of the tsar standing over me, weeping and sobbing, as though I were dead. And I saw myself lying naked, wounded in many places but still alive, for I had on my very strong ancestral armour; but still more I was favoured by the grace of my Christ, who commanded His angels to watch over me in all my ways, unworthy though I am. And afterwards I learned that all those noble men, about three hundred

аки со триста, яже обещались и устремитися были со мною вкупе и на них ударити, да погладили¹ возле полка их, не сразився с ними, — подобно для того, иже предних их некоторых зело поранили, близу собя припустя их, или негли убояшеся толщи ради полку, — возвратився паки, ззади оного бусурманского полку сещи начаша, наезжаючи и топчючи их. Чело же их иде невозбранно, чрез широкий луг, к великому блату, идеже конем не возможно; а тамо уже, за блатом, великий лес.

Потом, глаголют, приспел он, мой брат предреченный, иже первие на стену градскую взыде: аки бы среди оного лугу ещеᵃ застал их, и в самое чело их зело быстро, всеми уздами распустя коня, вразився в них, так мужественно, так храбро, иже вере неподобно, яко всем свидетельствовати: аки два крот проехал посреди их, секуще их и обращающе конем посреде их. Егда же в третий раз вразился в них, поможе ему некоторый благородный воин, помогающе ему, вкупе бьюще бусурманов, всем же со града зрящим и дивящимся; которые же не ведяще о цареве отданию, мняще царя Казанского между их ездяща. И так его уранили, иже по пятиᵇ стрел в ногах ему было, кроме иных ран;ᶜ но живот сохранен был Божиею благодатию, понеже сбрую на собе зело крепку имел. И такого был мужественнагоᵈ сердца, егда уже тот конь под ним ураниша так, иже с места не може двигнутися, другаго коня обрел, просто водяща у единаго дворянина царева брата, и испрося его, и забывши, паче же нерадящий так о прелютых своих ранах, угонив паки полк бусурманский, секуще их со другими воины, аж до самого блата. И воистинну имел таковаго брата храбра, и мужественна, и добронравна, и к тому зело разумна, иже во всем войску християнском не обреташеся храбрейший и лутши, паче его; аще бы обрелся хто, Господи Боже, да

ᵃ Patr., Pog., T. юще: Ar.   ᵇ Patr., Pog. пати: Ar.
ᶜ Patr., Pog., T. вран: Ar.   ᵈ T. множествен: Ar.

---

¹ A conjecture for the unintelligible да погладили.
² It seems as though the punctuation, and perhaps the word-order, is at fault here and that брата (брат?) should precede испрося.

of whom had collected and who had agreed to gallop together with me and to attack them, had ridden[1] alongside the enemy's army without fighting them—perhaps because some of those in front had been seriously wounded while letting the enemy get too close to them, or probably because they were afraid of the density of the Tatar force—and had gone back and had begun to strike the Mussulman army from behind, attacking them and trampling on them. But their front line moved unhampered across the broad meadow towards the great marsh where horses cannot go; and there, behind the marsh, lies the great forest.

Then, so they say, my brother, whom I have talked about above and who was the first to mount the citadel wall, arrived. He found the enemy while they were still in the middle of the meadow, and, galloping at full speed, he swiftly fought his way into their very foremost ranks, so boldly and courageously that, as all bear witness, it was unbelievable. Twice he rode through their ranks, fighting and turning his horse around in their midst. And when for the third time he fought his way into them, a certain noble soldier helped him, bringing him aid and fighting the Mussulmans at the same time, while everyone watched him from the fortress in amazement. Those who did not know that the khan of Kazan' had been handed over thought that he was riding in their midst. And so my brother was wounded—with five arrows in his legs apart from other wounds. But thanks to the grace of God his life was preserved, for he was wearing very strong armour. And he was so brave of heart than when the horse he was riding received such wounds that it could not move, he found another horse which was merely being led by one of the tsar's service men. My brother asked him for the horse,[2] and then, forgetting and having no care for his fierce wounds, again fought against the Mussulman army together with other soldiers and drove it back as far as the very marsh. Indeed, my brother was so brave and courageous and virtuous and, furthermore, so very wise, that in the whole Christian army there was no man braver or better than he. Should there ever be such a man [as brave and good as he], then, O Lord God, grant that he might be like him! And,

таков же бы был! Паче же мне зело был превозлюблен, и воистинну мел бы за него душу свою положити и животом своим здравие его откупити, понеже умре потом, на другое лето, подобно от тех лютых ран.

Сие конец краткого писания о Казанского великого града бусурманского взятию.

what is more, he was dearly loved by me and indeed I would have laid down my soul for him and would have ransomed his safety with my own life; for he died in the following year, evidently from those same fierce wounds.

And so ends my short description of the capture of the great Mussulman city of Kazan'.

III

По оной же преславной победе, аки бы на третий день, царь наш отрыгнул нечто неблагодарно, вместо благодарения, воеводам и всему воинству своему; на единаго разгневался, таковое слово рекл: "Ныне, рече, оборонил мя Бог от вас!" Аки бы рекл: "Не возмогл есмя вас мучити, поки[a] Казань стояла сама в собе, бо ми естя потребны были всячески; а ныне уже вольно мне всякую злость и мучительство над вами показовати." О слово сатанинское, являемое неизреченную[1] лютость человеческому роду! О наполнения меры кровопивства отческого![2] Паче к нам, християном, достоило рещи ото всего сердца человекови сицевое слово, между благодарными глаголы ко Богу всемогущему: "Благодарю тя, Господи, иже ныне оборонил еси нас от врагов наших!" Приявши же сатана человеческий скверный язык, яко орудие, сице похвалился губити роды християнския со своим стаинником, аки бы мстяще християнскому воинству, иже воином его, скверных Измаильтян, мужеством храбрости своей, Богу им помогающу, побили.

Царь же вниде в совет о устроению града нововзятаго: и советоваше ему все мудрые и разумные, иже бы ту пребыл[b] зиму, аж до весны, со всем воинством, — бо запасов было всяких множество с Руския земли кгалиями направажено, яко же и в той земле бесчисленное богатство всяких достатков —, и до конца выгубил бы воинство бусурманское и царство оное себе покорив и усмирил землю на веки; бо, кроме Татарска языка, в том царстве пять различных языков: Мордовский, Чюважский, Черемиский, Войтецкий або Арский, пятый Башкирский — те живут Башкирды вверх великие реки Камы, в лесах, яже в Волгу впадает, ниже

---

[a] Т. паки: Ar.   [b] Patr. прибыл: Ar.

---

[1] A strange use of the present passive participle *являемое vice* the present active participle.
[2] Matt. xxiii. 32.

III

On about the third day after that most glorious victory our tsar, instead of showing gratitude, uttered some ungrateful words to his *voevody* and to all his soldiery; he grew angry with one and said the following: "Now God has protected me from you!"—as if to say: "I was not able to torment you while Kazan' stood on its own, for I had need of you then in all manner of ways; but now I am free to exercise upon you every kind of evil and torment." O word of Satan which manifests[1] unspeakable ferocity towards mankind! O filling up of your father's measure of bloodthirstiness![2] Especially to us Christians was it befitting for a man to say such a word with all his heart in the midst of words of thanks to God Almighty: "I thank thee, O Lord, who hast now defended us from our enemies"! But Satan, having taken the vile tongue of man as a weapon, thus boasted that he would destroy mankind together with his minions, taking vengeance upon the Christian soldiery, who, with the help of God and by their heroic bravery, defeated his warriors, the foul Ishmaelites.

Now the tsar held counsel concerning the administration of the newly-captured city, and all his wise and judicious counsellors advised him to remain there with all his army throughout the winter, even up to spring,—for a vast amount of all kinds of provisions had been sent there from the Russian land in galleys, and also in that land there is immense wealth and all kinds of plenty—and they advised him to annihilate the Mussulman soldiery and, having subjugated the kingdom, to enthrall the land for ever; for apart from the Tatars there are five different tribes in that kingdom: the Mordvinian, the Chuvashian, the Cheremisian, the Votiak or Arsky, and, fifth, the Bashkir tribe.[3] (These Bashkirs live in the forests up the great Kama river, which flows into the Volga twelve miles

[3] All five tribes living in the area of the middle reaches of the Volga and Kama rivers. For the Chuvashians, or Hill Cheremisians, see above, p. 31, n. 2, p. 39, n. 5.

73

Казани дванадесять миль. — Он же совета мудрых воевод своих не послушал; послушал же совета шурей своих: они бо шептаху ему во уши, да споспишетца ко царице своей, сестре их; но и других ласкателей направили с попами.[1]

Он же, стояв неделю и оставя часть воинства в месте и огненые стрельбы с потребу, и вседши в суды ехал к Новугороду Нижнему, еже есть крайнее место великое Руское, которое лежит от Казани шездесят миль; а кони наши все послал не тою доброю дорогою, еюже сам шол х Казани, но водле Волгу, зело притрутными стезями, по великим горам лежащими, на нихъже Чювашский язык обитает, и того ради погубил у всего воинства своего кони тогда: бо у кого было сто або двесте коней, едва два або три вышли. Се сия первая дума человекоугоднича![2] Егда же приехав в Новъгород Нижний, и пребывал тамо три дни и распустил по домом воинство все; сам же пустился на подводах сто мил до главнаго места своего, Москвы: бо уродился ему был тогда сын Димитрий, егож своим безумием погубил, яко напреди вкратце о сем повем. Приехав же до Москвы, аки по двух месяцах или по трех, разболелся зело тяжким огненым недугом так, иже никто же уже ему жити надеялся. Не по малых днях, по малу оздравляти почал.

Егда же уже оздравел, обещался, скоро по недузе оном, и умыслил ехати сто миль от Москвы до единого монастыря, глаголемаго Кирилова. После же великого дня Воскресения Христова, аки на третьей или на четвертой недели, поехал первие в монастырь Троицы Живоначальные, глаголемый Сергиев, яже лежит от Москвы дванадесять

---

[1] I.e. Tsaritsa Anastasia's brothers, Daniil and Nikita Romanovich Yur'ev-Zakhar'in, who were both present at the siege of Kazan'. See *PSRL* XIII, pp. 200, 515; XIX, p. 473; *DRK*, pp. 152, 153, 157.

[2] Presumably in order to urge Ivan to return to Moscow from Kazan'. The chronicles make no mention of the advice given to Ivan; they merely state that on 11 October 1552 Ivan "decided with Prince Vladimir Andreevich and with all the boyars to go to Moscow" (*PSRL* XIII, pp. 222, 516).

[3] I.e. across country, through Murom and Sviyazhsk. See above, p. 31.

below Kazan'). But he did not listen to the advice of his wise *voevody*; he listened instead to the advice of his brothers-in-law;[1] for they whispered in his ears that he should hurry to his tsaritsa, their sister; and they sent other flatterers with priests.[2]

And after staying there a week he left part of his army and such firearms as were necessary in the town, and having embarked on ships went to Nizhny Novgorod, which is the furthest great Russian city [from Moscow] and which is sixty miles distant from Kazan'. All our horses, however, he sent not by that good route which he himself had taken on his way to Kazan',[3] but along the Volga on very difficult tracks running over great hills where the Chuvashian tribe dwells;[4] as a result of this he destroyed the horses of all his army at that time: for if anyone had a hundred or two hundred horses, barely two or three of them survived. Such was the first counsel of men-pleasers! And when he came to Nizhny Novgorod he stayed there for three days and dismissed all his army, sending them to their homes; but he himself set off in carriages to cover the hundred miles to his capital city Moscow; for at that time his son Dmitry was born, whom he destroyed in his madness, as I shall briefly narrate below. When he came to Moscow, after about two or three months, he fell ill with such a very grievous fever that no one expected him to live. After several days he began to recover a little.[5]

Now soon after he had recovered from that illness, he took a vow and decided to travel a hundred miles from Moscow to a monastery called St Kirill's monastery.[6] In about the third or fourth week after the great day of Christ's resurrection he set off first of all to the monastery of the life-giving Trinity, called St Sergy's monastery, which is situated twelve miles from

---

[4] I.e along the right (or south) bank of the Volga.

[5] Ivan arrived back in Moscow before the end of October 1552 (*PSRL* XIII, pp. 223, 518). His illness occurred in March 1553. For details of the so-called Boyar rebellion which took place at the time of the illness, see *Correspondence*, p. 94, n. 6; I. I. Smirnov, *Ocherki*, pp. 264–86; A. A. Zimin, *Reformy*, pp. 406–18.

[6] The Kirillo-Belozersky monastery, situated south-east of the town of Beloozero and the White Lake, was founded by St Kirill (d. 1427) at the end of the fourteenth century.

миль, на великой дорозе, которая идет к Студеному морю. Поехал же не один, но со царицею своею и с новорожденным отрочатем, на так долгий путь, и пребыл в Сергиеве монастыре аки три дни, опочиваючи собе, бо еще был не зело оздравел.

А в том тогда монастырю обитал Максим преподобный, мних святые горы Афонские, Ватапеда монастыря, Грек родом, муж зело мудрый, и не токмо в риторском искустве мног, но и философ искусен, и уже в летех превосходные старости умащен, и по Бозе в терпению исповедническом украшен; много бо претерпел ото отца его многолетных и тяжких оков[a] и многолетнаго заточения в прегорчайших темницах, и других родов мученей искусил неповинне, по зависти Данила митрополита, прегордаго и лютаго, и ото вселукавых мнихов, глаголемых Осифлянских; а он был его из заточения свободил, по совету некоторых синглитов своих, исповедающих ему, иже отнюдь неповинне стражет таковый блаженный муж. Той предреченный мних Максим начал советывати ему, да не едет на так далекий путь, наипаче же со женою и с новорожденным отрочатком.

"Аще, рече, и обещался еси тамо ехати, подвижуще святаго Кирила на молитву ко Богу; но[b] обеты таковые с разумом не согласуют. А то сего ради: егда доставал еси так прегордаго и сильнаго бусурманского царства, тогда и воинства християнского храброго тамо не мало от поганов падоша, яже брашася с ними крепще по Бозе за православие, и тех избиенных жены и дети осиротели и матери обещадели, во слезах многих и в скорбех пребывают. И далеко, рече,

[a] Т. онов: Ar.   [b] Patr. на: Ar.

[1] The great Trinity monastery founded in the fourteenth century by St Sergy of Radonezh. The Frozen Sea was the name given by the Russians to what was later called the Barents Sea. According to the chronicle Ivan set off in May 1553 (*PSRL* xiii, p. 231).
[2] Maksim the Greek was born in Italy in about 1475. After spending ten years in the Vatopedi monastery on Mount Athos he was invited to Moscow by Vasily III in order to help with the translation of sacred books. He remained in Moscow for the rest of his life, interesting himself in such controversial questions as monastic landownership and the position of the

Moscow on the great road which leads to the Frozen Sea.[1] He did not set off alone on such a long journey but with his tsaritsa and his newly-born child, and he stayed in St Sergy's monastery about three days, resting, for he had not yet completely recovered.

In that monastery there dwelt at that time the venerable Maksim, a monk from the monastery of Vatopedi on Mount Athos, the holy mountain; he was a Greek by birth, a very wise man, and not only was he great in the art of rhetorics, but also he was a skilled philosopher; and he was a man of ripe and venerable old age, adorned by God for his long-suffering as a confessor; for at the hands of his [Ivan's] father [Vasily III] he had endured much—long-lasting and grievous chains and long-lasting imprisonment in the direst prisons—and in his innocence he had suffered other kinds of torments because of the envy of Metropolitan Daniil, that most proud and fierce man, and at the hands of those evil monks who are called Josephians; and the grand prince had freed him from imprisonment on the advice of certain of his advisers, who told him that so blessed a man was suffering although he was completely guiltless. Now this monk Maksim, whom we have been talking about, began to advise him not to go on so distant a journey, especially as he had with him his wife and his newly-born infant.[2]

"Although", he said, "you promised to go there to urge St Kirill to pray for you to God, such vows are not in accordance with wisdom. The reason for this is as follows: when you were conquering the proud strong Mussulman kingdom, there fell at the hands of the pagans many who with God fought firmly against them for the Orthodox faith; and the wives of those who were killed were widowed, their children were orphaned and their mothers lost their sons, and they continue to lament

Church vis-à-vis the State. He was put on trial (1525 and 1531) for his ecclesiastical views, which ran counter to those of the Josephian hierarchy, for "heretical" opinions and for treacherously conspiring with one Skinder, the sultan's ambassador in Moscow. From 1525 to 1531 he was imprisoned in the Josephian monastery of Volokolamsk; after his second trial in 1531 he was sent to the Tver' Otroch' monastery; in 1551 he was allowed to move to the Trinity monastery of St Sergy where he died in 1556.

лутше тех тобе пожаловати и устроити, утешающе их от таковых бед и скорбей, собравше их ко своему царственнейшему граду, нежели те обещания не по разуму исполняти. А Бог, рече, везде сый, все исполняет и всюды зрит недреманным своии оком, яко пророк рече: сей не воздремлет, ни уснет, храняще Израиля; а другий пророк: у него ж, рече, очи седм крат солнца светлейши. Тем же не токмо святый Кирил духом, но и все первородных праведных духи, написанные на небесех, иже предстоят ныне у престола Господня, имуще очи духовные острозрительнейше, паче с высоты, нежели богатый во аде,[a] и молятся Христу за всех человеков, на земном кругу обитающих, паче же за кающихся грехов и волею обращающихса от беззаконий своих ко Богу, понеже Бог и святые Его не по месту объятия молитвам нашим внимают, но по лоброй воле нашей и по самовластию. И аще, рече, послушаеши мене, здрав будеши и многолетен, со женою и отрочатем.'' И иными словесы множайшими наказуя его, воистинну сладчайшими паче меда, каплющаго ото уст его преподобных.

Он же, яко гордый человек, упрямяся, толико ''ехати, да ехати'', рече, ''ко святому Кирилу''; к тому ласкающе его и поджигающе миролюбцом и любоименным мнихом и похваляюще умиление царево, аки богоугодное обещание; бо те мнихи[b] боготолюбные не зрят богоугоднаго, а ни[c] советуют по разуму духовному, чему были должны суще паче в мире живущих человеков, но всячески со прилежанием слухают, что бы угодно было царю и властем, сииречь, чем бы выманити имения к монастырем, или богатство многое, и жити в сладострастиях скверных, яко свиньям питающеся, а не глаголю, в кале валяющеся. Прочее же умолчим, да не речем чего горшаго и сквернейшаго, и ко предреченным возвратимся, о оном добром совете глаголюще.

[a] Patr., Pog., T. ад: Ar.   [b] Patr., Pog., T. мниги: Ar.
[c] Patr., Pog., T. аки: Ar.

---

[1] Ps. cxxi. 4.
[2] Ecclus. xxiii. 19. In the Slavonic text: тмами тем *vice* седм.
[3] Lit. ''according to the area of their compass''.

and to grieve much. And, he said, it would be far better to reward them and to settle them, comforting them in such troubles and sorrows and calling them to your ruling city, rather than to fulfil promises which are contrary to wisdom. For God, he said, who is everywhere, fulfils all things and sees in all places with His unslumbering eye, as the prophet said: 'He that keepeth Israel shall neither slumber nor sleep.'[1] And another prophet said: 'The eyes of the Lord are seven times brighter than the sun.'[2] Likewise not only St Kirill [sees] in spirit, but so do all the spirits of our just forefathers, whose names are inscribed in the heavens and who now serve at the throne of the Lord; for they have most sharp-sighted eyes of the spirit, which see more from on high than does the rich man in hell; and they pray to Christ for all men who dwell on the globe of the earth, especially for those who repent their sins and willingly turn from their transgressions to God; for God and His saints listen to our prayers not according to their length,[3] but according to our good will and according to our free will. And if, he said, you listen to me, you will enjoy health and long life with your wife and infant." And he instructed him with very many other words, which were indeed sweeter than honey dripping from his venerable lips.

But the tsar, like a proud man, was stubborn and merely said: "We must go, we must go to Saint Kirill", and he was flattered and urged to do this by those monks who love the world and love possessions; and they praised the tsar's piety as though his promise were pleasing to God; for those wealth-loving monks do not consider that which is pleasing to God, nor do they give advice according to spiritual wisdom, which they, more than those who live in the world [i.e. laymen], ought to do. But they are always zealously on the watch for what might be pleasing to the tsar and to the powers, in other words how they might wheedle out of them estates or great wealth for the monasteries and how they might live in foul lusts, feeding like swine, to say nothing of wallowing in filth. But let us be silent on the rest, so as not to say anything still worse and still more foul, and let us return to what we were talking about before and speak of that good advice. When the

Егда же видев преподобный Максим, иже презрел его совет и ко еханию безгодному устремился царь, и исполнився духа пророческого, начал прорицати ему: "Аще, рече, не послушаеши мене, по Бозе советующаго ти, и забудеши крови оных мучеников, избиенных от поганов за правоверие, и презриши слезы сирот оных и вдовиц, и поедеши со упрямством, — ведай[a] о сем, иже сын твой умрет и не возвратитца оттуды жив; аще послушаеши и возвратишися, здрав будеши, яко сам, так и сын твой." И сия словеса приказал ему четырмя нами: первый исповедник его, презвитер Андрей протопоп,[b] другий Иоанн княжа Мстиславский,[c] а третей Алексей Адашев, ложничей его, четвертый мною; и те слова, слышав от святаго, исповедахом ему по ряду. Он же не радяще о сем, и поехал оттуды до града, глаголемаго Дмитрова, а оттуды до монастыря единаго, реченнаго на Песочне, яже лежит при реце Яхроме: туто имел суды уготованы ко плаванию.

Ту ми зри со прилежанием, что враг наш непримирительный, диавол, умышляет и к чему человека окояннаго приводит и на что подвижет, влагающе ему аки благочестие ложное и обещание к Богу, сопротивное разуму! И аки бы стрелою по примете, царем стрелил до того монастыря, идеже епископ, уже престаревшейся во днех мнозех, пребывал; прежде был мних от Осифлянские оные лукавые четы, яже был великий похлебник отца его и, вкупе со прегордым и проклятым Данилом митрополитом, предречен-

---

[a] Pog., T. ведый: Ar.   [b] Patr. Протопопов: Ar.   [c] Patr., Pog., T. Мстивлаский: Ar.

---

[1] Andrey was archpriest of the Blagoveshchensky (Annunciation) cathedral in the Kremlin and spiritual father of the tsar. He later took the tonsure and, under the name of Afanasy, succeeded Makary as metropolitan. Prince Ivan Fedorovich Mstislavsky was a member of the Privy Council (*Blizhnyaya duma*) during the fifties and was a close associate of the tsar (his grandmother was a daughter of Ivan III). He was later made governor (*namestnik*) of Novgorod. As for Aleksey Adashev, he was also at the time of the "pilgrimage" a member of the Privy Council. Kurbsky here (and once again later, see below, p. 122 n. 2) calls him *lozhnichy* (cf. Polish łożniczy),

venerable Maksim saw that the tsar disregarded his advice and was determined to go on his useless journey, he was filled with the spirit of prophecy and began to prophesy to him: "If, he said, you do not listen to me who advise you according to God, and if you forget the blood of those martyrs who were slaughtered by the pagans in the name of Orthodoxy, and if you overlook the tears of those orphans and widows and set off with stubbornness, then know that your son shall die and shall not return from there alive; but if you listen to me and return, you shall enjoy health, both you and your son." And he enjoined four of us to convey these words to him: first, his confessor, the archpriest Andrey; second, Prince Ivan Mstislavsky; third, Aleksey Adashev, his gentleman of the bed-chamber; and fourthly, me.[1] And having heard these words from the saint we told them to him. But he took no notice of this and went from there to the town called Dmitrov, and from there to a certain monastery called the monastery on the Pesnosha, which lies on the river Yakhroma; there he had boats ready for sailing.[2]

Consider now with attentiveness what our implacable enemy the devil devises, what he leads sinful man to and what he urges him to do, inspiring him with false piety and promises to God which are contrary to reason. And just as though he [the devil] was shooting an arrow at a target,[3] he shot the tsar to that monastery where dwelt a bishop of ripe old age; formerly he had been a monk of that cunning Josephian band, and he had been a toady of his father [i.e. of Vasily III], and together with that most proud and accursed Metropolitan Daniil he

a translation of the Russian *postel'nichy*, i.e. gentleman of the bed-chamber. Adashev, however, is not known to have held this rank at any time during his career. I. M. Veshnyakov (whom Kurbsky also calls *lozhnichy*, see below, pp. 122-3) was in fact Ivan's *postel'nichy* from 1552 to 1561 (I. I. Smirnov, *Ocherki*, p. 228). Probably Kurbsky is confusing the term with *spal'nik*, a lower rank in the court hierarchy than *postel'nichy*, for both Mstislavsky and Adashev were *spal'niki* at Ivan IV's wedding (*DRV*, vol. 13, p. 34).

[2] The Pesnosha monastery of St Nicholas (*Pesnoshsky-Nikolaevsky*) was founded in 1361 by St Sergy's pupil, Mefody, on the right bank of the Yakhroma river, at the place where the Pesnosha stream joins it, some 25 versts from Dmitrov.

[3] See above, p. 66, n. 1.

ных оных мужей многими лжесшиваньми оклеветаша и велико гонение на них воздвигоша. Той-то митрополит Силвана преподобнаго, Максимова ученика, обоего любомудрия внешняго и духовнаго искуснаго мужа, во своем епискупском[a] дому злою смертию за малые дни уморил; и скоро по смерти князя великого Василия, яко митрополита Московскаго, так того Коломенского епископа, не токмо по совету всех синглитов, но и всенародне, изгнано от престолов их, явственныя ради злости.

Что же тогда приключишася? Таково то воистинну: иж приходит царь до оного старца в келью и, ведая, яже отцу его единосоветен был и во всем угоден и согласен, вопрошает его: "Како бы могл[b] добре царствовати и великих и сильных своих в послушестве имети?" И подобало рещи ему: самому царю достоит быти яко главе, и любити мудрых советников своих, яко свои уды, и иными множайшими словесы от священных писаней ему подобало о сем советывати и наказати царя християнъского, яко достоило епископу некогда бывшу, паче же престаревшемуся уже в летех довольных. Он же что рече? Абие начал шептати ему во ухо, по древней своей обыкновенной злости, яко и отцу его древле ложное сиковацие шептал, и таково[c] слово рекл: "И аще хощеши самодержец быти, не держи собе советника ни единаго мудрейшаго собя, понеже сам еси всех лутчши; тако будеши тверд на царстве, и всех имети будеши в руках своих. И аще будеши имел мудрейших близу собя, по нужде будеши послушен им." И сице соплете силлогизм сотанинский. Царь же абие руку его поцеловал и рече: "О, аще и отец был бы ми жив, таковаго глагола полезнаго не поведал бы ми!"

[a] Т. своем епископством: Ar.   [b] Pog., Т. могк: Ar.
[c] Patr., Pog., Т. такобо: Ar.

---

[1] I.e. Maksim and his followers.

[2] Selivan (Sil'van), a monk of the Trinity monastery, was attached to Maksim to assist him in his work as translator. Together with Maksim he was tried by Metropolitan Daniil in 1525. According to one source he was

had slandered those above-mentioned men[1] with many tissues of lies and had inflicted upon them great persecution. And that same metropolitan in a few days cruelly put to death in his palace the venerable Sil'van, a pupil of Maksim, a man skilled in both worldly and spiritual wisdom.[2] And shortly after the death of Grand Prince Vasily, both the metropolitan of Moscow and the bishop of Kolomna were driven from their sees on the advice not only of all the counsellors but also of all the people, because of their manifest wickedness.[3]

And what happened then? The following, in truth: the tsar came to that elder in his cell and knowing that he had been of one accord with his father and had been pleasing to him and in agreement with him in everything, he asked him: "How might I rule well and hold my great and powerful subjects in obedience?" And he should have answered: "The tsar himself ought to be the head [of the body] and he ought to love his wise counsellors as though they were his own limbs", and with a great many other words from the sacred writings he should have advised and instructed the Christian tsar about this, as is fitting for one who was once a bishop and especially for a man of ripe old age. But what did he say? He straightway began to whisper in his ear according to his old evil custom, just as of old he used to whisper false sycophancy in his father's ear; and this is what he said: "If you wish to be an autocrat, do not keep beside you a single counsellor wiser than yourself, for you yourself are better than all; thus you shall be firm in the realm and you shall hold all men in your hands. And if you keep near you men wiser than yourself, then perforce you will be subject to them." And thus he spun his satanic syllogism. But the tsar immediately kissed his hand and said: "O, even if my father had been alive, he would not have given me such useful advice!"

imprisoned in the monastery of Volokolamsk with Maksim where he was put to death (see E. Golubinsky, *Istoriya Russkoy Tserkvi*, vol. II, part I, p. 719, n. 1); yet another source indicates that he died a natural death (*AE*, vol. I, no. 289, p. 337).

[3] For the dismissal of Metropolitan Daniil (1539) and Bishop Vassian Toporkov of Kolomna, see *Correspondence*, pp. 74, n. 4, and 236, n. 2.

Ту ми розсмотри[a] прилежно, яко согласует древний глас отечь с новым гласом сына! Искони отец, прежде бывшей Офорос, глаголет, видев себя пресветла и сильна и надо многими полки ангельскими чиноначальником от Бога поставлена, и забыв, иже сотворение есть, рече себе: "Погублю землю и море и поставлю престол мой выше облак небесных и буду равен Превышнему." Аки бы рекл: "и могу сопротивитися Ему"; и абие денница низпаде восходящая заутра, и низпаде аж в преисподнее: возгордев бо и не сохранив своего чина, яко писано есть: и от Осфора Сатана наречен, сииречь отступник. Тому древнему отступнику и сын глас подобен провещал, паче же он сам, точию действовал устнами престаревшимися старца, и рече: "ты лутче всех, и недостоит ти никого имети мудраго"; аки бы рекл: "понеже еси Богу равен".

О глас воистинну дияволи, всякие злости и презорства и забвения преполон! Забыл ли еси, епископе, во Втором царстве реченного? Егда советовал Давыд со синглиты своими, хотяще[b] считати людей Исраительских, яко речено: советоваше ему все синглитове, да не сочитает, понеже умножил Господь люд Исраилев, по обещанию своему ко Аврааму, аки песок морский, и превозможе, рече, глагол царев, сиречь не послушал советников своих, и повелел считати люд, дани ради болше. Забыл ли еси, что принесло непослушание синглитскаго совета, и яковую беду навел Бог сего ради? Мало весь Исраиль не погибе, аще бы царь покаянием и слезами многими не предварил. Запомнил ли еси, что гордость и совет юных, и[c] презрении старейших совету, Ровоаму безумному принесло? И иные все безчисленные во священных писаниях о сем учащие оставя, вместо тех шепътанный, пребеззаконный глагол царю християнскому, покаянием очищену сущу, во уши всеял еси.

[a] Patr., Pog., T. разсмотрити: Ar. [b] Patr., Pog. ходяще: Ar.
[c] T. о: Ar.

---

[1] *Oforos*: Phosphorus, Lucifer.
[2] Or perhaps, "whose was the Creation".   [3] Is. xiv. 13, 14.
[4] Is. xiv. 12.   [5] I.e. the second Book of Samuel.

Consider now diligently how the old voice of the father is in accord with the new voice of the son! In the beginning the father, who was formerly Lucifer,[1] seeing that he was brilliant and strong and appointed by God as commander over the many angelic hosts and forgetting that this was God's Creation,[2] said to himself: "I will destroy the earth and the sea and I will place my throne above the clouds in the heavens and I will be like unto the Most High."[3] It was as though he said: "I can even oppose Him"; and straightway the morning star, which arises in the morning, fell,[4] and fell even to the nether regions; for he was filled with pride and kept not his rank, as it is written: Lucifer was called Satan, that is to say the apostate. And like that ancient apostate the son too gave utterance, or rather he spoke only through the venerable lips of the elder and said: "You are better than all men, and it is not befitting for you to have any wise man beside you"—as though he were saying: "for you are equal to God".

O truly diabolical voice, full of all kinds of evil, pride and forgetfulness! Have you forgotten, O bishop, that which is said in the second Book of Kings?[5] When David took counsel with his advisers as he was about to number the people of Israel, then, according to the scriptures, all his counsellors advised him not to number the people, for the Lord had increased the people of Israel as the sand of the sea according to His promise to Abraham, and the king's word prevailed, that is to say he did not listen to his counsellors, and he ordered that the people be numbered for the sake of greater taxation. Have you forgotten what were the results of his failure to listen to his counsellors' advice and what misfortune God inflicted because of this? Almost all Israel [would have] perished had not the king forestalled [disaster] by penitence and many tears.[6] And have you forgotten what pride and the counsel of young men and the forsaking of the counsel of the old men brought to foolish Rehoboam?[7] And you left aside all the other countless teachings on this which are found in the holy scriptures, and instead of them you sowed in the ears of the tsar, who had been purified by penitence, most iniquitous whispered words. And

[6] 2 Sam. xxiv.   [7] 1 Kings xii.

Подобно ленился еси прочести златыми усты вещающаго о сем во слове о Духу Святом, емуже начало: Вчера от нас любимицы, тако же и во другом слове, в последних, похвале о святом Павле, сиречь во 9-м, емуж начало: Обличили нас друзи некоторые, яко он похваляет нарицающе дар духа совет от Бога данный, идеже в них разсуждает о различных дарованиях духа, яко мертвых воскрещати и предивные чюдеса творити и различными языки глаголати дары духа нарицает, тако же и советовати полезные на прибыль царства дар совета нарицает, и свидетельство на то приводит не худаго мужа, ни незнаемого, но самого славного Моисея, со Богом беседовавшаго, моря разделителя, и Фараонова бога и пресельных Амалехитов потребителя, и предивных чюдес делателя, а дара совета неимеюща, яко писано: но принял, рече, совет от окромнаго, сииречь от чюжеземца або от страннаго человека, от тестя своего; и не токмо, рече, Бог совет Рагуила тестя его похвалил, но и в закон написал, яко пространнее в предреченных его словесах зрится. Царь же, аще и почтен царством, а дарований которых от Бога не получил, должен искати добраго и полезнаго совета не токмо у советников, но и у всеродных[a] человек, понеже дар духа дается не по богатеству внешнему и по силе царства, но по правости душевной; ибо не зрит Бог на могутство и гордость, но на правость сердечную, и дает дары, сиречь елико хто вместит добрым произволеньем.[b] Ты[c] же все сие забыл! Отрыгнул же еси вместо благоухания смрад! И еще к тому, что запамятовал еси или не веси, иж

[a] Patr. всенародных: Т.; вседронных: Ar.   [b] Тако же зри о добром совете в Златоустого в (в omitted in Patr., Pog., Т.) толковании (толкованию: Т.) втораго послания х (х omitted in Patr., Pog., Т.) коринфом (коринфом omitted in Patr., Pog., Т.) Павловых словес во нравочении (нравоучении: Т.) от бесед 18: in margin of Ar., Patr., Pog.; in text of T.   [c] Patr., Pog. ы же: Ar.

[1] See *PG*, vol. 52, cols. 813–26. St John Chrysostom's Sermon on the Holy Spirit begins "Yesterday, O lovers of Christ, the coming of the... Holy Spirit was celebrated by us."

likewise you were too lazy to read what he who speaks with the golden mouth [St John Chrysostom] says about this in the homily on the Holy Spirit, which begins: "Yesterday by us, O beloved... "[1] and also in another homily, towards the end, concerning praise for St Paul, that is the ninth homily, which begins: "Certain friends have accused us", [you did not read] how he gives praise, calling the advice given by God the gift of the spirit; and in the places where he discusses the various gifts of the spirit, he not only calls resurrecting the dead and working most wondrous miracles and talking in various tongues "gifts of the spirit", but he also calls counselling that which is useful for the weal of the realm "the gift of counsel", bringing as an example of this no poor man, no unknown man, but the most glorious Moses, who conversed with God, who divided the sea, who destroyed the god of Pharaoh and the mighty Amalekites, who worked most wondrous miracles, and yet who did not possess the gift of counsel, as it is written: "he took advice from an outsider", that is to say from a foreigner or from a stranger, from his father-in-law; and not only did God praise the counsel of Raguel, his father-in-law, but he even inscribed it in the law, as can be seen in greater length in his [i.e. St John Chrysostom's] above-mentioned homilies.[2] Now a tsar, if he is honoured by his realm but has not received certain gifts from God, must seek good and useful counsel not only from his advisers, but also from all kinds of men,[3] for the gift of the spirit is granted not according to worldly wealth and the strength of the realm, but according to righteousness of soul; for God does not regard power and pride, but righteousness of heart, and He gives gifts—that is to say He grants as much as anyone can accept of good will.[4] But you forgot all this! You belched forth stench instead of fragrance! And furthermore have you forgotten or do you not know that all

---

[2] See *PG*, vol. 51, cols. 131, 134–6.

[3] Or, according to another reading (всенародных) "from men of all stations", i.e. men representing all walks of life, or "common people".

[4] A marginal note reads as follows: "See also concerning good counsel in Chrysostom's commentary on St Paul's words on teaching in the second epistle to the Corinthians, from the eighteenth homily." See *PG*, vol. 61, cols. 523 *sq*. (*In secundam ad Corinthios epistolam commentarius*).

все безсловесные душевные есътеством несутся, або принуждаются, и чювством правятся; а словесные, не токмо человецы плотные, но и самые безтелесные силы, сиречь святые ангели, советом и разумом управляютца, яко Дионисий Ареопагит и другий великий учитель[a] пишут о сем. А что древных оных блаженных лик исчитал бы? Иже всем еще тамо во устех обносится, о том мало достоит воспомянути, сииречь деда того царя, Иоанна князя великого, так далече границы свои разширивши, и к тому еще дивнейшаго, у негож в неволе был, великого царя Ордынского изгнал и юрт его разорил, не кровопиянства ради своего и любимаго для грабления, не буди, но воистинну многаго его совета ради с мудрыми и мужественными сигклиты его; бо зело, глаголют, его любосоветна быти, и ничто же починати без глубочайшаго и многаго совета. Ты же, аки сопротив всех оных, не токмо древних оных великих святых предреченных, но и новаго того славнаго вашего сопротив стал, понеже все те согласне вещают: любяй совет, любит свою душу; а ты рече: ''не дерши советников мудрейшии собя!''[b]

О сыну диаволь! про что человеческаго естества, вкратце рещи, жилы пресекл еси, и всю крепость разрушити и отъяти хотяща, таковую искру безбожную в сердце царя християнского всеял, от неяже во всей Святоруской земли таков пожар лют возгорелся, о немъже свидетельствовати словесы мню не потреба? Понеже делом сия прелютейшая

---

[a] Ar. и другие великие учители: Т.   [b] Зри сопротивнаго и надхненнаго от сатаны поветреннаго совету, тысящу крат горша совета Ахитофелова, от негоже храбрый и непобедимый преодолетель страшных и ужасных гигинтов (гигантов: Patr., Pog.) боготец Давыд вострепетал, не царя юна и всего растейскаго (исраилтескаго: Patr., Pog.) войска бояся и от совета лукаваго онаго мужа ужасается, яко писано во книг (книгах: Patr., Pog.) царьст вторых: in margin of Ar., Patr., Pog. но лучше бы тому прелукавому епископу таков конец был; но лучше Бог весть, еже попусти сему быти за грехи наша по неизреченным праведным судбам своим: in margin of Patr. and Pog. only.

---

[1] I.e. by instinct. I have taken душевные to be an error for душевным.
[2] Or, according to a variant, ''other great teachers''. See *De Coelesti*

animals are moved or constrained by the nature of the heart[1] and are governed by feeling? Whereas humans—not only fleshly men, but the bodiless powers themselves, that is to say the holy angels—are governed by counsel and reason, as Dionysius the Areopagite and another great teacher write concerning this?[2] And would you have considered many of those ancient blessed men?[3] It is hardly worth mentioning him who is still on the lips of everyone there [in Russia], namely the grandfather of the tsar, Grand Prince Ioann [Ivan], who increased his frontiers to such an extent, and, still more wondrous, drove out the khan of the Great Horde in whose bondage he had been, and destroyed his *yurt*,[4] not because of bloodthirstiness and love of plunder, no, but, in truth, because he took frequent counsel with his wise and bold advisers; for they say that he greatly loved counsel and ventured on nothing without much profound counsel. But you opposed all those people, not only those above-mentioned great saints of old, but also that recent glorious grandfather of yours, for all proclaim with one consent: "he who loves counsel, loves his own soul";[5] but you have said: "Keep not counsellors wiser than yourself."[6]

O son of the devil! Why, in short, did you sever the veins of human nature and, intending to destroy and remove all strength, sow in the heart of the Christian tsar such a godless spark, from which throughout the whole Holy Russian land so fierce a conflagration blazed up? There is, I think, no need to expatiate on this. For by this deed the fiercest evil was en-

Hierarchia of St Dionysius the Areopagite, ch. IV, sect. 1 (*PG*, vol. 3, cols. 177–8).

[3] Lit. "the number of...". This seems to be the general sense of this confusing sentence.

[4] I.e. his capital. See above, p. 64, n. 1.   [5] Prov. xv. 32.

[6] A marginal note reads as follows: "See the evil pestilential counsel inspired by Satan, a thousand times worse than the counsel of Ahithophel, before which the brave invincible conqueror of the terrible dread giants, David, the ancestor of God, trembled; fearing not the young king and all the host of Israel, he was afraid of the counsel of that evil man, as is written in the second book of Kings." In two MSS. the note continues: "But it would have been better if that most evil bishop had had a similar end; but God knows better—according to His untold just judgements He allowed this to happen because of our sins."

злость произвелася, якова никогда же в нашем языце бывала, от тебя беды начало приемше, яко напреди нами плод твоих прелютых дел вкратце изъявитца.[a] Воистинну мало по наречению твоему и дело твое показася, бо наречение ти Топорков; а ты не топорком, сиречь малою секеркою, воистинну великою и широкою, и самым оскордом благородных и славных мужей по великой Руси постинал еси. К тому, яко многое воинство, так бесчисленное множество всенародных человеков ни от кого прежде, по добром покаянию своему, только от тебя Васьяна Топоркова царь будучи прелютостию наквашен, всех тех предреченных различными смерти погубил. И сие оставя, да предреченным возвратимся.

Напившися царь християнский от православного епископа таковаго смертоноснаго яду, поплыл в путь свой Яхромою рекою[b] аж до Волги; Волгою же плыл колько десять миль до Шексны реки великие, и Шексною вверх аж до езера великаго Белаго, на немъже место и град стоит. И не доезжаючи монастыря Кирилова, еще Шексною рекою плывучи, сын ему, по[c] пророчеству святаго, умре. Се первая радость за молитвами оного предреченнаго епископа! Се получение мзда за обещания не по разуму, паче же не богоугодных! И оттуду приехал до оного Кирилова монастыря в печали мнозе и в тузе, и возвратился тощими руками во мнозей скорби до Москвы.

К тому и то достоит вкратце воспомянути, перваго ради презрения совета добраго, яже, еще в Казани будуще, советовали ему синклитове не исходити оттуды, дондеже до конца искоренит от земли оные бусурманских властелей, яко преже написахом. Что же, смиряюще его гордость, попущает Бог? Паки ополчаютца против его оставшие князи Казанские, вкупе со предреченными протчими языки

[a] Patr., Pog. изъявятца: Ar. [b] Patr., Pog., T. рукою: Ar.
[c] Patr., Pog., T. по omitted in Ar.

[1] A pun on Vassian's name, Toporkov, which is formed from the diminutive *toporok*, a little chopper.

gendered, such as has never been before amongst our people, and misfortune stemmed from you—later on we shall show briefly the fruit of your evil deeds. In truth this deed of yours has shown itself to have a little in common with your name, for your name is Toporkov; and not with a little chopper, that is to say a small hatchet, but indeed with a great and broad one, with a very axe, did you behead noble, glorious men in great Russia.[1] Furthermore the tsar killed both many of his soldiers and countless numbers of men of all stations, not having been urged on[2] in ferocity by anyone previously (thanks to his good penitence), but urged on only by you, Vassian Toporkov—all those above-mentioned men he destroyed with various forms of death. But let us leave this and return to what we were talking about before.

When the Christian tsar had been made to drink his fill of such deadly poison by the Orthodox bishop, he set off by boat on his journey along the Yakhroma river as far as the Volga; and along the Volga he sailed several tens of miles as far as the great Sheksna river; and he sailed up the Sheksna river as far as the great White Lake, on which stand the town and fortress [of Beloozero]. And before reaching the monastery of St Kirill, while still sailing along the river Sheksna, his son died, as the holy man had prophesied.[3] Such was the first joy resulting from the prayers of that bishop we have been talking about! Such was the reward received for promises which were not in accordance with reason and, what is more, were not pleasing to God! And from there he went to the monastery of St Kirill in much grief and affliction, and he returned with empty hands and in great sorrow to Moscow.

In addition to this I must briefly recall how he spurned the good advice which his counsellors gave him while still in Kazan', telling him not to go away from there before utterly eradicating from that land the Mussulman rulers, as I have written above. What then did God, humbling his pride, send as a result of this? The remaining princes of Kazan' again took up arms against him together with those other heathen

[2] Lit. "leavened", "fermented".
[3] According to the Nikon Chronicle, Dmitry died in June 1553 on the return journey to Moscow (*PSRL* xiii, p. 232).

поганскими, и воюют зелне, не токмо на град Казанъский приходяще с великих лесов, но и на землю Муромскую и Новаграда Нижнего наезжают и пленят. Того было беспрестанне, аки шесть лет после взятия места Казанского, иже во оной земле грады новопоставленные, некоторые же и Руской земле, в осаде были от них. И свели тогда битву з гетманом его, мужем нарочитым, емуже имя было Борис Морозов, глаголемый Салтыков: и падоша полки християнские от поганов и сам же гетман поиман. И держаша его жива, аки два лета, и потом убиша его; не хотеша его а ни на откуп, а ни отмену своих дати. И в тую шесть лет битвы многие быша с ними и воевания; и толикое множество в то время погибе войска[a] християнского, биющеся и воюющеся с ними безпрестанно, иже вере неподобно.

И по шестом лете собра войско не мало царь наш, вящей нежели от тридесять тысещей, и поставил над ними воевод трех: Иоанна Шереметева, мужа зело мудраго и острозрительнаго и от младости своея в богатырских вещах искуснаго, и предреченнаго князя Симеона Микулинского, и меня; и с нами немало стратилатов, светлых, и храбрых и великородных мужей. Мы же пришедше в Казань и, опочинув мало воинству, поидохом в пределы оныя далеко, идеже князие Казанские с воинствы бусурманскими и другими поганскими ополчашесь. И было их во ополчению вящей, нежели пятьнадесят тысящей, и поставляху битвы с нами и со предними полки нашими; сражашеся мало на двадесять крат, памятамися, бо им удобно бываше, яко знаемым во своей их земле; паче же с лесов прихождаху, сопротивляющиижеся нам крепце; и везде, за благодатию Божиею, поражаеми были от християн. И к тому погодное время Бог дал нам на них, понеже зело в тую зиму снеги

[a] Patr., Pog., T. воинска: Ar.

---

[1] For details of the local rebellions against Muscovite rule and of the fighting in the Kazan' area during the years following the submission of the khanate, see *PSRL* xiii, pp. 228 *sq.* In early 1553 Boris Ivanovich Saltykov, a *voevoda* attached to the commander-in-chief in the Muscovite fortress of

tribes which I have mentioned before, and they fought fiercely, not only coming from the great forests against the town of Kazan', but also attacking the lands of Murom and Nizhny Novgorod and taking the people prisoner. And this happened incessantly for about six years after the capture of the town of Kazan'; and newly-founded fortresses in that land [i.e. the district of Kazan']—as well as some even in the Russian land—were besieged by them. And they joined battle with his *hetman*, a distinguished man whose name was Boris Morozov-Saltykov: and the Christian regiments fell before the heathens and the *hetman* himself was captured. And they kept him alive for about two years and then killed him; they did not want to return him either for ransom or in exchange for their own prisoners. And during those six years there were many battles and skirmishes with them. And during that time so many Christian soldiers perished, battling and fighting with them incessantly, that it is beyond belief.[1]

And after the sixth year our tsar collected a large army, more than thirty thousand strong, and over it he placed three *voevody*: Ivan Sheremetev, a very wise and sharp-sighted man, skilled from his youth in deeds of valour, and Prince Semen Mikulinsky, whom I have mentioned above, and myself; and with us were many commanders, brilliant, brave and high-born men. Now when we came to Kazan' and when the troops had rested a little, we set off for those distant parts where the princes of Kazan' stood in arms with the Mussulman and other pagan troops. And in their army there were more than fifteen thousand men, and they joined battle with us and with our advance regiments; and they fought with us almost[2] twenty times, I remember, for it was convenient for them as they were known in their own land, especially when they emerged from the forests, resisting us strongly. Yet in every place they were beaten by the Christians thanks to the grace of God. And furthermore God granted weather that was favourable to us against them, for that winter there were very great snows with-

Sviyazhsk, was beaten and taken prisoner when trying to subdue Tatar detachments which had been harassing the Russians.
[2] A scribe's error for мало не.

были великие без северов;[a] и того ради мало что их осталось, понеже хождаху за ними месяц целый, а предние полки наши гоняху за ними аж за Уржум и Мет реку, за лесы великие, и оттуду аж до Башкирска языка, яж по Каме реке вверх ко Сибири протязается. И что их было осталося, те покоришася нам. И воистинну было что писати по ряду о оных сражаниях з бусурманы, да[b] краткости ради оставляется, бо тогда больши десяти тысящей воинства бусурманского погубихом со аттаманы их; тогда же славных кровопийцов христианских, Янчюру Измаильтянина и Алеку Черемисина, и других князей их немало погубихом. И возвратихомся, за Божиею благодатию, во отечество со пресветлою победою и со множайшими корыстьми. И оттуду начала усмирятися и покорятися Казанская земля цареви нашему.

И потом, того же лета, прииде весть ко царю нашему, иже царь Перекопский, со всеми силами своими препроводясь чрез проливы морския, пошел воевати[c] землю Черкасов Пятигорских; и сего ради послал царь наш войска на Перекопь аки тринадесят тысящей, над нимиже поставил гетманом Иоанна Шереметева и других с ним стратилатов. Егда же наши поидоша чрез поле великое к Перекопи дорогою лежащею, глаголемою на[d] Изюм-курган, царем же бусурманским, яко есть обычай издавна, инуды лук потянут, а инуды стрелять, — сиречь на иную страну славу пустят, аки бы хотяще воевати, а инуды поидут, — и возвративши войска от Черкаския земли, поиде на Русь

---

[a] Ar. серенов: Patr., Pog. T. [b] Patr., Pog. до: Ar.
[c] Patr., Pog., T. воевади: Ar. [d] T. но: Ar., Patr., Pog.

---

[1] Other MSS. read серенов, which could mean either (a) "without frozen snow", i.e. without a hard crust of snow (see Sreznevsky, *Materialy*, vol. III, col. 339), or (b) "without clear days" (cf. Latin *serenum*).

[2] The Urzhumka river, on which the town of Urzhum lies, is a tributary of the Vyatka; the Mesha river, on which the rebellious Kazanites had built a stronghold (*PSRL* XIII, p. 230), is a tributary of the Kama river. According to the chronicle the Russians ranged as far as "250 versts from

94

out north winds;[1] and few of them survived, because our advance regiments followed them for a whole month and chased after them as far as beyond the Urzhumka and Mesha rivers, beyond the great forests, and from there even as far as the territory of the Bashkir tribe, which stretches up along the Kama river towards Siberia.[2] And those of them who survived surrendered to us. And indeed there was plenty to narrate about those battles with the Mussulmans, but for the sake of brevity I abstain from doing this. At that time we destroyed more than ten thousand men of the Mussulman army together with their leaders; and also at that time we slew those renowned drinkers of Christian blood, Yamchura the Ishmaelite and Aleka the Cheremisian[3] and many others of their princes. And thanks to the grace of God we returned to our fatherland with a brilliant victory and with a vast amount of booty. And from that time onwards the land of Kazan' began to be subdued and to be subjugated to our tsar.[4]

And then, in that same year, news came to our tsar that the khan of Perekop, having crossed the straits with all his forces, had set off to wage war on the land of the Circassians of the Five Hills;[5] and therefore our tsar sent troops against Perekop, about thirteen thousand strong, and over them he placed Ivan Sheremetev as *hetman*, and he sent other commanders with him. Now when our troops set off across the great steppe along the road which leads towards Perekop, called the road to Izyum Hill, then the khan—as has long been the custom of the Mussulman khans, namely to draw their bows in one direction but to shoot in another, that is to say they spread the rumour that they are about to war in one direction and move off in another—withdrew his troops from the Circassian land and set

Kazan' up the Kama river and 200 versts from the Volga across the Vyatka" (*PSRL* xiii, p. 239).

[3] The chronicles make no mention of Yamchura or Aleka.

[4] The army under Mikulinsky, Sheremetev and Kurbsky was assembled in September 1553; it returned after its highly successful campaign in the Kazan' district on 25 March 1554 (*PSRL* xiii, pp. 234, 238–9; *DRK*, p. 165). Kurbsky's dating, "after the sixth year", is clearly at fault.

[5] I.e. the Circassians of the Northern Caucasus. The town of Pyatigorsk was founded on the position of the Five Hills.

95

дорогою, глаголемою[a] на Великий перевоз, от тое дороги, иже лежит на Изюм-курган, аки день езду конем; и не ведяше о християнском[b] войску. Ианн же, яко муж разумный, имяше стражу со обоих боков зело прилежную и подъезды под шляхи, и уведявше[c] о цареве хождению на Рускую землю, и абие послал весть ко царю нашему до Москвы, иже грядет недруг его на него в силе тяжстей; а сам заиде ему созади: хотяше на него ударити в то время, егда в Руской земле войска распустит.[d] Потом, уведав[e] о коше царя Перекопскаго, послал на него аки третину войска, бо от шляху был, имъже Иоан идяше, аки полднища в стране; бо обычай есть всегда Перекопскаго царя днищ за пять, або за шесть, оставляти половину коней всего воинства своего, пригоды ради.

Писари же наши Руские, имъже князь великий зело верит, — а избирает их не от шляхетского роду, ни от благородна, но паче от поповичов, или от простаго всенародства, а что ненавидячи творит вельмож своих, подобно, по пророку глаголющему, хотяще един вселитися[f] на земли, — что же тые сотворили писари? То воистинну: что было таити,[g] сие всем велегласно проповедали. "Се, рекше, изчезнет убо царь Перекопский со всеми силами своими! Царь наш грядет со множеством воинства против его, а Иоан Шереметев над главою его идет за хрептом." И то во все украины написали проповедающе. Царь же Перекопский, до самых Руских пределов прешедши, ни о чем же не ведяше; но так был Бог дал, иже ни единаго человека не возможе нигде обрести, и о том зело тружашеся, тамо и овамо по странам ищуще языка; последи же, по несчастию,

---

[a] Patr., Pog., T. глаголемаго: Ar.   [b] T. християнскому: Ar.
[c] Patr. увидевше: Ar.   [d] Patr., T. войско распустят: Ar.
[e] Patr. уведал: Ar.   [f] Patr., Pog., T. един един веселитися: Ar.   [g] Pog., T. тоити: Ar.

---

[1] Izyum Hill and Veliky Perevoz (Great Ferry) are near the confluence of the Oskol and Seversky Donets rivers.

[2] Presumably the meaning of подъезды под шляхи. See Sreznevsky,

off against Russia along the road called the road to the Great Ferry, which is about a day's horse-ride distant from the road to Izyum Hill.[1] And they did not know about the Christian army. But Ivan [Sheremetev], like a sensible man, had very watchful guards on both flanks and reconnaissance patrols on the enemy's steppe routes,[2] and learning of the khan's march against the Russian land he straightway sent a message to our tsar in Moscow, saying that the enemy was marching against him in strength; and he himself went behind the enemy, intending to attack him the moment he dispersed his troops in the Russian land. Then, learning about the baggage train of the khan of Perekop, he sent about a third of his force against it—it was about half a day's journey away from the route along which Ivan [Sheremetev] was marching; for it is always the habit of the khan of Perekop to leave half the horses of all his army five or six days journey behind, in case they should be needed.

Now our Russian clerks, whom the grand prince puts great faith in—he chooses them not from noble or high-born stock but rather from priests' sons or from the rank and file, and this makes him hate his grandees, as in the words of the prophet who says: "wishing to be placed alone in the midst of the earth"[3]—well, what did these clerks do? This, in truth, is what they did: that which should have been concealed they announced with a loud voice to all the people, saying: "Now the khan of Perekop will disappear with all his forces! Our tsar is marching with a large number of troops against him, while Ivan Sheremetev is marching secretly[4] behind his back." This they wrote, proclaiming it to all the frontier districts. Now when the khan of Perekop arrived in the Russian lands themselves, he knew nothing [of the Russian plans]—God had so granted that it was impossible to find a single person anywhere, and the khan was in grave difficulty, seeking a prisoner on all sides and in all

Materialy, vol. II, col. 1073 under подъезжьчик. The *shlyakhi* or *shlyagi* were paths along which the Tatars invaded Muscovy.

[3] Is. v. 8.

[4] A possible rendering of над главою его. Or perhaps "at the head [of an army]"?

наиде дву: един же ему вся по ряду исповеда, муки не пре-
терпев, еже написали мудрые наши писари. И первие
тогда, глаголют, во велицее ужасе тогда был и в недоумению
со всеми своими, и абие возвратился шляхом своим к орде.
И по дву днях встретился с войском нашим, и то не со всем,
понеже еще не пришла была оная предреченная часть
войска, яже на кош была послана; и снидошася оба войска
о полудни в среду, и битва пребывала аж до самыя нощи.
И так было перваго дня посчастил Бог над бусурманы, иже
множество побито их; во християнском же войску зело
мало шкоды быша. И по излишному смельству вразишася
некоторые наши в полки бусурманские, и убит един зацнаго
отца сын, а два[a] шляхтича изымано живых, от Татар при-
ведено их пред царя. Царь же нача со прещением и муками
пытати их; един же поведал ему то, яко достоило храброму
воину и благородному; а другий, безумный, устрашился
мук, поведал ему по ряду: "иже, рече, малый люд, и того
вяще и четвертая часть на кош твой послано".
Царь же Татарский, аще и хотяше[b] нощию тою отоити и
бежати в орду — зело бо бояшеся ззади войска християнского и самого князя великого, — но он его, предреченный
безумник, во всем утвердил, и сего ради задержался. На
утро же, в четверг, дню светающа, паки битва начашася, и
пребывала аж до полудня; так бишася крепце и мужественне
теми малыми людьми, иже все были полки Татарские
розогнали. Царь же един остался между анчары (бо было
с ним аки тысяща с ручницами и дел не мало). И по грехом
нашим, в том часу сам гетман воинства християнского зелне
ранен, и к тому конь застрелиша под ним, иже еще к тому
збил его с себя (яко обычай раненым конем), и оброниша
его храбрые воины некоторые едва жива и наполы мертва.
Татаровя же, видевше царя своего между янычары при

<hr/>

[a] два omitted in Ar.   [b] Patr., Pog., T.   аще и не хотяще: Ar.

<hr/>

[1] I.e. members of the *szlachta*, minor service nobility or gentry.

98

directions. And after a while he unfortunately found two: one of them, being unable to bear the torture, told him everything which our wise clerks had written. And then for the first time, they say, the khan was greatly afraid and did not know what to do with all his men, and straightway he set off back to his horde by the route he had come by. Two days later he met our army—but not all of it, for that part of the army which, as we mentioned above, had been sent against the Tatar baggage train had not yet arrived. And both armies joined battle on Wednesday at mid-day, and the battle lasted right until the very night. And on the first day God granted us such good fortune against the Mussulmans that a large number of them were killed, while in the Christian army there were very few losses. And with excessive boldness some of our men struck their way into the Mussulman ranks, and one of them, the son of a distinguished father, was killed, and two noblemen[1] were caught alive and brought before the khan by the Tatars. The khan began to question them with threats and torments, and one of them answered him as befits a brave and noble soldier; but the other, the foolish man, was frightened of the tortures and told him: "There are only a few of them, as just over a quarter of the army has been sent against your baggage train."

Now the Tatar khan, even though he had intended to withdraw that night and flee to the horde—for he was very afraid of the Christian army in his rear and of the grand prince himself—was convinced of everything which that above-mentioned foolish man said, and so he delayed. And on the next day, Thursday, at daybreak, the battle began again, and it lasted right until mid-day; and with their small forces the Russians fought so firmly and so bravely that they dispelled all the Tatar regiments. And the khan remained in the midst of his janissaries (for he had with him about a thousand men with muskets and several guns). And because of our sins the *hetman* himself of the Christian army was seriously wounded at that time, and furthermore his horse was shot dead beneath him and threw him, as usually happens with wounded horses; and certain brave soldiers of his protected him while he was half-alive, half-dead. And when the Tatars saw their khan by the guns in the

делех, паки обратишася; а нашим уже справа без гетмана помешалася: аще и были другие воеводы, но не были так храбры и справны. Потом еще трвала битва мала не на две годины, яко глаголют пословицу: "аще бы и львов стадо было, без добраго пастыря неспоро". И большую половицу войска християнского разогнаша Татаровя, овых побиша, храбрых же мужей не мало же и живых поимано; а другая часть, аки две тысящи и вящей, в байраку едином обсекошася. К ним же царь со всем войском своим три краты того же дни приступал, добывающе их; и отбишась от него, и поиде от них пред солнечным заходом с великою тщетою. Поиде же скоро ко орде своей, бояшебося ззади нашего войска за собою. И приехаша те все стратилати с воями здравы ко царю нашему.

Царь же наш, егда о поражении своих не ведяше, скоро шел и со великим потшанием сопротив царю Перекопскому, ибо егда пришел от Москвы ко Оке реке, не стал тамо, идеже обычай бывал издавна застановлятися християнскому войску против царей Татарских, но, превезшеся за великую Оку реку, пошел оттуду к месту Туле: хотяше с ним битву великую свести. Егда же аки половину отъиде от Оки до Тулы, прииде ему весть, иже пораженно войско християнское от царя Татарскаго;[a] потом, аки по године, раненые наши воины нецыи усретошася. Цареви же нашему и многим советником его абие мысль отмениша, и начаша иноко советовати[b] ему, сииречь: да идешь паки за Оку, а оттуды к Москве. Нецыи мужественнейшии укрепляюще его и глаголюще, да не даст хрепта врагу своему, да не посрамит прежние славы своея добрые и лиц всех храбрых своих, и да грядет мужественне сопротив врага креста Христова. И рече: "Аще он и выиграл, за грехи християнские, битву, но обаче уже утружденно войско имеет, тако

---

[a] Т. перскаго: Ar.   [b] Т. советова: Ar.

[1] Lit. "the affair (Polish *sprawa*) for our men was confused...".

[2] Cf. *PSRL* xiii, p. 257: в дуброве...осеклися. The number of Russians given in the chronicle is "about five or six thousand".

midst of the janissaries, they turned again. And our men fell into confusion without their *hetman*:[1] even though there were other *voevody*, they were not so brave or so skilled. And the battle lasted nearly two hours after this, as the saying goes: "Even a pack of lions can do nothing without a good shepherd." And the Tatars dispersed the greater half of the Christian army: some they killed, and many brave men were captured alive. And the other part of the army, about two thousand or more, took up a defensive position in a hollow.[2] Three times that day the khan assaulted them with all his army, trying to finish them off,[3] but they repulsed him, and he withdrew from them before sunset with great losses. And in a short time he set off for his horde, for he was afraid of our army behind him. And all the generals returned safely to our tsar with their troops.[4]

Now before our tsar knew about the defeat of his men, he marched quickly and with great eagerness against the khan of Perekop; indeed, when he arrived from Moscow at the Oka river, he did not stop in the place where it had long been the custom for Christian armies facing Tatar khans to stop, but he crossed the great Oka river and went from there to the town of Tula, intending to fight a great battle with him. But when he had gone about half-way from the Oka to Tula, news came to him that the Christian army had been defeated by the Tatar khan; then, about an hour later, some of our wounded soldiers met him. And our tsar and many of his counsellors immediately changed their minds, and they began to advise him to do the opposite, that is: go back across the Oka and from there to Moscow. But some who were braver strengthened his purpose and told him not to show his back to the enemy and not to bring shame upon his former good repute and upon all his brave men, but to march boldly against the enemy of the Cross of Christ. And they said: "Even if the khan won the battle because of the sins of the Christians, nevertheless his army is

---

[3] Or "trying to reach them".

[4] For details of Khan Devlet Girey's invasion of 1555, culminating in the defeat of Sheremetev at Sudbishchi (150 versts from Tula), see *PSRL* xiii, pp. 256–8. Ivan in his first letter to Kurbsky called Sheremetev's defeat "a disaster for Orthodox Christianity" (*Correspondence*, pp. 116–17).

же множество раненых и побитых; бо брань крепкая с нашими пребывала два дни.'' Ибо сице ему добрый и полезный совет подающе, понеже еще того неведующе, иже царь пошел уже к орде, начающе его, что час, пришествия. Царь же наш абие совета храбрых послушав, а совет страшливых отверг: иде к Туле месту, хотящи сразитися с бусурманы за православное християнство. Се таков наш царь был, поки любил окола себя добрых и правду советующих, а не презлых ласкателей, над нихже губительнейшаго[a] и горшаго во царстве ничто же может быти! Егда же приехал на Тулу, тогда сьехашася к нему немало разогнаннаго войска, и оные предреченные приехаша со своими стротилаты, яже от царя отбишася, аки две тысящи их, и поведаша: ''уже, аки третий день, царь поиде к орде''.

Потом паки, аки бы в покаяние вниде, и не мало лет царствовал добре; ужаснулся бо о наказании оных от Бога, ово Перекопским царем, ово Казанским возмущением, о нихже мало пред тем рекох, понеже так уже, глаголют, было от тех Казанцов изнемогло воинство християнское и в нищету пришло, иже уже у множайших нас и последних стяжаней не[b] стало; к тому болезни различныя и моры частые бывали тамо, яко многим уже советовати со вопиянием, да покинет место Казанские и град, и воинство християнское сведет оттуду; а рада то была богатых и ленивых мнихов и мирских, яко глаголют пословицу: добре бывает, кому родити, тому и кормити младенца, или попечение о нем имети, сиречь: хто тружался зело, и болезновать о сем тому достоило и советовати о таковых.

А потом взяла была Черемиса Луговая царя собе с Нагайские орды, бронящеся[c] християном и воююще; бо тот Черемиский язык не мал есть и зело кровопииствен, а обирается их, глаголют, вящей двадесять тысящей войска; потом же, егда разсмотривши, иже[d] мало им прибыли с того царя, убиша его и сущих с ним Татар, аки триста, и главу

[a] T. любительнейшаго: Ar.   [b] Patr., Pog. не omitted in Ar.
[c] T. броняшеся: Ar.   [d] T. и: Ar.

already wearied and he has many wounded and killed; for the fierce battle with our men lasted two days." And they gave him this good useful advice, for they did not yet know that the khan had already set off to the horde, but they expected him to come any time.[1] Our tsar immediately took the advice of the brave men and rejected that of the cowards: he set off to the town of Tula, intending to fight the Mussulmans for Orthodox Christianity. Such a man was our tsar so long as he loved to have about him good men and those who counsel what is right, and not evil flatterers, than whom there can be nothing more destructive or worse in the tsardom! But when he arrived at Tula, much of the army which had been scattered gathered and met him; and these men, about whom we have written above and who had repulsed the khan, came to him, some two thousand strong, together with their commanders, and they told him: "The khan set off to the horde the day before yesterday."

And then it seemed as though he once again repented, and he ruled well for some years. For he was horrified by the punishments inflicted by God, that is to say the invasion of the khan of Perekop and the Kazan' uprising, about which I have spoken above, for, they say, the Christian army was so weakened by the men of Kazan' and so impoverished that very many of us were deprived of even our last possessions; furthermore, there were various sicknesses and frequent epidemics there, so that many cried out and advised him to quit the city and fortress of Kazan' and to lead the Christian army away from there; and such was the counsel of rich idle monks and laymen, as the saying goes: "It is right that one who gives birth should feed the child or care for it", in other words: he who has toiled much should worry about this and should give advice on such matters.

And after that the Meadow Cheremisians took a khan for themselves from the Nogay Horde, resisting the Christians and fighting; for that Cheremisian tribe is large and very blood-thirsty, and, so they say, they can muster more than twenty thousand soldiers. But when they saw that this khan was of little use to them, they killed him and the Tatars who were

---

[1] начающе: evidently a corruption of но чающе. For что час, cf. Polish co czas.

ему отсекоша и на высокое древо взоткнули и глаголали: "Мы было взяли тебя того ради на царство, з двором твоим, да обороняеши нас; а ты и сущие с тобою не сотворил нам помощи столько, сколько волов и коров наших поел: а ныне глава твоя да царствует на высоком коле!" Потом, избравше собе своих атаманов, бьющеся и воююще с нами крепце, аки два лета; и паки потом ово примиряхуся, ово паки брань начинаху. Но иные оставя в те лета бывшие, х краткости историйки тое зряще, но се воспомянем.

---

¹ For further details on this rebellion, which took place in 1556, see *PSRL* xiii, pp. 265, 266.

with him, some three hundred strong, and they cut off his head, stuck it on a tall pole and said: "We chose you as khan together with your retinue so that you might defend us; but you and those with you have not so much helped us as eaten our oxen and our cows: may your head now rule on a tall stake!"[1] After that they chose their own leaders and fought and warred fiercely with us for about two years. Then they would either become subjected to us again or they would start fighting again. Now let us leave aside the various other things which happened during these years, having regard for the brevity of this little history, and let us mention the following.

IV

В тех же летех премирие[a] минуло с Лифлянскою землею, и приехаша послове от них, просяще миру. Царь же наш начал упоминатися дани, яже еще дед его в привилью воспомянул об ней, и от того времяни, аки пятьдесят лет, не плачено было[b] от них; а Немцы не хотяще ему дани дати оныя, и за тем война зачалася. И послал тогда нас трех великих воевод, и с нами других стратилатов, и войска аки четыредесять тысящей и вящей, не градов и мест добывати, но землю их воевати. И воевахом ее месяц целый, и нигдеже опрошася нам битвою; точию со единаго града изошли сопротив посылок наших, и тамо поражено их. И шли есмя их землею, воююще вдоль вяще четыредесять миль, и изыдохом в землю[c] в Ифлянскую с великого места Пскова, а вышли есми совсем здраво с их земли, аж на Иванъград, вколо их землею ходяще. И изнесохом[d] с собою множество различных корыстей, понеже там земля зело была богатая и жители в ней быша так горды зело, иже и веры християнские отступили и обычаев и дел добрых праотец своих, но удалилися и ринулися все ко широкому и пространному пути, сиречь ко пьянству многому, и невоздержанию, и ко долгому спанию, и ленивству, к неправдам и кровопролиянию междоусобному, яко есть обычай, презлых ради догматов, таковым и делам последовати. И сих ради, мню, и

[a] Т. премирне: Ar.   [b] Patr., Pog., Т. были: Ar.   [c] Т. бо в землю: Ar.   [d] Т. изнесоша: Ar.

---

[1] In 1503, at the end of the Russo-Lithuanian war, Ivan III compelled his enemy's ally, the Master of the Livonian Order, to make a humiliating peace with his representatives in Novgorod and Pskov (see Fennell, *Ivan the Great*, p. 272). According to the treaty the Master, Von Plettenberg, had to agree to the renewal of the perpetual payment of tribute for the possession of the town of Derpt (Dorpat, Tartu, Yur'ev), which had formed part of the early Kievan state.

The Livonian ambassadors arrived in Moscow in 1554 and requested a renewal of the treaty for thirty years. Ivan IV agreed to a renewal for

IV

In those years the truce with the Livonian land ended, and envoys came from the Livonians asking for peace. And our tsar began to press for the tribute which his grandfather had mentioned in a charter—from that time onwards for about fifty years, no payment had been made by them.[1] But the Germans had no wish to pay him that tribute, and for this reason the war began. And at that time he sent us, three great *voevody*, and other generals with us, and about forty thousand troops or more, not to take fortresses and towns, but to war on their land.[2] And we waged war on it for a whole month and nowhere did they offer us resistance in battle; only from one fortress did they make a sortie against our attacks, and there they were defeated.[3] And we went through their land, fighting on a front of more than forty miles; we entered the Livonian land from the great city of Pskov and came out safe and sound from their land as far [north] as Ivangorod, having gone all round their country. And we brought out with us much booty of various kinds, for the land there was very rich and the inhabitants were so very proud that they had even departed from the Christian faith and customs and good deeds of their ancestors and had gone far afield, rushing towards that broad extensive path, that is to say towards much drunkenness and intemperance, long sleeping and idleness, injustice and internecine bloodshed; for it is customary to pursue such deeds for

fifteen years on the condition that the Derpt tribute be paid and that the arrears for the past fifty years be paid off in three years. See *PSRL* xiii, p. 240.

[2] Among the commanders of the army, which assembled in November 1557, were the ex-khan of Kazan', Shah Ali (C. in C.), Mikhail Vasil'evich Glinsky, Ivan Vasil'evich Sheremetev and Kurbsky (i.c. the Guard Corps, *storozhevoy polk*). See *PSRL* xiii, pp. 286-7; *PL* ii, p. 235. Cf. *DRK*, pp. 197-8.

[3] The only town to have offered the Russians any opposition during their first invasion of Livonia was Derpt (*PSRL* xiii, pp. 289-90). The Russian operations which took place in January 1558 were in fact more a reconnaissance in strength than a full-scale attack.

не попустил их Бог быти в покою и в долготу дней владети отчизнами своими.

Потом же они[a] упросили были премирья на полроку, хотяще себе взяти о той предреченной дани на размышление; и, сами упросивши, не пребыли в том дву месяцей. Сице разрушили тое премирье: яко всем есть ведомо, иже Немецкое место, глаголемое Нарви, и Руское Иванъград об едину реку стоят, а оба града и места не малые, паче же той Русии многонароден; и на самый день, в оньже Господь наш Исус Христос за человеческий род плотию пострадал, — и в той день, Ему по силе своей кождый християнин подобяся, страстем Его терпит, в посте и в воздержанию пребывающе, — а их милость Немцы, велеможные и гордые, сами себе новое имя изобретше, нарекшеся Евангелики, в начале еще дня того ужравшися и упившися, над надежду всех из великих дел стреляти на место Руское начали, и побиша люду немало християнского, со женами и детками, и пролияша кровь християнскую в такие великие и святые дни; бо безпрестани били три дни, и на самый день Христова Воскресения не унелися, будучи в премирию, присягами утвержденном. А на Иванегороде воевода, не смеюче без царева ведома премирья нарушити, и дал скоро до Москвы знаки; царь же вниде в совет о том и по совете на том положил, иже, по нужде за их початком, повелел бронитися и стреляти з дел на их град и место; бо уже было и великих дел с Москвы припроважено тамо и немало, и к тому послал стратилатов и повелел двема пятинам Новгородским воинству сбиратися к ним. Наши же, егда заточиша дела великие на место их, и начаша бити по граду и по полотом их, тако же и верхними делы стреляти кулями каменными великими, — они же, яко отнюдь тому неискусные, живша

[a] Patr., Pog., T. аки: Ar.

---

[1] Cf. *PSRL* xiii, p. 290 *sub fin.*, where the date of the Master's letter to Ivan IV is given as 1 March 1558. The chronicles make no mention of a six-months truce.
[2] I.e. the Narova river.

the sake of wicked beliefs. For this reason, I believe, God did not let them live in peace and hold their native lands for long.

Then they asked for a truce for half a year, wishing to consider the question of the tribute we have already talked about; and having themselves asked for a truce, they did not keep it even for two months.[1] And this is how they broke the truce. As everyone knows, there is a German town called Narva and a Russian town called Ivangorod which stand on [both sides of] one river,[2] and both fortresses and towns are not small—the Russian town is particularly populous. Now on the very day on which our Lord Jesus Christ suffered in the flesh for mankind— on that day when every Christian, emulating Him to the best of his ability, suffers His passion, abiding in fasting and restraint —their lordships the Germans, noble and proud, who have devised for themselves a new name, calling themselves Evangelicals, having gorged and guzzled early on that day, began, to the surprise of all, to fire from the great guns at the Russian town; and they killed many Christian people, including women and children, and they spilled Christian blood on these great and holy days; for they bombarded [Ivangorod] for three days without ceasing, and on the very day of Christ's Resurrection they did not stop, although they were still under the truce which had been confirmed by oaths. Now the *voevoda* of Ivangorod, not daring to break the truce without the knowledge of the tsar, quickly sent word to Moscow; the tsar took counsel on this, and as a result of this counsel decided that, compelled [to break the truce], as the enemy had done so first, he would order [the garrison] to defend itself and to shoot from the guns at their fortress and town, for several large guns had already been brought there from Moscow. Furthermore he sent commanders there and ordered two Novgorod *pyatiny*[3] to muster their forces under them. Now when our men had trained the great guns on the town and had begun to bombard their fortress and their houses and to shoot large stone cannon balls from the upper guns, the people of Narva, as they were completely inexperi-

[3] I.e. districts. The territory of Novgorod (in other words, all the lands in the vicinity of the capital which had been dependent on the republic before its annexation in 1478) was divided into five *pyatiny*.

множество лет в покою, гордость отложа, абие начаша просити премирья, аки на 4 недели, беручи себе на розмышление о поданию места и града. И выправили до Москвы ко царю нашему двух бурмистров своих, к тому же трех мужей богатых, обещающи за четыре недели место и град подати. Ко маистру же Лифлянскому и по другим властем Немецким послаша, просяще помощь: "Аще ли, рече, не дадите помощи, мы от такой великие стрельбы не можем терпети: подадим град и место." Маистр же абие дал им в помощь антипата Фелинского,[a] а другаго с Ревля, и с ними четыре тысящи люду Немецкаго, и конных и пеших.

Егда же приидоша войско Немецкое во град, аки во дву неделях потом, наши же не начинающи брани, дондеже минет оный месяць премирью; они же не престаша обыкновения своего, сиречь пиянства многаго и ругания над догъматы християнскими, и обретши икону пресвятые Богородицы, у неяше на руку написан по плоти превечный младенец, Господь наш Исус Христос, в коморах оных, идеже купцы Руские у них некогда обитали, возревше на нее господин дому с некоторыми новопришедшими Немцы, начаша ругатися, глаголюще: "сей болван поставлен был купцов ради Руских, а нам уже ныне не потребен; приидем и истребим его". Яко пророк некогда рече о таковых безумных: сечивом и теслою разрушающе, и огнем зжигающе светило Божие; сему подобно и те безумные южики сотвориша. И взявше образ со стены и пришедше ко великому огню, идеже потребные питья свои в котле варяще, и ввергше абие во огнь. О Христе! неизреченные силы чудес Твоих, имиже[b] обличаеши хотящих дерзати и на имя Твое беззаконновавших! Абие, паче пращи, прутко летящие, або из якого великого дела, весь огнь он испот котла ударил вверх, — воистинну яко при Халдейской пещи[c],— и не обретесь ничто же огня тамо, идеже образ вержен, и абие

[a] Т. Фелийскаго: Ar.   [b] Pog., Т. имже: Ar.   [c] Pog., Т. яко приехав дейской: Ar.

[1] Cf. Greek ἀνθύπατος.

enced in such matters and as they had lived for many years in peace, cast their pride aside and immediately asked for a truce for four weeks, having in mind the surrender of the town and fortress. And they sent two of their burgomasters to our tsar in Moscow and three rich men as well, promising to hand over the town and fortress in four weeks. But they also sent to the Livonian Master and to other German authorities as well, asking for help: "If", they said, "you do not give us help, we cannot resist such heavy shooting: we shall surrender the fortress and town." The master immediately sent them the governor[1] of Fellin (Viljandi) and another from Revel', and with them four thousand German troops, both cavalry and infantry.

When the German army arrived at the fortress, about two weeks later, our men did not begin fighting, as they were waiting for the month of the truce to pass. But the Germans did not desist from their habits, that is to say from much drunkenness and mockery at Christian beliefs. And in those rooms where the Russian merchants had formerly dwelt they found an ikon of the most holy Mother of God, in whose arms was painted after the flesh the eternal child, our Lord Jesus Christ; and looking at it, the master of the house and several Germans, who had recently arrived, began to jeer, saying: "This idol was put here because of the Russian merchants; we no longer need it. Come, let us destroy it." As the prophet once said of such foolish people: "destroying with axe and adze, and burning with fire the sanctuary of God".[2] And these foolish men[3] acted in this manner. They took the ikon from the wall and went to the large fire on which they were brewing in a pot the beverages they required, and straightway threw it on the fire. O Christ, ineffable are the powers of Your miracles, by which You denounce those who would be bold and those who have transgressed against Your name! Straightway, flying swiftly as from a siege-gun[4] or from some great cannon, all that fire struck upwards from underneath the pot—indeed, just like the Chaldaean fiery furnace—and there were no traces of fire where the ikon had been thrown; and immediately the top of

[2] Ps. lxxiv. 6, 7.   [3] Lit. "relatives", "kinsmen".
[4] Lit. "more than a siege-gun".

в верху палаты загорелось. Сия жь быша, аки по третьей године, в день неделный. Аеру чисту бывшу и тиху, и абие внезапу прииде буря великая, и загорелося место так скоро, же за малый час все место обьяло.

Людие же Немецкие все от места избегоша во град от огня великого и не возмогоша ни мало помощи себе. Народи же Руские, видевше, иже стены меские пусты, абие устремишася чрез реку, овии в кораблецех различных, овии на дщицах, овии ж врата вымающе от домов своих, и поплыша. Потом и воинство устремилося, аще и воеводам крепце возбраняющим им о сем, премирья ради; они же, не послушав, видевше явственный Божий гнев на них пущенный, а нашим подающи помощь. И абие разломавши врата железные и проломавши стены, внидоша в место; бе бо буря она зелная, от места на град возбураше огнь. Егда же приидоша с места ко граду войско наше, тогда начаша Немцы противитися им, исходяще из врат Вышеградских, и бишася с нами, аки на две годины. И взявше наши дела, яже во вратех места Немецкого и которые на стенах стояли, и начаша на них стреляти из дел оных. Потом приспеша стрельцы Руские с[a] стратилаты их, тако же и стрел множество от наших вкупе с ручничною стрельбою пущаемо на них. Абие втиснуша их во Вышъград; и ово от великого духа огня, ово от стрельбы, яже из их дел на них по вратом Вышеградцким стреляно, ово от великого множества народу, бо он вышеград был тесен, начаша абие просити, да повеленно будет им розмовити. Егда же утишишася[b] с обоих стран войска, изыдоша из града и начаша постановляти с нашими, да[c] дадут им вольное исхождение и да пустят

[a] T.   c omitted in Ar., Patr. and Pog.   [b] Patr., Pog. утишися:
Ar.   [c] Patr., Pog., T. еда: Ar.

[1] For a somewhat different version of the incident, see *PSRL* XIII, p. 295; *PL* II, pp. 235–6.
[2] Vyshgorod was the fortress or Kremlin of Narva, situated in the upper part of the town. See P. Semenov, *Slovar' Rossiysskoy imperii*, vol. 3, p. 389.

the room caught fire. This happened after the third hour on Sunday. The air was clear and calm; then suddenly a great storm came and the town caught fire so quickly that in a short time the whole town was enveloped in flames.[1]

The Germans all ran from the town to the fortress in order to escape the great fire, but they were unable to help themselves in any way. Now when the Russian townsfolk saw that the town walls were unmanned, they immediately rushed across the river, some in various kinds of little boats, others on small planks, while yet others removed the doors of their houses and sailed on them. Then our soldiers too rushed off to the town, although the *voevody* strictly forbade them to do this because of the truce; but they did not listen to them, for they had seen the manifest wrath of God which had been visited upon the people of Narva and which was helping our men. And having smashed the iron gates and broken through the walls they entered the town, for the storm, which blew the fire from the town up to the fortress, was very violent. And when our troops came from the town to the fortress, the Germans began to resist them, coming out of the Vyshgorod[2] gates, and they fought with us for about two hours. And our men seized the guns which stood in the gates of the German town and on the walls, and they began to fire at the enemy from those guns. Then the Russian archers came with their commanders, and a great number of arrows was shot at them by our men as well as musket-fire. Immediately they drove them back into Vyshgorod; and both because of the great heat of the fire, and because of the shooting which was directed at them [and] at the gates of Vyshgorod from their own guns, and because of the large number of people (for space in the citadel was very confined), they immediately began to ask that orders be given for a parley. Now when the fighting had died down,[3] they came out of the fortress and began to discuss terms with our men, requesting that they be given free exit and be allowed to go safe and

Elsewhere Kurbsky uses the word *vyshgorod* simply to denote a citadel. See below, p. 150.

[3] Lit. "when the troops on both sides had calmed down".

здравых совсем. И на том постановили: и пустили их со оружием, яже точию при бедрах, новопришедших во град воинство их, а тутошних жителей со женами и з детьми токмо, а богатество и стяжания во граде оставили; а нецыи произволиша ту в домех своих остати: то пущено на волю их.

Се такова мзда ругателей, яже уподобляют Христов образ, по плоти написан, и рождшия Его болваном поганских богов! Се иконома̀хом[a] воздаяние! Абие, яко за четыре годины, або за пять, ото всех отчин и от превысоких полат и домов златописанных лишены и премногих богатств и стяжаней обнажены, со уничижением и постыдением и со многою срамотою отоидоша, аки нази: воистинну знамение суда прежде суда на них изъявленно, да протчие накажутся и убоятся не хулити святыни. Сице первое место Немецкое вкупе взято со градом. О образе же оном того же дня исповедано стратилатом нашим. Егда же до конца погашен огнь в той нощи, обретен образ Пречистые в пепеле, идеже был ввержен, наутрии цел ничем же не рушен, Божия ради благодати; потом в новосозданной великой церкви поставлен, и поднесь всеми зрим.

Потом, аки неделя едина, взят град другий Немецкий, оттуду шесть миль, Сыренеск глаголемый, яже стоит на реке Нарве, идеже она исходит из великого езера Чюцкого, — та есть река не мала, еюже от места Пскова порт, аж до мест оных предреченных, — и били з дел по нем только три дни и подали его Немцы нашим. Мы же от Пскова поидоша под Немецкий град, нарицаемый Новый, яже дежит от границы Псковские аки полторы мили; стояхом же под ним вящей, нежели месяц, заточившии дела великие: едва

---

[a] Pog. кономахом: Ar.

---

[1] Narva fell on 11 May 1558. For a detailed description of the Russo-Livonian negotiations and the fighting in Narva preceding the fall of the town, see *PSRL* xiii, pp. 291–5.

[2] The meaningless поднесь is perhaps a scribe's error for подпись. For this meaning of подпись, see Sreznevsky, *Materialy*, vol. 2, col. 1066.

[3] For this meaning of the word порт, see below, p. 246, n. 2.

sound. And this they agreed upon: they were let out only with the weapons which they had at their hips—that is to say, the army which had recently come into the town; and the local inhabitants were let out only with their wives and children—their wealth and possessions they left behind in the fortress; but some of them preferred to stay there in their houses: this they were allowed to do.[1]

Such is the reward of the mockers, who liken the image of Christ, painted after the flesh, and that of His Mother to the idols of the heathen Gods! Such is the recompense of the iconoclasts! After about four or five hours, deprived of all their hereditary possessions, of their lofty mansions and gilded houses, stripped of their great wealth and property they departed like naked people in great abasement and shame and in much disgrace: in truth the sign of judgement, before the day of judgement, was manifested upon them, so that others might be instructed and might learn by fear not to revile holy things. This was the first German town taken together with its citadel. On that day our generals were told about the ikon. And after the fire had been completely extinguished during the night, the ikon of the most pure Mother of God was found next morning in the ashes where it had been cast, whole and undamaged, thanks to God's grace. Then it was placed in the newly-built great church, and the painting[2] was seen by all.

Then, about a week later, another German town was taken, six miles from there; it is called Syrenesk and it stands on the river Narova where it comes out from the great lake Chudskoe —that river is large and on it goods can be conveyed[3] from the town of Pskov as far as those towns we have been talking about —and the town was bombarded by our cannons for only three days, and the Germans surrendered it to our troops.[4] Then we marched from Pskov against the German fortress called New Town[5] which lies about one and a half miles from the Pskov border; and we besieged it for more than a month, having placed the great guns in position; and we were barely able to

[4] Syrenesk (Gmn. *Neuschloss*, Est. *Vaskanarva*) was captured on 6 June 1558 by troops from Narva and Novgorod (*PSRL* XIII, pp. 297–9).

[5] Novgorodok (Gmn. *Neuhausen*, Est. *Vastseliina*), situated on the Pizhma river which flows into Lake Pskovskoe.

возмогохом взяти его, бо зело тверд был. Маистр же Лиф-лянский, со всеми бискупы и властели земли оные, пошел ко граду тому на помощь сопротив нас, имеюще войска Немецкого с собою вящей, нежели осмь тысящей, и не доходя от нас стал аки за пять миль, за великими крепостьми блат и за рекою единою; к нам же дале не пошел, подобно боялся, бо на едином месте стоял, окопався, четыре недели обозом. Егда же послышал, иже стены града розбиты, и град уже взят, поиде назад к месту своему Кеси, а бискупово войска ко Юрьеву граду. И не допущено их до места и поражено. За маистром же сами мы поидохом, и отоиде от нас.

Мы же возвратихомся оттуды, и поидохом до великого места Немецкаго, глаголемаго Дерпта, в немже бискуп сам затворился со бурмистры великими и со жители града, и к тому аки две тысящи заморских Немец,[a] еже к ним приидоша за пенези. И стояли есмо под тем великим местом и градом две недели, пришанцовався и заточа дела и все место тое облегши,[b] от негоже не могоша уже ни исходити, ни входити в него; и бишася с нами крепце, броняще града и места, яко огненою стрелбою, тако частые вытечки творяще на войско наше, воистинну яко достоит рыцерским мужем. Егда же уже мы стены меские из великих дел розбихом, так же из верхних дел стреляюще, ово огнистыми кулями, ово каменными, немалую тщету в людех сотворихом, — тогда они начали роковати с нами, и выезжали к нам из града о постановлению четыре крат дня единаго, о немъже бы долго писати, но вкратце рещи: здали места и град. И оставлен кождый при домех своих п при

---

[a] Patr., Pog., T. месяць: Ar.   [b] Patr., Pog., T. облебши: Ar.

---

[1] Neuhausen was captured by the Russians under command of Prince Petr Ivanovich Shuysky and Kurbsky on 30 June 1558. The Master and the bishop of Derpt were in the nearby Livonian fortress of Kirepega during the siege of Neuhausen. The Russians took Kirepega and chased the Master and the bishop. The former managed to escape, but the latter was caught 25 versts from Derpt, where he was defeated. After the battle he managed to get back into Derpt with his army. See *PSRL* xiii, pp. 303–4; *PL* ii, p. 236.

take it, for it was very strong. And the Livonian Master with all the bishops and rulers of the land came to the help of that fortress against us with more than eight thousand German troops. And he halted about five miles before us, behind great defences afforded by marshes and behind a river. And he did not come any closer to us, as though he were afraid; and he dug himself in and stopped in one place with his baggage-train for four weeks. But when he heard that the walls of the fortress had been smashed and that the fortress had been taken, he went back to his town of Kes' [Wenden], while the bishop's army went to Yur'ev [Derpt]. And they [the bishop's army] were not allowed to get as far as the town and they were beaten. And we went after the Master, but he got away from us.[1]

We returned from there and set off towards the great German town called Derpt, in which the bishop had shut himself up together with the great burgomasters and the inhabitants of the town; and furthermore there were about two thousand Germans from over the sea[2] who had joined them for money. And we besieged that great town and fortress for two weeks, having entrenched ourselves close to the walls and put our guns in position and surrounded the whole town so that it was impossible to come out of it or to go into it; and they fought fiercely with us, defending the town and the fortress, both by shooting from firearms and by making frequent sorties against our troops, as is indeed befitting for chivalrous men. And when we had broken down the town walls with the great guns and had caused considerable losses among the people, shooting also from the upper guns[3] both with incendiary[4] and with stone cannon-balls, then they began to parley with us; and they came out to us from the fortress to discuss terms four times in one day. One might write for a long time about this, but to put it briefly —they surrendered the town and fortress. And all the people

[2] I.e. Swedes. The presence of mercenaries "from across the seas" is also mentioned in the chronicle account. See *PSRL* XIII, p. 304.

[3] Perhaps guns mounted on turrets or on earth ramparts. The same expression is used by Kurbsky in his description of the capture of Narva. See above, pp. 108–9.

[4] Lit. "fiery", "of fire". Probably hollow cannon-balls containing incendiary material.

всех стяжаниях; токмо бискуп выехал из места до кляштора своего, аки бы миля велика от места Дерпта; и пребыл тамо до повеления царя нашего, и потом поехал к Москве, и тамо был дан ему удел до живота его, сиречь град един со великою властию.[1]

И того лета взяхом градов Немецких с месты близу двадесяти числом;[2] и пребыхом в той земле аж до самого первозимия, и возвратихомся ко царю нашему со великою и светлою победою, бо и по взятью града, где и сопротивляшеся Немецкое войско к нам, везде поражаху их от нас посланными на то ротмистры. И скоро по отшествию нашем, аки во две неделях, собравшися маистр[a] сотворил немалую шкоду во Псковских властех, и оттуды пошел к Дерпту и, не доходя места великого, облек един градок, по иговскому языку зовут его Рындех, аки за четыре мили от места Дерпта; и стоял, его облегши, аки три дни и, выбив стену, припустил штурм, и за третьим приступом взял: и которого ротмистра на нем взял, с тремасты воины,[3] тех мало не всех во презлых темницах гладом и зимою поморил. А помощи дати тому граду не возмогохом, для далечайшаго пути, презлые[b] ради первозимные дороги, бо от Москвы место до Дерпта миль сто и осмьдесят есть, и войско было уже зело утружденно. И к тому тое зимы пошел был царь Перекопский со всею ордою на князя великого; бо дана была с Москвы от Татар весть, аки бы князь великий[c] со всеми силами своими на Лифлянты к месту Ризе пошел. Егда жь пришел до Украины, аки за полтора днища, тогда взял на поле, на ловех рыбных и бобровых, козаков наших и доведался, иже князь великий на Москве есть, и войско от Лифлянские земли возвратилось здраво, взявше Немецкое[4]

---

[a] Pog. наистр: Ar. [b] Patr., Pog., T. первые: Ar. [c] T. великими: Ar.

---

[1] Lit. "appanage (or share) for life".
[2] Derpt fell on 18 July 1558 (*PSRL* xiii, pp. 304–5).
[3] The same number is given by the chronicler (*ibid.* p. 306).
[4] See *PSRL* xiii, pp. 312–13; *PL* ii, p. 237. Kettler, the new Master of

were left in their houses with all their possessions; only the bishop quit the town for his monastery about one great mile from Derpt. And he stayed there until he received the command of our tsar, and then he went to Moscow where he was given a life estate,[1] that is to say a town and a large domain.[2]

And that year we took close on twenty German fortresses and towns;[3] and we stayed in that land up to the beginning of winter and returned to our tsar, having won a great and brilliant victory, for even after the capture of a town the German troops, if they resisted us, were always beaten by the cavalry commanders, who were sent by us for this purpose. And soon after our departure, about two weeks later, the Master collected his forces and caused considerable damage in the Pskov districts; and from there he marched towards Derpt; and before he got to the great city, he surrounded a small fortress which is called in their language Ryndekh [Gmn. *Ringen*, Est. *Rõngu*], about four miles from the town of Derpt. And having surrounded it, he stood there for about three days, and having breached the wall he launched an assault; and after the third attack he took it. And he captured a certain cavalry commander there and three hundred soldiers, and he killed nearly all of them by starvation and cold in the direst dungeons.[4] And we were unable to help that fortress because of the great distance and because of the very bad state of the roads in early winter; for from the town of Moscow to Derpt it is a hundred and eighty miles, and the army was already extremely tired. Furthermore that winter the khan of Perekop had set off with all his horde against the grand prince, for news had been sent from Tatars in Moscow to the effect that the grand prince had marched with all his forces against the Livonians in the direction of the town of Riga. But when the khan came to about one and a half days' march from the frontier district, he captured some of our cossacks in the steppes while they were fishing and hunting beavers, and he found out that the grand prince was in Moscow and that the army had returned safe from the Livonian land, having captured the great German town of

the Livonian Order, held Ringen for only six weeks (October–November 1558).

место великое Дерпт и других о двадесят градов. Он же не повоевал, оттуды возвратился к орде со всеми силами своими, со великиою тщетою и срамом; бо та зима зело была студена и снеги великие, и того ради кони собе все погубили, и множество их от зимы и самых померло; к тому и наши за ними гоняли, аж до реки до Донца, глаголемаго Северского, и тамо, по зимовищам их обретая, губили. Паки на тую же зиму царь наш послал с войском своим не малых гетманов своих, Ивана княжа Мстиславское и Петра Шуйского, с роду княжат Суздальских: и взяли вшедше един град зело прекрасен, стоит среди немалого озера, на такой выспе,[a] яко велико местечко и град; а зовут его, иговским языком, Алвист, а по Немецкии Наримборх.

В те же то лета, яко прежде воспомянухом, иже был царь наш смирился и добре царствовал и по пути Господня законна шествовал, тогда ни о чесом же, яко рече пророк, враги его смирил и на наступающих языков народу християнскому возлогал руку свою. И произволение человеческое Господь прещедрый паче добротою наводит и утвержает, нежели казнею; аще ли же уже зело жестоко и непокориво[b] обращутся, тогда прещением, с милосердием смешенным, наказует; егда ж уже неисцелено будет, тогда казни, на образ хотящим беззаконновати. Приложил же еще и другое милосердие, яко рехом, дарующе и утешающе в покояния суща царя християнского.

В тех же летех, аки мало пред тем, даровал ему х Казанскому другое царство Астроханское; а се[c] вкратце извещу о сем. Послал тридесять тысящей войска в кгалиях рекою Волгою на царя Астараханского; а над ними поставил стратига, Юрья именем, с роду княжат Пронских, яко

<hr />

[a] Patr. выcте: Ar.   [b] Т. непориво: Ar.   [c] Patr., Pog. a сем: Ar.

<hr />

[1] See *PSRL* xiii, pp. 314–15. According to this source Khan Devlet Girey sent his son with 100,000 men to attack Ryazan', Tula and Kashira in December 1558.

[2] Marienburg (Latv. *Aluksne*) was captured by a large Russian army in February 1560 (*PSRL* xiii, p. 325; *DRK*, pp. 215–17). Kurbsky makes

Derpt and some twenty other towns. And the khan did not wage war, but returned from there to his horde with all his forces, having suffered great loss and shame; for that winter was very cold and there was much snow, and therefore they lost all their horses, and a great number of the Tatars themselves perished from the cold. What is more, our men chased after them as far as the river Donets, which is called the Seversky Donets, and they found them there in their winter quarters and destroyed them.[1] And again during that winter our tsar sent several of his generals with their troops—Princes Ivan Mstislavsky and Petr Shuysky from the kin of the princes of Suzdal'; and they entered and took an exceedingly fine fortress which stands in the middle of a large lake on an island like a great town and citadel. And it is called in their language Alvist, and in German Marienburg.[2]

In those years, as I have previously mentioned, when our tsar humbled himself and ruled well and walked in the way of the Lord's law, he subdued his enemies with no difficulty, as the prophet said, and raised his hand against the nations afflicting the Christian people.[3] The most bounteous Lord directs and strengthens human will with goodness rather than with punishment; and should anyone be found behaving cruelly and unsubmissively, He instructs with rebuke mixed with mercy. And should anyone be incurable, He punishes as an example to those who would transgress. And he added yet a further mercy, as I have said, by favouring and comforting our Christian tsar while he was in a state of penitence.

And in those years, or a little before that time, God granted him another khanate, that of Astrakhan', in addition to the khanate of Kazan'; and now I shall tell about it in brief. He sent thirty thousand troops in galleys along the river Volga against the khan of Astrakhan'; over them he placed a general, Yury by name, from the kin of the princes of Pronsk—I men-

no mention either of the unsuccessful Russian attack on Revel' in August 1558, or of the attempt to take Riga in January 1559, or of the Russo-Livonian truce (March–November 1559).

[3] Ps. lxxxi. 13–14. The unintelligible ни о чесом же is a calque from the Greek ἐν τῷ μηδενί, which translates the Hebrew "easily", "quickly".

рехом прежде о нем (о Казанском взятью пишучи), и к нему прилучил другаго мужа Игнатья, реченнаго Вешнякова, ложничего своего, мужа воистинну храброго и нарочитого. Они же шедши взяша оное царство, лежащие близу Каспийскаго моря; царь же утече пред ними; а цариц его и детей побрали и со скарбы царскими; и все людие, яже во царстве оном, ему покорили, и возвратишася со светлою победою, здравы со всем воинством.

Потом в тех же летех мор пущен был от Бога Нагайскую орду, сиречь на Заволских Татар, и сице наведе его: пустил на них так зиму зело люте студеную, еже[a] и весь скот их помер, яко стада конские, так и других скотов, а на лето и сами изчезоша, так бо они живятся млеком точию от стад различных скотов своих, а хлеб тамо а ни именуется. Видевше же остатные, иже явственне на них гнев Божий пущен, поидоша, препитания ради, до Перекопские орды. Господь же и тамо поражаше их так: от горения солнечнаго наведе сухоту и безводие; идеже реки текли, там не токмо вода обретесь, но, и копавши три сажени в землю, едва негде мало что обреташеся. И так того народу Измаильтескаго мало за Волгою осталося, едва пять тысячей военных людей, егож было число подобно песку морскому. Но и с Перекопи тех Нагайских Татар выгнано, тако же мало что их осташася, понеже и тамо глад был и мор великий. Некоторые самовидцы наши, тамо мужие бывше, свидетельствовали, иже и в той орде Перекопской[b] десяти тысящей коней от тое язвы не осталось. Тогда время было пад бусурманы християнским царем мститися за многолетную кровь християнскую, беспрестанне проливаему от них, и успокоити собя и отечества свои[c] вечне, ибо ничего ради[d]

[a] Pog.   же: Ar.   [b] Patr., Pog.   перекопский: Ar.   [c] T. свое: Ar.   [d] Patr., T.   роди: Ar.

[1] See above, pp. 36–7.
[2] I.e. *postel'nichy.* For the term ложничий, see above, p. 80, n. 1.
[3] For the expedition of Prince Yury Shemyakin-Pronsky to Astrakhan'

tioned him previously when writing about the capture of Kazan'[1]—and to him he attached another man, Ignaty Veshnyakov, his gentleman of the bed-chamber,[2] a man who was indeed brave and distinguished. And they went and took that khanate, which lies hard by the Caspian Sea; and the khan ran away from them; and they seized his wives and children together with his royal treasures. And they subjugated to him [Ivan IV] all the people who were in that kingdom, and they returned, having won a brilliant victory, safe and sound, with all the army.[3]

Then in those years a pestilence was sent by God against the Nogay horde, that is to say against the trans-Volga Tatars. And this is how God brought it about: He sent them such a fiercely cold winter that all their cattle died, both their herds of horses and other cattle too; and they themselves disappeared for the summer, for they live only by the milk from their various herds of cattle, and as for corn, there is none of it there.[4] Now when the survivors saw that God's wrath had been manifestly sent against them, they went to the horde of Perekop [i.e. the Crimean horde] in search of food. But there too the Lord struck them in the following manner: by means of the heat of the sun He brought about a drought and an absence of water; where rivers had flowed, there was not only no water, but even if you dug three *sazhen'* into the earth there was barely anything to be found anywhere. And so there remained few of that Ishmaelite people beyond the Volga, barely five thousand soldiers—and their number had been as the sand of the sea.[5] But even from Perekop were those Nogay Tatars driven, so that few of them survived; for there too there was famine and great pestilence. Certain eye-witnesses of ours, men who were there at the time, testified that in the horde of Perekop ten thousand horses perished from the pestilence. Then was the time for the Christian tsars to take their revenge on the Mussulmans for the Christian blood which had been shed by them continuously for many years, and to achieve everlasting peace for themselves and

(1554) and the subsequent annexation of Astrakhan' (1556), see *PSRL* XIII, pp. 236, 274.
[4] Lit. "it is not even named there".   [5] Hos. i. 10.

другаго, но точию того ради и помазаны бывают, еже прямо судити и царства, врученные им от Бога, оброняти от нахождения варваров. Понеже и нашему тогда цареви советницы некоторые, мужие храбрые и мужественные, советовали и стужали, да подвигнется сам, с своею главою, со великими войски на Перекопского, времени на то зовущу и Богу на се подвижущу и помощь на сие истое хотящу подати, аки самым перстом показующу[a] погубити врагов своих старовечных, християнских кровопивцов, и избавити пленных множайши[b] от древле заведенныя работы, яко от самых адских пропастей. Яще бы на свой сан помазания царскаго памятал, и послушал добрых и мужественных стратигов совету, яко премногая бы похвала и на сем свете была, но паче тмами крат премножайше во оном веце, у самого создателя, Христа Бога, иже надрожайшее крови своея не пощадил за человеческий погибающий род излияти! Аще бы и души наши случилось положити за плененных многими леты бедных християн, воистинну всех добродетелей сия добродетель любви вышшей[c] пред ним обрелабыся, яко сам рече: больши сея добродетели ничто ж есть, аще кто душу свою положит за други своя.

Добро бы, и паки реку, зело добро избавити в орде плененных от многолетныя работы, и разрешити окованных от претехчайшие неволи; но наш царь о сем тогда мало радяше, аще и едва послал с пять тысящей всего воинства с Вишнивецким Дмитром, Днепром рекою, на Перекопскую орду, а на другое лето с Данилом Адашевым и з другими стратилаты со осмь тысящей, тако же водою, посла. Они же выплыша Днепром на море и, над надежду Татарскую, немало тщету учиниша в орде: яко самых побиша, тако же жен и детей их немало плениша, и християнских людей от работы свободили немало, и возвратишася восвояси здравы.

[a] Patr. показующе: Ar.   [b] Pog. множайшах: Ar.   [c] T. любвии вышший: Ar.

---

[1] Or perhaps "himself at the head of the army".
[2] Lit. "the time calling [him] to this".   [3] John xv. 13.

for their fatherlands: for tsars are not anointed for anything else but this—to judge justly and to defend the tsardoms entrusted to them by God from the incursion of barbarians. At that time certain counsellors, heroic and courageous men, advised and importuned our tsar to march himself, in person,[1] with great forces against the khan of Perekop, for the time was ripe[2] and God urged him on and was willing to give him help for this just venture, showing him, as it were, with His very finger how to destroy his ancient enemies, the drinkers of Christian blood, and how to free the great multitude of prisoners from their long-established slavery, as from the very pit of hell. And had he remembered the ceremony of his own anointment and had he listened to the advice of his good and brave generals, how exceedingly great would have been his glory in this world, and how many thousand times greater would it have been in the life to come, before the Creator Himself, Christ our God, who did not shrink from shedding His dearest blood for the perishing human race! For had we had to lay down our lives for those poor Christians who had been prisoners for many years, then indeed the virtue of love would have been higher in His eyes than all virtues, for He Himself said: there is nothing greater than this virtue, that a man lay down his life for his friends.[3]

It would have been a good thing—and I say it again, it would have been an exceedingly good thing—to have freed the prisoners in the horde from their many years of slavery and to have delivered those who were fettered from their most grievous bondage; but our tsar took little notice of this at that time, although he did send some five thousand troops in all with Dmitry Vishnevetsky down the Dnepr river against the horde of Perekop, and in the next year he sent about eight thousand with Danilo Adashev and other generals, also by water. And they sailed by the Dnepr to the sea, and, to the surprise of the Tatars, caused considerable damage in the horde: they killed the Tatars themselves, took many of their wives and children prisoner, freed many Christians from slavery and returned home safe and sound.[4] And again and again we importuned

[4] In early 1558 Prince Dmitry Ivanovich Vishnevetsky, who in the previous year had transferred his allegiance from the Polish king to the tsar, was

Мы же паки о сем, и паки ко царю стужали и советовали: или бы сам потщился итти, или бы войско великое послал в то время на орду; он же не послушал, прещкаждающе нам сие и помогающе ему ласкателие, добрые и верные товарыщи трапез и купков и различных наслажаней друзии; и подобно уже на своих сродных и единоколенных остроту оружия паче, нежели поганом, готовал, крыюще в себе оное семя, всеянное от пререче則наго епископа, глаголемаго Топорка.

А здешнему было королеви и зело ближайши; да подобна его кролевская высота и величество не к тому обращалося умом, но паче в различныя плясания много и в преиспещренныя машкары. Тако же и властели земли тоя драгоценныя колачи со безчисленными проторы гортань и чрево с марцыпаны натыкающе, и якобы в утлые делвы дражайшие различные вина безмерне льюще, и с печенеги вкупе высоко скачяще и воздух биюще, и так прехвалне и прегорде друг друга пьяни возхвалящи, иже не токмо Москву, або Костянтинополь, но аще бы на небе[a] был Турок, совлещи его со другими неприятельми своими обещевающе. Егда же возлягут на одрех своих между толстыми перинами, тогда, едва по полудню проспавшись, со связанными головами с похмелья, едва живы, и выочутясь востанут; на протчие дни паки гнусны и ленивы, многолетнаго ради обыкновения. И сего ради забыли таковаго благополучнаго времени на бусурманы, и не радящи, горши предреченных тех, о своем отечестве, не токмо о оных заведеных, о нихже выше мало прежде рекох, во многолетней работе сущих, но на каждое лето пред очима их жен и деток, тако же и подручных во плен множество

[a] Т. себе: Ar.

---

sent by Ivan with a small expeditionary force along the Dnepr. The khan, warned by King Sigismund of Poland of the Russians' advance, withdrew into the Crimean peninsula, and Vishnevetsky was recalled to Moscow, having had no contact with the Tatars. In February 1559 a double expedition was sent by Ivan against the Crimea: Vishnevetsky was sent by the Don, Daniil Adashev by the Dnepr. Vishnevetsky won a small victory in

the tsar and counselled him either to endeavour to march himself or to send a great army at that time against the horde. But he did not listen to us, for his flatterers, those good and trusty comrades of the table and the cups, his friends in various amusements, hampered us while helping him. It was as though he were already testing the sharpness of his weapons against his relatives and kinsmen rather than against the pagans, hiding within himself the seed which had been sowed by that bishop named Toporok, about whom we have talked before.

It was just like the behaviour of the king of this country [Sigismund II]; in the same way the mind of his royal highness and majesty was turned not towards that [i.e. fighting the Tatars], but towards many different kinds of dancing and to gaudy masquerades.[1] And likewise the rulers of this land stuff their gullets and bellies with costly buns and almond cakes[2] at incalculable expense and immoderately pour down various kinds of dearest wines, as it were into leaky casks, leaping high and striking the air together with their hangers-on, and in their drunkenness praising one another so exceedingly boastfully and proudly that they promise not only [to capture] Moscow or Constantinople, but, even if the Turk were in the sky, to drag him down with their other enemies. And when they lie down on their beds between thick down quilts, they sleep off their drunkenness almost till mid-day and, coming to, they get up, barely alive and racked with drunken headaches. And on other days they are slothful and idle because of this long-standing habit of theirs. And therefore they have forgotten that the opportunity is so favourable for fighting the Mussulmans, and, worse than those people I mentioned above, they have no care for their fatherland; and not only do they have no care for those who were long ago taken prisoner and have been many years in captivity (about these I spoke a little before this), but also they care not for their own subjects, who every year are led off

the neighbourhood of Azov, but Adashev managed to sail from the mouth of the Dnepr, land in the Crimea and cause considerable damage there. He was pursued back up the Dnepr by Khan Devlet Girey, who failed to catch him. (*PSRL* xiii, pp. 288, 315–16, 318–20.)

[1] Lit. "to many-coloured masks".
[2] Cf. above, p. 32, n. 1.

веденных, не пекущеся о них, но паче же те то[a] предреченные печенеги они оброняюще их. Но, аще и срама ради великого и нарекания многаслезнаго от народу, аки бы выедут, ополчатся, грядуще издалека во след полков бусурманских, боящеся наступити и ударити на враги креста Христова, и попошедчи за ними два дни або три, паки возвратятся восвояси; а что было остало от Татар, або сохраненно убогих християн на лесех нечто со стяжанием яковым, або скотов, все поядят, и последное розграбят, и ничто же бедным и окоянным оставляюще оных слезных остатков.

А издавна ли тые народы и тые люди нерадивии и немилосерди так зело о их языце[b] и о своих сродных? Но воистинну не издавна, но ново: первие в них обретахуся мужие храбры чюйны о своем отечестве. Но что ныне таково есть и чего ради им таковая приключишася? Заисте того ради: егда беша о вере християнской и в церковных дохметех утверженны и в делех житейских мерне и воздержне хранящеся, тогда яко едины человецы наилепшие во всех пребывающе,[1] себя и отечество броняще. Внегда же путь Господень оставили и веру церковную отринули, многаго ради преизлишняго покоя и возлюбивша же ринушася во спространный и широкий путь,[2] сиречь в пропасть ереси Люторские и других различных сект, паче же пребогатейшие их властели на сие непреподобие дерзнуша, — тогда от того им приключишася. Паче же нецыи и велможи их богатые, в великих властех постановленные у них, на сие самовластие ум свой[c] обратишася; на них же зряще не токмо подрученныя их, но братия их мнейшая произволение естественное самоизвольне на таковыя слабости, непреподобне и неразсудне, устремишась, яко глаголют мудрыя пословицу: идеже начальницы произволяют, тамо и всенародства воля

___

[a] Т. лето: Ar.   [b] Pog. языцеи: Ar.   [c] Patr., Pog. своей: Ar.

___

[1] Or "the best men in all things".

[2] A possible rendering of the obscure многаго ради…покоя и возлюбивша.

into captivity before the very eyes of their wives and children. And as for those hangers-on I mentioned before—it is they whom they defend. But if, as a result of great reproach and tearful imploration by the people, they take up arms and set out, then they follow the Mussulman forces from afar, fearing to attack and to strike at the foe of the Cross of Christ; and having followed them for two or three days they return home again. And should anything survive the depredations of the Tatars—either poor Christians remaining alive in the forests with some possessions or other, or cattle—all this they consume, and they plunder everything that remains, leaving not one of those miserable relics to the poor and the wretched.

But has this nation, have these people, long been so exceedingly heedless and merciless about their own folk and about their relatives? No, indeed, it has not been like this long; this is something recent. At first there were amongst them men who were brave and who watched over their fatherland. But why is there such a state of affairs now and for what reason have such things happened to them? This, in truth, is the reason: when they were firm in the Christian faith and in the dogmas of the Church, and when in things that pertain to this life they behaved with moderation and restraint, then being the best amongst all men,[1] they defended themselves and their fatherland. But when they left the way of the Lord and cast aside the faith of the Church, then, because they loved excessive tranquillity,[2] they rushed on to the broad wide way,[3] in other words into the pit of the Lutheran heresy and of various other sects; and, what is more, it was the richest of their rulers who dared to commit this impiety. That was the beginning of it for them at that time. And again, certain of their rich grandees, who were appointed to positions of great power, turned their minds to this act of free will;[4] not only were they watched by their subjects, but also their lesser brethren of their own accord impiously and unreasoningly directed their natural will towards such weaknesses; as the saying of the wise men goes: "where those in power act arbitrarily, thither is borne or

[3] Matt. vii. 13–14.
[4] Or, perhaps, "self-will".

несется, або устремляется. А что еще и горшаго видех от сих сладострастей приключившихся им, — ибо много от них, не токмо зацные их некоторые, и княжата так боязливы и раздроченныи от жен своих, яко послышат варварское нахождение, так забьются в претвердые грады; и воистинну смеху достойно: вооружившися в зброи, сядут за столом за кубками, да бают фабулы с пьяными бабами своими, а ни из врат градских изыти хотяще, аще и пред самым местом, або под градом, сеча от бусурман на християны была. Сие воистинну дивное сам очима своима видех, не во едином от градов, но и в других некоторых.

Во едином же граде случилось нам таково видети: идеже была пятерица великородных з дворы их, к тому два ротмистра с полки своими, и ту же под самым местом, яко некоторых воинов, так человеков всенародных биющеся немало с мимошедшим полком Татарским, яже уже со пленом из земли шол и поражаеми суть и гоними неединократ[a] от бусурман християне; а оные предреченныя властели ни един от града изыде на помощь им: седящих их в то время глаголют и пиющих великими полными алавастры. О пирование зело непохвальное! О алавастр, ни вина, ни меду сладкого, но самые крови християнские налиянны! И при конце битва тое, аще бы не Волынский полк, прутко гонящий за оными поганы, приспел, и всех бы до конца избили. Но егда видевше бусурманы за ними скоро грядущ полк християнский, посекши часть большую плену, а других живых пометали и, все оставя, в бегство обратишася. Тако же и во других градех, яко мало вышши рехом, очима своима богатых и благородных, вооруженных в зброях, видех, а не токмо сопротив врагов хотящих исходити, ани[b] во след их гонити хотяще, или подобно и следу их боящеся, понеже а ни[c] лакоть един которые вельможи вооруженные дерзнули изыти из градов.

Се таковые ужасно слышательные, паче же смеху достой-

---

a T. но поединократ: Ar.   b Pog. аки: Ar.   c Pog. о ни: Ar.

---

1 I.e. civilians.

directed the will of the common people". And I have seen yet worse things befall them as a result of these voluptuous pleasures: many of them, not only certain of their noblemen but also their princes, are so timorous and so exhausted by their wives that when they hear of an invasion by the barbarians they shut themselves up in strong fortresses, and—this is indeed ridiculous —having put on their armour, they sit down at table before their cups and tell tales to their drunken women, and they show no desire to go out of the gates of the fortress, even though in front of the town itself or at the walls of the citadel a battle were raging between Mussulmans and Christians. This truly wondrous thing I have seen with my own eyes, not just in one particular fortress, but in several others as well.

Now in one fortress we happened to see the following: there were five noblemen there with their retinues, as well as two cavalry commanders with their regiments; and there, at the very walls of the town, there were several soldiers as well as common men[1] fighting with a Tatar regiment which was passing by on its way out of the country with prisoners; and the Christians were beaten and driven back several times by the Mussulmans. Yet not one of those above-mentioned lords came out of the fortress to help them—they were said to be sitting there at that time and drinking from great full alabaster jugs. O most unpraiseworthy feasting! O alabaster jugs, filled not with wine, not with sweet mead, but with the very blood of Christians! And at the end of that battle, had not the Volynian regiment, which swiftly pursued those pagans, arrived in time, they would have massacred everyone. But when the Mussulmans saw the Christian regiment coming quickly after them, they slew a large part of the prisoners and others they left alive, and, abandoning everything, they turned to flight. And also in other fortresses, as I have said a little before, I saw with my own eyes rich and noble men clad in their armour, who not only had no wish to come out against the enemy, but had no desire even to chase after them—it was as though they were afraid to pursue them: for some grandees, when armed, did not care to go as much as a cubit from their fortress.

Such things which are dreadful to hear and, what is more,

ные, от роскошей и от презлых различных вер приключаются християнским предстателем, прежде бывшим храбрым и мужественным славным воином женовидные и боязни исполненные случаются! А о тех Волынцах не токмо в кронниках мужество их описуется, но и новыми повестьми храбрость их свидетельствуется, яко мало прежде и о других рехом: егда быша в вере православной, пребывающе во обычаех мерных, и к тому имеюще над собою гетмана храбраго и славнаго Констянтина, в правоверных дохматах светлаго и во всяком благочестии сияющаго, яко славнии и похвалнии в делех ратных явишася, отечество свое оброняюще, ни единова, ни дважды, но многожды показашася нарочиты. Но впала сия повесть, мнитмися, преизлишие;[a] а сего ради оставя сию, ко предреченным возвратимся.

Преминувшу ми много о Лифлянской войне, мало нечто вкратце о битвах некоторых и взятью градов оных воспомянем, к сокращению истории и к концу зряще. И яко напреди воспомянухом оных дву добрых мужей,[b] исповедника царскаго, другаго ложжничего, которые достойны нарещися друзи его и советницы духовные, яко сам Господь рече: идеже два или три собрани о имени моем, ту есмь аз посреди их; и воистинну был Господь посреди, сиречь многая помощь Божия, когда было сердца их и душа тех едина, и к тому советницы оные мудрые и мужественные близ царя со искусными и мужественными стратилаты, и храброе воинство цело и весело было. Тогда, глаголю, царь всюду прославляем был, и земля Руская доброю славою цвела, и грады предтвертыя Аламанския разбивахуся, и пределы християнския разширяхуся, и на диких полях

 ᵃ Pog. произлишие: Ar.   ᵇ T. мужех: Ar.

---

¹ For the expression "champions of Christianity", here used sarcastically, see *Correspondence*, pp. 2–3, 106–7.
² A reference to either Prince Konstantin Ivanovich Ostrozhsky (*c.* 1460–1530), one of the greatest West Russian generals of the fifteenth and sixteenth centuries, distinguished for his campaigns against the Tatars and the Muscovites, or his equally distinguished son Konstantin Konstantinovich.

worthy of ridicule, happen to the champions of Christianity[1] because of luxuries and various wicked beliefs, and those who were formerly bold and brave glorious warriors become effeminate and filled with fear. But as for those Volynians, not only is their courage described in the chronicles, but also their bravery is attested in new stories, as I said shortly before about others. For when they were of the Orthodox faith, keeping to moderate habits and furthermore having over them a brave and glorious *hetman*, Konstantin, who was a brilliant exponent of the Orthodox beliefs and resplendent in every kind of piety, then they were glorious and praiseworthy in deeds of war, and, while defending their fatherland, they proved themselves distinguished, not once, not twice, but many times.[2] But this story has, I think, turned out to be too long. Therefore let us leave it and return to what we were talking about before.

Having omitted a great deal about the Livonian war, I must now briefly recall some of the battles and the capture of some of the towns, with a view to curtailing and finishing my history. Now as I have mentioned before, those two good men, the tsar's confessor and the other one, his gentleman of the bed-chamber,[3] were worthy[4] to be called his friends and spiritual advisers, as the Lord Himself said: "where two or three are gathered together in my name, there am I in the midst of them".[5] And in truth the Lord was in their midst, that is to say there was much help from God, when their hearts and souls were one; and furthermore when those wise courageous advisers were near the tsar with skilled courageous generals, then the brave army too was safe and happy. Then, I say, the tsar was glorified everywhere, and the land of Russia flourished in good renown, and the strong German towns were shattered, and the Christian boundaries were enlarged, and the towns in the steppes which

The large estates of the Ostrozhsky family (including the town of Ostrog) were in Volynia.

[3] I.e. Sil'vestr and Adashev. Sil'vestr was not, in fact, Ivan's confessor, nor was Adashev his gentleman of the bed-chamber. See above, p. 80, n. 1.

[4] Lit. "who were worthy". I have made the relative clause the main sentence, as there is no main verb.

[5] Matt. xviii. 20.

133

древле плененыя грады от Батыя безбожнаго и паки воздвизахуся, и сопротивники царевы и врази креста Христова падаху, а другии покаряхуся, нецыи же от них и ко благочестию обращахуся, огласився и научився от клириков верою, Христу присвояхуся, от лютых варваров, аки от кровеядных зверей, в крототсь овчю прелагахуся и ко Христове чреде присовокупляхуся.

Потом же, аки на четвертое лето по Дерпском взятью, последняя власть Лифлянская разрушилася, понеже оставшая часть их кралеви Польскому, ко великому княжеству Литовскому поддашеся; зане Кесь, столечный свой град, новоизбранный маист отдал и забежал, подобно от страха, за Двину реку, упрося себе у краля Курлянскую землю, и протчие грады, яко рекох, сие с Кесью все оставил, яже обою страну отсюду Двины[a] реки великие; а другие Швецкому кролю поддашася, яко место великое Ревль; а другие Дунскому. А в месте, реченном Вильяне, а по-Немецкому Филине, маистр старый Фиштемъберкл остал, и при нем кортуны великие, ижзе многою ценою из-за моря з Любка, места великого, от Германов своих достали было, и вся стрельба огненая многая.

На тот же Филин князь великий войско свое с нами великое послал; а первие, до того аки за два месяца еще, в самую весну, пришел аз в Дерпт, послан от царя, того ради, понеже было у воинства его зело сердце сокрушенно от Немец, зане егда обращали искусных воевод и стратилатов своих сопротив царя Перекопскаго, храняще пределов своих, а вместо тех случилось посылати в Вифлянские городы неискусных и необыкновенных в полкуустроениях,

[a] Т. дивны: Ar.

---

[1] Probably a scribe's error for об ту страну. The Duchy of Courland and Semigallia, which Kettler received from the king, lay south-west (i.e. *this* side, from Kurbsky's point of view) of the Dvina river.

[2] On 28 November 1561 (just over *three* years after the capture of Derpt) Kettler, who had succeeded Fürstenberg as Master of the Livonian Order, and the Archbishop of Riga concluded a treaty with King Sigismund in Vilna, whereby those parts of Livonia which had not been previously

had long ago been captured by the godless Baty rose up again, and the enemies of the tsar and the foes of the Cross of Christ fell, and others were subjected: some of them were converted to piety, instructed and taught in the faith by clerics, and they joined Christ and they were converted from fierce barbarians or bloodthirsty beasts into gentle lambs, and they joined the flock of Christ.

Then, about the fourth year after the capture of Derpt the last remnants of Livonian power were destroyed, for what remained unconquered submitted to the king of Poland and to the grand principality of Lithuania: the newly-elected Master surrendered his capital town Kes' [Wenden] and ran, as if in fear, across the Dvina and asked the king for the land of Courland. And as for the other towns which are on the other side[1] of the great river Dvina from here, he left them all [to Poland], as I have said, together with Kes'; other towns, such as the great city of Revel', surrendered to the Swedish king, and others to the Danish king. But in the town called Viljandi—Fellin in German—the old Master Fürstenberg remained, and with him were the great siege-guns, which had been brought from the Germans at great cost from over the sea from the great city of Lübeck, and all the many firearms.[2]

Now against this same Fellin the grand prince sent his great army with us in it. Before this, about two months earlier, in the spring, I had come to Derpt, having been sent by the tsar, for the following reason: the heart of the soldiery had been broken by the Germans, for when the tsar turned his skilled *voevody* and generals against the khan of Perekop to protect his frontiers, in their place he had to send to the Livonian towns men who were unskilled and inexperienced in military affairs;[3]

occupied by Sweden (Northern Estonia, including Revel') or Denmark (Oesel) were handed over to Poland–Lithuania, Kettler becoming a vassal of the king with the newly-created duchy of Courland and Semigallia as his fief.

Kurbsky's chronology is somewhat awry here. Fürstenberg was in Fellin in 1560, some eighteen months before the treaty of Vilna. Indeed, in the following paragraph Kurbsky's narrative deals with events which took place in 1560.

[3] Lit. "army organization".

и того ради многажды были поражени от Немец, не токмо от равных полков, но уже и от малых людей великие бегали. Но, сего ради, введе мя царь в ложницу свою и глагола ми словесами, милосердием разстворенными и зело любовными, и к тому[a] со обещаньми многими: "Принужден бых, рече, ото оных пробегших[b] воевод моих, або сам итти сопротив Лафлянтов, або тебя, любимаго моего, послати, да охрабрится паки воинство мое, Богу помогающу ти; сего ради иди и послужи ми верне." Аз же с подщанием поидох: послушлив был, яко верный слуга, повелению царя моего.

И тогда в те два месяца, нежели пришли другие стратихи, аз ходил два крат: первие[c] под Белый камень, от Дерпта осмьнадесять миль, на зело богатые волости, и тамо поразих гуфец Немецкий, под самым градом, яже был на стражи; и доведахся от тех вязней о маистре и о других ротмистрех Немецких, еже стояли во ополчению немалом, оттуду аки в осми милях, за великими блаты. Аз же, со пленом отпустя к Дерпту и избрав войско, поидохом к ним в нощи и приидохом во утрии ко оным великим блатам, и препровожахомся лехким войском день целый чрез них. И аще бы ту встретились с нами, поразили бы нас, аще бы и трикратно было нашего войска, а со мною невеликое тогда было воинство, аки пять тысящ было; но они, яко гордыя, стояли на широком поле от тех блат, ждуще нас, аки две мили, ко сражению. Но мы, яко рехом, препроводясь те нужные месца, починути дали, аки годину едину, конем; пред солнечным захождением аки за годину, поидохом ко сражению, и уже приидохом к ним аки в половину нощи — нощь же бе лунна; а наипаче близу моря, тамо светлы нощи бывают, нежели где инде, — и сразихомся; с нами, на широком поле, первие предние гуфцы сражахуся. И пребыла битва аки на полторы годины, и не так в нощи воз-

[a] Patr., Pog., T. к кому: Ar.   [b] T. прибегших: Ar.   [c] T. первый: Ar.

<hr/>

[1] It is hard to see what recent military defeats in Livonia Kurbsky is referring to. In February 1560, just before Kurbsky was sent to Derpt

and therefore they were often beaten by the Germans—not only were they beaten by forces of the same size, but large numbers ran from small numbers. And so the tsar took me into his bed-chamber and said to me in words which were mixed with kindness and which were exceedingly amiable (and with many promises as well): "I have been forced by those of my *voevody* who have run away either to go myself against the Livonians or to send you, my beloved friend, so that, God aiding you, my troops may become brave again: go, therefore, and serve me truly." And I went with haste; like a true servant I obeyed the order of my tsar.[1]

And during those two months, before the other commanders arrived, I carried out two expeditions: first, against White Stone,[2] eighteen miles from Derpt, in very rich territory; and there, by the fortress itself, I beat a small German detachment which was on guard, and I learned from prisoners that the Master and other German cavalry commanders were situated in some force about eight miles away, beyond the great marshes. Now when I had sent a party with prisoners back to Derpt and when I had selected a force, we marched towards them during the night and arrived in the morning at those great marshes, and with lightly armed troops we spent a whole day crossing them. And had they met us there they would have beaten us, even if we had had three times as many troops (at that time I had a small number of men with me—about five thousand). But like proud men they stood in a broad field, some two miles from those marshes, waiting for us to join battle with them. Now when, as I have said, we had crossed those difficult places, we gave our horses about an hour to rest; then, about an hour before sunset, we set off to the battle; and we reached them at about midnight, and it was a moonlit night: the nights near the sea are brighter than anywhere else; and we joined battle. First of all their vanguard fought with us on the broad field. And the battle lasted for about an hour and a half; and their shooting from firearms by night was not so much use to them

from Moscow, the Russians had captured Marienburg (see above, p. 120).
  [2] I.e. Weissenstein (Paide).

могла им огненная стрельба, яко наши стрелы ко блистанию огней их. Егда же прииде помощь к нашим от большаго полка, тогда сразишась с ними вручь и сопроша их наши; а потом на бегство Германи устремишась, и гнаша их наши аки милю до единыя реки, на нейже бе мост; егда же прибегоша на мост, к тому несчастию их, еще под ними мост подломился, и тамо погибоша до конца. Егда же возвратихомся от сечи, и уже восиявшу солнцу, тогда на том предреченном поле, идеже битва была, обретохом пеших их кнегтов, по житом и инде расховавшихся лежащих, бо было их четыре полки конных, а пять пеших; тогда, кроме побиенных, взяхом их живых сто семдесят нарочитых воинов; а наших убиенных особ шляхты шестьнадесять, кроме служащих их.

И оттуду возвратихомся паки к Дерпту. И опочивши войско аки 10 дней к тому, своею охотою непосланных на то[a] к нам прибыло аки 2,000 войска, або и вящей, паки поидохом к Фелину, идеже бе маистр старый предреченный. И укрывши все войско, послахом един полк Татарский, аки предместия жещи; он же, мняще мал си люд, выехал сам бронити со всеми людьми, яже бе во граде, и поразихом его засадою; едва сам утече. И воевах потом тыждень целый, и возвратихомся с великими богатствы и корыстьми, и вкратце рещи: седмь, або осем крат того лета битв имехом великих и малых, и везде, за Божиею помощию, одоление получихом. А срам бы ми было самому о своих делех вся по ряду писати; а сего ради множайшие оставляю, яко о Татарских битвах, яже во младости моей бывали с Казанцы и Перекопцы, так и со другими языки; бо вем сие добре, иже подвиги християнских воинов не суть забвенни, а ни малейшии, пред Богом, не токмо подвизи, по Бозе за правоверие со доброю ревностию производимыя, или сопротив чювствен-

1 Or, perhaps, "the light of their fires".
2 A possible interpretation of the obscure своею охотою непосланных на то[м?].

as our arrows were to us, [guided] by the flash of their shots.¹ And when help came to our troops from the Great Regiment, our men fought with them hand to hand and drove them back. Then the Germans turned to flight, and our men chased them for about a mile, as far as a river, over which there was a bridge. But when they ran on to the bridge, unfortunately for them it collapsed beneath them and they all perished there. Now when we returned from that skirmish the sun had already begun to shine, and in that field which I have talked about above, where the [main] battle had been fought, we found their foot-soldiers lying hidden amongst the corn and elsewhere—they had had four cavalry regiments and five infantry regiments. And at that time, apart from those who had been killed, we took a hundred and seventy warriors of rank prisoner; and on our side there were sixteen noblemen killed, apart from those who served them.

And from there we came back again to Derpt. And after the army had rested about ten days, some two thousand troops or more, not very pleased to be sent on this mission,² joined us, and again we marched towards Fellin, where the old Master, whom I mentioned above, was. And having concealed the whole army, we sent a Tatar regiment to burn the outskirts. But the Master, thinking that there were few of us, came out himself with all his people, who were in the fortress, to defend the town, and we beat him by means of an ambush, so that he himself barely escaped. And after that I fought for a whole week, and we returned with great riches and booty—in short, seven or eight times we fought great and small battles that year and everywhere, with the help of God, we won victories. It would be shameful for me myself to narrate all these things about my own deeds. Therefore I shall omit a great many things both about Tatar battles which I fought in my youth with the Kazan' and Perekop Tatars, and about battles with other peoples. For this I know well—that the exploits of Christian warriors are not forgotten by God, not even the smallest; for not only are our exploits numbered which are carried out with good zeal in God's name for Orthodoxy or against the enemies of the senses or the mind, but "the

ных врагов или мысленных, но и власы на главах наших изочтени суть, яко сам Господь рече.[1]

Егда же приидоша гетмани со другим великим войском к нам, к Дерпту, с ними же было воинства вящей тридесять тысящ конного, и пеших 10,000 стрельцов и казаков, и дел великих четыредесять, тако же и других дел аки 50, имиже огненной бой с стен збивают, а и мнейшие по полторы сажени, — и повеление прииде от царя нам итти под Фелин. Мы же,[a] взявши ведомость, иже маистр хощет выпроводити кортуны великие предреченные и другие дела и скарбы свои во град Гупсал, иже на самом море стоит, тогда абие послахом 12,000 с стратилаты, да обгонят Фелин; а сами поидохом с другою частию войска иным путем, а дела все препровадихом Имбеком рекою вверх, и оттуды езером, аж за две мили от Фелина выкладахом их на брег з кгалей; а оные стратилаты, прежде посланные от нас к Фелину, идяху путем[b] поблизу града Немецка Армуса, аки за милю.

Филип же, ленсъмаршалок,[2] муж храбрый и в военых вещах искусный, мающе с собою аки 500 человек райторов[c] Немцов, и аки бы другую 500 або 400 пеших, не ведяше о таком великом люду, мнящи мои посылки, аж не един крат посылал воевати под той град прежде, даижь великое еще войско пришло со предреченными стратихи: и изыде на них со дерзновением скоро, — а наипаче, яко Немцы мало бывают в день трезвы, — взявши от бегающих в осаду[d] ведомость,[3] а не выведавшися совершение, яковое войско грядет. Наши же еще и ведали о нем, но не надеялись, иже так малым людом дерзнет ударити на так неравное собе войско. И пред полуднем, но[e] опочивании, ударили на едину часть смешавшися со стражею наших, потом пришли до коней наших, и битва сточися. Стратилаты же другие, ведавше

[a] Т. иже: Ar., Patr., Pog.   [b] Patr., Pog., Т. потем: Ar.
[c] Patr., Pog. ратайров: Ar.   [d] Patr., Pog. по саду: Ar.
[e] sic.

---

[1] Matt. x. 30.   [2] I.e. Marshal of the province.
[3] Lit. "running into the siege".

very hairs of our heads are numbered",[1] as the Lord Himself said.

Now when the generals arrived with the other great army in Derpt, they had with them more than thirty thousand cavalry and ten thousand foot archers and cossacks, and forty great guns and also about fifty other guns with which the enemy's fire-power is struck down from the walls, as well as smaller guns one and a half *sazhen'* long. And the order came to us from the tsar to march against Fellin. Now when we heard the news that the Master was going to take the great siege-guns which I mentioned before and other guns and all his goods and put them in the fortress of Hapsal [Est. Haapsalu], which stands by the sea, we immediately sent twelve thousand men with their commanders to cut off Fellin. And we ourselves set off with another part of the army by another route and we transported all the guns up the Embakh [Est. Emajõgi] river, and from there by lake, and we landed them from galleys on the shore just two miles from Fellin. And the commanders who had been sent by us ahead to Fellin went by a route near the German fortress of Ermes [Latv. Ergemes], about a mile away. Now Philipp [von Bell], the Landmarschall,[2] a brave man skilled in military matters, who had with him about five hundred German knights and another four or five hundred infantrymen, did not know that there were so many troops, thinking that this was one of my expeditions, which I had several times previously dispatched against that fortress, [nor did he know] that it was the great army that had arrived with the above-mentioned commanders; and he quickly marched out against them with boldness—all the more boldly, in that the Germans are rarely sober in the daytime—having heard the news from those who were hastening to shut themselves up in the fortress,[3] but without having found out exactly what sort of force was approaching. Now although our men knew about him, they did not reckon that with so few people he would dare to attack a force so unequal to his own. And just before midday, while we were resting, they attacked a unit of our men which was mixed with the advance guard, and then they reached our horses, and battle was joined. But as the other

141

со полки своими, имеюще вожей добрых, ведомых о месцах, обыдоша чрез лесы вкось, и поразиша их так, иже едва колько их убеже з битвы, и самого онаго храбраго мужа и славнаго в их языцех, иже воистинну последняго, и защитника и надежду Лифлянского народу, Алексея Адашева пахолик жива поимал, и с ним единнатцать кунтуров жиых взято и сто двадесять шляхтичей Немецких, кроме других. Мы же, о сем не ведавше, приидохом под место Фелин и тамо обретохом наших стратилатов не токмо здравых, но и пресветлою победою здравых, и славнаго начальника Лифлянского, храброго мужа Филиппа ленсъмаршалка со единатцатьма кунторы и со другими в руках имуща.

Егда же повелехом привести его и поставити пред нами, и начаша о некоторых вещах вопрошати его, яко есть обычай, тогда же он муж светлым и веселым лицем (мнился, яко пострадавшей за отечество), нимало ужаснувся,[а] начал со дерзновением отвещевати нам; бе бо муж, яко разсмотрихом его добре, не токмо мужественный и храбрый, но и словества полон, и остр разум и добру память имущы. Иные ответы к нам его, разумом роствореные, оставлю, но сие точию едино, яже в память ми приходит, оплаковательное его вещание о Лифлянской земли, воспомяну. Седящему ему у нас некогда на обеде (бо аще и вязнем случилося ему быти, но обаче в почести его имехом, яко достоило светлаго рода мужу), и между иными беседованьми, яко обычай бывает при столех, начал вещати нам:

"Согласяся все королеве западные вкупе з самым папою Римским и з самым цесарем християнским, выправивши множество воинов крестоносных, овых земли пустошеные християнские от нахождения срацынскаго помощи ради, овых в земли варварские поседания ради и научения для и познания веры, яже во Христа (яко и ныне соделываемо кролем Ишпанскии и Португальским во Индии); тогда

ᵃ Pog., T. ужаснулся: Ar.

---

[1] Cf. German *Komtur*, commander of the Order.

142

commanders, who had good experienced guides in their units, knew about the locality, they made a circuit through the forests and attacked them, so that barely any of them escaped from the battle; and that brave man, renowned amongst their peoples, who is indeed the last defender and hope of the Livonian nation, was captured alive by the squire of Aleksey Adashev, and with him eleven commanders[1] and one hundred and twenty German noblemen [i.e. knights] were taken prisoner as well as others. But we, knowing nothing of this, arrived at the town of Fellin and there we found our generals not only safe and sound, but rejoicing in a brilliant victory, with the glorious Livonian leader, the brave Landmarschall Philipp, as well as eleven commanders and others as prisoners.[2]

Now when we ordered him to be brought before us and when we began to question him about certain things, as is the custom, then that man, showing no fear whatsoever, began to answer us boldly, with a bright and cheerful face (for he had previously looked like one who had suffered for his fatherland); for, as [we found out after] we had investigated him thoroughly, he was a man who was not only brave and courageous, but also full of eloquence and possessed of a keen intellect and a good memory. Some of his answers to us, which were illumined by his intellect,[3] I will omit, but I will recall only this one thing alone which comes to my memory—his lamentable narrative of the Livonian land. He was once sitting at dinner with us (for although he happened to be a prisoner, nevertheless we held him in esteem, as was befitting a man of brilliant birth), and while we were talking of various things, as is the custom at table, he began to narrate the following to us:

"When all the western kings were in accord with the pope of Rome and the Christian emperor himself, they sent off a large number of cross-bearing warriors, some to help the Christian lands which had been laid waste by the Saracen invasion and others to settle in barbarian lands and to teach and [instil] knowledge of the belief in Christ, just as is now done in India by the kings of Spain and Portugal. At that time they

---

[2] The battle of Ermes took place in August 1560 (*PSRL* xiii, p. 330).
[3] Lit. "opened up by his intellect".

оное предреченное войско разделиша по три гетмана, и пустишася морем едино к полудню, а два к полунощи. И яже к полудню пловущие приплыша к Родису,[a] спустошенному от предреченных Срацын, несогласия ради безумных Греков: тогда, обретше его в конец спустошен, обновиша его с прочими грады и месты другими, и укрепив их и осадя, обладаше тамо со остатними живущими обладали. А яже к полунощи пловущие, приплыша един, идеже бе Прусы, и тамо живущими обладали;[b] а третьи в ту землю; и обретоша тут языцы зело жестоки и непокорных варваров, и заложиша град и место первое Ригу, потом Ревл, и бишася много со живущими оными предреченными варвары, и едва возмогоша ими обладати, и наклонити их немалыми леты ко познанию християнския веры.

Егда же усвоиша тую землю ко Христову наречению, тогда обещашася в возложение Господеви, и на похвалу имяни пречистые Его Богоматере. Внегда же пребывахом в католицкой вере и жительствовахом мерне и целомудренне, тогда Господь наш зде живущих везде покрывал ото врагов наших и помогал нам во всем, яко от Руских княжат, находящих на землю сию, так и от Литовских. (Другие оставя) едину же исповем, иже зело крепку битву имехом со великим княжатем Листовским Витовтом, иже у нас во един день шесть маистров было поставлено, и един по единому побиты, и так крепце сражахомся, яже нощь темная розвела битву ту. Тако же и недавными леты (яко лутче, мню, вам ведомо есть сие) князь великий Иоан

[a] Егда же той Родис взял Турецкий царь Сулиман, долго сам в себе царствоваше, тогда тому Родискому опату, сиречь архимандриту, дали паки вси царие западнии остров, глаголемый Малегу, сииречь Мелетии, егоже Лука в плавании Павловом в Деяних поминает, в немъже сотвориша грады тверды зело, яко и недавно войско от того же Сулимана посланное поразиша под ним и два пашей великих убили ковалеры опатовы, помогающи ему кралеви Гишпанскому и папе: in margin of Ar., Pog., T.; in text of Patr.   [b] Patr., T. обладани: Ar., Pog.

---

[1] A marginal note reads as follows: "When the Turkish sultan Suleiman, who had long ruled independently, took this island of Rhodes, then all the

divided the army I have spoken of between three generals, and one of them set off southwards by sea, and two northwards. and those who sailed south came to Rhodes[1] which had been laid waste by the above-mentioned Saracens owing to the disagreement of the foolish Greeks: and finding it utterly ravaged, they restored it with other fortresses and towns, and having strengthened and fortified them they ruled them together with the other rulers[2] who lived there. And those who sailed north came first to the place where the Prussians dwelt and they ruled those who lived there. And the third party came to this land; and here they found very cruel tribes and indocile barbarians, and they founded firstly the fortress and town of Riga, then Revel'; and they fought a great deal with those above-mentioned barbarians who lived there, and with difficulty they were able to rule them and to incline them after several years to the knowledge of the Christian faith.

Now when they had converted this land to Christianity[3] they pledged themselves to the service of the Lord and to the praise of the name of His most pure Mother. And while we remained in the Catholic faith and lived in moderation and chastity, our Lord helped us in all things and protected those who lived here from our enemies, both from the Russian princes who attacked this land and from the Lithuanians. Leaving other things aside, I will tell of one very fierce battle which we had with Grand Prince Vitovt of Lithuania, when in one day six Masters were appointed and one after another they were killed, and we fought fiercely until the darkness of night dispersed the battle.[4] And also in recent years (as is better known to you, I think) Grand Prince Ivan of Moscow, the grandfather of the present

Western kings gave the abbot, or archimandrite, of Rhodes the island called Malta, that is to say Melita, which Luke mentions in St Paul's voyage in the Acts and in which exceedingly strong fortresses were built—recently the knights of the abbot, with the help of the king of Spain and the pope, defeated a great army sent there by that same Suleiman and killed two great pashas."

[2] I have taken обладали to be a corruption of обладатели (instrumental plural) "rulers".

[3] Lit. "adapted to the name of Christ".

[4] The battle of Grunwald, 1410.

Московский, дед того настоящего, умыслил был тую землю взяти, и крепце бронихомся, яко и со гетманом его Данилом сведохом колько битв, и две одержахом. Но обаче, еликими нибудь обычаи, ублагахом оных предреченных силных, Богу тогда, яко рехом, помогающу праотцом нашим, и при своих отчинах устояли. Ныне же, егда отступихом от веры церковные, и дерзнухом, и опровергохом законы и уставы святые, и прияхом веру новоизбретенную, и за тем в невоздержание ко широкому и пространному пути вдахомся, вводящему в погибель, — и явственно ныне обличающу Господу[a] грехи наши и казнящу нас за беззакония наши, предал нас в руки вам, врагом нашим. И яже сооружили были прародители наши нам грады высокие и места твердые, полаты и дворы пресветлые, вы, о том не трудившися, ни проторов многих налагающе, внидоша в них; садов же и виноградов наших не насадивше, наслаждаетесь, и других таковых устроеней наших домовых ко житию потребных.

А что глаголю о вас, яже аки бы, мните, мечем побрасте? Другие же без меча в наши богатства и стяжания туне внидоша, ни мало, ни в чесом же трудившеся, обещевающе нам помощь и оброненя. Се добра их помощь, иже стоим пред враги связаны! О, о, коль[b] жалоно ми и зело скорбно; но воспоминаю, иже пред очима нашима все сие лютые быша, за грехи наши, веденны и милое отечество разорено суще! И сего ради не мните, иже вы силою своею нам таковые сотвориша; но вся сия Богу на нас попущающу, за преступление наше, иже предал нас в руки врагом нашим!''

И сие ему, со текущими слезами, к нам глаголющу, яко и нам всем слез исполнитися, на него зрящим и таковая от него слыщащим. По сем же, утерши слезы, радостным лицем провеща: ''Но обаче благодарю Бога и радуюся, иже связан бых и стражу за любимое отечество; аще ми за него

[a] Pog. господь: Ar.   [b] Patr. кол: Ar.

_____

[1] The major Russo-Livonian clashes in Ivan III's reign took place in 1480 and during the Russo-Lithuanian war of 1500–1503. In August 1501 the Livonians defeated the Muscovites under Prince Daniil Penkov on the

grand prince, planned to take this land, but we resisted strongly
—we fought several battles with his *hetman* Daniil and won two
of them.[1] But nevertheless, by some means or other, we made
peace with those strong men I have been talking about, for at
that time, as I have said, God helped our forefathers, and we
remained in possession of our patrimonies. But now that we
have departed from the faith of the Church and have become
bold and have overturned the laws and the sacred statutes and
have accepted a newly-invented faith, and have set foot on the
broad and extensive path of intemperance which leads to
destruction, the Lord, clearly reproving us for our sins and
punishing us for our transgressions, has handed us over to you,
our enemies. And as for the tall fortresses and strong towns,
houses and most fair courts which our forefathers built for us—
into these you have entered without having laboured or in-
curred great expense; and without having planted our gardens
and vineyards, you enjoy them, as well as other such buildings
of ours which are used for dwelling.

But what shall I say of you, who, so you think, have taken
our country by the sword? Others have entered freely into our
wealth and possessions without the sword, not having laboured
in any way whatsoever, promising us help and defence.
Look how good their help is—we now stand bound before our
enemies! Oh, how sad and how very grievous! But I recall
how before our very eyes all these cruel things were brought
about because of our sins, and how our dear fatherland was
destroyed. Therefore do not think that by your strength you
have done such things to us: all this was visited upon us because
of our crime by God, who has handed us over to our enemies!"

This he said to us with flowing tears, and all our eyes were
filled with tears as we looked at him and heard such things
from him. Then, wiping his tears away, he told us with joyful
countenance: "But nevertheless I thank God and rejoice that
I have been taken prisoner and that I suffer for my beloved

river Seritsa, south of Izborsk. In September they captured the town of
Ostrov in the district of Pskov. These were the only battles which could be
described as victories for the Livonians. See Fennell, *Ivan the Great*, pp.
73–4, 240–1.

и умрети случится, воистинну драга ми сия смерть будет и прелюбезна." Сие ему изрекшу,[a] умолчал; мы же все удивишась разуму мужа и словеству, и держахом в почести его за стражею; потом послахом его до царя нашего и со протчими властели Лифлянскими к Москве, и молихом царя много чрез епистолию, да не кажет погубити его. И аще бы послушал нас, могл[b] бы всю землю Лифлянъскую по нем мети, понеже имяху его все Лифлянты, яко отца. Но егда же приведен был пред царя и вопрошаем жестоце, отвещал: "иже, рече, неправдою и кровопивством отечество наше посядаешь, а не яко достоит царю християнскому". Он же, разгоревся гневом, повелел абие погубити его, понеже уже лют и бесчеловечен начал быти.

И тогда под тем Филином стояхом, памятамись, три недели и вяще, заточа шанцы и биюще по граду из дел великих. И яже аз тогда ходих к Кеси имех три битвы, и единаго поразих новаго ленсъмаршалка, под Волмарем градом, на того место избраннаго, и яко пришедши под Кесь ротмистры, посланные на нас от Еронима Хоткевича, поражении, и яко стоящи под Кесю,[c] посылахом к Ризе войну, и яко слышачи Ероним о пороженю своих, и ужаснувся, поиде скоро из земли Лифлянские, ажь за Двину реку великую от нас, — сие премину и оставлю по ряду писати, сокращения ради истории; ко предреченному же о Фелинском взятью возвращаюся. Егда же уже разбихом стены меские, — еще крепце сопротивляющеся нам Немцы, — тогда в нощи стреляюще огненными кулями, и едина куля упаде в самое яблоко церковное, яже в верху великие церкви их бе, и другие кули инде и инде, и абие загорелося место: тогда начаша сущеи во граде и маистр просити времяни о постановлению, обещавающе град и место подати, и прошаще вольнаго проезду со всеми сущими во граде и скарбы своими. Мы же так не поволяше;

[a] Patr., Pog. изрекше: Ar. [b] T. многл: Ar., Patr.
[c] Patr., T. ксею: Ar., Pog.

[1] See *PL* п, p. 239. [2] See *PL* п, p. 240.

fatherland. Should I have to die for it, then indeed such a death would be dear to me and most sweet." Having said this he became silent. And we were all astonished at the intellect and eloquence of the man, and we held him in esteem while he was our prisoner. Then we sent him together with other Livonian rulers to our tsar in Moscow, and we implored the tsar in a letter not to have him put to death. Had he listened to us he might have had the whole land of Livonia under him, for all the Livonians held him [Bell] as a father. But when he was brought before the tsar and cruelly interrogated, he answered: "you are conquering our fatherland with injustice and bloodshed, and not as befits a Christian tsar". And the tsar, blazing with anger, ordered him to be put to death immediately; for he had already begun to be fierce and in-human.[1]

And at that time, I remember, we stood at the walls of Fellin for three weeks or more, setting trenches and shooting at the fortress from the great guns. And as for how at that time I marched to Kes' and fought three battles and at Wolmar defeated the new Landmarschall, who had been chosen in the place of the other one; and how the cavalry commanders, who had been sent against us by Ieronim Khodkevich, were defeated on arrival at Kes'; and how we sent an expedition to Riga while we were at Kes', and how Ieronim, when he heard about the defeat of his men, was frightened and quickly left the Livonian land and went away from us right across the great Dvina river[2]—I will omit all this and forbear to describe it in order to keep my story short. I will return to the capture of Fellin, which I was talking about before. Now when we had smashed the town walls, while the Germans were still fiercely resisting us, we fired incendiary cannon-balls by night, and one of them fell into the very dome which was at the top of their great church, and other balls fell in other places, and the town immediately caught fire. Then the Master and those who were in the fortress began to ask for time to discuss terms, promising to surrender the fortress and town, and they asked to be allowed to leave freely with all those who were in the fortress and to take their goods with them. But we did not desire this, and the

а на том стало: желнерей всех выпустити вольно и жителей градских, елицы хотеша, а его не выпущали и со скарбы, милость ему обещевающе от царя; яко и даде ему град на Москве до живота его, и скарбы оные его, елицы были взяты, возвращенны ему потом. И сице взяша град и место; и огнь в месте угасихом. А к тому тогда взяхом два, або три грады, в нихже быша наместники того маистра Фиштемберкга. Егда же внидохом в место и во град Фелин, тогда узрехом от места стоящи еще три вышеграды, и так крепки и от претвердых каменей сооружени, и рвы глубоки у них, иже вере не подобно, бо и рвы оные, зело глубокие, каменьми гладкими тесаными выведены; и обретохом в нем великих дел стенобитных осмьнадесять, а под теми великих и малых всех полпятаста на граде и месте, и запасов и всех достатков множество; а в самом граде вышнем не токмо церковь, или полаты, или сам град, но и кухня и стайни толстыми оловяными тщицами были крыты.^a И тую всю кровлю абие князь великий повелел сняти, и в то место кровлю от древа сотворити.

^a Т. крысти: Аг.

---

¹ Fellin was captured in August 1560. The old Master, Fürstenberg, had been replaced by Kettler in 1559. For the capture of Fellin and Ivan's pardon of Fürstenberg, see *PSRL* xiii, pp. 330–1.

following was agreed upon: we allowed all the soldiers and the inhabitants of the town, as many as wanted to, to depart freely; but we did not let the Master go or take his possessions, but we promised him mercy from the tsar—and the tsar gave him a town in Muscovy on life tenure, and the goods which were taken from him were returned to him later.[1] And thus the fortress and town were captured; and we put out the fire in the town. And furthermore we took two or three fortresses in which were stationed the governors of the Master Fürstenberg.[2] Now when we entered the town and fortress of Fellin we saw three more citadels[3] which were so strong and built of such very hard stone and with such deep moats, that it was hard to believe: for those moats, which were very deep, were faced with smooth hewn stones. And in the fortress we found eighteen large siege-guns and below them in the fortress and the town four hundred and fifty large and small guns and a great abundance of all kinds of supplies. And in the fortress itself not only the church and the houses and the citadel, but also the kitchen and the stables were covered with thick sheets of lead; and the grand prince immediately ordered all this roofing to be removed and to be replaced by a wooden roof.

[2] See *PSRL* XIII, p. 330. The Russian operations in Livonia in the summer of 1560 resulted in the complete military collapse of the Order.

[3] See above, p. 112.

V

Что же по сем царь наш начинает? Егда же убо обронился, Божиею помощию, храбрыми своими от окресных врагов его, тогда воздает им! Тогда платит презлыми за предобрейшие, прелютыми за превозлюбленнейшее, лукавствы и хитролествы за простые и верные их служды. А яко же сие начинает? Сице: первие, отгоняет дву мужей оных от себя предреченных, Селивестра, глаголю, презвитера, и Алексея предреченнаго, Адашева, туне и ни в чем же пред ним согрешивших, отворивши оба ухи свои презлым ласкателем (над нихже, уже яко многажды рехом, ни един прыщ смертный во царстве поветреннейши быти может), яже[a] ему уже клеветаша и сикованции во уши шептаху заочне на оных святых, паче же шурья ево и другие с ними нечестивые губители всего тамошнего царства. А чего же ради сие творяху? Того ради воистинну: да не будет обличенна злость их и да невозбранно будет им всеми нами владети и, суд превращающе, посулы грабити и другие злости плодити скверныя, пожитки свои умножающе. Что же клевещут и шепчют во ухо? Тогда цареви жена умре: они же реша, аки бы счеровали ее оные мужи (подобно, чему сами искусны и во что веруют, сие на святых мужей и добрых возлагали). Царь же, буйства исполнився, абие им веру ял. Услышавши же сие, Селиверстр и Алексей начаша молити, ово епистолиями посылающи,[b] ово чрез митрополита Руского, да будет очевистное глаголание с ними. "Не отрицаемся, рече, аще повинни будем, смерти; но да будет суд явственный пред тобою и предо всем сенатом твоим."

Презлые же к сему что умышляют? Епистолей не допущают до царя; епископу старому запрещают и грозят;

---

[a] Patr., Pog. яко: Ar.   [b] Patr. посылающу: Ar.

[1] According to *PSRL* XIII, p. 328, Anastasia died on 7 August 1560, "on the day of the holy martyr Diomid". St Diomid's day, however, is 16 August.

152

V

Now what did our tsar begin to do after this? When with God's help he had defended himself against his enemies on every side thanks to his brave men, then he repaid them! Then he recompensed them with extreme evil for extreme good, with ferocity for loving-kindness, with cunning and deceit for their simple and faithful service. And how did he set about this? In the following manner: firstly, he unjustly dismissed those two men I have talked about above, I mean Sil'vestr the priest and Aleksey Adashev (although they had not sinned in any way before him), opening his ears to those wicked flatterers, than whom, as I have already said many times, not a single deathly boil can be more pestilential in the tsardom, and who had already accused those holy men and in their absence whispered sycophancy in his ears against them—especially his brothers-in-law and other impious destroyers of all the tsardom. But why did they do this? This, in truth, is the reason: so that their wickedness should not be exposed and so that they might freely rule us all, and, perverting justice, take bribes and multiply other foul wicked deeds, thus increasing their possessions. But what accusations do they whisper in the tsar's ear? At that time the wife of the tsar died,[1] and they said that those men had bewitched her (it was as though they were accusing those good and holy men of what they themselves were skilled in and believed in). And the tsar, being filled with folly, straightway believed them. And hearing this, Sil'vestr and Adashev began to beg him, both by means of epistles and through the metropolitan of Russia, to talk to them face to face. "We do not shun death if we are guilty, but let there be open judgement before you and before all your senate."[2]

And what did the wicked ones devise to counter this? They did not let the epistles reach the tsar; they forbade the old bishop[3]

---

[2] I.e. before the Boyar Council.
[3] Metropolitan Makary was 78 or 79 at the time. He was born c. 1481/2. See A. A. Zimin, *Peresvetov*, p. 72.

цареви же глаголют: "Аще, рече, припустишь их к себе на очи, очаруют тебя и детей твоих; а к тому, любяще их все твое воинство и народ, нежели тобя самого, побиют тебя и нас камением. Аще ли и сего не будет, обьвяжут тя паки и покорят тя аки в неволю себе. Так худые люди и ничему же годные чаровницы тебя, государя, так великого и славнаго и мудраго, боговенчаннаго царя, держали пред тем, аки в оковах, повелевающе тебе в меру ясти и пити и со царицею жити, не дающе тебе ни в чесом же своей воли, а ни в мале, а ни в великом, а ни людей своих миловати, а ни царством твоим владеть. А аще бы не они были при тебе, так при государе мужественом и храбром и пресильном, и тебя не держали аки уздою, уже бы еси мало не всею вселенною обладал, а то творили они своими чаровствы, аки очи твои закрывающе, не дали ни на что ж зрети, хотяще сами царствовати и нами всеми владети. И аще на очи припустишь[a] их, паки тя, очаровавши, осляпят. Ныне же, егда отогнал еси их, воистинну образумился еси, сиречь во свой разум пришел, и отворил еси себе очи, зряще уже свободно на все свое царство, яко помазанец Божий, и никто же ин, точию сам един, тое управляюще и им владеюще."

И иными таковыми мношайшими и бесчисленными лжесчивалцы, согласе со отцем своим дияволом — паче же рещи, воистинну язык ему и уста самому глаголанию бывают на пагубу роду християнскому, — сице подходят ласкательными глаголы мужа, и сице опровергают царя християнского душу, добре живущаго и в покаянию сущаго, и сице растерзают пленицу оную, Богом соплетенную в любовь духовную (яко же сам Господь рече: идеже собрани два или три во имя мое, ту аз посреди их); ис[b] посреди Бога отгоняют оные, проклятые, и паки реку: сицевыми прелестными глаголы царя християнского губяще, добраго бывшаго много лет, покаянием украшенного и ко Богу усвоенного, в воздержанию всяком и в чистоте пребывающа.

ᵃ Patr. приступишь: Ar., Pog.   ᵇ Patr., Pog. и: Ar.

¹ Matt. xviii. 20.

[to intercede] and threatened him; they said to the tsar: "if you admit these men to your presence, they will bewitch you and your children. Furthermore, all your army and your people, who love them more than they love you yourself, will stone you and us. Even if this does not happen, they will bind you and subject you again to themselves in servitude. Thus did these evil men and worthless sorcerers hold you before, as it were in chains, you, the sovereign, so great and glorious and wise, the tsar crowned by God, ordering you to eat and drink and to live with your tsaritsa with moderation, not granting you your own will in anything great or small, and not allowing you to have mercy on your people or to rule your tsardom! Had they not been with you—so courageous, so brave and so powerful a sovereign—and had they not held you as it were with a bridle, then you would have ruled almost all the universe. And this they did by their magic charms, closing your eyes; they did not allow you to supervise anything, for they wanted to reign themselves and to rule us all. And if you admit them to your presence, then again they will bewitch you and blind you. But now that you have dismissed them, you have indeed seen reason; that is to say you have come to your senses and you have opened your eyes, freely supervising all your tsardom like the anointed of God, and no one else, but yourself alone, governs and rules it."

And thus, with countless other tissues of lies, in agreement with their father the devil—indeed, one might say that when his tongue and mouth speak, they lead to the downfall of Christianity—they deceived their man with flattering words and overthrew the soul of the Christian tsar, who was living righteously and in penitence, and thus they broke that bond which was woven by God for spiritual love (as the Lord Himself said: "where two or three are gathered together in my name, there am I in the midst of them"[1]); and those accursed ones drove him away from the vicinity of God; and again I say: with such deceptive words they destroyed the Christian tsar, who for many years had been good and who had been adorned with penitence and had been brought close to God, abiding in every kind of restraint and purity. O wicked men, filled with

О злые и всякия презлости и лукавства исполненыя, своего отечества губители, паче же рещи, всего Святоруского царства! Что вам принесет сие за полезное? Вмале узрите над собою делом исполняемо и над чады своими, и услышите от грядущих родов проклятие всегдашное!

Царь же, напився от окаянных, со сладостным ласканием смешаннаго, смертоноснаго яду, и сам, лукавства, паче же глупости, наполнився, похваляет совет, и любит и усвояет их в дружбу и присягами себе и их обвязует, вооружающеся на святых неповинных, к тому и на всех добрых и добро хотящих ему и душу за него полагающих, аки на врагов своих:ᵃ и собрав и учинив уже окрест себя яко пресильный и великий полк сотанинский. И что же еще к тому первие начинает и делает? Собирает соборище не токмо весь сенат свой мирский, но и духовных всех, сиречь митрополита и градских епископов призывает, и к тому присовокупляет прелукавых некоторых мнихов, Мисаила, глаголемого Сукина, издавна преславнаго в злостях, и Васьяна Беснаго, по истинне реченнаго, неистового, и других с ними таковых тем подобных, исполненых лицемерия и всякого безстыдия диявола и дерзости; и посаждает их близу себя, благодарне послушающе их, вещающих и клевещущих ложное на святых и глаголющих на праведных беззаконие, со премногою гордынею и уничижением. Что же на том соборище производят? Чтут пописавши вины оных мужей заочне, яко и митрополит тогда пред всеми рекл: "Подобает, рече, приведенным им быти зде пред нас, да очевисте на них

ᵃ зело достойно зде вкратце рещи Римскую древнюю пословицу, о прелом и прелукавом Котелине, реченную их языком, (in T. only: ерретуус имижекусь амикорум суор) — понеже такова царя нашего учинили ласкатели и таков стался, — сииречь в Рускую беседу (Pog. беду: Ar.) рекше: вечный и всегдашний враг или неприятель приятелей своих: in margin of Ar., Pog. and T.; in text of Patr.

---

¹ A marginal note reads as follows: "It would be very fitting here briefly to mention an ancient Roman saying, which was uttered in their language concerning that most evil and cunning man, Catiline: (for flatterers made our tsar what he is, and such did he become), that is to say in Russian:

all kinds of evil and cunning, the destroyers of their fatherland, still more of all the holy Russian tsardom! What good will this bring you? Soon you shall see the result of this deed upon yourselves and upon your children, and from generations to come you shall hear an everlasting curse!

Now the tsar, having been made by the accursed ones to drink his fill of this deadly poison mixed with sweet flattery, and being filled with cunning, or rather stupidity, praised their counsel and loved them and drew them into friendship and bound them to him with oaths, taking up arms against the holy innocent men—and furthermore against all good men and against all who wished him well and who [were ready to] lay down their lives for him, as though against his enemies;[1] and he gathered together and collected around him an exceedingly strong and great satanic host. And what did he then embark upon and do first of all? He summoned a council, including not only all his lay senate, but also all the clergy, that is to say he called for the metropolitan and the bishops of the towns, and to these he added certain very cunning monks, Misail Sukin, who had long been renowned for his iniquities, and Vassian Besny, who was rightly named "the Mad",[2] and others like them, filled with hypocrisy and all kinds of diabolical shamelessness and boldness; and he seated them near himself, listening to them with gratitude as they uttered false accusations against the holy men and said lawless things against the just with exceedingly great pride and contempt. And what was done at that council? Having written down the charges against these men they read them out in their absence; but the metropolitan then said in the presence of all: "It is right that they should be brought here before us so that the charges may be brought

'the everlasting and constant foe or enemy of his friends'." The actual Latin quotation is clearly missing here, but it is given in one copy as "erretuus imizhekus amikorum suor" (*perennis inimicus amicorum suorum*).

[2] *Besny* means "possessed of a devil" and may perhaps be a nickname invented by Kurbsky for Bishop Vassian Toporkov. Misail Sukin came from a family of *d'yaki* connected with the court of Ivan IV (see Zimin, *Peresvetov*, p. 49, n. 168). In December 1559 A. Adashev and Fedor Ivanovich Sukin, who was treasurer (*kaznachey*) at the time, received a delegation in Moscow (*PSRL* xiii, p. 322).

клеветы будут, и нам убо слышети воистинну достоит, что они на то отвещают." И всем ему добрым согласующе, тако же рекшим; губительнейшие же ласкатели вкупе со царем возопиша: "Не подобает, рече, о епискупе! Понеже ведомые сие злодеи и чаровницы велицы, очаруют царя и нас погубят, аще приидут." И тако осудиша их заочне.[a] О смеху достойное, паче же беды исполненое, осуждение прельщеннаго от ласкателей царя!

Заточен бывает от него Селивестр презвитер, исповедник его, аж на остров, яже на Студеном море, в монастырь Соловецкий, край Корелска языка, в Лопи дикой лежащь.[b] А Олексей отгоняется от очей его, без суда, в нововзятый град от нас Фелин, и тамо антипат бывает на мало время. Егда же услышали презлые, иже и тамо Бог помогает ему — понеже не мало градов Вифлянских, еще не взятых, хотяще поддатись ему, его ради доброты, ибо, и в беде будуще положен, служаше царю своему верне, — они же паки клеветы клеветам, шептание к шептанию, лжесщивание ко лжесщиванием цареви прилогают, на мужа онаго и праведнаго и добраго. И абие повелел оттуду свести в Дерпт и держан быти под стражею; и по дву месяцех потом в недуг огненный впал: исповедався и взяв святые Христа Бога нашего тайны, к Нему отъиде. Егда же о смерти его услышавше, клеветницы возопиша цареви: "Се твой изменик сам себе задал яд смертоносный и умре."[c]

[a] Patr., Pog., T. заочие: Ar.   [b] Patr., T. лежаш: Ar.
[c] зри зде Златоустом реченное исполнено, яко он негде глаголет, иже все страсти и злости человеческия житием разрушаются, а ненависть и по смерти не угаснет, яко и на самого Христа нашего от богоборных Иудеов, ведущих волею лжесшивано по премногому лукавству их, учаще воинов лгати: "рцыте, рече, яко нам спящим украдоша Его ученицы" и проч(ее); и промчеся то слово между ими и доселе, такожде и между теми нечестивыми промчеся лгабство их, аки бы муж святый, и святою смертию отшедший, сам себе яд задал: in margin of Ar., Pog. and T.; in text of Patr.

---

[1] There is no other information in the chronicles on the Council of 1560, at which Sil'vestr and Adashev were condemned.

[2] In January 1560 Aleksey Adashev was still active in Moscow; he received an embassy from Lithuania in that month (*PSRL* XIII, p. 324); in

against them in their presence, for it is indeed right that we should hear what they have to say in reply." And all the good men agreed with him and said the same thing. But those most pernicious flatterers shouted with the tsar: "It is not right, O bishop! These men are recognized evil-doers and great sorcerers, and they will bewitch the tsar and will destroy us if they come!" And so they were condemned in their absence. Oh judgement worthy of ridicule, still more, replete with calamity, passed by a tsar who was deceived by flatterers.[1]

The priest Sil'vestr, his confessor, was imprisoned by him and sent as far as an island in the Frozen Sea, to the monastery of Solovki in the land of the Korelian people, amongst the wild Lapps. And Aleksey was banished from his sight without judgement to the town of Fellin, which had recently been taken by us, and was governor there for a short time.[2] But when the evil ones heard that even there God was helping him—several Livonian towns which had not yet been taken wanted to surrender to him because of his goodness, for even though he was in a calamitous position he served his tsar faithfully—then again in the tsar's ears they added accusation to accusation, whisper to whisper, tissue of lies to tissue of lies against that just and good man. And straightway he ordered him to be taken away from there to Derpt and kept under guard; and two months later he fell into a fever. Having confessed and having taken the holy sacraments of Christ our God, he departed to Him. And when his accusers heard about his death they cried in the tsar's ear: "Now your traitor has given himself deadly poison and has died."[3]

February his brother Daniil was sent to Livonia (*ibid.* p. 326) and in May 1560 he himself was sent as 3 i/c the Great Regiment to Livonia (*ibid.* p. 327; *DRK*, p. 222). After the capture of Fellin he was appointed one of the governors of the town (*DRK*, p. 225).

[3] A marginal note reads as follows: "See, here is the fulfilment of that which was spoken by Chrysostom, for somewhere he said that all passions and human wickednesses are destroyed by life, whereas hatred will not be quenched even after death, as the hatred of the God-destroying Jews for our Christ Himself, for they knew that tissues of lies had been deliberately woven according to their great cunning, and they taught the soldiers to lie, saying: 'Say ye, His disciples came...and stole Him away while we slept', and so forth, and this saying is commonly reported among them unto this day [cf.

А той Селивестр пресвитер, еже преже даже не изгнан был, видев его, иж уже не по[a] Бозе всякие вещи начинает, претив ему и наказуя много, да во страсе Божии пребывает и в воздержанию жительствует, и иными множайшими словесы Божественными поучая и наказуя много; он же отнюдь того не внимаше и ко ласкателем ум свой и уши приклонил: разсмотрив же вся сия, презвитер, иже уже лице свое от него отвратил, отшел был в монастырь, сто миль от Москвы лежашь, а тамо во мнишестве будуще, нарочитое и чистое свое жительство препровожал. Клеветницы же, слышавше, иже тамо в чести имеют оные мниси его, сего ради, завистию разседаеми, ово завидяще мужу славы, ово боящеся, да не услышит царь о сем и паки да не возвратит его к собе, и да не обличатся их неправды и привращение судов, и много-взимателныя, любимыя издавна обыкновения их, посулы, и новоначатыя пиянства и нечистоты паки не пресекутся от оного святаго, — и оттуды похватиша его и заведоша на Соловки, аж преже рехом, идеже бы и слух его не обрелся, похваляющись, аки бы то соборне осудиша его, мужа нарочитаго и готоваго отвещати на клеветы.

Где таков суд слышан[b] под солнцем, без очевистнаго вещания? Яко и Златоустый пишет во епистолии своей ко Инокентию, папе Римскому, нарекающе на Феофила и на царицу и на все соборище его о неправедном изгнанею своем, емуже начало: "Первие нежели отдани суть еписто-лии наши, мню, благочестие твое слышавше, яковый зде мятеж творити дерзнула неправда"; и паки при конце в той же: "И аще противники обрели, иже так презрение сотво-рили, и еще замышляют ложные клеветы, понеже нас безвинне изгнали, не давше нам а ни[c] преписей, а ни книжец,

[a] Patr., Pog. бо: Ar.   [b] Pog., Т. слышав: Ar.   [c] Т. они: Ar., Patr., Pog.

Matt. xxviii. 13, 15], just as among these impious men their lying statement is reported, to the effect that this holy man, who died a holy death, gave himself poison."

[1] Presumably the White Lake Monastery of St Kirill, which Kurbsky elsewhere describes as "a hundred miles from Moscow" (see above, pp.

Now before the priest Sil'vestr had been driven out, he saw that the tsar was starting all sorts of things in an ungodly manner, and he rebuked him and instructed him so that he might abide in the fear of God and live with restraint, and he taught and instructed him with very many divine words; but the tsar did not listen to him at all, but inclined his mind and ear to the flatterers. And the priest, having considered all these things and [seeing] that the tsar had turned his face from him, departed to a monastery, which lies a hundred miles from Moscow, and there, as a monk, he led a pure and distinguished life.[1] But his accusers, hearing that the monks held him in honour, were bursting with envy, both because they coveted his glory and because they were afraid that the tsar would hear of this and bring him back and that their wrong deeds and their perversion of justice would be exposed, and that their highly acquisitive habits which they had long practised, their bribes, their recently-resumed drunkenness and impurity would be stopped by that holy man—and they seized him and took him from there to Solovki, as I have previously said, where no more would be heard of him; and they boasted that he—that distinguished man, who was prepared to answer their accusations— had been condemned by a council.

Where under the sun is such judgement—without confrontation—heard of? As Chrysostom, rebuking Theophilus and his empress and all his council for his unjust banishment, wrote in his epistle to Innocent, the pope of Rome, which begins: "Before our epistles were handed to you, I think your holiness heard what confusion injustice dared to create here";[2] and again, at the end of the same epistle: "and if our adversaries, who have acted so evilly,[3] should still plan false accusations, because of which we were banished without guilt, without giving us records or written accusations[4] and without declaring

74–5). Ivan IV, in his first letter to Kurbsky, describes Sil'vestr's departure as voluntary (*Correspondence*, pp. 98–9).

[2] See *PG* vol. 51, cols. 529–30.

[3] презрение should read презле (οἱ τὰ τοιαῦτα παρανομήσαντες—иже так презле сотворили). The presence of the word обрели is hard to explain.

[4] Cf. ὑπομνημάτων...λιβέλλων.

а ни обьявивша клеветников имети и оброняти, и мы суд[a] будем и покажем оных самых, а не нас, быти винными, что на нас возкладают, понеже неповинне есмя. И сопротив иже[b] они сотворили? Сопротив всех правилом, сопротив всем церковным каноном. И что глаголю каноном церковным? а не в поганских судех, а ни в варварских престолех таковые когда случились; а ни Скифы, а ни Сармацы когда судили суд[c] повелети единой стороне заочне оклеветанных[''] и прочие, тем подобные, яко в том его посланию лучше, читаючи, разсмотрится. Сей соборный царя нашего християнскаго таков суд! Се декрет, знамените произведен от вселукаваго сонмища ласкателей, грядущим родом на срамоту вечныя памяти и уничижения Рускому языку! понеже у них в земли уродилися таковые лукавые, презлые, ехитнины отроды, уже у матери своей чрево прогрызли, сиречь земли Святоруские, яже породила их и воспитала, воистинну на свою беду и пустошенье!

Что же по сих за плод от преславных ласкателей, паче жь презлых губителей, возрастает? и во что вещи обращаются? и что царь от них приобретает и получает? Абие с ними диявол умышляет первый вход ко злости, сопротив ускаго и мернаго путя Христова, по преславном и широком пути свободное хождение. А яко же сие начинают и како царева жития прежнюю мерность разоряют, еже нарицали неволею обвязана? Начинают пиры частые со многими пиянствы, от нихъже всякие нечистоты родятся. И что еще к тому прилагают? чаши великие, воистинну дияволу обещанные, и чаши таковые: наложивши в них зело пьянаго питья, и советуют первую цареви выпити, потом всем сущим пирующим с ним, и аще ли теми да обоумертвия, паче же до неистовства, не упиются, они другие и третье прилагают, и не хотящих их пити и̃ таковая беззакония творити закли-

[a] Т. сут: Ar.   [b] Т. же: Ar.   [c] Patr., Т. суть: Ar.

[1] оброняти is misplaced. Cf. Greek: καὶ δικασόμεθα, καὶ ἀπολογησόμεθα.

who the accusers are[1]. . .,[2] then we shall stand trial and defend ourselves, and we shall show that they, and not we, are guilty of the things they accuse us of; for we are innocent. And against what did they act? Against all rules, against all ecclesiastical canons. And why say I ecclesiastical canons? Neither in pagan law-courts nor in barbarian places of justice[3] have such things ever happened. Neither Scythians nor Sarmatians ever gave judgement on one side only in the absence of the accused",[4] and other things like this, as can best be seen if you read them in that epistle. Such, then, was the justice meted out by the council of our Christian tsar! Such was the decree, notoriously set forth by the all-cunning gathering of flatterers, to shame the everlasting memory of generations to come and to humiliate the Russian race! For in their land was born such cunning, wicked progeny of vipers who gnawed through their mothers' wombs—in other words the holy Russian land, which begat them and nourished them, indeed to its own affliction and desolation.

And what fruit grew from these most glorious flatterers, or rather should I say, most evil destroyers? And what did things turn into? And what did the tsar acquire and receive from them? Together with them the devil straightway devised the first entry into evil, the free passage along that most glorious broad path, compared to the narrow and moderate path of Christ. And in what way did they set about this, and how did they destroy the early moderation of the tsar's way of life, which they called "bound by servitude"? They began with frequent feasts and much drunkenness, from which all kinds of impurities sprang. And what did they add to this? Great beakers, pledged, in truth, to the devil, and beakers which were filled with extremely heady drink; and they advised the tsar to drink the first beaker followed by all those who are feasting with him; and if they did not drink themselves into a stupor, or rather a frenzy, then they added a second and a third beaker; and those who had no wish to drink or to commit such transgressions they

[2] The clause δικαστηρίου καθίσαντος ἀδεκάστου ("should there be impartial judges") has been omitted here.

[3] Lit. "thrones". In the Greek: ἐν βαρβαρικῷ δικαστηρίῳ.

[4] Ibid. cols. 534–5.

нают со великими прещеньми; цареви же вопиют: "Се, рече, онъсице, и онъсица, имя рекше, не хощет на твоем пиру весел быти, подобно тебя и нас осуждает и насмевает, аки пьяниц, являющь праведный лицемерием. И подобно твои суть недоброхоты, иже с тобою не согласуют и тебя не слушают, и еще Селивестров или Алексеев дух, сиречь обычай, не вышел из них!" И иными словесы бесовскими множайшими, нежели тех, многих трезвых мужей и мерных во жительстве добром и во нраве наругают и посрамащают, льюще на них чаши оные проклятые, имиже не хотяще упиватися, або[a] отнюдь не могуще, и к тому им смертьми и различными муками претяще, яко и мало последи многих того ради погубиша. О воистинну новое идолослужение, и обещание и приношение не балвану Аполонову и прочим, но самому Сатоне и бесом его; не жертвы волов и козлов приношаще, влекомые насилием на заколение, но самые души свои и телеса самовластною волею, сребролюбия ради и славы мира сего ослепше, сия творяще! И сице первие царьское честное и воздержанное жительство разоряют, презлые и окаянные!

Се, царю, получил еси от шепчущих ти во уши любимых твоих ласкателей: вместо святаго поста твоего и воздержания прежняго, пиянство губительное со обещанными дияволими чашами[1]; и вместо целомудреннаго и святаго жительства твоего, нечистоты, всяких скверн исполненныя; вместо же крепости и суда твоего царского, на лютость и безчеловечие подвигоша тя; вместо же молитв тихих и кротких, имиже ко Богу твоему беседовал еси, лености и долгому спанию научиша тя, и по сне зиянию, главоболию с похмелия и другим злостям неизмерным и неисповедимым. А еже восхваляше тя, и возношаше и глаголаше тя царя велика, непобедима и храбра, и воистинну таков был еси, егда во страсе Божии жительствовал. Егда же надут от них и прельщен, что получил еси? Вместо мужества твоего и храбрости, бегун пред врагом и храняка. Царь великий

[a] T. обо: Ar.

[1] Lit. "with pledged devilish beakers".

adjured with great rebuke, while they shouted at the tsar: "Behold, this one here, and this one (naming him) does not wish to be joyful at your feast, as though he condemns and mocks you and us as drunkards, hypocritically pretending to be righteous! It looks as though those people are not your well-wishers who are not in agreement with you and who do not listen to you and from whom the spirit, that is to say the custom, of Sil'vestr and Aleksey has not yet departed!" And with other still more devilish words than these they abused many men who were sober and moderate in their good way of life and habits, and they put them to shame, pouring those accursed beakers on them, with which they did not wish—or were quite unable—to become drunk, and they threatened them with death and various tortures, in the same way as they destroyed many people a little later for this reason. O, new idolatry, in truth, a pledge and an offering not to the statue of Apollo and others, but to Satan himself and to his devils! They brought not a sacrifice of oxen and goats led by force to the slaughter, but brought their very souls and bodies of their own free will, because of the love of money and the glory of this world—this they did in their blindness! And thus those most evil and accursed men first of all destroyed the pious and moderate way of life of the tsar!

This then, o tsar, is what you have received from your beloved flatterers who whisper in your ears: instead of your former holy fasting and restraint—pernicious drunkenness, with beakers pledged to the devil;[1] and instead of your chaste and holy way of life—impurities filled with all kinds of filthiness; and instead of strength and your royal justice they urged you on to ferocity and inhumanity; instead of quiet and gentle prayers by means of which you conversed with God, they taught you idleness and long sleeping and yawning after sleep, drunken headaches and other immeasurable and unspeakable evils. And as for praising you and exalting you and calling you a great tsar, unconquerable and brave—this indeed you were when you lived in the fear of God. But when you were puffed up and deceived by them, what did you get? Instead of being brave and courageous, you ran from the enemy and hid. The great Christian tsar [fled]

християнский, пред бусурманским волком, яже преже пред нами места не нашол и на диком поле, бегая. А за советом любимых твоих ласкателей и за молитвами Чюдовского Левки и прочих вселукавых мнихов, что добраго и полезнаго и похвальнаго и Богу угоднаго приобрел еси? Развее спустошение земли твоея, ово от тебя самого с кромешники твоими, ово от предреченнаго пса бусурманского, и к тому злую славу от окрестных суседов, и проклятие и нарекание слезное ото всего народу. И что еще прегоршаго и срамотнейшаго и ко слушанию претехчайшаго, — самое отечество твое, превеликое место и многонародное, град Москву, во вселенней[a] славный, созжен и потреблен со безчисленными народы християнскими[b] внезапу. О беда претехчайшая и ко слышанию жалостна! Али не час было образумитися и покаятися ко Богу, яко Монасия, и отклонити волю естественнаго самовластия по естеству ко своему Сотворителю, искупившему нас надражайшею[c] кровию своею, нежели то самовластие со произволением самовольным покаряти чрез естество супостату человеческому и внимати верным слугам его, глаголю, презлым ласкателем его?

Еще[d] ли ся не разсмотришь, о царю, к чему тя привели человекоугодницы? и чем тя сотворили любимыя маньяки твои? и яко опровергли и опроказили прежде святую и многоденную, покаянием украшенную, совесть души твоей? И аще нам не веришь, нарицающе нас туне изменниками прелукавыми, да прочтет величество[e] твое во слове, златовещательными устнами изреченном,[f] о Ироде, емужь начало: "Днесь нам Иоанново преподобие, Иродова лютость егда

---

[a] Т. вселенныи: Ar.   [b] Patr., Т. християн с ними: Ar., Pog.
[c] надражайшаго: Ar. надражайшего: Patr., Pog.   [d] аще: Ar., Patr.   [e] Patr., Pog., Т. величества: Ar.   [f] Т. изреченному: Ar.

---

[1] This sentence and the following sentences are very close in content and style to a passage in Kurbsky's third letter to Ivan (1578). See *Correspondence*, pp. 204–7.

from the Mussulman wolf, who formerly found no place [of rest] in his flight from us over the steppe.[1] But thanks to the advice of your beloved flatterers and thanks to the prayers of Levky of the Chudov monastery[2] and of other most cunning monks, what did you win that was good and useful and praiseworthy and pleasing to God? What apart from the laying waste of your land, both by you yourself and by your children of darkness[3] and by that Mussulman dog I have mentioned above,[4] as well as evil repute in the eyes of your neighbours and cursing and tearful entreaty from all the people? And—still worse and more shameful and most grevous to the ears—your own inheritance, that great and populous town, the city of Moscow, glorious throughout the universe, was suddenly burned and destroyed with its countless Christian peoples.[5] O calamity most grievous and sad to the ears! Was it not time to come to your senses and to repent before God like Manasseh,[6] and according to nature to turn your natural free will[7] to your Creator, who redeemed us by His dearest blood, rather than, contrary to nature, to subject that free will voluntarily to the enemy of man and to listen to his true servants, I mean to his most wicked flatterers?

Will you not further consider, o tsar, what your man-pleasers have led you to and what your beloved maniacs have turned you into, and how they have overthrown and harmed the conscience of your soul which was formerly holy and of great value,[8] adorned with penitence? And if you do not believe us, vainly calling us most cunning traitors, let your majesty read the sermon on Herod, uttered by the lips which speak words of gold, which begins: "Today, when the virtues of John and the

---

[2] Levky was archimandrite of the Chudov monastery in the Kremlin from 1554 to 1568 (Stroev, *Spiski*, col. 163). Ivan IV, in his letter to the monastery of St Kirill, mentions him as being most successful in raising the importance of the monastery. See *Poslaniya Ivana Groznogo*, p. 173.

[3] I.e. members of the *Oprichnina*. See *Correspondence*, p. 205.

[4] A reference to the invasion of Devlet Girey in 1571 (*ibid.* p. 205, n. 1).

[5] *Ibid.* pp. 204–5.

[6] 2 Chron. xxxiii.

[7] Lit. "the will (freedom) of your natural free will".

[8] многоденную clearly an error for многоценную.

возвещалась, смутились внутренные, сердца вострепетали, зрак помрачился, разум притупился. Или что твердо в чювствах человеческих, егда погубляет добродетелей величество злостей множество?" И паки мало пониже: "Достойне убо смущалися внутренные, сердца трепетали, понеже Ирод осквернил церковь, иерейство отнял", — яко ты аще не Иоанна Крестителя, но Филиппа архиепископа с другими святыми смутил, — "чин скверно соделал, царство сокрушил; что было благочестия, что правил, что жития, что обычаев, что веры, что наказания — погубил и смесил. Ирод, рече, мучитель гражан, воинов, разбойник, другов спустошитель"; твоего же величества произобилие злости, иже не токмо другов, но и всея Святоруския земли с кромешники твоими спустошения, домов их грабитель и убийца сынов. От сего, Боже, сохрани тебя и не попусти тому быти, Господи Царю веком! Бо уже и то аки на острею сабли висит, понеже аще не сынов, но соплемянных и ближних в роде братею уже погубил еси, наполняюще меру кровопийцев, отца и матери твоей и деда. Яко отец твой и мати, иже всем ведомо, колико погубили, так же и дед твой, со Гречкою бабою твоею, сына предобраго Иоанна, от первыя жены своея, от Тверския княжны святые Марии рожденна, наимужественнейшаго и преславнаго в богатырских исправлениях, и от него рожденнаго, боговенчаннаго внука своего, царя Димитрия, с материю его святою Еленою, оваго смертоносным ядом, а того многолетным заключением темничным, последи же удавлением погубиша, отрекшись и забывшись любови сродста. И не удовлевся тем! К тому брата единоутробнаго, Андрея Углицкого, мужа зело раз-

---

[1] See above, pp. 8–9.
[2] For the murder of Metropolitan Philipp, see below, pp. 240–1.
[3] Lit. "the abundance of your majesty's wickedness".
[4] Matt. xxiii. 32.
[5] Ivan Ivanovich died of gout in 1490; it is most unlikely that Ivan III had anything to do with his death. Sofia Palaeologa, "the Greek", Ivan's second wife, may have been suspected of having a hand in her stepson's death, as the doctor who treated him had in fact been brought to Moscow

ferocity of Herod were announced to us, our innermost parts were disturbed, our hearts trembled, our vision was dimmed, our mind was blunted. Or what is firm in the feelings of man when the multitude of evils destroys the majesty of virtues?"[1] And again, a little lower: "Rightly were our innermost parts disturbed and our hearts trembled, for Herod defiled the Church, removed the priesthood"—just as you destroyed, if not John the Baptist, then Archbishop Philipp and other holy men[2]—"befouled the priestly order, shattered the kingdom; what there was of piety, of rules, of life, of customs, of faith, of instruction—he ruined all this and put it to confusion. Herod —the torturer of citizens and warriors, the robber, the destroyer of his friends"; but your majesty's wickedness is still greater,[3] for with your children of darkness you not only destroy your friends, but also you lay waste the whole holy Russian land, you, the pillager of their houses and the murderer of sons (from which may God protect you, and may the Lord, the everlasting king, not allow this to be!). For already this, as it were, hangs on the edge of the sabre, since you have already slain, if not sons, then kinsmen and brothers of those close to your kin, filling up the measure of the bloodthirsty ones,[4] your father and your mother and your grandfather. Not only did your father and mother, as everyone knows, kill many people, but also your grandfather together with your grandmother, the Greek, killed his son Ioann, most excellent and glorious in exploits of valour, who was born of his first wife, the holy princess Maria of Tver', and his grandson, Tsar Dmitry, crowned by God, together with his holy mother Elena,—the former was killed with deadly poison and the latter was imprisoned for many years and then strangled, for he [Ivan III] had renounced and forgotten his love of kinship.[5] And he was not satisfied with that! As well as this he put his own[6] brother, Andrey of Uglich, a man of great intellect

by Sofia's brother. Ivan III's grandson, Dmitry Ivanovich (Ivan Ivanovich's son), who was crowned grand prince of Vladimir, Moscow and All Russia in 1498, fell from favour in 1502 and was sent to prison where he died, or was killed, seven years later. See Fennell, *Ivan the Great*, pp. 334, 337, 342.

[6] Lit. "of one womb".

умнаго и мудраго, тяжкими веригами в темнице за малые дни удавил, и двух сынов его, от сесец матерних оторвавши. О умиленно ко услышанию и тяжко ко изречению! Человеческая злость в толикую презлость превозрастаемо, паче же от християнских начальников! — многолетным заключением темничным нещадно поморил. Князя Симеона же, глаголемаго Ряполовского, мужа зело пресильнаго и разумнаго, влекомаго от роду великаго Владимера, главным посечением убил. И других братию свою, ближних ему в роде, овых разогнал до чюждых земель, яко Верейскаго Михаила и Василия Ярославича; а других, во отроческом веку еще сущих, тамо же темничным заключением, на скверной и проклятой заветной грамоте — о увы, о беда ко слышанию тяжка — заклинающе сына своего Василья, повелел неповинных погубити неотрочне. Тако же сотворили и иным многим, ихъже, долготы ради писания, зде оставляется. Ко предреченному Златоустову возвращаюся, о Ироде пишущу: "Окресных, рече, мужеубийца, напаяюще землю кровию, в жажде крове содержался". Сия Златоустый о Ироде во слове своем рече, и прочие.

О царю, прежде зело любимый[a] от нас! не хотел бы малыя сея части презлости твоей изрещи, но преодолен бых и принужден любовию Христа моего, и ревностию любви распаляхся по мученицех, от тебя избиенных неповинне, братиях наших. Яко и от тебя самаго не токмо слышах, но и видех и делом исполняемо, и о сем, еще аки хвалящеся, глаголал еси: "Аз, рече, избиенных от отца и деда моего одеваю гробы их драгоценными аксамиты и украшаю раки неповинне избиенных праведных." Се Господне слово збылося на тебя, к Жидам реченное: А сего ради, рече, согласуете и соблаговоляете, наполняюще меру, делы

[a] Patr., T. любимых: Ar.

---

[1] Cf. *Correspondence*, pp. 210–11. Andrey Vasil'evich was imprisoned in 1491 and died in prison two years later; it is not certain if he died a natural death. His two sons were imprisoned in Pereyaslavl'. See Fennell, *Ivan the Great*, pp. 304–5.

and wisdom, in heavy chains and after a few days in prison had him strangled; and he tore his [Andrey's] two sons from their mother's breasts—O pitiful to hear and hard to utter! Human wickedness which has been made into such extreme evil, especially by Christian rulers!—and mercilessly killed them by many years of imprisonment.[1] And Prince Semen Ryapolov-sky, a man of great strength and understanding, who was descended from the great Vladimir, he killed by beheading.[2] And as for others of his cousins who were close to him in kin, some he drove away to foreign lands, like Mikhail of Vereya and Vasily Yaroslavich,[3] while others, imprisoned while still in their childhood—alas! O calamity, grievous to the ear!—he ordered, innocent though they were, to be killed without fail, adjuring his son Vasily in his foul accursed will to do this. Such things were done to many others too, but for brevity's sake they are here omitted. I return to what Chrysostom wrote about Herod: "The murderer of those around him, he soaked the earth in blood and persisted in blood-thirstiness." These things Chrysostom said in his sermon on Herod, and so forth.

O tsar, formerly most loved by us, I would rather not tell of this small part of your wickedness, but I have been overcome and forced by the love of my Christ, and I have been enflamed by the zeal of my love for the martyrs, our brothers, who were slain in their innocence by you. For I have not only heard this from you yourself, but I have even seen these things per-formed in action, and you yourself, still boasting, said: "I clothe the tombs of those who were slain by my father and by my grandfather with costly velvets and I garnish the sepulchres of the righteous[4] who were slain in their innocence." Lo, the word of the Lord which He spoke to the Jews has come to pass upon you: "Wherefore you agree and allow, filling the measure,

[2] For the arrest and execution of S. I. Ryapolovsky, see *ibid.* pp. 338 *sq.* For the expression влеком от рода великого Владимира, see *Corres-pondence*, p. 182.

[3] Mikhail of Vereya was not "driven away" by Ivan III: his son Vasily was—to Lithuania (see Fennell, *Ivan the Great*, pp. 307 *sq.*). For the fate of Vasily Yaroslavich, ex-prince of Serpukhov and Borovsk, see *Correspondence*, p. 210, n. 3.

[4] Matt. xxiii. 29.

презлыми, убивство презлости отцов ваших, и показуете сами себе, сиречь свидетельствуете сами о собе, иже есте сынове убийцов исповедающеся. А от тебя и от твоих кромешников, твоим повелением, безсчисленных убиенных мучеников кто будет украшати гробы и позлащати раки их? О воистинну смех достойно, со многим плачем смешенным, и непотребное сие отнюдь, аще бы было то от сынов твоих действуемо, которые бы хотели, от чего Боже сохрани, меру твою сохраняти. Но яко, а ни Бог, а ни те избиенные от человекоубийцов древних того не желали, иже бы неповинне избиенни были, тако и от сынов, произволением злым согласующих отцем своим, не желают сего по смерти, не токмо гробом и ракам украшаемым и позлащаемым быти, но и самым величаемым и похваляемым; но праведные от праведных, мученики от кротких и по закону Божию жительствующих похваляеми и почитаеми быти достоят. А сему уже и конец положим, понеже и сие краткое сего ради произволихом написати, да не отнюдь в забвение приидут, ибо того ради славныя и нарочитыя исправления великих мужей от мудрых человеков историями описашася, да ревнуют им грядущие роды; а презлых и лукавых пагубные и скверные дела того ради пописани, иже бы стреглись и соблюдались от них человецы, яко от смертоносных ядов, или поветрия, не токмо телеснаго, но и душевнаго. Тако же и мы вкратце написахом малую часть, яко прежде многажды рехом, все оставляющу Божию суду нелицеприятному, хотящему воздати и сокрушити главы врагов своих, аж и до влас приходящих во прегрешениях своих, сиречь: отомстит и намалейшую обиду убогих своих, от пресильных; и паки той же: озлобления ради нищих и воздыхания убогих, ныне воскресну, глаголет Господь: положуся во спасение и не обинюся о нем; яко инде тем же пророком рекл: помыслил еси, рече, беззаконие, аки был бы тебе подобен; обличю тя

---

[1] A somewhat incoherent amalgam of Matt. xxiii. 31–2 and Luke xi. 48.
[2] Ps. lxviii. 21.

the most wicked deeds of your fathers, most wicked murder, and you show yourselves, that is to say you bear witness unto yourselves, confessing that you are the children of murderers."[1] But who will garnish the tombs and gild the sepulchres of those countless martyrs killed by you and, at your command, by your children of darkness? Oh, it would indeed be worthy of laughter mixed with much weeping and completely indecorous, were this to be done by your sons who might wish—God forbid! —to preserve your measure! But just as neither God nor those slain by the murderers of old desired that they be slain without guilt, so too they have no desire that after death their tombs and sepulchres be garnished and gilded and that they themselves be glorified and praised by the sons who correspond to their fathers in evil intent. But the righteous ought to be praised and esteemed by the righteous, the martyrs—by the meek and by those who live according to the law of God.

But let us now put an end to this, for I only wanted to write a brief account of this so that men should not completely forget —this is the reason why the glorious and distinguished exploits of the great have been described by wise men in histories, so that coming generations might emulate them; while the pernicious and foul deeds of wicked, cunning men are written of, so that men might beware and preserve themselves from them, as from deadly poisons or pestilence, not only bodily but also spiritual. And so too we have briefly written down a small part, as I have said many times before, leaving all the rest to the impartial judgement of God, who will repay and will wound the head of the enemies, even to the hair of those who go on in their trespasses,[2] that is to say: He will avenge even the least wrong done to His needy ones by the mighty; and again, likewise: for the oppression of the poor, for the sighing of the needy, now will I arise, saith the Lord: I will place myself in salvation and will speak freely about him;[3] and in another place He said through the same prophet: "You thought it a sin that I should be like you; I will reprove you and set your sins before your

---

[3] Ps. xii. 5. Cf. the text of the A.V.: "I will set him in safety from him that puffeth at him." The Greek text of the LXX reads as follows: θήσομαι ἐν σωτηρίᾳ, παρρησιάσομαι ἐν αὐτῷ.

и поставлю пред лицем твоим грехи твоя; аки бы рекл: аще не покаетеся о неправдах своих и о обидах убогих Закъхсеевым покаянием. А к тому до наилепшей памяти тамо живущим оставляю, понежь аз, еще во среду беды тое презелные, отъидох от отечества моего; а уже и тогда виденнаго и слышаннаго о таковых злостях и гонениях не могл бы на целу книгу написати, яко вмале и вкратце воспомянух о сем в предисловию, от нас написанном на книгу словес Златоустовых, глаголемую Новый Моргарит, емуж начало: "В лето осмыя тысящи, веку звериннаго, яко глаголет во святой Апоколепси", и прочие. Но достоит ми убиенных оных без правды благородных и светлых мужей, — светлых, глаголю, не токмо в родех, но и в обычаех, — воспомянути, колико память ми снесет, паче же благодать Святаго Духа подаст, уже во старости немощным телом сущу, бывшу ми паче же бедами и напастьми от ту живущих человеков и всякими ненавистьми обьяту. Аще что и забудется, да оставитца ми, молю, от острозрительных в разуме, и в памяти должайшей и неутружденно сущих. Се уже по возможности моей начну изчитати имена благородных мужей и юнош, паче же достоит со дерзновением нарицати их — страдальцов и[a] новых мучеников, неповинных сущих, избиенных.

[a] T. a: Ar.

---

[1] Ps. l. 21. Again there is considerable discrepancy between the text of the LXX, which the Church Slavonic version follows, and that of the A.V.

face."[1] It was as though He said: if you do not repent with the repentance of Zacchaeus for your unrighteousness and the wrongs you have done to the needy. Furthermore I leave these things to the excellent memory of those who live in that country, for in the very midst of that most grievous calamity I departed from my fatherland; and I would not have been able to write a whole book about what I saw and heard at that time of such evils and persecutions—I mentioned this briefly and in short in the introduction to the book of the sayings of Chrysostom called The New Pearl, which begins: "In the year eight thousand, the age of the beast, as is said in the holy Revelation", and so forth.[2] But I must mention those noble and brilliant men (brilliant, I say, not only by birth but in their ways) who were unjustly slain, in so far as my memory permits and, especially, the grace of the Holy Spirit grants, for in my old age my body is already weak and furthermore I have been beset with misfortunes and troubles and all kinds of hatred by those who live here. Should I forget anything, may it be forgiven me, I pray, by those who are sharp-sighted in understanding and who have a long and unwearied memory. Now, to the best of my ability I shall begin to enumerate the names of those noble men and youths—indeed I must name them with boldness— the sufferers and the new martyrs, who were slain in their innocence.

[2] See Kurbsky's Introduction to his *Novy Margarit* ("New Pearl"). Ustryalov, *Skazaniya*, pp. 269 *sq.*

VI

Скоро по Алексееве смерти и по Селивестрову изгнанию
воскурилося гонение великое, и пожар лютости в земле
Руской возгорелся; и гонение воистинну таковое неслыханное не токмо в Руской земле никогда же бывало а ни у
древних поганских царей: бо и при нечестивых мучителех[a]
християня, исповедающие веровати Христу и богом поган-
ским ругающися, имаеми и мучими были, а неисповедающих
и крыемых внутрь себя веру, аще и ту стоящих, аще и
знаемых, аще и братию и сродников, не имано, а ни мучено.
А наш новоявленный зверь первие начал сродников Алексе-
евых и Селивестровых писати имяна, а не токмо сродных,
но о ком послышал от[b] тех же клеветников своих, и друзей
и соседов знаемых, аще и мало знаемых, многих же отнюдь
и не знаемых, их богатеств ради и стяжания, оклеветаемо
от тех, многих имати повелел и мучити различными муками;
а других множайших ото имений их из домов изгоняти в
дальные грады. А про что же тех мучил неповинных? Про
то, понеже земля возопияла о тех праведных в неповинном
изгнанию, нарекающе и кленуще тех предреченных ласкателей, соблазнивших царя; он же вкупе с ними, ово аки
оправдаяся предо всеми, ово яко стрегущесь чаровства, не
вем якого, мучити повелел оных, ни единого, ни дву, но
народ цел, ихъже имян тех неповинных, яже в тех муках
помроша, множества ради исписати невозможно.

Тогда-то убиенна Мария преподобная, нарицаемая Могда-
лыня, с пятьми сынами своими; понеже была родом
Ляховица, потом исправилися в правоверие, и была великая
и превосходная посница, многажды в год единова в седмицу

---

[a] Pog., T. мучителей: Ar.　　　[b] Patr., Pog. о: Ar.

VI

Soon after the death of Aleksey and the banishment of Sil'vestr a great persecution flared up and a fire of ferocity blazed in the Russian land; and indeed there had never before been such unheard-of persecution, not only in the Russian land but even at the time of the ancient pagan tsars: for even under those impious tormentors, while Christians who confessed their belief in Christ and reviled the pagan gods were seized and tortured, those who did not confess their beliefs but hid them within themselves,—even if they were standing there [with those who openly confessed], even if they were known [to be believers], even if they were their brothers or relatives—were not seized and were not tortured. But this beast of ours, who has recently appeared, first of all began to proscribe the relatives of Aleksey and Sil'vestr—and not only their relatives, but anybody he heard about from those accusers of his,—and their friends and neighbours and those who were known, however slightly, to be their friends and neighbours, and even many of those who were not recognized at all as such, were accused by them because of their wealth and possessions; and he ordered many to be seized and subjected to various forms of torture, and very many others to be banished from their estates and houses to distant towns. And why did he persecute those innocent men? Because the land cried out on behalf of those just men who had been banished in their innocence, naming and cursing those above-mentioned flatterers who had seduced the tsar; and he, together with them, now as it were justifying himself before all men, now on his guard against I know not what sorcery, ordered them to be tortured—not one, nor two, but a whole race: it would be impossible to enumerate the names of all the guiltless ones who died in those tortures, there are so many of them.

At that time the venerable Maria Magdalina was put to death with her five sons. She was by birth a Pole; later she was converted to Orthodoxy. She was a great and excellent faster, many times a year eating only once a week, and to such an

вкушающи, и так во святом вдовстве провозсиявшия, яко на преподобном теле ея носити ей вериги тяжкие железные, тело порабощающе, да духу покорит его; и прочих святых дел ея и добродетелей исписати тамо живущим оставлю. Оклеветана же пред царем, аки бы то была чаровница и Алексеева согласница, того ради ея погубити повелел и со чады ея, и многих других с нею; понеже той был Алексей не токмо сам добродетелен, но и друг и причастник, яко Давыд рече, всем боящимся Господа и сообщник всем хранящим заповеди его, и колько десять имел прокаженных в дому своем, тайне питающе и обмывающи[a] их, многажды же сам руками своими гной их отирающи.[b]

Но тогда ж убиен в том гонению един муж Иоан, нареченный Шишкин, со женою и з детками; сродник был Алексеев и муж воистинну праведный и зело разумный, в роде благороден и богат. Потом по летех двух, або трех, убиенни[c] благороднии мужие: Данило, брат единоутробный Алексеев, и с[d] сыном Тархом, яже был еще во младенческом веку, лет аки двунадесять, и тесть Данила оного, Петр Туров, и Феодор, и Алексей и Андрей Сатины, ихже была сестра, за Алексеем предреченным, и других с ними. А Петру оному, аки за месяц пред смертию, видение божественное дивное явилося, проповедающее смерть мученическую — яже мне сам исповедал, — которое ту, краткости ради писания, оставляю.[e]

ᵃ Patr., Pog. обмывающа: Ar.   ᵇ Patr., Pog. отирающа: Ar.
ᶜ Patr. убиенна: Ar.   ᵈ Т. с omitted in Patr. and Pog.   ᵉ Т. оставляют: Ar.

---

[1] Who Maria Magdalina was is not known; only Kurbsky mentions her.
[2] Ps. cxix. 63.
[3] Lit. "several tens of lepers".
[4] In March 1563 M. Ya. Morozov, who at the time was one of the *voevody* of Smolensk, reported to Ivan that Ivan Shishkin-Ol'gov, a close relative of Adashev, and V. Funikov, who were stationed at Starodub, planned to hand over the town to the king of Poland. They were both arrested and sent to Moscow. Shishkin's execution presumably took place

extent did she shine forth in her holy widowhood that she wore
heavy iron chains on her venerable body, enslaving her flesh
in order to subject it to the spirit. As for her other holy deeds
and virtues, I leave it to those who live there [i.e. in Russia] to
enumerate them. She was accused before the tsar of having
been a sorceress and a confederate of Aleksey, and so he ordered
her and her children to be put to death, and many others with
her;[1] for that Aleksey was not only virtuous himself, but, as
David said, the friend and companion of all them that fear the
Lord and the accomplice of all them that keep His precepts;[2]
and he would keep scores of sick men[3] in his house, secretly
feeding them and washing them, and many a time wiping their
sores with his own hands.

And at that time, during that persecution, a man by the
name of Ioann Shishkin was put to death together with his wife
and little children; he was a relation of Aleksey and a man of
true righteousness and great wisdom, noble of birth and rich.[4]
Then, about two or three years after, the following noble men
were put to death: Danilo, Aleksey's own brother,[5] with his
son Torkh who was still a child of about twelve years old, and
Danilo's father-in-law, Petr Turov, and Fedor, Aleksey and
Andrey Satin, whose sister was married to the Aleksey about
whom I have been talking, and others with them. And there
appeared to Petr [Turov] about a month before his death a
wondrous divine vision announcing his martyr's death—he told
me about it himself;[6] I must leave it out, however, in order to
keep my story short.

in the late spring of 1563. See R. G. Skrynnikov, *Kurbsky i ego pis'ma*,
p. 104; A. A. Zimin, *Sostav Boyarskoy dumy*, p. 71.
  [5] See above, p. 169, n. 6.
  [6] Kurbsky's chronology would appear to be at fault here. If D. and T.
Adashev, P. Turov and the three Satin brothers were executed "about two
or three years after [Shishkin's execution]", the date would be 1565 or 1566.
As, however, Turov himself narrated his "vision" to Kurbsky and as
Kurbsky could only have seen Turov for the last time in March 1563 (see
Skrynnikov, *Kurbsky i ego pis'ma*, p. 104, n. 42), the execution must have
taken place in or around April 1563, probably shortly after that of Shishkin.
Thus "two or three years after" must refer to the time which elapsed after
the removal of A. Adashev and Sil'vestr (1560). Cf. Zimin, *Sostav Boyarskoy
dumy*, p. 71.

Паки убит от него тогда князь Дмитрей Овчинин, егоже отец зде много лет страдал за него и умре ту. Сие вызлужил на сына! Бо еще во юношеском веку, аки лет двадесяти или мало боле, заклан от самого его руки.

Тогда же убиен от него князь Михайло, глаголемый Репнин, уже в сиглитском сану сущ. А за что же убиен и за якую вину? Начал пити, с некоторыми любимыми ласкатели своими, оными предреченными великими, обещанными дьяволу, чашами, идеже и он по прилучаю призван был — хотяще бо его тем аки в дружбе себе присвоити — и упившися начал и с^a скоморохами в машкарах плясати, и сущие пирующие с ним; видев же сие бесчиние, он муж нарочитый и благородный начал плакати и глаголати ему, иже не достоит ти, о царю християнский, таковых творити. Он же начал нудити его, глаголюще: "Веселися и играй с нами!" и взявши машкару класти начал на лице его; он же отверже ю и потоптал и рече: "Не буди ми се безумие и безчиние сотворити, в советническом чину сущу мужу!" Царь же, ярости исполнився, отогнал его ото очей своих, и по коликих днех потом, в день неделный, на всенощном бдению стоящу ему в церкви, в час чтения евангельского, повелел воином бесчеловечным и лютым заклати его, близу самого олтаря стояща, аки агнца Божия неповиннаго.

И тое же нощи убити повелел синглита своего князя Юрья, глаголемаго Кашина, тако же ко церкви грядуща^b на молитву утренную: и заклан на самом празе церковном, и наполниша помост церковный весь кровию его святою.

^{a} Pog.   c omitted in Ar. and Patr. ^{b} Pog.   грядуще: Ar., Patr.

---

[1] Prince Dmitry Fedorovich Ovchinin-Obolensky was executed probably in 1564. See Zimin, *Sostav Boyarskoy dumy*, p. 72, n. 364; Skrynnikov, *Kurbsky i ego pis'ma*, p. 109. According to the Italian traveller Guagnini he was killed for accusing Ivan's favourite, Fedor Basmanov, of pederastic relations with the tsar. His father, Fedor Vasil'evich Telepnev-Ovchina-Obolensky, *namestnik* and *voevoda* of Starodub, was taken prisoner by the Lithuanians in July 1535 (*PSRL* VIII, p. 290; cf. S. B. Veselovsky, *Sinodik*, p. 318, where the date is given erroneously as 1527). Dmitry must, therefore, have been nearer thirty than twenty.

And at that time Prince Dmitry Ovchinin was put to death by him—his father suffered here [i.e. in Poland–Lithuania] for many years on his [Ivan IV's] behalf and died here. Thus did the tsar repay his son! For while he was still a youth, about twenty years old or a little more, he was slain by his very hand.[1]

And at that time Prince Mikhaylo Repnin, who already held the rank of counsellor,[2] was put to death by him. But why was he killed, for what offence? The tsar began drinking from those great beakers, pledged to the devil, which I have talked about above,[3] with certain favourite flatterers of his, and he [Repnin] was, as it happened, summoned—for he [Ivan] wanted thereby to attach him to himself in friendship. And having drunk his fill the tsar began dancing in masks together with the *skomorokhi*,[4] and so did those who were feasting with him. Now when that distinguished and noble man saw this indecorum, he began to weep and to say to him: "It is not fitting for you, O Christian tsar, to do such things." But the tsar began to press him, saying: "Be cheerful and play with us", and taking a mask he started putting it on his face; but he [Repnin] threw it away and trampled on it and said: "May I not perform such indecorous and mad acts, I who am a man of the rank of counsellor!" And the tsar was filled with fury and banished him from his sight. And a few days later, on Sunday, when he was standing in church during the all-night vigil,[5] at the time of the reading of the Gospel, he ordered his inhuman and fierce soldiers to slay him as he stood near the very altar like an innocent lamb of God.

And on the same night he ordered his counsellor, Prince Yury Kashin, to be put to death while he too was on his way to church for Matins; and he was slain on the very threshold of the church and the floor of the church was covered with his holy blood.[6]

---

[2] I.e. was a member of the Boyar Duma.

[3] See above, p. 163.

[4] See above, p. 23, n. 4.

[5] I.e. the service consisting of Vespers and Matins.

[6] Princes Mikhail Repnin-Obolensky and Yury Ivanovich Kashin-Obolensky, both members of the Boyar Duma, were executed on 31 January 1564 (Skrynnikov, *Kurbsky i ego pis'ma*, p. 106; Zimin, *Sostav Boyar-*

Потом убиен того Юрья брат, князь Иоан. И сродник их князь Дмитрей, глаголемый Шовырев, на кол посажен. И глаголют его день быти жива и аки не чювши муки тоя лютыя: на коле, яко на престоле седящ, воспевал канон изо уст Господу нашему Исусу Христу, а другий канон благодарственный пречистой Богородицы, с ними же вкупе правило немалое, глаголемое акафист, еже в нем замыкается все плотское Божие смотрение; и по скончанию пения оного, дух святой предал Господеви. И тогда же и других княжат немало того же роду побито; а стрыя тех княжат Дмитрея, глаголемаго Курлетева, постричи во мнихи повеле — неслыханное беззаконие, — силою повеле, всеродне, сиречь со женою и с сущими малыми детками, плачющих, вопиющих. А по колевых летех подавлено их всех. А сей был князь Дмитрей муж совершенъный и нарочитый в разуме синклит, избранный в роде.[a]

Потом убьен от него Петр Оболенский, глаголемый Сребреный, синклитским саном украшен и муж нарочит в воинстве и богат. Потом того же роду княжат побиенно: Александра Ярославова и князя Владимера Курлетова, сыновца оного Дмитрея. И были те оба, паче же Александр, мужие воистинну ангелом подобные жительством и разумом; бо были так искусны в книжном разуме православных догмат, иже все священные писания во устех имели; к тому и в военных делех светлы и нарочиты, по роду влекомы от великого Владимера, от пленицы великого князя Михаила Черниговского, яже убиен от безбожнаго Батыя за то, иже

[a] Ar. избранные роды: Т.

---

skoy dumy, p. 72). For the details of their military careers, see Veselovsky, *Sinodik*, pp. 328, 293.

In the beginning of his first letter to Ivan, Kurbsky asks the tsar: "why have you spilt their [the boyars'] holy blood in the churches of God...and stained the thresholds of the churches with their blood of martyrs?" (*Correspondence*, pp. 2–3).

[1] Princes Ivan Ivanovich Kashin and Dmitry Andreevich Shevyrev, both members of the Obolensky family, were executed "for their great treacherous deeds" together with A. B. Gorbaty (see below, pp. 184–5) in February 1565 (*PSRL* XIII, p. 395).

Then the brother of this Yury, Prince Ioann, was put to death, and their relative, Prince Dmitry Shevyrev, was impaled. And they say that he was alive for a whole day and that he did not feel that fierce pain: when on the stake, as it were sitting on a throne, he sang a canon to our Lord Jesus Christ and another canon of thanksgiving to the most pure Mother of God, and as well as these a long office called an acathistus, in which is enclosed all God's human Providence; and when he had finished singing this he gave up his holy spirit to the Lord.[1] And at that same time several other princes of the same kin were killed; he ordered Dmitry Kurlyatev, the uncle of those princes, to be forcibly tonsured—an unheard-of crime—with all his family, that is to say with his wife and his little children at the breast, weeping and wailing. And after a few years they were all strangled. And this Prince Dmitry was a man of integrity and excellent birth and a counsellor distinguished for his wisdom.[2]

Then Petr Obolensky-Serebryany was killed by him, a man honoured with the rank of counsellor, distinguished in warfare, and rich.[3] Then the following princes of the same family were put to death: Aleksandr Yaroslavov and Prince Vladimir Kurlyatev, the nephew of Dmitry Kurlyatev. And both of them, especially Aleksandr, were truly like angels in their way of life and in their wisdom; for they were so versed in the bookish wisdom of the Orthodox teachings that they had all the holy scriptures on their lips; furthermore, they were brilliant and distinguished in military matters, and they traced their descent from the great Vladimir, from the branch of Grand Prince Mikhail of Chernigov, who was slain by the godless

[2] Or, perhaps, according to another reading (T.), "a member of the Chosen Council". For information on D. I. Kurlyatev (Shkurlyatev)-Obolensky, see *Correspondence*, pp. 89, n. 6, 96–7, 190–1. Kurlyatev was disgraced for "his great treacherous deeds" on 29 October 1562 (*PSRL* xiii, p. 344).

[3] Prince Petr Semenovich Obolensky-Serebryany, a distinguished general and a member of the Boyar Duma, was executed in 1571 (see Zimin, *Sostav Boyarskoy dumy*, pp. 64, 78). According to an interpolation in the Sinodal MS. of the Nikon Chronicle (*PSRL* xiii, p. 238) P. S. Serebryany was a member of Lobanov-Rostovsky's conspiracy during the tsar's illness in 1553 (see below, p. 188, n. 1).

боги его насмевал и Христа Бога пред мучителем, так сильным и грозным, со дерзновением проповедал. Но и те сродницы его, кровию венчавшеся, приложени суть, пострадавшия неповинне, к пострадавшему за Христа, и преставлени мученики к мученику. Тогда же убиен от него княжа Суздальское Александр, глаголемый Горбатый, со единочадным своим сыном Петром, в первом цвете возраста, аки в седминадесяти летех. И того же дня убиен с ним шурин его Петр Ховрин, муж Гретцкого роду, зело благородного и богатого, сын подскарбия земского; а потом и брат его Михаил Петрович. О том-то Александре Горбатом воспомянух, пишучи повесть о взятью Казанском; бо те княжата Суздальские влекомы от роду великого Владимера, и была на них власть старшая Руская, между всеми княжаты, боле дву сот лет, и владел от них един Андрей,ᵃ княжа Суздальское, Волгою рекою, аж до моря Каспиского, от негоже, памятамись, и великие княжата Тверские изыдоша, яко лутче о сем знаменует в летописной книге Руской. Но и той был, новоубиенный Александр,

ᵃ тех же той был княжат Суждальских сродичь Нижнаго Новаграда отчичь славный богатырь в землях Руских князь Иоанн крепкой лук. Аще бы о нем по ряду воспомянути, была бы целая повесть рыцерства его: in margin of Ar., Pog.; in text of Patr.

---

[1] See below, p. 200, n. 1.

[2] Prince Vladimir Konstantinovich Kurlyatev was *voevoda* in Polotsk in 1564–5 and in Bryansk in 1565–6. He is last mentioned as being alive in 1568 (see Veselovsky, *Sinodik*, p. 303). According to Kurbsky he was executed together with Chulkov, F. Bulgakov and G. S. Sidorov (in Epifan'?) some time between 1568 and 1570 (see below, pp. 224–5). Prince Aleksandr Ivanovich Yaroslavov is last mentioned as being alive in 1567 when he was *namestnik* in Novgorod-Seversky (see Veselovsky, *Sinodik*, p. 366). Both Kurlyatev and Yaroslavov were members of the Obolensky family.

[3] *Podskarbi* was a rank in Poland and Lithuania corresponding roughly to the Russian *kaznachey*.

Petr Petrovich's father, Petr Ivanovich Khovrin-Golovin, was in fact *kaznachey* during Vasily III's reign (Zimin, *O sostave dvortsovykh uchrezhdeniy*, pp. 187, 204). The ancestors of the Khovrin-Golovin family, Stefan Komnin and his son Grigory, emigrated to Russia in 1399 from Kaffa in the Crimea.

Baty for mocking his gods and boldly confessing Christ our God before so strong and dread a tormentor.[1] But those kinsmen of his, crowned with blood, who suffered in innocence, were joined to him who suffered for Christ, and martyrs were added to martyrs.[2]

Then the prince of Suzdal', Aleksandr Gorbaty, was put to death by him, together with his only son Petr, who was about seventeen years old and in the first flower of his youth. And on the same day his brother-in-law, Petr Khovrin, was put to death with him, a man of Greek stock, very noble and rich, the son of the State Treasurer,[3] and after that his brother too, Mikhail Petrovich.[4] I mentioned this Aleksandr Gorbaty when writing the story of the capture of Kazan';[5] the princes of Suzdal' trace their descent from the kin of the great Vladimir, and for more than two hundred years they owned the largest[6] districts amongst all the princes; and one of them, Andrey,[7] prince of Suzdal', owned [the land along] the Volga river right as far as the Caspian Sea, and from him, I remember, sprang the grand princes of Tver', as is better described in the Russian chronicle book. But that Aleksandr, who has recently been

[4] Prince Aleksandr Borisovich Gorbaty-Suzdal'sky, his son Petr, and the two Khovrin-Golovin brothers, Petr and Mikhail Petrovich, were executed together with I. I. Kashin and D. A. Shevyrev (see above, pp. 182–3) in February 1565 (*PSRL* xiii, p. 395; Zimin, *Sostav Boyarskoy dumy*, p. 73). Cf. the *posluzhny spisok*, or list of Boyar counsellors, which gives the date as 1566, *DRV*, vol. xx, p. 47. Cf. also the evidence of Taube and Kruse, the two Livonian adventurers in Ivan IV's service who deserted the tsar in 1571, where the same date is given for Gorbaty's execution (*Poslanie Taube i Kruze*, p. 38). The Khovrin-Golovins were related both to Gorbaty and to A. Adashev (Zimin, *ibid.*).   [5] See above, pp. 46–9.

[6] Or, perhaps, "theirs was the senior district" (i.e. appanage) or "the senior authority".

[7] A marginal note reads as follows: "a relative of these same princes of Suzdal' was the inheritor of Nizhny Novgorod, the glorious hero of the Russian lands, Prince Ioann Strong-Bow [or Stiff-Bow]. Were I to mention him properly there would be a whole story of his knightly deeds."

There was indeed a Prince Ivan Tugoy-Luk amongst the princes of Suzdal' (Ustryalov, *Skazaniya*, p. 318, n. 129). The Andrey here mentioned is either Andrey Bogolyubsky, grand prince of Rostov-Suzdal' (d. 1174), or Grand Prince Andrey of Suzdal' (d. 1264), from whom stemmed the princes of Suzdal'. The princes of Tver', however, stemmed from neither, but from Yaroslav Yaroslavich, fifth son of Grand Prince Yaroslav Vsevolodovich.

муж глубокого разума и искусный[a] зело в военных вещах, и к тому последователь тшаливой священных писаний, яко и при самой смерти их радостны и надежны быша, и неповинне от него посечени, яко агнцы Бога живаго. И глаголют о них при том бывшия и на то зрящи: егда уже приведены к самому посечению,[b] тогда глаголют сына его первие со потщанием приклонивша выю к мечю; отец же возбранив ему и рече: "О чадо превозлюбленное и единородный сыне мой! да не узрят очи мои отсечения главы твоея!" И первие сам княжа усечен; младенец же оный храбрый, взяв мученическую честную главу отца своего, и поцеловав, и возрев на небо, рече: "Благодарю тя, о царю веком, Исусе Христе Боже наш, царствующий со Отцем и со Святым Духом, иже сподобил еси нас неповинным убиенным быти, яко и сам от богоборных Жидов заклан еси, неповинный агнче! А сего ради приими души наша в животательные руце твои, Господи!" И, сие изрекши, приклонився под оскорд ко усечению главы своея святые. Со таковым упованием и со многою верою ко Христу своему отоидоша.

Тогда, в те же лета, або пред тем еще мало, убит за повелением его[c] княжа Ряполовское Дмитрей, муж в разуме многом и зело храбр, искусен же и свидетельствован от младости своей в богатырских вещах, бо не мало, яко всем тамо ведомо, выиграл битв над безбожными Измаильтяны, аж на дикое поле за ними далеко ходяще. Се выслужил! Главою заплатил. От жены и деток оторвал и внезапу смерти предати повелел.

Паки побиени от него того же лета княжата Ростовское Семен, Андрей и Василей и друзии с ними. Паки потом тех же княжат Ростовских, иже и здесь страдал за него, Василей

---

[a] Patr., Pog., T. искусные: Ar.   [b] T. посещению: Ar., Patr., Pog.   [c] T. сего: Ar.

---

[1] тшаливой: a corrupt form, probably derived from тщание. See below, p. 264, line 13.

[2] Lit. "for" or "as".

slain, was a man of deep understanding and highly skilled in military matters; furthermore, he was a zealous[1] follower of the holy scriptures, and[2] at their very death they [i.e. father and son] were joyful and full of hope, and they were slaughtered by him in their innocence, like lambs of the living God. And those who were present at their death and who saw them said of them: when they were led to the place of execution, then the son first of all bent his neck to the sword with zeal; but his father stopped him, saying: "O my dearly beloved child and only-begotten son! Let not my eyes behold the cutting-off of your head!" And the prince himself was the first to be beheaded; and the brave child took the holy martyr's head of his father and kissed it and looking up towards heaven said: "I thank thee, O King of Ages, Jesus Christ our God, who reigneth with the Father and the Holy Spirit, who hath deemed us worthy to be killed in our innocence, as Thou Thyself, the innocent lamb, wert slain by the God-destroying Jews. Therefore receive our souls in Thy life-giving hands, O Lord!" And having said this he bowed his holy head beneath the blade [lit. axe]. With such hope and with great faith he departed to his Christ.

Then, in those years, or a little before, Prince Dmitry Ryapolovsky was put to death at his orders—a man of much wisdom and great bravery, skilled and tested from his youth in deeds of valour, for, as is known to all men in Russia, he won not a few battles over the godless Ishmaelites, chasing far over the Wild Field[3] after them. This was his reward! He paid with his head. The tsar tore him from his wife and little children and ordered him to be put to a sudden death.[4]

Then again in that year the princes of Rostov, Semen, Andrey and Vasily, and others with them were put to death. Then another of those same princes of Rostov, Vasily Temkin, who had suffered here too [i.e. in Lithuania] on the tsar's be-

---

[3] I.e. the barren steppe-lands south of the Oka river.

[4] Dmitry Ivanovich Ryapolovsky was one of the members of I. P. Chelyadnin-Fedorov's conspiracy against Ivan IV (1567) (P. A. Sadikov, *Ocherki*, pp. 29–32; cf. below, p. 193, n. 4). He was executed together with Fedorov in September 1568 (S. M. Solov'ev, *Istoriya Rossii*, II, col. 169). For an account of his military career, see Veselovsky, *Sinodik*, p. 332.

Темкин и со сыном своим разсеканы от кромешников его, катов изобранных, за повелением его.

Паки убьен княжа Петр, глаголемый Щенятев, внук княжати Литовского Патрикея. Муж зело благородный был и богатый, и оставя все богатство и многое стяжание, мнишествовати был произволил, и нестяжательное, христоподражательное жительство возлюбил; но и тамо мучитель мучити его повеле, на железной сковраде огнем разженой[a] жещи и за ногти иглы бити. И в сицевых муках скончался. Тако же и единоколенных братию его, Петра, Иоанна, княжат нарочитых, погубил.

В те же лета побиты братия мои, княжата Ярославские, влекомые от роду княжати Смоленского, святаго Феодора Ростиславича, правнука великого Владимера Мономаха. Имяна их были: князь Феодор Львов, муж зело храбрый и святаго жительства, и от младости своей, аж до четыредесятного лета, служил ему верне, многажды над поганскими языки светлыя одоления поставлял, крововяще руку свою, паче же освящающе во крови бусурманской сущих врагов

[a] Patr., T. розженный: Ar.

---

[1] According to an interpolation in the Synodal copy of the Nikon Codex, Prince Semen Vasil'evich Lobanov-Rostovsky was one of the leading conspirators during the illness of Ivan IV in 1553; in 1554 he attempted to flee to Lithuania but was caught and disgraced (*Correspondence*, p. 96, n. 1). Prince Andrey Ivanovich Rostovsky-Katyrev was also a member of the same conspiracy (he was, however, made a member of the Boyar Duma in 1557). Both were executed *c.* 1566 (Zimin, *Sostav Boyarskoy dumy*, pp. 67, 73). One "Vasily Volk Rostovsky" is mentioned in Ivan's *Sinodik* (Veselovsky, *Sinodik*, p. 328).

As for Prince Vasily Ivanovich Temkin-Rostovsky, he was originally closely connected with the court of Prince Vladimir Andreevich of Staritsa. During the Livonian war he was taken prisoner, but later released. In 1567 he was accepted by Ivan IV as a member of the *Oprichnina*, in which his career was short but distinguished. In 1571 he was executed, probably for his shortcomings as C.-in-C. of the *Oprichnina* army in that year. For details of his life, see V. B. Kobrin, *Sostav oprichnogo dvora Ivana Groznogo*, pp. 76–8.

[2] During the minority of Ivan IV P. M. Shchenyatev was a close supporter of the Bel'sky faction and was banished to Yaroslavl' after the coup of January 1542 (*Correspondence*, p. 78, n. 2). By 1549 or 1550 he was a member of the Boyar Duma. According to the interpolations in the Nikon

half, was beheaded together with his son at the tsar's command by his children of darkness, his chosen executors.[1]

And Prince Petr Shchenyatev, the descendant of Prince Patriky of Lithuania, was put to death. He was a very noble and rich man; and abandoning all his wealth and many possessions he chose to become a monk, and he grew to love the way of life of the non-possessors and imitators of Christ. But even though he was a monk, the torturer ordered him to be tortured, to be burned on an iron pan which had been made red-hot on a fire and to have needles driven under his nails. And in such torments he died. And he also slew his [Shchenyatev's] cousins of the same kin, the distinguished princes, Petr and Ioann.[2]

And in those years my cousins, the princes of Yaroslavl', were put to death; they trace their descent from the prince of Smolensk, Saint Fedor Rostislavich, the descendant of the great Vladimir Monomakh. Their names were: Prince Fedor L'vovich, a man of great bravery and holy life, who from his youth to his fortieth year served the tsar faithfully and many times won brilliant victories over the pagan peoples, staining his hand with blood, or rather sanctifying it with the pagan

chronicle, he was a member of Rostovsky-Lobanov's conspiracy during the illness of Ivan IV in 1553 (*PSRL* xiii, p. 238), but he managed to avoid disgrace until 1565 (in October 1564 he was *voevoda* in Polotsk, *PSRL* xiii, p. 390. At the inception of the *Oprichnina* in January 1565 he was still a member of the Boyar Duma, *ibid.* p. 394). In the autumn of 1565, during the Tatar attack on Bolkhov (north of Orel) he was disgraced as a result of a squabble with other Russian commanders. Without the tsar's permission he took the tonsure. This failed to save him. In 1566 Ivan had him tortured. So severe was the torture that he died from it (see Sadikov, *Ocherki*, pp. 25–6). Taube and Kruse say that he was flogged to death together with Pronsky-Turuntay, i.e. in 1569 (see below, p. 192, n. 2). Zimin gives August 1565 as the date of his execution (*Sostav Boyarskoy dumy*, p. 62, n. 243).

Shchenyatev was the great-grandson of Vasily Yur'evich Patrikeev, who himself was the grandson of Patriky Narimuntovich.

"Petr and Ioann" were Shchenyatev's second cousins, Petr Andreevich and Ivan Andreevich Kurakin. The latter was forcibly tonsured in February 1565. The former was sent to "honourable exile" in Kazan' in the spring or summer of 1565 and was executed *c.* 1575 (i.e. probably *after* Kurbsky wrote his History). See Zimin, *Kogda Kurbsky napisal*, p. 307. These Kurakins may have been involved in Lobanov-Rostovsky's conspiracy in 1553 (see *PSRL* xiii, p. 238, where among his accomplices are mentioned "*Korakiny rodom*").

креста Христова; другаго князя Феодора, внука славнаго князя Феодора Романовича, яже прадеду того у царя, губителя нашего, в орде будучи, — даже еще в неволи были княжата Руские у[a] ординского царя и от его руки власти приимовали, — помог: за его попечением, на государство свое возведен бысть. Се так службы и доброхотствования прародителей наших ко своим прародителем воспомянул и заплатил! Княжата наши Ярославские никогда же от его прародителей не бывали отступни в бедах и в напастех их,[b] яко верные и доброхотныя братия, сущая по роду влекомы от единаго славнаго и блаженнаго Владимера Манамаха. За тем-то князем Феодором была сестра его, за двух рожденная, тщи князя Михаила Глинского, славнаго рыцаря, егоже погубила неповинне мати его, сущаго стрыя своего, обличающе ее за беззаконие. Тако же и других тое же пленицы княжат не мало погубил. Единого от них своею рукою булавою на смерть убил на Невле месте, идучи к Полотцу, реченного Иоанна Шаховского; и потом Василья и Александра и Михаила княжат, глаголемых Прозоровских, и других княжат того же роду, Ушатых нареченных, сродных братий их, сущих тех же княжат Ярославских роду, погубил всеродне: нонеже имели отчины великие, мню, негли ис того их погубил.

[a] Pog., T. и: Ar.   [b] T. иже: Ar., Patr., Pog.

---

[1] Who Princes Fedor L'vovich Yaroslavsky (or perhaps Fedor L'vov) and Fedor Romanovich Yaroslavsky were is not known. No Yaroslavsky is recorded as having helped Vasily II in his legal conflict with Yury Dmitrievich at the horde in 1432. For Fedor Rostislavich, prince of Yaroslavl' (d. 1299), the ancestor of Kurbsky and the princes of Yaroslavl', see *Correspondence*, pp. 6–7. Another unidentified Yaroslavsky prince, Ivan Semenovich, was mentioned by Ivan in his first letter to Kurbsky as an adherent of the "treacherous" Prince Andrey of Staritsa, Ivan's uncle (*ibid.* pp. 70–1).

[2] Fedor Yaroslavsky's wife was, therefore, first cousin of Elena Vasil'evna [Glinsky], Ivan IV's mother. For the death of his father-in-law, Mikhail L'vovich Glinsky in 1534, see Smirnov, *Ocherki*, pp. 33–44; Zimin, *Reformy*, pp. 230 sq.

[3] Ivan Shakhovskoy was evidently executed in January 1563 when Ivan IV halted in Nevel' on his way to Polotsk (Skrynnikov, *Kurbsky i ego pis'ma*,

blood of the enemies of the Cross of Christ; and another Prince Fedor, the descendant of the glorious Prince Fedor Romanovich, who aided the great-grandfather of this our pernicious tsar while he was in the horde (for Russian princes were indeed prisoners of the khan of the horde and used to receive their authority from his hand), and as a result of his efforts he [Vasily II] was raised to sovereignty. This is how he [Ivan IV] remembered and recompensed the service and well-wishing which our forefathers gave to his forefathers! Our princes of Yaroslavl', like true and well-wishing brothers who traced their descent from the same glorious and blessed Vladimir Monomakh, never left his forefathers during their times of trouble and adversity.[1] The former Prince Fedor [i.e. F. L. Yaroslavsky] was married to his second cousin, the daughter of Prince Mikhail Glinsky, that glorious knight, whom the tsar's mother put to death in his innocence (though he was her uncle), because he rebuked her for her transgression.[2] And also he put to death several others of that same family of princes. One of them named Ioann Shakhovskoy he personally slew with a mace at the town of Nevel' when he was on his way to Polotsk.[3] Then Princes Vasily, Aleksandr and Mikhail Prozorovsky and other princes of the same family, named Ushaty, their cousins, who were also of the same kin as the princes of Yaroslavl', were utterly destroyed by him; for they owned great patrimonies, and I think it was probably for this reason that he destroyed them.[4]

p. 104). The Shakhovskoy family was descended from Gleb Vasil'evich, great-grandson of Fedor Rostislavich of Yaroslavl'.

[4] The Prozorovskys and Ushatys were descended from Mikhail Davidovich, grandson of Fedor Rostislavich of Yaroslavl'. The Prozorovskys were evidently large landowners in the former principality of Yaroslavl'. See Ivan's remarks in his first letter to Kurbsky (*Correspondence*, pp. 190–1); cf. M. N. Tikhomirov, *Rossiya v XVI stoletii*, pp. 203, 210.

When the Prozorovskys and Ushatys were executed is not known, but it was probably after 1567, the date when Vasily Ivanovich Prozorovsky is last mentioned. His brother Aleksandr and his cousin Mikhail Fedorovich Prozorovsky (Kurbsky's brother-in-law) are last mentioned in 1566 and 1565 respectively (Veselovsky, *Sinodik*, p. 326). Kurbsky later on states that Nikita Ivanovich Prozorovsky was forced by Ivan IV to kill his brother Vasily. See below, pp. 288–9.

Потом Иоанна княжа Пронское, от роду великих князей Рязанских, мужа престаревшагося уже во днех, и от младости его служаща не токмо ему, еще и отцу его много лет, и многажды гетманом великим бывша и сигклитским саном почтенного. Последи же мнишество возлюбил и в монастыре едином остриже власы и отрекшеся всеа суеты мира сего, Христа своего ради. Он же так мужа престаревшаго в днех мнозех и во старости мастисте от чреды спасенныя извлече и в реце утопити повелел. И другаго княжа Пронское Василий, глаголемого Рыбина, погубил.

В той же день и иных не мало благородных мужей нарочитых воин, аки двести, избиенно; а нецыи глаголют и вящей.

Тогда же убил Владимера, стрыечного[a] брата своего, с матерью того Ефросиньею, княжною Хаванскою, яже беша от роду князя великого Литовского Алгерда, отца Ягайла короля Польского, и воистинну святую и постницу великую, во святом вдовстве и во мнишестве провосиявшую. Тогда же разстреляти с ручниц повелел жену брата своего Евдокию, княжну Одоевскую, тако же воистинну святую, и зело кроткую, и священных писаней искусную, и пения божественнаго всего навыкшую, и два младенцов, сынов брата своего, от тое святыя рожденных; единому было имя Василий, аки в десяти летех, а другий мнейший. Запамятах уже, яко было имя его; но лутчи в книгах животных написан, приснопамятных, на небесех, у самого Христа Бога нашего. И иныи мнози слузи их верныя избиенны, не токмо мужи и юноши благородные, но и жены и девицы светлых родов и благородных шляхецких.

[a] Patr., Pog. стричнаго: Ar.

---

[1] чреда in error for среда, "milieu", "society".

[2] Prince Ivan Ivanovich Pronsky-Turuntay, one of the leading supporters of Vladimir Andreevich of Staritsa in the succession crisis of 1553 (*PSRL* xiii, pp. 238, 525), was executed probably in 1569 (Zimin, *Sostav Boyarskoy dumy*, p. 74). Taube and Kruse say he was flogged to death with Shchenyatev (i.e. in August 1566); however, he was still alive in 1567/8. His cousin, Prince Vasily Fedorovich Pronsky-Rybin, was executed in late 1566 for objecting to Ivan IV's policy at the Zemsky Sobor of 1566, which had been

Then [he put to death] Ioann, prince of Pronsk, from the kin of the grand princes of Ryazan', a man of great old age, who from his youth had served not only the tsar, but also, for many years, his father, and who had many a time been his great *hetman* [i.e. commander-in-chief] and who had been honoured with the rank of counsellor. And later he grew to love monasticism and he took the tonsure in a certain monastery and renounced all the vanity of this world for the sake of his Christ. And the tsar dragged the old man, who was of great and venerable age, from his place[1] of salvation and ordered him to be drowned in the river. And he killed another prince of Pronsk, Vasily Rybin.[2]

And on that same day several other noble and distinguished warriors—about two hundred—were put to death; some say even more.

And then he put to death his first cousin[3] Vladimir together with his [Vladimir's] mother Evfrosinya, [*née*] Princess Khovansky, who was of the kin of Grand Prince Ol'gerd of Lithuania, the father of King Jagiello of Poland, a truly holy and truly great faster, who shone forth in holy widowhood and monasticism. Then he ordered to be shot by musket the wife of his cousin, Evdokia, [*née*] Princess Odoevsky, who was likewise truly holy and very meek and versed in the holy scriptures and an adept in all kinds of sacred singing, and also two infants, the sons of his cousin, who were born of that holy woman: one of them was called Vasily—he was about ten years old,— and the other was younger. I have already forgotten what his name was, but it is inscribed in the ever-memorable books of life, in the heavens, with Christ our God Himself. And many others of their true servants were slain, not only noble men and youths, but also wives and maidens of distinguished stock and well-born noble families.[4]

summoned to discuss the war with Lithuania (Zimin, *Sostav Boyarskoy dumy*, p. 73, n. 378; Zimin, *Zemsky sobor 1566*, pp. 230–1; Sadikov, *Ocherki*, p. 29).

[3] Lit. "his avuncular cousin". Vladimir was the son of his father's brother, Andrey Ivanovich.

[4] The execution of Prince Vladimir Andreevich took place in 1569 (Zimin, *Sostav Boyarskoy dumy*, p. 74, n. 399; cf. Ustryalov, *Skazaniya*, pp. 321–5). Ever since his illness in 1553, when Vladimir Andreevich had been

Потом убиен славный и между княжаты Рускими Михаил Воротынской и Микита княжа Одоевской, сродный его, со младенчики детками своими, един аки седми лет, а другий мнейший, и со женою его: всеродне погубленъно их, глаголют; его же была сестра, предреченная Евдокия святая, за братом царевым Владимером. А что же сему за вина была княжати Воротынскому? Негли тая точию: егда, по сожжению великого славнаго места Московского, многонароднаго, от Перекопскаго царя и по спустошению, умиленом и жалостном ко слышанию, Руския земли от безбожных варваров, аки год един спустя, той же царь Перекопский, хотяще уже до конца спустошити[a] землю оную и самого того князя великого выгнати из царства его, и поиде яко лев кровоядец, рыкая, розиня лютую пащеку на пожрения христиан,[b] со всеми силами своими бусурманскими; услышав же сие, наше чюдо забежал пред ним сто и двадесят мил с Москвы, аж в Новгород великий; а того Михаила Воротынского поставил с войском,[c] и яко могучи, земли оныя спустошенныя и окаянные бронити повелел. Он же, яко муж крепкий и мужественной, в полкоустроениях[d] зело искусный, с тем так сильным зверем бусурманским битву великую сведе: не дал ему распростертися, а ни на мнее воевати убогих християн; но бияшеся крепце зело с ним, и, глаголют, колько дней брань она пребывала. И поможе Бог християном, благоумнаго мужа полкоустроением, и падоша от воинства християнского бусурманские полки, и самого царя сынове два, глаголют, убиени, а един жив изыман на той-то битве; царь же сам едва в орду утече, а хоругвей

[a] Patr., Pog., T. спустошите: Ar. [b] Patr., T. на пожрении християны: Ar. [c] T. войским: Ar. [d] T. в полкоустроения же: Ar., Patr., Pog.

---

openly chosen by many of the boyars as candidate for the moribund tsar's throne, Ivan had bided his time, waiting, as it were, for a suitable opportunity to rid himself of his cousin, who afforded the obvious rallying-point for the discontented opposition. In 1567 a vast conspiracy, headed by I. P. Chelyadnin-Fedorov (see above, p. 187, n. 4), to kidnap Ivan during the autumn operations in Lithuania and hand him over to King Sigismund of Poland was discovered. Once again Vladimir Andreevich, who was a party

Then Mikhail Vorotynsky, glorious among the Russian princes, was put to death, as well as his relative, Prince Nikita Odoevsky,[1] with his little children—one about seven years old and the other less—and his wife: the whole family was destroyed, they say, for his [Odoevsky's] sister, the holy Evdokia, whom we have just mentioned, was married to Vladimir, the tsar's cousin. And what was the guilt of Prince Vorotynsky? Forsooth, only the following: when about a year after the burning of the great, glorious and many-peopled city of Moscow by the khan of Perekop and after the devastation of the Russian land by the godless barbarians, which is so grievous and piteous to the hearing, that same khan of Perekop, who wanted to devastate the land utterly and to drive the grand prince himself out of his tsardom, marched with all his Mussulman forces, roaring like a bloodthirsty lion with jaws gaping to swallow up Christians— then, hearing this, our wonder-tsar ran before him, a hundred and twenty miles from Moscow, as far as Novgorod the Great. And he placed Mikhail Vorotynsky at the head of the army and ordered him to defend that ravaged and hapless land as best he could. And he, like a strong and brave man, highly skilled in military matters, fought a mighty battle with that powerful Mussulman beast; he did not let him deploy and still less war on the wretched Christians; but he fought fiercely with him, and, they say, the battle lasted several days. And God helped the Christians, thanks to the military skill of that keen-witted man, and the Mussulman regiments fell at the hands of the Christian soldiers; and they say that two sons of the khan were killed and that one was captured alive during the very battle, while the khan himself barely escaped to his horde, running

to the plot, was designated by certain of the conspirators as successor to Ivan IV. When the conspiracy was discovered, Vladimir confessed all he knew to the tsar in an effort to save his neck. (Sadikov, *Ocherki*, pp. 29–34.)

[1] A. A. Zimin considers that the final section of Chapter VI (the execution of Vorotynsky and Odoevsky), as well as the final paragraph of Chapter VII (the execution of Morozov), were added by Kurbsky after he had finished his History in 1573. Vorotynsky, Odoevsky and Morozov were all put to death in the summer of 1573; theirs were chronologically the last executions to be mentioned by Kurbsky, with the exception of that of I. I. Khabarov (see below, pp. 210–11). (Zimin, *Kogda Kurbsky napisal*, pp. 306–7.)

великих бусурманских и шатров своих отбежал в нощи. На
той же битве и гетмана его славнаго, кровопийцу християнского, Дивея мурзу изымано жива; и всех тех, яко гетмана
и сына царева,[a] так и хоруговь царскую и шатры его послал
до нашего хороняки и бегуна, храброго же и прелютого на
своих единоплемянных и единоязычных, не противящихся
ему.

Что же воздал за сию ему службу? Послушай, молю,
прилежно прегорчайшия тоя и жалостныя ко слышанию
трагедии! Аки лето едино потом спустя, оного победоносца
и обранителя своего и всеа Руские земли изымати и связанна
привести и пред собою поставити повелел; и обретши единого раба его, ократшаго того господина своего — а мню,
научен от него, бо еще те княжата были на своих уделех, и
велия отчины под собою имели; околико тысящ с них по чту
воинства было слуг их имже он зазречи того ради губил
их[b] — и рече ему: "Се на тя свидетельствует слуга твой,
иже мя еси хотел счаровати и добывал еси на меня баб
шепчющих." Он же, яко княжа от младости своея святый,
отвещал: "Не научихся, о царю, и не навыкох от прародите-

[a] Patr. цареви: Ar.   [b] Patr., Pog., T. имже он зазречи того
ради губил их omitted in Ar.

---

[1] Divey-mirza was commander-in-chief of Devlet Girey's army. For his
behaviour on capture, see Staden, *Aufzeichnungen über den Moskauer Staat*,
pp. 78–9; and for his subsequent fate, see *Poslaniya Ivana Groznogo*, p. 641.

[2] Prince Mikhail Ivanovich Vorotynsky was one of the leading military
figures of Ivan IV's reign. He was one of the first to suffer disgrace and
imprisonment—in 1562 he was banished to Beloozero with his family
(Zimin, *Sostav Boyarskoy dumy*, p. 71). In 1565 he was pardoned, made a
member of the Boyar Council and given back his estates (*ibid.* p. 73; Sadikov,
Ocherki, p. 26. Cf., however, Veselovsky, *Sinodik*, p. 273; Skrynnikov,
Oprichnaya zemel'naya reforma, p. 249). In the summer of 1572 he was
appointed commander-in-chief of the Russian forces when Khan Devlet
Girey with 120,000 troops, including Turkish reinforcements, invaded
Russia (Ivan was in Novgorod at the time). He won a brilliant victory over
the Tatars on the river Lopasnya, 50 versts south of Moscow, after which
the khan was forced to retreat. In April 1573 he was on "bank service"
(i.e. in command of defensive forces on the Oka river) (Zimin, *Kogda
Kurbsky napisal*, p. 307). On 12 June 1573 he was executed with Odoevsky
and Morozov (Zimin, *Sostav Boyarskoy dumy*, p. 73). According to Sadikov,

away by night from his mighty Mussulman banners and tents. And in that same battle his glorious *hetman*, the drinker of Christian blood, Divey-mirza, was captured alive.[1] And he [Vorotynsky] sent all of them—the *hetman* and the khan's son, as well as the khan's banner and his tents—to our coward and runaway, who is brave and ferocious only when it comes to dealing with those of his own family and race who cannot resist him.[2]

And how did he reward him for this service? Listen attentively, I pray you, to this tragedy which is most bitter and piteous to the hearing. About a year afterwards he ordered the victor and defender of him and of all the Russian land to be seized and to be led to him in chains and to be placed before him. And having found a servant of his who had robbed his master—I think he had been instructed to do so by the tsar, for those princes were still masters of their appanages, and they had under them large patrimonies, and in the army their own servants numbered several thousands: it was because he coveted these that he destroyed them;[3]—the tsar said to Vorotynsky: "See, your servant bears witness against you, saying that you wanted to bewitch me and that you got whispering women to cast a spell over me." And he answered (for the prince had led a holy life from his youth on): "I have not learned, o tsar, nor

he was accused of sabotaging the artillery during Devlet Girey's invasion of 1571 and of plotting against Ivan.

Prince Nikita Romanovich Odoevsky, Vladimir Andreevich's brother-in-law, after a fairly distinguished military career, became a member of the *Oprichnina* in 1570. In July–August 1572 he was commander of the "Right Hand" in the army which repulsed Devlet Girey's invasion. In April 1573, like Vorotynsky and Morozov, he was on "bank service" on the Oka (Kobrin, *Sostav oprichnogo dvora*, pp. 53–4).

The real reason for the execution of Vorotynsky and Odoevsky is not known; Kobrin thinks it was connected with "Ivan's desire to liquidate the last appanages". Their wealth may have tempted Ivan, but a political cause seems more likely.

[3] The Vorotynskys and Odoevskys were the last of what might be called the "service appanage princes" who still controlled their estates in the trans-Oka districts with some degree of autonomy (Tikhomirov, *Rossiya v XVI stoletii*, p. 50). The Vorotynskys and Odoevskys were among the first of the so-called "Upper Oka princes" to transfer their allegiance to Moscow in the 70's and 80's of the fifteenth century (Fennell, *Ivan the Great*, p. 133).

лей своих чаровати и в^a бесовство верити; но Бога единого хвалити, и в Троице славимаго, и тебе, цареви, государю своему, служити верне. А сей клеветник мой есть раб и утече от мене, окравше мя: не подобает ти сему верити и ни свидетельства от такова приимати, яко от злодея и от предателя моего, лжеклевещущаго на мя.''

Он же абие повеле, связана положа на древо между двема огни, жещи мужа в роде паче^b же в разуме и в делех насветлейшаго; и притекша глаголют самого, яко начального ката к катом, мучащим^c победоносца, и подгребающе углие горящие жезлом своим проклятым под тело его святое. Такожде и предреченного Одоевского Никиту мучити различне повелел, ово срачицу его прозникнувши в перси его, тамо и овамо торгати: той же в таковых абие мучениях скончался. Онаго же преодолетеля славнаго, смученна и изжена огнем неповинне, наполы мертва и едва дышуща, в темницу на Белое озеро повести повелел; и отвезен аки три мили с того прелютаго пути на путь прохладный и радостный небеснаго возхождения, — ко Христу своему отъиде.

О мужу налепший и наикрепъчайший, и многаго разума исполнены, велия и преславная суть память твоя блаженная! Аще негли недостаточна в оной,^d глаголю варварской земле, в том нашем неблагодарном отечестве, но зде и везде, мню, в чуждых странах паче, нежели тамо, преславнейшая, не токмо во християнских пределех, но у главных бусурманов, сиречь у Турков, понеже немало от Турецкого войска на той-то предреченной битве тогда быша, наипаче же от Багмета баши великого двора мнози быша на помощь послани Перекопскому цареви, и за твоим благоразумием все изчезоша, и не возвратился, глаголют, ни един в Костянтинополь. А^e что глаголю о твоей славе, на земли сущей? Но и на небеси, у ангельского царя, преславна быша память твоя, яко сущаго мученика и победоносца, яко

^a Patr., Pog. в omitted in Ar. ^b T. по сих: Ar. ^c T. мучащив: Ar. ^d Patr., T. оном: Ar. ^e T. и: Ar.

have I received the custom from my ancestors, to practise magic and to believe in devilry; but I have learned to praise one God, who is glorified in the Trinity, and to serve you, my tsar and sovereign, truly. This man accusing me is a servant of mine who ran away from me after robbing me. You should not believe him, nor should you accept evidence from such a man, for he is an evil-doer and has betrayed me, bearing false evidence against me."

And the tsar immediately ordered that man, who was most brilliant in birth and especially in intellect and deed, to be tied to a stake between two fires and to be burned. And they say that he himself ran up, as the chief executioner to those who were torturing the victorious man, and with his accursed staff heaped up the burning coals under his holy body. And he also ordered Nikita Odoevsky, whom I have been talking about, to be subjected to various forms of torture—they stuffed his shirt through his breast and tugged it to and fro: he died immediately in such tortures. And he ordered that glorious conqueror, tortured and burned by fire in his innocence, half-dead and barely breathing, to be taken to a prison by the White Lake; and having been conveyed about three miles, he departed from the path of agony to the path of rest and heavenly joy, and ascended to his Christ.

O most excellent and most steadfast of men, filled with much understanding, great and glorious is your blessed memory! If the memory of you is wanting in that land, in that barbaric land, I say, in that ungrateful fatherland of ours, then here and everywhere else, I think, in foreign lands more than in Russia, it is most glorious—not only in Christian countries, but also in the countries of the chief Mussulmans, that is to say of the Turks; for there were not a few men from the Turkish army in that battle which I have mentioned—many were sent from the great court of Mehmed Pasha[1] to the aid of the khan of Perekop, and thanks to your great wisdom they all disappeared; and not one, they say, returned to Constantinople. But why do I speak of your glory on earth? In heaven, in the realm of the angelic King, your memory was most glorious, both as martyr and as

[1] Mehmed Pasha Sokollu, Grand Vizier 1565-79.

199

за оную[a] пресветлую победу[b] над бусурманы, еяже произвел еси и поставил мужеством храбрости своея, оброняющи[c] християнский род; наипаче же сподобился[d] еси мзду премногую получити, еже пострадал еси неповинне от оного кровопийцы, и сподобился еси со всеми оными великими мученики венцов от Христа Бога нашего, во царьствию Его, яже за Его овцы, супротив волку бусурманскому, много от младости своей храброствовал, аж без мала до шездесятого лета.

Те два сице блиско сродныя между себя от мучителя вкупе пострадали: бо и те княжата Воротынские и Одоевские от роду мученика князя Михаила Черниговского, закланнаго ото внешняго врага церковнаго, Батыя безбожнаго; тако же и сей Михайло, победоносец тезоименитый и оному сродник, созжен от внутренняго дракона церковнаго, губителя християнского, боящагося чаров: бо отец его Василий со оною предреченною законопреступъною женою, юною сущею, сам стар будущи, искал чаровников презлых отовсюду, да помогут ему ко плодотворению, не хотяще бо властеля быти брата его по нем, бо имел брата Юрья зело мужественнаго и добронравнаго, яко и повелел, заповедающе жене своей и окаянным советником своим, скоро по смерти своей убити его; яко и убиен есть. О чаровницех же оных так печашесь, посылаше по них тамо и овамо, аж до Корелы еже есть Филяндия и аж до дикия Ляпунии, яже той язык седит[e] на великих горах, подле Студеного моря — и оттуду провожаху их к нему летущих оных и презлых советников сатанинских; и за помощию их от прескверных семян, по произволению презлому (а не по естеству от Бога вложенному) уродилися ему два сына: един таковый пре-

[a] Pog., T. очную: Ar.   [b] T. победу omitted in Ar., Patr. and Pog.   [c] T. победу оброняющи: Ar., Pog.   [d] Patr., Pog., T. сподобил: Ar.   [e] T. аж до Корелы еже есть филя — сидит: Ar.

[1] Prince Mikhail of Chernigov, who was killed in the horde in 1246, was the ancestor of most of the Upper Oka princes.

victor, for you won that most brilliant victory over the Mussulmans thanks to your heroic bravery while defending the Christian race; but above all you have been counted worthy to receive the very great reward by suffering in your innocence at the hands of that drinker of blood, and you have been counted worthy together with all the great martyrs to receive crowns from Christ our God in His Kingdom, in that from your youth up to a little before your sixtieth year you many a time bravely defended His sheep against the Mussulman wolf.

These two men, who were closely related to one another in the following manner, suffered together at the hands of the torturer: both the princes of Vorotynsk and the princes of Odoev are from the kin of the martyr, Prince Mikhail of Chernigov, who was slain by the external foe of the Church, the godless Baty;[1] so too was this Mikhail, the conqueror who bears the same name as, and is related to, that Mikhail, burned by that monstrous internal[2] foe [lit. dragon] of the Church, the destroyer of Christianity, who is afraid of magic: for his [Ivan IV's] father Vasily, together with that law-breaking wife of his whom I have mentioned above, while he was old and she was young,[3] sought wicked magicians everywhere to help him become fertile—for he did not want his brother to be ruler after him—he had a brother Yury, who was very brave and virtuous, —and so he instructed his wife and his accursed advisers, ordering them to kill him soon after his death; and so he was killed. And he took such pains to get those sorceresses, sending hither and thither for them even as far as Korelia, that is to say, Finland, and as far as the wild Lapps, the tribe settled in the great hills by the Frozen Sea—and from there they brought to him those "healers",[4] those wicked counsellors of Satan. And with their help from his most foul seed were born two sons according to wicked design and not according to divinely decreed nature: one of them was so savage and bloodthirsty

[2] For this contrast of "internal" (or spiritual) and "external" (or bodily), see below, pp. 286-7.

[3] In fact, Vasily III was just under 48 at the time of his second marriage.

[4] летущих is perhaps an error for лекующих, "healing". Ustryalov hazards лехтущих, "stimulating", "titillating". Cf. Polish lechtać, "to tickle".

лютый и кровопийца и погубитель отечества, иже не токмо в Руской земле такова чюда и дива не слыхано, но воистинну нигде же никогда же, мню, зане и Нерона презлаго превзыде лютостию и различными ниисповедимыми сквернами; паче же не внешний, непримирительный враг и гонитель церкви[a] Божии бысть, но внутренный змий ядовитый, жруще и растерзающе рабов Божиих; а другий был без ума и без памяти и безсловесен, тако же аки див якой родился.

Ту ми зрите и прилежно созерцайте, християнскии родове, яже держат непреподобне приводити себе на помощь и к деткам своим, мужей,[b] презлых чаровников и баб, смывалей и шептуней, и иными различными чары чарующих, общующе[c] со дияволом и призывающе его на помощь, что за полезную и якову помощь от того имеете, в предреченной неслыханной лютости, разсмотрите! Мнози бо, яко слышахом многажды, за мало сие себе важат и смеющесь глаголют: "Мал сей грех, и удобне покаянием исправится." Аз же глаголю: не мал и воистинну превелик зело, понеже тем Божию заповедь великую во обетованию разоряете; бо Господь глаголет: да не убоишись никого же, а ни послужишись, сиречь: ни у кого же помощи не имаши[d] разве Меня,[e] а ни небеси горе, а ни на земли низу, а ни под безднами; и паки еще: кто отвержется Мене пред человеки, отвергуся и Аз его пред Отцем Моим небесным. И вы, забывше таковые страшные заповеди Господа нашего, течете к дияволу, просяще его[f] чрез чаровники! А чары, яко всем есть ведомо, без отвержения Божия и без согласия со дияволом не бывают. Воистинну,[g] яко мню, и се неисцелимый грех есть тем, еже внимают им; и ко покаянию неудобен: неисцельный, и того ради, зане за малый его собе мните; неудобен же ко покаянию, понеже без отвержения

[a] Patr. церквий: Ar.   [b] Т. своих, мужем: Ar.   [c] Pog. общуяще: Ar.   [d] Patr., Pog. не имам: Ar.   [e] Pog. мена: Ar. [f] Patr. просящего: Ar.   [g] Patr. воистинно: Ar.

[1] Yury Vasil'evich, died 1563.

and such a destroyer of his fatherland that not only in the Russian land have such strange and wondrous things never been heard of before, but in truth nowhere, I think, and at no time, for in ferocity and unmentionable foul practices he has even exceeded the evil Nero; furthermore, he was not an implacable external foe and persecutor of the Church of God, but a poisonous internal serpent, devouring and torturing the servants of God; and the other one, just as strange and wondrous, was born without mind, memory or speech.[1]

Consider and ponder attentively, O Christian peoples, how men dare in unholy manner to get evil magicians and women, those who cast spells by sprinkling water or by whispering,[2] and those who bewitch with various other charms, in order to help them and their children, communing with the devil and calling him to help,—consider what advantage and what help you have in this unheard-of period of ferocity which we have been talking about! For many people, so I have often heard, consider this to be but a trifle and say laughingly: "This is a small sin and it can easily be atoned for by penitence." But I say: it is not small; indeed it is extremely great, since in this manner you are destroying the commandment of God which is great in promise: for the Lord says: "You shall not fear anybody, nor shall you serve them",[3] that is to say: you shall have no help from anybody except from Me, "nor in heaven above, nor on earth below, nor beneath the depths";[4] and again, "whosoever shall deny Me before men, him will I also deny before My Father which is in heaven".[5] And you, forgetting such fearsome commandments of our Lord, run to the devil, asking for him by means of sorcerers! Yet, as is known to all people, there are no spells without denial of God and without agreement with the devil. Indeed, I think that it is also an irremediable sin to hearken to sorcerers, and hard to atone for by penitence: irremediable in that you consider it to be a small sin; hard to atone for by penitence, since without Judas's betrayal of

---

[2] One of the common Russian methods of casting healing spells was by whispering incantations on bread or water (*nasheptyvanie*); another, by sprinkling the patient with water over which spells had been said (*smyvanie*).

[3] Ex. xx. 5.   [4] Ex. xx. 4.   [5] Matt. x. 33.

Июдина, чары и относы и смывание, прежние ради купели, и стирания солью мира ради[a] святаго помазания, шептания же скверные, явственных ради обещаней ко Христу на святом крещению, и относы,[b] приношения ради на святом жертвоннице у пречистаго агнца, и без согласия, сиречь, без обещания дияволу и без отвержения Христова, яко рехом, чаровницы сих не могут действовати; но всяко дияволом, тех ради всех, от предреченных презлых человеков согласников дияволих умышлено. Господь Бог наш, премногия ради благодати своея, да избавит всех правоверных от таковых! Аще же[c] кто таковым не внимает, тому и боятись не подобает, понеже яко дым от знамения честнаго креста изчезают и от простых людей, верующих во Христа, не токмо от искусных християн, доброю совестию живущих, у которых бывают на сердцах скрижалеи плотяных написаны заповедей Христовых евангельские словеса. О сем бо и сам Бог-Слово свидетельствует в молитве оной, еюже поучал ученики свои молитися, — при конце глаголюще:[d] яко Твое есть царьство и сила, и протчие. Блаженный же Златоуст ясно толкует в беседе 19, еже от Матвея евангелие: ''Иже несть царьство, а ни сила иная, а ни боятись кого достоит християном, разве единого Бога, аще и дияволь негде на нас возмогает мученьми, сие Богу попущающу; а он без воли[e] Божии, аще и злорадный и прелютый и непримирительный враг наш, не токмо на нас человеков не возмогает, ни на свиниях, ни на воловых стадах, а ни на других скотех, без Божии воли.'' Яково все свидетельствуется и во евангелии. А лепей, прочитаючи, узрите во оном священном толкованию златаго языка.

Сиих еликих[f] памятью могл объъяти;[g] напишу о княжецких родех.

[a] Т. и стирания союзми ради: Ar.   [b] Patr., Pog., Т. отиносы: Ar.   [c] Patr., Pog., Т. ше: Ar.   [d] Т. глаголю: Ar.   [e] Patr. волии: Ar.   [f] Patr., Т. великих: Ar.   [g] Patr., Pog., Т. объявити: Ar.

---

[1] *Otnosy* are small bundles containing coal, ash and burned clay, used for healing sicknesses (Dal', *Tolkovy Slovar'*, vol. ii, col. 1921). For *smyvanie*, see

Christ, spells and charms and asperging [are ineffective] because of the former baptismal font, so too is rubbing with salt[1] because of the oil of holy chrismation, and also foul whisperings because of clear promises made to Christ at holy baptism, and also charms because of offerings at the altar of the most pure Lamb—and without agreement with, that is to say without promises to, the devil and without the denial of Christ, as I have said before, sorcerers cannot make these things work; but it is all the work of the devil on behalf of all those people, and it is planned by those above-mentioned wicked men who are in agreement with the devil. May our Lord God, because of His exceedingly great grace, deliver all the Orthodox from such people! Should anyone not hearken to such people, he need not fear, for they disappear like smoke from the sign of the holy Cross and from simple people who believe in Christ, not only from practised Christians who live in good conscience and on the tables of whose fleshly hearts[2] are written the evangelical words of the commandments of Christ. For God the Word testifies about this in the prayer by means of which He taught His disciples to pray and which says at the end: "For Thine is the kingdom, the power", etcetera, while the blessed Chrysostom clearly explains in his nineteenth homily on the gospel of St Matthew that "there is no other kingdom and no other power, and Christians should fear no one except God alone, even if the devil in some places prevails against us with tortures, God permitting this; but without the will of God, even though he is our evil and ferocious and irreconcilable enemy, he cannot prevail not only against us but also against swine and herds of oxen and other cattle, without God's will".[3] And this is all testified in the gospel as well. But you will see better when you have read it in the sacred commentary by the Golden Tongue [i.e. Chrysostom].

I have written about as many of these princely families as I could encompass with my memory.

above, p. 203, n. 2. "Rubbing with salt" is probably another form of magic connected with spell-casting. [2] Prov. iii. 3.

[3] A very rough rendering of St John Chrysostom's 19th Homily on St Matthew (*PG*, vol. 57, col. 282).

VII

О побиении болярских и дворянских родов

О великих же панов родех, а по их о боярских, аще елико Господь памяти подаст, покушусь написати. Убил мужа, в роде светла, Иоанна Петровича, уже в совершенном веку бывша; и жену его Марью, воистинну святую, погубил, у неяже прежде, еще во младости своей, единочаднаго, возлюбленнаго сына от недр оторвавши[a] усекнул, Иоанна, княжа Дорогобужского, с роду великих князей Тверских. Его был отец от Татар Казанских на битве убит; а тот отрочатко остался у сосцу един у матери; она же во святом вдовстве своем питала его до осминадесяти лет; о егоже убиению мало преже воспомянух в кронице пишучи, иже вкупе убиени суть со нарочитым юношею стрыечным братом своим, с князем Федором Овчинным. И так на того Иоанна разгневался, иже не токмо слуг его шляхетных мужей всеродне погубил и различными муками помучил, но и места и села — бе зело много отчины имел — все пожег, сам ездя с коромешники своими, елико где обрелись, со женами и детками их, ссущих[b] от сосцов матерних, не пощадил;[c] наконец, глаголют, а ни скота единого живити повелел.

[a] Patr., Pog., Т. оторварьши: Ar.   [b] Patr., Pog. сущих: Ar.
[c] Т. пощадою: Ar., Pog.

---

[1] For the conspiracy of I. P. Chelyadnin-Fedorov, which was discovered in 1567, see above, p. 193, n. 4. For details of his variegated and distinguished political career, as well as for the problem of the exact date of his execution (September 1568), see Zimin, *Sostav Boyarskoy dumy*, p. 60, n. 223.

[2] See above, pp. 12–13. Ivan Ivanovich Dorogobuzhsky's father, Ivan Osipovich, was killed on the 1530 expedition to Kazan' (*PSRL* xxvi, p. 314)

VII

Concerning the Slaying of the Boyar and Noble Families

I will attempt to write about the families of the great *pans*, or, in their language, boyars, in as far as the Lord grants me memory.

He put to death Ioann Petrovich, a man of brilliant birth, who was already of ripe old age;[1] and he slew his wife Maria, who was indeed a holy woman and whose only-begotten beloved son, Ioann, prince of Dorogobuzh, from the kin of the grand princes of Tver', he had earlier torn from her bosom and beheaded. His father had been killed in battle by the Tatars of Kazan'; and that infant remained alone at his mother's breasts; and in her holy widowhood she nurtured him until the age of eighteen; as for his execution, I mentioned it a little earlier when writing in my chronicle—he was put to death with his cousin, that distinguished youth, Prince Fedor Ovchinin.[2] And the tsar was so angry with this Ioann [Chelyadnin] that he not only slew every one of his service noblemen[3] and subjected them to various kinds of torture, but he burned all his towns and villages—he had a very large patrimony—while he himself travelled with his children of darkness, and wherever any of them were found, he did not spare them, nor their wives, nor their little children sucking at their mothers' breasts; and they say that he even ordered that not a single animal be left alive.[4]

just over seventeen years before his son's death. When his widow married I. P. Chelyadnin-Fedorov is not known.

[3] I.e. his "boyar children"—presumably the meaning of слуги шляхетные.

[4] Chelyadnin's large estates were in the Beloozero district. See Tikhomirov, *Rossiya v XVI stoletii*, pp. 236–7; S. B. Veselovsky, *Feodal'noe zemlevladenie*, pp. 54, 179.

О Иоанне Шереметеве

В начале же мучительства своего, мудраго советника своего Иоанна, глаголю Шереметева, о немъже многажды в кронице воспомянух, мучил такою презлою ускою темницею, острым помостом приправлену, иже вере неподобно, и оковал тяжкими веригами по вые, по рукам и по ногам, и к тому еще и по чреслам обруч толстый железный, и к тому обручю десять пудов железа привесити повелел, и в таковой беде аки день и нощь мужа мучил. Потом пришел глаголати с ним; ему же, наполы мертву сущу и едва дышущу, в таковых тяжких оковах и на таковом остром помосте лежащу повержену, начал между иными вопросы о сем пытати его: "Где, рече, многи скорбы твои? Скажи ми. Вем бо, яко богат еси зело, бо не обретох их, ихъже надеялся в сокровишницах твоих обрести." Отвещал Иоан: "Целы, рече, сокровенны лежат, идеже уже не можешь достати их." Он же рече: "Скажи ми о них, аще ли ни муки к мукам приложу ти." Иоан же отвеща: "Твори, еже хощеши. Уже бо ми близ пристанище." Царь же рече: "Повеждь ми, прошу тя, о скарбех твоих." Иоан отвеща: "Аще бы и исповедал ти о них, яко уже рекох, не можешь их держати; пренесох бо их убогих руками в небесное сокровище, ко Христу моему." И другие ответы зело премудрыя, яко един премудрейший философ, или учитель великий, отвещал ему тогда. Он же, умилився мало, повелел от тех тяжких узов разрешити его и отвести в лехчайшую темницу; и обаче того дня повелел удавити брата его, Никиту, уже в сигклитском сану почтенна суща, мужа храбраго и на телеси от варварских рук немало ран имуща. Иоанн же потом — сокрушено[a] уж тело — насилием колико лет поживе при нем, оставя все последне стяжание свое, паче же во убогих и во странных,

[a] Pog. сокрушенну: Ar.

---

[1] Lit. "Ioann, I say, Sheremetev". Probably глаголю is an error for глаголемого, "called", Kurbsky's habitual method of appellation.

[2] Or perhaps "floor". The usual meaning of помост is "floor", but it is sometimes used (in connection with churches) to mean "dais".

Concerning Ioann Sheremetev

Now at the beginning of his period of torturing he had his wise counsellor, Ioann Sheremetev,[1] whom I have mentioned many times in my chronicle, tortured in an unbelievably dire and cramped prison cell, fitted with a rough platform,[2] and he fettered him with heavy chains around his neck and on his arms and on his legs, and he ordered a thick iron hoop to be placed around his loins and ten weights of iron[3] to be hung from that hoop; and in such affliction he tortured the man day and night. Then he came to talk to him; and as he lay there, prostrated on his rough platform and wearing his heavy fetters, half-alive and barely breathing, the tsar began, amongst other questions, to interrogate him in the following manner: "Where", he said, "are your many treasures? Tell me. For I know that you are very rich, yet I have not found what I hoped to find in your treasure-house." And Ioann answered: "They lie untouched and hidden where you cannot get them." And he said: "Tell me about them, or I shall add torture to torture." But Ioann answered: "Do what you wish. My haven is already near." And the tsar said: "Tell me, I beg you, about your treasures." And Ioann answered: "If I were to tell you about them, as I have already said, you would not be able to keep them; for by the hands of the poor I have transferred them to the heavenly treasure, to my Christ." And like an exceedingly wise philosopher or great teacher he gave him other very wise answers at that time. And the tsar had slight compassion and ordered him to be freed from those heavy bonds and to be taken to a milder prison; however, on that same day he ordered his brother Nikita, who was already honoured with the rank of counsellor, to be strangled—a brave man, with many wounds on his body inflicted by barbarian hands. After that Ioann, having forced himself to continue living for several years with his body already broken, abandoned the last of his possessions, and having once more joined the poor and the wretched,[4]

---

[3] Or, perhaps, "ten *pudy* of iron". A *pud* is a measure of weight, the equivalent of 16·3 kilograms.

[4] Lit. "strangers", "wanderers".

в духовную лихву и мздовоздаятелю Христу Богу вдав, во един от монастырей изыде, во святый и монашеский образ облечеся. И не вем, аще и там не повелел ли уморяти его.

Потом убиен от него брат стрыечный жены его, Семен Яковлевич, муж благородный и богатый, тако же и сын его, еще во отроческом веку удавлен.

Паки убиени от него мужи: Грецка роду, именем Хозяин, нареченный Тютин, муж зело богатый, и еже был у него подскарбием земским, и погублен всеродно, сиречь со женою и з детками и со другими южики; тако же и другие мужие нарочитые и богатые,[a] ихъже имен[b] невместно писати, широкости ради, бо околико тысящ их не токмо в месте Московском великом, но и во других великих местех и во градех побито.

Потом разграбил синглита своево скарбы великие, от праотец его еще собраны, емуже было имя Иоан, по наречению Хабаров, роду старожитного, яже нарицались Добрынские. Он же муж мало радяше о тех своих сокровищах, утешашеся Богом, понеже был муж наполы в книжном разуме искусен. По трех же летех убити его повелел со единочадным сыном его, из отчины, понеже великии вотчины имел во многих поветех.

[a] T. богатых: Ar.   [b] Patr., Pog. именем: Ar.

---

[1] Ivan Vasil'evich Bol'shoy-Sheremetev became a member of the Boyar Council in 1549. As a close supporter of A. Adashev and as a general with considerable experience of fighting the Tatars of Kazan' and the Crimea, he was one of the leading military and political figures of the fifties. In 1564 he was arrested and imprisoned, suspected of planning to flee the country. He was tonsured between May 1570 and July 1571 in the White Lake monastery of St Kirill, taking the monastic name of Iona (Jonah). He was still alive in September 1573 when Ivan IV wrote to the abbot of the White Lake monastery. (Zimin, *Sostav Boyarskoy dumy*, pp. 61, 72; *Poslaniya Ivana Groznogo*, pp. 162 *sq*.)

Nothing is known of the execution of Nikita Sheremetev. In the *posluzhny spisok* he is shown as having died in 1565 (*DRV*, vol. xx, p. 46).

[2] Who Semen Yakovlevich was is not known. Ustryalov suggests Semen Vasil'evich Yakovlya (or Yakovlev) (Ustryalov, *Skazaniya*, pp. 328–9). The Yakovlyas were in fact close relatives of the Zakhar'ins, the family of Ivan

handed over everything into spiritual usury and to the recompenser, Christ our God, and left for a monastery, putting on the holy monastic habit. I know not if the tsar ordered him to be killed there.[1]

After that the cousin of his wife, Semen Yakovlevich, a noble and rich man, was put to death, and his son too, while still a boy, was strangled.[2]

And a man of Greek stock, Khozyain Tyutin by name, who was very rich and who was his Great Treasurer, was also put to death by him, and he was killed with all his family, that is to say with his wife and children and other relatives.[3] And likewise he put to death other rich and distinguished men, whose names there is no room to write, because there are so many of them; for several thousands of them were slain, not only in the great city of Moscow, but in other great cities and towns as well.

Then he plundered the great possessions of one of his counsellors which had been gathered together by his ancestors: his name was Ioann Khabarov, and he came from an ancient family called Dobrynsky. He was a man who cared little for those treasurers of his but who consoled himself in God, for he was partly skilled in bookish wisdom. But three years later he ordered him to be killed together with his only-begotten son because of his patrimony, for he owned large estates in many districts.[4]

IV's first wife, Anastasia (Smirnov, *Ocherki*, pp. 177, 188), and were rich landowners in the Kolomna district (Tikhomirov, *Rossiya v XVI stoletii*, p. 117). S. V. Yakovlya, who was *dvoretsky* of Nizhny Novgorod from 1556 to 1566 (Zimin, *O sostave dvortsovykh uchrezhdeniy*, p. 198) was evidently beheaded in July 1570 (Sadikov, *Ocherki*, p. 367).

[3] Khozyain Yur'evich Tyutin held the post of "treasurer" (*kaznachey*) from 1551 until 1568, when, it appears, he was executed. The reason for his execution is not known. See Zimin, *O sostave dvortsovykh uchrezhdeniy*, p. 195; cf. Sadikov, *Ocherki*, p. 208. For *podskarbi*, see above, p. 184, n. 3.

[4] Ivan Ivanovich Khabarov was descended from Konstantin Ivanovich Dobrynsky (himself a descendant of the eleventh-century Kasogian chieftain Rededya). He had a distinguished military career, being made boyar in 1547 and governor of Smolensk in 1548. In 1558 he probably took the tonsure (according to the *posluzhny spisok* he died in this year: see *DRV*, vol. xx, p. 42). In September 1573 he was still alive, under the monastic

В тех же летех[a] убил светлаго рода мужа, Михаила Матфеевича Лыкова, и с ним ближняго сродника его, юношу зело прекрасного, в самом наусию, яже был послан на науку за море, во Германию, и тамо навык добре Аляманскому языку и писанию: бо там пребывал, учась, немало лет, и объездил всю землю Немецкую, и возвратился был к нам во отечество, и по колких летех смерть вкусил от мучителя неповинне. А той-то Матфей Лыков, отец ево Михаилов, блаженные памяти, созжен, пострадал за отечество тогда, когда возвратишася от Стародуба войско Ляцкое и Литовское со гетманы своими: тогда немало градов Северских разориша; Матфей же той, видев, иже не может избавлен быти град его, первие выпустил жену и детки свои во плен, потом не хотяше сам видети взатья[b] града от супостатов, и потоль[c] броняше стен градцких вкупе с народом, иже произволил созжен быти с ними, нежели супостатом град здати. Жена же и дети его отведены быша, яко пленники, до короля старого Сигизмунда. Кроль же, воистинну яко сущий святый християнский, повелел их питати не яко пленников, но яко своих сущих, не токмо питати во своих царских полатах, но и доктором своим повелел их научити шляшецких наук и языку Римскому. Потом по колких летех, послы Московские великие (Василей Морозов и Федор Воронцов) в Кракове упросиша их у кроля во отечество, глаголю воистинно неблагодарное и недостойное ученых мужей, в землю лютых варваров, идеже един от них,

[a] Т. местех: Ar.   [b] Т. взятые: Ar., Patr., Pog.   [c] Patr., Pog., Т. потом: Ar.

---

name of Ioasaf, in St Kirill's monastery (Ivan IV, in his letter of that date to the monastery, states that this was his sixth or seventh monastery; see *Poslaniya Ivana Groznogo*, p. 191). S. A. Belokurov considers that he died in 1581. Assuming that Kurbsky finished his History in 1573, his information on Khabarov's execution is clearly wrong. (Zimin, *Sostav Boyarskoy dumy*, p. 60, n. 225; S. A. Belokurov, *Nadgrobnye plity XVI v.*, pp. 24–8.)

[1] M. M. Lykov was given the rank of *okol'nichy* in 1560 or 1561. He was executed in 1571 for no known reason. (Zimin, *Sostav Boyarskoy dumy*, p. 70, n. 340, p. 75; Skrynnikov, *Oprichnaya zemel'naya reforma*, p. 238). Who the

And in those years he put to death a man of noble stock, Mikhail Matfeevich Lykov, and with him a close relative of his, a very fair youth, with the first down of manhood still on his cheeks, who had been sent overseas to Germany to acquire learning, and there he had learned to speak and write German well: for he had stayed there studying for several years and had travelled all over the German land and had returned home to us; and after several years he tasted death in his innocence at the hands of the torturer.[1] Now the father of that Mikhail, Matfey Lykov of blessed memory, who was burned, suffered for his fatherland at the time when the Polish and Lithuanian army returned with its generals from Starodub: at that time many towns in the district of Seversk[2] were destroyed; and Matfey, seeing that his town could not be saved, first of all let his wife and children out of the town into captivity; then, not wishing to see the town taken by the enemy, he so defended the walls together with the townsfolk that he preferred to be burned with them rather than surrender the town to the enemy.[3] His wife and children were taken away as prisoners to the old king Sigismund. And the king, who was indeed a holy Christian, ordered them to be fed not like prisoners but like his own family; and not only did he order that they be fed in his royal palace, but he even told his doctors to instruct them in noble sciences and the Roman tongue. Then, several years later, in Cracow, the ambassadors of Moscow, Vasily Morozov and Fedor Vorontsov, asked the king to let them go back to their fatherland,[4] to that land which was, I say, indeed ungrateful and unworthy to receive learned men, to the land of the fierce barbarians; and[5] one of them [i.e. of Matfey Lykov's sons],

noble young man was is not known. He must have been one of the earliest Muscovites ever to have been sent abroad for educational purposes.

[2] I.e. the lands east of the Dnepr watered by the Desna and Seym rivers.

[3] According to the chronicles, Matfey Lykov was *namestnik* of Radogoshch, which was burned by the Poles and Lithuanians in the autumn of 1534 (*PSRL* xiii, pp. 80, 421).

[4] For the embassy of Vasily Grigor'evich Morozov and Fedor Semenovich Vorontsov of June 1542, see *PSRL* xiii, p. 203.

[5] Lit. "where". Evidently something has been omitted just before this clause. The "land of fierce barbarians" obviously refers to Russia; whereas the following clauses all refer to Livonia.

Иоан имянем, изыман жив на битве и уморен от маистра Лифлянского в прелютой темнице: яко достоило мужу ученому, пострадал за отечество; а другий той, предреченный Михаил, был остался и был воеводою в Ругодеве; там убиен, яко рехом, от оного мучителя, варварского царя. Так убо он, грубый и прелютый варвар, не памятуючи отеческих и братских служеб, воздает своим, светлыми делы украшенным, верным служащем ему мужем!

Потом погубил род Колычовых, тако же и мужей светлых и нарочитых в роде, единоплемянных сущих Шереметевых, бо прародитель их, муж светлый и знаменитый, от Немецкие земли выехал, емуже имя было Михаил: глаголют его быти с роду княжат решких. А побил[a] их тое ради вины, иже разгневался зело на стрыя их, Филиппа архиепископа, обличающа его за презлыя беззакония, о немъже вкратце последи повем. И бысть тогда знамение[b] не худо от Бога явленно над единым от тех, емуже имя было Иоан Борисович Колычов; чюдо же воистинну таково, яко слышах от самовидца, при том зрящаго: егда зело возъярился, паче же рещи, неистовился от непримирительнаго[c] врага человеческаго, бесовские сожительницы раждежен, яко прежде рекох, ездя палил места и веси и дворы оного Иоанна Петровича со живущими в них, тогда обрел храмину, глаголют, зело высоку, по их же обыкновенному слову, нарицают ее повалуша; в самых верхних коморах привязати повелел крепко оного предреченного мужа, и як под тую-то[d] храмину, тако и под другие, близу тое стоящие, в нихже бяше полно человеков нагнано[e] и затворенно, неколико бочек порохов повелел поставити, и сам стал издалеча в полкоустроениях, иже под супостатным[f] градом, ожидающе, егда взорвет храмину. Егда же уже взорвало и

---

[a] Patr., Pog., T.   а бобил: Ar.   [b] Patr.   знамения: Ar.   [c] T. неприятнаго: Ar.   [d] Patr., T.   тою-то: Ar.   [e] Pog.   нагнаты: Ar.
[f] T.   сустатным Ar.

---

[1] One Ivan Lykov was indeed taken prisoner by Kettler when he captured Ringen in 1558. See above, pp. 118–19; *PSRL* xiii, p. 313.
[2] For решких, see above, pp. 12–13.

Ioann by name, was captured alive in a battle and put to death by the Livonian Master in a very dire dungeon;[1] and as befits a learned man, he suffered for his fatherland; and the other one, Mikhail, whom I mentioned above, stayed [in Livonia] and was *voevoda* in Rugodiv [Narva]; and there he was killed, as I have said, by that torturer, the barbaric tsar. Thus does he, that crude fierce barbarian, remembering not the services rendered by fathers and brothers, repay his servants who are bedecked with brilliant deeds, the men who serve him faithfully!

Then he destroyed the kin of the Kolychevs, who were also men of brilliant and distinguished birth and of the same family as the Sheremetevs, for their ancestor, a brilliant and renowned man by name of Mikhail, came out of the German land; they say he was from the kin of the imperial princes.[2] And he slew them for this reason—because he was very angry with their uncle, Archbishop Philipp, who upbraided him for his wicked transgressions and about whom I shall briefly narrate afterwards.[3] And at that time no mean sign was manifested by God over one of them whose name was Ioann Borisovich Kolychev; indeed the miracle was just as I heard it from an eye-witness who was there and watched it: when he became angry, or, one should say, flared up in a rage, enflamed by the implacable enemy of man, the concubine of the devil, and, as I have said above,[4] travelled around and burned the towns and villages and courts of Ioann Petrovich [Chelyadnin-Fedorov] together with those who lived in them, he came across a house which, they say, was very high and which they normally call a *pova-lusha*;[5] and he ordered that man whom I mentioned above to be securely bound in the very top rooms, and he ordered several barrels of powder to be placed beneath that house as well as beneath others standing near it which were full of people who had been herded together and locked in; and he himself stood at a distance with his troops drawn up, as though under the walls of an enemy town, waiting for the house to blow up. And

[3] See below, pp. 232 *sq.*   [4] See above, pp. 206–7.
[5] повалуша is described by Sreznevsky as meaning "one of the buildings belonging to a house" (see Sreznevsky, *Materialy*, vol. II, col. 993). The word can also be used to describe one of the rooms in a house.

разметало не токмо тую храмину, но и другие близ стоящие, тогда он со всеми кромешники своими, яко воистинну бесной со неистовящимися, со всем оным полком диявольским, все велегласно возопивше, яко на брани супостатов, и аки пресветлое одоление получиша, всеми уздами конскою скоростию расторганых телес християнских зрети поскочиша; бо бе множество в тех храминах, под нихже порохи подставлены быша, повязани и затворени бяше. Тогда же потом, далече на поле, обретено того Иоанна, единою рукою привязана ко великому бревну, на земли цела седяща, а ничем же ни мало вредима, прославляюще Господа, троряще чюдеса; а тамо был, растягненый, связан руками и ногама. Егда же сие исповедано кромешником его, тогда един безчеловечный и прелютый устремился и прибеже прутко на коне первие к нему, и видев его здрава и псалмы благодарные Господеви поющи, абие отсече ему саблею главу и принесе ее, аки дар многоценный, подобному лютостию цареви своему. Он же абие повелел в кожаный мех зашити и послал ее ко стрыю его, архиепископу предреченному, заточенному в темницу, глаголюще: "Се сродного твоего глава! Не помогли ему твои чары!" Тех же Колычовых около десять роду; в них же беша нецыи мужие храбрыи и нарочитые, некоторые же от них и сигклитским саном почтеныи, а нецыи стратилаты быша; а погублени суть всеродне.[a]

Потом убиен от него муж зело храбрый и разумный, и к тому священных писаней[b] последователь, Василей, глаго-

[a] Т. всеродние: Ar.   [b] Patr. писаниих: Ar.

---

[1] It is hard to see whom exactly Kurbsky had in mind when he talked of "some ten...Kolychevs", who were put to death "in their entirety" by Ivan. Assuming that Kurbsky wrote his *History* in 1573 (Zimin, *Kogda Kurbsky napisal*), the following members of the Kolychev clan must be excluded: Vasily Ivanovich and Fedor Ivanovich Kolychev-Umnoy, cousins of Metropolitan Philipp (ex-Fedor Stepanovich Kolychev)—both members of the *Oprichnina*; the former was executed in Autumn 1575 and the latter died as a monk in St Kirill's monastery in 1574 (Zimin, *Sostav Boyarskoy dumy*, pp. 68, 73, 77; Kobrin, *Sostav oprichnogo dvora*, pp. 43-4); Vasily

when not only the house but the others standing near it blew up and were shattered, then he and all his children of darkness, verily like a madman surrounded by raving men, with all that devilish host, yelling at the top of their voiçes like enemies in battle and like men who have won a glorious victory, galloped at full rein to gaze upon the mangled corpses of the Christians. For a great number of people had been tied up and locked in those houses, beneath which the powder had been placed. Then, far away in the open, Ioann was found, tied by one arm to a great beam and sitting safe and sound upon the ground, unharmed by aught, and praising the Lord who works miracles; yet in the house he had been stretched out and tied by his arms and legs. Now when this was told to his children of darkness, one of them, a savage and inhuman man, rushed off and galloped up to him before the others. And when he saw him safe and singing psalms of thanksgiving to the Lord, he straightway cut off his head with a sabre and brought it like a priceless gift to the tsar, his equal in savagery. And the tsar immediately had it sewn up in a leather bag and he sent it to his uncle, the archbishop, whom I mentioned above and who was imprisoned, saying: "Here is the head of your relative! Your spells were of no avail to him!" There were some ten of the family of those Kolychevs; and amongst them were some brave and distinguished men; and several of them were honoured with the rank of counsellor, and some of them were generals; and they were destroyed in their entirety.[1]

Then a man of great bravery and intellect, who was, furthermore, versed in the holy scriptures, was put to death by him;

Grigor'evich Kolychev, died 1578/9 (Zimin, *op. cit.* p. 77); Grigory Grigor'evich Kolychev (*ibid.* p. 77). Of all the known Kolychevs probably only Mikhail Ivanovich Kolychev was executed in connection with Metropolitan Philipp's protest against the *Oprichnina* in March 1568 (*ibid.* p. 74).

The Ivan Borisovich Kolychev mentioned here by Kurbsky was probably I. B. Kolychev-Khlyznev, a close relative of one Bogdan Nikitich Kolychev-Khlyznev, who betrayed his country in 1563 (*PSRL* xiii, p. 350). Veselovsky thinks that his execution was connected rather with his relative's treachery and his past service (with many other Kolychevs) at the court of Prince Vladimir of Staritsa than with the protest of Metropolitan Philipp (Veselovsky, *Sinodik*, pp. 297-8).

лемый Разладин, роду славнаго Иоанна Родионовича, нареченного Квашни. А глаголют и матерь его Феодосию пострадавшу, от мучителя многими муками мучиму, вдовицу старую сущую, многолетную, неповинне терпящу. Только три сыны у ней были, мужи зело храбрыи: един предреченный Василей, а другий Иоанн, третий Никифор, убиени на битвах еще во юношеском веку от Германов (но[a] всяко тогда пораженны суть Германи); мужие зело быша храбрые и мужественные, и не токмо телеси благолепны, но воистинну нравы благими и душами преукрашенны быша.

Тогда же убиен от него Дмитрей, по наречению Пушкин, тако же муж зело разумный и храбрый, и уже в совершенных летех; единоплемянен же бе Челядниным.

Потом убиен от него стратилат славный, Крик Тыртов по наречению, муж не токмо храбрый, мужественный и священных писаней последователь, но воистинне в разуме мног, к тому кроток и тих был, зело всякими благими нравы преукрашен, и обычаими добрыми прелюбезен, и к тому — что еще ноилепнейшаго и дивнейшаго — от порождения матери своей чист и непорочен; в воинстве християнском знаменит и славим, понеже многие рани[b] на телеси имел, на многих битвах от различных варваров; младу же еще ему сущу, храбре юношествовал в Казанское взятие, и ока единаго

[a] Patr., T.   на: Ar.   [b] ради: Ar., Patr.   н in margin of Patr.

---

[1] When and why Vasily Vasil'evich Razladin-Kvashnin was executed is not known. According to the second Novgorod Chronicle, his wife (not his mother) was tonsured in June 1572—perhaps as a result of her husband's execution ? (Veselovsky, *Sinodik*, p. 294.)

It is interesting to note that in the "Tale of the Capture of Andrey of Staritsa", which describes Andrey's rebellion of 1537, one Vasily Prokof'evich Razladin was in command of the vanguard of Telepnev-Obolensky's army, while one "Ivan Borisovich Kolychev" was in command of Andrey's rearguard (M. N. Tikhomirov, *Maloizvestnye letopisnye pamyatniki XVI v.*, p. 87).

In 1558 V. Razladin and Boris Stepanovich Kolychev (perhaps Metropolitan Philipp's brother and the father of the Kolychev whose head, according to Kurbsky, was sent to Philipp in a bag—see above, p. 216, n. 1)

his name was Vasily Razladin and he was of the family of the glorious Ioann Rodionovich Kvashnya. And they say that his mother Feodosia endured many tortures at the hands of the tormentor when she was a widow of great old age, and that she suffered although she was innocent. She had only three sons, men of great bravery: one of them was Vasily whom I have mentioned; the second was Ioann and the third Nikifor, both of whom were killed in battle by the Germans while still in their youth (but nevertheless the Germans were beaten at that time); they were very brave and courageous men, and not only were they beautiful in body, but, in truth, they were adorned with fair morals and fair souls.[1]

And Dmitry Pushkin was put to death by him; he was also a man of great bravery and intellect and already of mature years; he was a relative of the Chelyadnins.[2]

Then a glorious general, Krik [Kirik?] Tyrtov by name, was put to death by him; he was a man not only brave and courageous and versed in the holy scriptures, but indeed great in intellect and, furthermore, meek and gentle, adorned with excellent morals and most pleasant in his good habits, and—still more splendid and remarkable—from the day his mother bore him he was pure and unsullied; he was distinguished and glorified in the Christian army, for he had many wounds inflicted by various barbarians in many battles. And when he was still young he was present[3] at the capture of Kazan', and as a result

were sent from Novgorod to take part in the capture of Syrenesk (Neu-schloss). (*PSRL* xiii, p. 297; see above, pp. 114–15). When Kirepega was captured in 1558 (see above, p. 116, n. 1) by A. I. Shein and D. F. Adashev, Razladin and one Semen Nashchekin were left there as *voevody*. (*PSRL* xiii, p. 303.)

Rodion Nestorovich and his son Ivan Kvashnya were distinguished boyars of Ivan I and Dmitry Donskoy respectively.

[2] It is not known who this Dmitry Pushkin was. There were nine Pushkins in the *Oprichnina*, and two of them are mentioned in Ivan's *Sinodik* as having been executed (Veselovsky, *Sinodik*, p. 327). Perhaps their father, Tret'yak-Dmitry Ivanovich Pushkin-Kurchev, is the one mentioned by Kurbsky, although when and how he died is not known. (Kobrin, *Sostav oprichnogo dvora*, p. 70.)

[3] Lit. "he was young"—i.e., presumably, he fought as a cadet or page. юношествовал, however, may be a corruption of юный шествовал.

пострадал, презельнаго ради и крепкого мужества. Но и таковаго мучитель кровопийственный не пощадил!

Тогда же, або мало пред тем, убиен от него муж благоверный, Андрей, внук славнаго и сильного рыцаря Дмитрея, глаголемаго Шеина, с роду Морозовых, яже еще вышли от Немец, вкупе с Рюриком, прародителем Руских княжат, седмь мужей храбрых и благородных. Той-то был Мисса Морозов един от них; а и Дмитрей он венец принял мученический от Казанскаго царя Магмедеминя, подвизающеся за правоверие. В те же лета убиени от него мужие, того же роду Морозовых, синглитским саном почтенныи. Владимер единому имя было; много лет темницею от него мучен, а потом и погубил его; а другому имя было Лев, по наречению Салтыков, с четырьмя або с пятьма сынами, еще во юношеском веку цветущими. Ныне, последи, слышах о Петре Морозове, аки жив есть; тако же и Львовы дети не все погублены: нецыи остави живы, глаголют.

Тогда же побиени Игнатей Заболацкий, Богдан и Феодосий и другия братия их, стратилаты нарочитые и юноши в роде благородные;[a] глаголют, иже и со единоплемянными их всеродне погублено.

[a] T. благородне: Ar.

_____

[1] Tyrtov was executed between the end of 1572 and March 1573 (Zimin, *Kogda Kurbsky napisal*, p. 307, n. 19; cf. Veselovsky, *Sinodik*, p. 351). He may be the same as Tikhon Tyrtov, who, when in 1558 Kurslav was captured by Shein and Adashev shortly after Kirepega (see above, p. 116, n. 1), was left there as one of the military commanders. Kurbsky, who played a considerable role in the fighting of 1558, would certainly have known him, just as he knew V. V. Razladin, who was also a minor figure in the 1558 campaign.

[2] Andrey Ivanovich Shein was executed in or about 1568 (Zimin, *Sostav Boyarskoy dumy*, p. 74; Veselovsky, *Sinodik*, p. 360).

[3] Мисса—evidently a corruption of Михаил, Миша. For Mikhail Yakovlevich Morozov, see below, pp. 230–1.

[4] Dmitry Vasil'evich Shein, one of Ivan III's most experienced generals, was taken prisoner and killed during the Kazan' expedition of 1514 (Veselovsky, *Sinodik*, p. 360).

[5] Vladimir Vasil'evich Morozov became a member of the Boyar Council in 1561 or 1562. He was imprisoned some time after 1563 and executed probably in 1568. (Zimin, *Sostav Boyarskoy dumy*, pp. 64, 71, 74; Veselovsky, *Sinodik*, p. 313.)

of his exceedingly great courage he lost an eye. Yet even such a man was not spared by the bloodthirsty torturer![1]

And at that time, or a little before, that true-believing man Andrey was put to death by him;[2] he was the grandson of the glorious and mighty knight, Dmitry Shein, from the kin of the Morozovs, who came from the Germans together with Ryurik, the ancestor of the Russian princes; and there were seven brave and noble men [of the Morozovs who were also put to death], and one of them was Mikhail[3] Morozov. And that Dmitry received a martyr's crown from Mehemmed Emin, the khan of Kazan', while fighting for Orthodoxy.[4] And in those years men of the same family of Morozovs who were honoured with the rank of counsellor were put to death by him. Vladimir was the name of one of them: he was tormented by him with many years of prison and then he was killed;[5] and yet another one was called Lev Saltykov—he was put to death with his four or five sons, who were still in the flower of their youth.[6] And now, afterwards, I have heard that Petr Morozov is alive; and also that the children of Lev were not all destroyed; he left some alive, so they say.[7]

And at that time Ignaty Zabolotsky, Bogdan, Fedosy and others of their brothers were put to death, distinguished generals and youths of noble birth; they say that together with all the members of their family they were entirely destroyed.[8]

---

[6] Lev Andreevich Saltykov, who appears to have been one of the "loyal" boyars during the crisis of 1553 (*PSRL* xiii, p. 525), was given the rank of *okol'nichy* in that year and of boyar in 1561 (Zimin, *Sostav Boyarskoy dumy*, p. 66, n. 291). In 1565 he was arrested by Ivan for his inefficient conduct of military affairs in 1564 and released again in the same year after taking a vow of loyalty (Sadikov, *Ocherki*, pp. 22–3). He joined the *Oprichnina* between 1567 and 1570. In 1571 (after forcible tonsure in the Trinity monastery, according to Taube and Kruse) he was executed (Zimin, *ibid.*; Kobrin, *Sostav oprichnogo dvora*, pp. 71–2). Which of his sons died with him is not known. He is known to have had only three: one of them predeceased him, while the other two survived him by several years (Veselovsky, *Sinodik*, p. 335).

[7] Evidently the last two sentences were added by Kurbsky after the completion of his History. Petr Vasil'evich Morozov was still alive in October 1580 (Zimin, *ibid.* p. 64, n. 273). Of the children of Lev Saltykov, Vasily certainly survived: he was last mentioned in the *razryady* in 1577 (Kobrin, *Sostav oprichnogo dvora*, pp. 71–2).

[8] Nothing is known of the execution of the Zabolotskys. One Ignaty Grigor'evich Zabolotsky was sent with Vishnevitsky's first, fruitless, expedi-

И паки побиени Василей и другия братия его, со единоплемянными своими, Бутурлины глаголемые, мужие светли в родех своих; сродницы же бяше оному предреченному Иоанну Петровичю.

Паки убиен от него Иоанн Воронцов, оного Феодора сын, яже во младости своей еще убил отца своего Феодора, со другими оными мужи, ихъже в кронице пишучи воспомянух.

Потом убиен от него муж велика роду и храбрый зело, со женою и со единочадным сыном своим, еще в отроческом веку, аки в пяти или в шести летех, младенческом; а был той человек роду великих Сабуровых, а наречение ему было Замятня. Его-то отца сестра единоутробная была за отцом его, Соломанида, преподобная мученица, о нейже первие в книжице сей воспомянух.

Побиени ж от него стратилаты, або ротмистры, мнози мужие храбрые[a] и искусные в военных вещах: Андрей, глаголемый Кашкаров, муж славный в знаменитых своих заслугах, и брат его, Азарий именем, тако же муж разумный и во священных писаниях искусный, з детками погублен и братиею их, Василей и Григорей, глаголемыя Тетерины; и других стрыев и братии их немало всеродне погубити повелел со женами и з детками их.

[a] Pog., T. храбрае: Ar.

---

tion against the Crimea in 1558 and again with D. Adashev in 1559 (see above, p. 125, n. 1; *PSRL* xiii, pp. 288, 315). Ivan's *Sinodik* mentions Bogdan, Ignaty and *Fedor* (Veselovsky, *Sinodik*, pp. 284–5; cf. Skrynnikov, *Oprichnaya zemel'naya reforma*, p. 237).

[1] Ivan's *Sinodik* mentions six Buturlins by name, including one Vasily (Andreevich) and one Dmitry (Andreevich). The latter served in the *Oprichnina* and was executed in 1575. When and why Vasily Buturlin died is not known. He is last mentioned as being alive in 1567 (Veselovsky, *Sinodik*, p. 268). One Vasily Buturlin is mentioned in the chronicles as having beaten off a Tatar raid at Pronsk in 1559 (*PSRL* xiii, p. 318). The common ancestor of the Buturlins, Ivan Andreevich Buturlya, was in fact the younger brother of Chelyadnin's great-great-grandfather.

[2] See above, pp. 12–13. Ivan Fedorovich Vorontsov was already a member of the *Oprichnina* in 1567. He was executed not earlier than 1571. His

And Vasily Buturlin and others of his cousins together with members of their families were put to death, men of distinguished birth; and they were relatives of Ioann Petrovich [Chelyadnin-Fedorov] whom I mentioned above.[1]

And Ioann Vorontsov was put to death by him; he was the son of that Fedor whom Ivan put to death in his youth together with other men whom I mentioned in my chronicle.[2]

After that a man of noble birth and extreme bravery was put to death by him together with his wife and only son, who was still a child, five or six years old. This man was of the kin of the great Saburovs and his name was Zamyatnya. The sister of his father, Solomonida, that holy martyr whom I mentioned earlier in this book, was married to the father of the tsar.[3]

And many generals and cavalry commanders were put to death by him, men brave and skilled in military matters: Andrey Kashkarov, a man glorious and renowned for his services, was executed, and his brother, Azary by name, who was also a man of intellect, versed in the holy scriptures, was put to death with his children and with their cousins, Vasily and Grigory Teterin. And he ordered several of their uncles and cousins to be put to death by whole families, together with their wives and children.[4]

younger brother Vasily, who died in battle in 1579, also served in the *Oprichnina*. (Kobrin, *Sostav oprichnogo dvora*, pp. 30–1.)

[3] When and why (Timofey) Zamyatnya Ivanovich Saburov, the son of Solomonia Saburov's brother, Ivan Yur'evich, was executed is not known. There is evidence of his active career at court and in the army from 1556 to 1559 (Veselovsky, *Sinodik*, p. 333; *PSRL* XIII, p. 320). In 1572 he was engaged in a squabble over precedence with one of the *oprichniki*, Prince V. A. Sitsky (Sadikov, *Ocherki*, p. 76, n. 2). Ustryalov thinks that he is the same as the "Iwan Zathania" mentioned by Taube and Kruse as having been executed together with Ivan Petrovich and Vasily Petrovich Yakovlev (1571) (Ustryalov, *Skazaniya*, pp. 330–1). Veselovsky, however, considers that he was executed and thrown in the Volkhov river in Novgorod by Ivan in 1570 (Veselovsky, *Sinodik*, p. 333).

[4] Andrey Kashkarov and Timofey Teterin, "archer captains" (*streletskie golovy*), were both active during the Livonian campaigns of 1558–60 and are usually mentioned together in the chronicles (see, for instance, *PSRL* XIII, pp. 293, 323). At the end of the 1550's Teterin was banished to the Siysky monastery and forcibly tonsured there. He managed, however, to escape to Lithuania shortly afterwards. Andrey Kashkarov was evidently

Такожде и от Резанские шляхты благородных мужей, зацных в родех, мужественных же и храбрых, и славными заслугами украшенных, Данила Чюлкова и других некоторых искусных поляниц и воеводителей, вкратце же рещи,[a] пагубников бусурманских, а оборонителей краин християнских, и ротмистра, нарочитова в мужестве Феодора Булгакова со братиями их и со другими многими единоплемянными их всеродне погубленно того жь лета и того единого дня, в новопоставленом[b] граде на самом Танаисе, посланными от него прелютыми кромешники, у нихже был воев демонских воевода, любовник его, Федор Басманов (яже последи зарезал рукою своею отца своего Алексея, преславного похлебника, а по их языку, маянка и губителя своего и Святоруские земли). О Боже праведный! коль праведен еси, Господи, и праведны[c] судьбы Твои! Что братиям готовал, то вскоре и сам вкусил.

Тогда же и того дня он убил предреченнаго, славного в доброте и пресветлаго княжа в роде, Владимера Курлетева; и тогда же он вкупе заклал с ним Григорея Степанова сына Сидорова, с роду великих синглитов Резанских. А той-то был Степан, отец его, муж славный в добродетелех, и в богатырских вещах искусен; служаше много лет, аж до осмидесяти лет, верне и трудолюбне зело империи Святоруской. Потом же, аки седмица едина преиде, нападоша на той же новопоставленный град поганый Измаильтеский со

[a] Т. вкратцех рещи   [b] Patr., Pog., Т. нопоставленом: Ar.
[c] Т. праведныи: Ar.

caught helping him to escape; presumably this was the reason for his execution. (*Poslaniya Ivana Groznogo*, p. 588; Veselovsky, *Sinodik*, p. 293; Skrynnikov, *Oprichnaya zemel'naya reforma*, p. 237.)

Who the two Teterins mentioned here were is not known (however, see below, p. 224, n. 2). There are several Teterins mentioned in Ivan's *Sinodik* (Veselovsky, *Sinodik*, pp. 346–7).

Andrey Fedorovich and Azary Fedorovich Kashkarov were probably executed in 1566 (Veselovsky, *Sinodik*, pp. 293–4).

[1] Ps. cxix. 137. судьбы is probably in error for суды.

[2] Both Basmanovs, formerly leading members of the *Oprichnina*, fell from favour in 1570 when they were accused of treachery and presumably

And also certain well-born men from the nobility of Ryazan',
distinguished in stock, brave and courageous, adorned with
glorious service, Danilo Chulkov and certain other men skilled
in capturing prisoners and leading troops—in short, destroyers
of the Mussulmans and defenders of the Christian frontier-
lands—and a cavalry commander who was distinguished for
his courage, Fedor Bulgakov, together with their brothers and
many other relations—all were put to death by whole families
in the same year and on the same day in the newly-built fortress
on the Tanais [Don] itself by his fierce children of darkness
whom he sent and who had as the leader of his satanic host his
favourite, Fedor Basmanov (afterwards with his own hands he
cut the throat of his father Aleksey, that most glorious flatterer,
or, in their tongue, maniac and destroyer of himself and of the
holy Russian land). O righteous God! How righteous art
Thou and upright are Thy judgements![1] What he [Fedor
Basmanov] prepared for his brethren he himself soon tasted.[2]

And on that very same day he put to death the prince whom
I have mentioned above and who was glorious in virtue and
brilliant in birth, Vladimir Kurlyatev; and together with him
he slew Grigory Stepanovich Sidorov from the kin of the great
counsellors of Ryazan'. Now his father Stepan was glorious in
virtue and skilled in deeds of valour; truly and most diligently
he served the holy Russian empire for many years until the
age of eighty. Then, after about a week had passed, the pagan
Ishmaelite attacked that very same newly-built fortress to-

put to death; only Kurbsky mentions the fact that Fedor cut his father's
throat and was later executed by Ivan.

Danilo Chulkov is mentioned frequently in the chronicles between 1554
and 1558 in connection with various military activities on the southern
borders. In 1558 he took part in Vishnevetsky's Crimean expedition (see
above, p. 125, n. 1) together with one Vasily Teterin, presumably the
Teterin mentioned above by Kurbsky (DRK, p. 192).

Who exactly Fedor Bulgakov was and which members of his family were
executed is not known—he is not mentioned in Ivan's Sinodik.

Where, when and why this massacre by the Basmanovs took place is not
known. The "newly-built fortress on the Don" may well have been the
steppe frontier town of Epifan', in the district of Ryazan', which prior to
1571-2 belonged to Ivan Fedorovich Mstislavsky and evidently housed a large
garrison of frontier troops. (Tikhomirov, Rossiya v XVI stoletii, pp. 388 sq.)

царевичи своими, аки в десяти тысящах; християнския же воини сопрошашася с ними крепце, бронящеся града и убогих християн, при том граде живущих, от наглаго нахождения поганского, и в том обронению подвизающеся храбре, овы зело уранены,[a] овы же, до смерти подвизающеся, посечени от поганов. И абие по той битве, аки[b] по трех днях — предивно и ужасно не токмо ко изречению, но и ко слышанию — случилося тяжко и изумению нечто: абие внезапу нападоша от того прелютаго зверя и Святоруские земли губителя, от того антихристова сына и стаинника, предреченные кромешники его на оставших християнских воинов, которые о ни непщеванни были еще остати от заклания их и ото Измаильтеска избиения; прибегших их глаголют во град, вопиющих, яко беснующихся, по домох или станех[c] рыщущих или оптекающих: "Где есть онъсица князь Андрей Мещерский и князь Никита брат его, и Григорей Иоаннов сын Сидорова, (предреченному стры-ечный)?" Слуги же их, показующе им телеса мученические, ото Измаильтян новоизбиенные; они же яко неистовые, уповающе еще их живых, вскочиша в домы их резати с мучительскими орудии уготованными;[d] видевше же уже их мертвых, абие поскочиша со постыдением ко зверю сеун-чевати сие.

Тако же случишася подобно и брату моему единоплемян-ному, княжати Ярославскому, емуже имя было Андрей, по наречению Аленкин, внук предреченнаго княжати пре-славнаго, Феодора Романовича. Ибо случилося ему бранити единаго места или града[e] Северских градов от нахождения

Patr., T. укранены: Ar. Patr., Pog. абие: Ar. T. и листех: Ar. T. уготованным: Ar., Patr., Pog. Patr., Pog., T. грады: Ar.

---

[1] Or "close by it".
[2] Lit. "who had not [o ни in error for ани ?] been thought to survive...".
[3] It is impossible to date accurately either of the two punitive expeditions led by F. Basmanov against Epifan'(?). However, as Vladimir Kurlyatev is last mentioned as being alive in 1568, and as the Basmanovs fell from favour

gether with his tsareviches, some ten thousand men strong. And the Christian troops fought fiercely with them, defending the fortress and the poor Christians living in it[1] from the insolent pagan attack; and in that defence some of those who fought valiantly were seriously wounded and others who fought to the death were slain by the pagans. And—most wondrous and awful not only to utter but also to hear—straightway after that battle, some three days later, something grievous and amazing occurred: suddenly those above-mentioned children of darkness, sent by that ferocious beast, that destroyer of the holy Russian land, that son and servant of the antichrist, fell upon the remaining Christian soldiers who had, beyond all expectation,[2] survived the [previous] slaughter [by the *Oprichnina*] and massacre by the Ishmaelites. They say that they ran into the fortress, shrieking like men possessed and scurrying and running around the houses and dwelling-places, saying: "Where is that Prince Andrey Meshchersky and Prince Nikita his brother and Grigory Ivanovich Sidorov (the cousin of the one I mentioned above)?" And their servants showed them their martyr's bodies recently slain by the Ishmaelites. And like frenzied men, hoping to find them still alive, they leaped into the houses to cut them down with their torturous weapons, which they had prepared; and when they saw that they were already dead, they straightway galloped off in shame to report this to the beast.[3]

And a similar thing happened to my cousin, the prince of Yaroslavl', whose name was Andrey Alenkin and who was the grandson of that most glorious prince, Fedor Romanovich.[4] He happened to be defending one of the towns or fortresses in the Seversk district from an insolent attack of the enemy, and

in 1570, the date must have been some time between 1568 and 1570 (see above, p. 184, n. 2, where Kurlyatev is mentioned).

Grigory Stepanovich Sidorov is last mentioned as serving in the Ryazan' towns of Pronsk and Mikhaylov between 1563 and 1567 (Veselovsky, *Sinodik*, p. 338).

Nothing is known of the careers of A. and N. Meshchersky and G. I. Sidorov. They were, presumably, connected with service on the southern front, as was G. S. Sidorov's father Stepan.

[4] For Fedor Romanovich, see above, p. 190, n. 1.

наглаго супостатов, и застрелен бысть из праща огненнаго, и умре на завтрее; а по третьем дни, прискочиша от мучителя кромешники заклати его, и обретоша уже его мертва, и поскочиша ко зверю сеунчевати. Зверь же кровоядный и ненасытимы,[a] по смерти святаго подвижника, отчизну того и все стяжание от жены и детков отнял, преселивши их в дальную землю от их отечества, и тамо, глаголют, всеродне тоскою погубил всех.

Сабуровых же других, глаголемых Долгих, а воистинну великих в мужестве и храбрости, и других, Сарыхозиных, всеродне погубити повелел. Абие ведено их, глаголют, вкупе осмьдесят душ со женами и з детьми, яко и младенцы, у сосцов сущие, в немотующим еще веку, на матерних руках играющеся, ко посечению носими.

В тех же летех, или мало пред тем, погубил зацного землянина имянем Никиту, по наречению Казаринова, и с[b] сыном единородным Феодором, во цветущем возрасте сущаго, служащаго много лет верне империи Святоруской. А погубил его таковым образом: егда избранных катов послал[c] изымати его, он же, видев их, уехал был пред ними[d] во един монастырь, на Оке реке лежащ, и тамо принял на ся великий ангельский образ; егда же посланные от мучителя кромешники[e] начаша пытатися о нем, он же, последующе Христу своему, уготовався, сиречь принявши святые тайны, изыде во стретение сим и рече со дерзновением: "Аз есми, егож ищете!" Они же яша и приведоша его связана пред него во кровопийственный град, глаголемую Слободу; зверь же словесный, егда узрел его во ангельском чину, абие возопил, яко сущей ругатель тайнам христианским: "Он, рече, ангел: подобает ему на небо возлетети." И абие

[a] Patr., Pog. нанасытимый: Ar. Pog.   [c] Patr., Pog. послан: Ar.   [e] T. кромешними: Ar., Pog.   [b] Patr.   c omitted in Ar. and   [d] T. ним: Ar., Patr., Pog.

---

[1] Lit. "striver", "fighter" in the spiritual sense.
[2] This is the only known reference to the death of Prince Andrey Fedorovich Alenkin or the confiscation of his property. He is last mentioned as serving in Shatsk (due east of Epifan') in 1567 (Veselovsky, *Sinodik*, p. 261).

he was shot by a siege-gun and he died on the following morning. Three days later the children of darkness came galloping up from the torturer to slay him, and finding him already dead they galloped back to report to the beast. And the bloodthirsty insatiable beast, after the death of that holy warrior,[1] took away his patrimonies and all his possessions from his wife and little children, whom he transferred to a land far away from their home; and there, they say, he destroyed the whole family by grief.[2]

And then he ordered some other Saburovs named Dolgy, who were truly great in courage and bravery, and some others called Sarykhozin to be put to death with all their families. And they say that they were all led to the slaughter straightway, altogether eighty souls with their wives and children; and the babes, sucking at the breast, who could not yet talk and were still playing in their mothers' arms, were carried off to the slaughter.[3]

And in those same years, or a little before this, he put to death a distinguished landowner by the name of Nikita Kazarinov together with his only-begotten son Fedor; he was in the prime of life and had served the holy Russian empire for many years. And he put him to death in the following manner: he sent his chosen executioners to seize him; but when he saw them coming, he went away and escaped to a monastery situated on the river Oka, and there he accepted the great angelic habit. And when the children of darkness who had been sent by the torturer began to make enquiries about him, he, following his Christ, prepared himself, that is to say he took the holy sacraments and went out to meet them, saying with boldness: "I am he whom you seek!" And they took him and led him to the tsar in chains, to that bloody fortress named [Aleksandrova] Sloboda; and when the human beast saw him in the angelic order, he immediately yelled out, like a very scoffer of the Christian sacraments, saying: "He is an angel: he ought to fly up to heaven!" And straightway he ordered a barrel or two

---

[3] Little is known either of the Dolgovo-Saburovs or of the Sarykhozins. One Mark Sarykhozin deserted to Lithuania together with Timofey Teterin. See above, p. 223, n. 4.

бочку пороху, або две, под един струбец повелел поставити и, привязавши тамо мужа, взорвати. Воистинну злым произволением согласяся со отцем своим, сатоною, неволею правду провещал еси прелукавыми усты! Яко древле Каияфа, бесящеся на Христа, неволительне пророчествующе, тако ж и ты зде, окаянный, рекл еси, ко восхождению небесному верующим во Христа, паче же мучеником, понеже Христос страстию своею, излиянием надражайшие крови своей, небо верным отворил ко возлетению или восхождению небесному.

И что излишне глаголю? Аще бы писал по родом и по имянам их, ихже памятую добре, мужей оных храбрых и нарочитых, благородных в родех, и, в книгу пишучи, не вместил бы. А что реку о тех, ихже памятью, немощи ради человеческие, не объях и забвение уже погрузило? Но имяна их в книгах животных лутше есть приснопамятныи; а ни намнейшая их страдания незабвенни пред Богом, мздовоздаятелем благим и сердцевидцем, тайных всех испытателем.

По тех же всех, уже предреченных, убиен от него же муж в роде славный, его же был сингклит избранные роды, Михаил Морозов с сыном Иоанном, аки в восминадесять[a] летех, с младенцем и со другим юнейшим, емуже имя забых, и со женою его Евдокиею, яже была дщерь князя Дмитрея Бельского, ближняго сродника Ягайла короля. И воистинну, глаголют ее во святом жительстве пребывающу, яко же последи и мученическим венцем с мужем своим со возлюблеными своими[b] вкупе украсилася, понеже вкупе пострадаша от мучителя.

[a] Т. осмидесяти: Ar.   [b] Pog. свои: Ar.

---

[1] John xi. 49–52.
[2] Little or nothing is known of Nikita Kazarinov or his son. He is last mentioned alive in 1561 (Veselovsky, *Sinodik*, p. 290).
[3] Or, perhaps, "Why do I say so much?" "Why do I speak excessively?"
[4] Or, perhaps, "they say she was a saint, as she was adorned...".

of powder to be placed beneath a small pile of wood, and having tied the man up there he ordered it to be exploded. Verily agreeing in evil intent with your father Satan did you unwittingly prophesy the truth with your wicked lips! Just as Caiaphas of old, raging against Christ, prophesied unwittingly,[1] so too did you, accursed one, speak of the heavenly ascent of those who believe in Christ—particularly of the martyrs; for by His passion, by the shedding of His dearest blood, Christ opened heaven to the faithful, so that they might fly up or ascend there.[2]

What more shall I say?[3] Were I to write about [all] the families and [to include all] the names of those whom I well remember—those brave distinguished men of noble birth—I would not be able to fit them into a book. But what say I of those whom, because of human frailty, I have not encompassed with my memory and who have already been plunged into oblivion? Their names are more permanently recorded in the books of life, and the least of their sufferings are not forgotten before God, who rewards the good and sees into men's hearts and who finds out all secrets.

Now after all these things which I have talked about, a man of glorious birth, a member of his Chosen Council, Mikhail Morozov, was put to death with his son Ioann, who was about eighteen, and with another child, who was still younger and whose name I have forgotten, and with his wife Evdokia, the daughter of Prince Dmitry Bel'sky, a close kinsman of King Jagiello; and they say that she lived a saintly life[4] and that afterwards she was adorned with a martyr's crown together with her husband and her beloved children; for together they all suffered at the hands of the torturer.[5]

[5] This final paragraph was probably added after Kurbsky had completed his History: the execution of Mikhail Yakovlevich Morozov only took place in the summer of 1573, at the same time as that of M. Vorotynsky and N. Odoevsky (see above, p. 195, n. 1; Zimin, *Kogda Kurbsky napisal*, p. 307).

Morozov's career as courtier, ambassador and general was long and successful. He became a member of the Boyar Council in 1549 or 1550. He had three sons: the one whose name Kurbsky forgot was probably Fedor. (Zimin, *Sostav Boyarskoy dumy*, p. 62, n. 244; Veselovsky, *Sinodik*, p. 314.)

VIII

О страдании священномученика Филиппа митрополита Московского

Не безбедно же ми мню,[a] умолчати о священномучениках, от него пострадавших; но достоит, яко возможно, вкратце претещи, оставляюще паче тамо живущим, сведомшим и ближайшим, паче же мудрейшим и разумнейшим. В недостатцех или в погрешенных молимся простити.[b]

По умертвии митрополита Московского Афонасия, или по изшествию его волею от престола, возведен бысть Филип, с Соловецкого острова игумен, на архиепископский престол Руские митрополии, муж, яко рехом, славна и велика рода, и от младости своея вольною мнишескою нищетою и священнолепным жительством украшен, в разуме же крепок и мужественнейш. Егда же уже епископом поставлен, тогда епископскими делы начат украшатися, паче же апостольски[c] по Бозе ревновати. Видев оного царя, не по Бозе ходяща, всяческими кровьми христианскими невинными обливаема, всякие неподобные и скверные дела исполняюща[d] и начал первие молити благовременне, яко апостол великий рече, и безвремменне належати; потом претити страшным судом Христовым, заклинающе, по данной ему от Бога епископской власти, и глаголати не стыдяся о свидениих Господних так прегордому и прелютому, безчеловечному царю. Он же многу с ним брань воздвиже и на потвари презлыя и сикованцы абие устремился. О неслыханныя

---

[a] Т. не небезбедно же, мню: Ar.   [b] рекше моего недостатка грубство напомнити (наполнити: Patr., Pog.) и, елико достоит исправлению о (от: Pog.) нас написанных о страдальцех, исправити и мучениския подвиги преукрасити и облаголепити, нели (нежели: Patr., Pog.) от нас в гонении крыющихся в дальных землях сущих: in margin of Ar., Pog. In text of Patr.   [c] Т. апостольскии: Ar.
[d] Patr., Т. исполняюще: Ar.

---

[1] A marginal note reads as follows: "That is to say [we pray you] to fill

VIII

Concerning the suffering of the holy martyr Philipp,
metropolitan of Moscow

It would be harmful for me, I think, to remain silent about the
holy martyrs who suffered at his hands; but it is fitting to mention them briefly, as far as I can, while leaving [most facts] to those
who live there and who are more informed and closer [to the
events], and, furthermore, who are wiser and more intelligent.
We pray to be forgiven our failings and shortcomings.[1]

After the death of Afanasy, metropolitan of Moscow, or after
his voluntary departure from the throne,[2] Philipp, abbot of the
monastery on the island of Solovki, was elevated to the archiepiscopal throne of the Russian metropolitanate; as I have said,
he was a man of glorious and noble stock, adorned from his
youth with voluntary monastic poverty and holy living, firm in
understanding and most courageous. And when he was made
bishop, he became distinguished for his episcopal deeds, and,
furthermore, he showed zeal for God, like an apostle. When he
saw the tsar not walking in God but soaked with the blood of all
kinds of innocent Christians and performing every kind of unholy and foul deed, he began first of all to beg him and to
insist, in season, out of season, as the great apostle said.[3] Then
he began to threaten him with the dreadful judgement of
Christ, adjuring him with the episcopal power given him by
God and being not ashamed to talk of the testimony of the
Lord to a tsar so exceedingly proud and fierce and inhuman.
And the tsar raised much strife against him and hastened forthwith to most evil slander and sycophancy. O deeds unheard-of

in the shortcomings caused by our ignorance, and, in as far as what we have
written about the sufferers can be corrected, to make corrections and to
embellish and to ennoble their martyrs' exploits, rather than that this be
done by us who are hiding in exile in distant lands."

[2] Metropolitan Afanasy quitted the metropolitanate in May 1566 and
retired to the Chudov monastery.

[3] 2 Tim. iv. 2.

вещи, и ко изглаголанию тяжки! Посылает по всей[a] тамо Руской земле ласкателей своих скверных, тамо и овамо рыщуще[b] и обтичюще, аки волцы разтерзатели от прелютейшаго зверя послани, ищуще и набывающе на[c] святаго епископа изметных вещей; лжесвидетелей же многими дарьми и великих властей обещаньми, где бы обрести могли, тамо и овамо обзирающе, со прилежанием изыскуют.[d]

О беды превеликия от неслыханныя и претягчайшие дерзости[e] бесовские! о замышления человеческия, безстудием диаволим поджигаеми! Кто слыхал где[f] епископа от мирских судима и испытуема? Яко пишет Григорий Богослов в слове о похвале Афонасия Великого, нарекающе на собор безбожных Агарян:[g] ''Иже, рече, посаждаху мирских людей и привождаху пред тех[h] на испытания епископов и презвитеров, им же а ни края уха не достоило таковых послушати'', и прочее. Где законы священные? где правила седьмостолпные? где уложения и уставы апостольские? Все попранны и наруганны от пресквернейшаго кровоядца зверя и от безумнейших человек, угодников его, пагубников отечества!

Что же по сих начинает? На святителя дерзающе, не посылает до патриарха Констянтинапольскаго (под егож судом Руские митрополиты) аще бы были оклеветанни от кого в чем, нигде инде, точию пред ним, достойни о собе ответ дати; а ни испрашает от престола патриаршеского ексарха на испытание епископъское. И воистинну, бесясь на святаго архиепископа, негли забыл еси[i] повесть свежую или не зело давную, устнама твоима, часто произносимую,

---

[a] Patr., T. своей: Ar. [b] T. рещуще: Ar., Patr., Pog.
[c] T. набывающеи: Ar. [d] Подобно сему суть (есть: Pog.) Симеон Метовраст в Златоустове житии воспоминает пиша, яко проклятаго сонмища Феофилова Акакий епископ Берийский испытовали святаго Златоустаго жития, хотяще вину на него изметную обрести, аще б негли одлити, яковое на него дело скверное обрели, яко писано: исчезоша испытающии испытания: in margin of Ar., Pog.; in text of Patr.
[e] T. претяжчанные дерзостны [f] Patr., Pog., T. зде: Ar.
[g] Patr. агирян: Ar. [h] Patr. тем: Ar. [i] T. есть: Ar.

and heavy to the utterance! He sent his foul flatterers through-out the whole Russian land, rushing to and fro and running around like devouring wolves sent by the most ferocious beast, seeking and finding evidence of apostasy[1] against the holy bishop. And searching in all directions, wherever they might find them, they diligently sought out false witnesses, [bribing them] with many gifts and with promises of great districts.[2]

O exceedingly great disaster caused by unheard-of and most grievous devilish arrogance! O human devices enflamed by the shamelessness of the devil! Who has ever heard of a bishop judged and questioned by laymen? As Gregory the Theologian writes in his oration praising Athanasius the Great, in which he complains of the council of the godless sons of Hagar: "Who placed laymen on the council and brought before them for questioning bishops and priests who should not have listened to such people even out of the corner of their ears",[3] and so forth. Where are the sacred laws? Where are the canons of the seven Oecumenical Councils?[4] Where are the decrees and rules of the Apostles? All are trampled on and abused by that most foul bloodthirsty beast and by those madmen, his toadies, the destroyers of their fatherland!

What did he do after this? In his presumptuous attitude towards the bishop he did not send to the patriarch of Con-stantinople, under whose jurisdiction are the Russian metro-politans; for should they·[the metropolitans] be accused of anything by anyone, they should not answer for themselves anywhere else but in front of the patriarch. Yet the tsar did not even ask the patriarchal throne for an exarch to question his bishop. Indeed, in your anger against the holy archbishop per-haps you forgot that story which is fresh, or not too old, and

---

[1] Presumably the meaning of изметные вещи.

[2] A marginal note reads as follows: "In like manner Symeon Meta-phrastes, writing in the Life of Chrysostom, recalls how Acacius, bishop of Beroea, [and others] on the accursed synod of Theophilus, investigated Chrysostom's holy life, wishing to find him guilty of apostasy, if only to find some evil deed committed since his youth, as it is written: those who carry out a search have disappeared" (Ps. lxiv. 6). For St Symeon Metaphrastes, see *Correspondence*, p. 234, n. 1.

[3] Migne, *PG*, vol. 35, col. 1107.   [4] Lit. "the seven-pillared canons".

о святом Петре сущую, Руском митрополите, на приключшуюся ему лжеклевету от Тверскаго епископа прегордаго? Тогда услышавше сие, вси велицыи княжата Руские не дерзнули разсмотряти между епископов, или судити священников; бо абие послали ко патриарху Констянтинопольскому о ексарха, да разсмотрит или разсудит о сем, яко пространнейшее пишет в литописней книзе Руской о сем. Або тебе не образ сие был, о зверю кровопивственный, яще ли еси християнин хотел быти?

Но собирает на святителя скверные свои соборища ереев Вельзавелиных и проклятое сонмище согласником Каиафиных, и мирует с ними, яко Ирод со Пилатом, и приходят вкупе со зверем в великую церковь, и садятся на месте святе — мерзость запустения со главою окружения их и со трудом устен их — и повелевают — о[a] смрадящие и проклятые власти! — привести пред ся епископа преподобнаго, во освященных одеждах оболчена, и поставляют лжеклеветателей, мужей скверных, предателей своего спасения — о коль тяжко и умиленно ко изречению! — и абие обдирают святительские[b] одежды с него, и катом отдают в руки святаго мужа, от младости в добродетелех превозсиявшаго, и нага влекут из церкви, и посаждают на вола опоко — окаянныи и скверныи! — и бичуют люте, нещадно, тело, многими леты удрученное от поста, водяще по позорищам града и места. Он же, боритель храбрый, всякия терпяще, яко не имущи тела, хвалами и песньми в таковых мучениях Бога благодаряще; безчисленных же народов, плачющих горце и рыдающих, священномученическою десницею своею благословяще.

Согласующи же во всем злостию прелютый зверь прелютейшему древнему дракану, губителю роду человеческого, еще не насытился крови священномученика, а ни удовлился

[a] Т. от: Ar., Patr., Pog.   [b] Patr., Т. спасительские: Ar.

---

[1] For the accusations of Bishop Andrey of Tver' levelled against Metropolitan Petr and the subsequent action of the patriarch, see *PSRL* xxi, pp. 326–7.

which your lips have so often uttered, about the false accusations brought by the arrogant bishop of Tver' against St Petr, the metropolitan of Russia? When they heard it, all the great Russian princes did not dare to investigate bishops or judge priests, but straightway they sent to the patriarch of Constantinople for an exarch to investigate or judge this matter, as is written concerning this at greater length in the Russian chronicle book.[1] And was not this an example to you, O bloodthirsty beast, if you wished to be a Christian?

But he gathered together against the bishop his foul councils of the priests of Beelzebub and his accursed collection of those in agreement with Caiaphas, and he was at peace with them, as was Herod with Pilate. And they all came together with the beast into the great church and sat down in the holy place—O abomination of desolation!—surrounding their leader and with poison on their lips,[2] and they ordered—O stinking, accursed powers!—the venerable bishop to be brought before them, clad in his sacred vestments; and they set up false witnesses, foul men who give up their own salvation—O how grievous and piteous to narrate!—and straightway they tore off his episcopal vestments from him and handed over the holy man, who had shone forth in virtue from his childhood, to the executioners and dragged him naked from the church and seated him back to front[3] on an ox—the accursed, foul men!—and fiercely and mercilessly they scourged his body, worn out by many years of fasting, and they led him through the city and the fortress on display.[4] And he, the brave fighter, suffering all things as though he had no body, thanked God in the midst of such torments with praise and song and blessed with his holy martyr's right hand the countless people who bitterly wept and sobbed.

But the savage beast, in agreement in all things evil with that most ferocious dragon of old, the destroyer of the human race, had not yet satiated himself with the blood of the holy martyr

---

[2] Lit. "with the head of their surrounding and the sickness of their lips". For this meaning of труд, see Sreznevsky, *Materialy*, vol. III, cols. 1008–9.

[3] опоко may be a corruption of опако, "backwards". Or it may be a corruption of о паки (окаянныи и скверныи!).

[4] Lit. "through the sights of the city and fortress [i.e. Kremlin]".

неслыханным от веков[a] безчестием оным над преподобным епископом: к тому повелевает его по рукам и ногам и по чрезлам претяжчайшими веригами оковавати и воврещи во ускую и мрачную темницу мужа смученного, престаревшагося, во трудех мнозех удрученного и немощнаго уже тела суща, и темницу оную повелел твердыми заклепы и замки заключити, и согласников своих в злости к темнице стражей приставил. Потом, аки день или два спустя, советников своих неяких посылает к темнице видети, аще уже умер. И глаголют их нецыи вшедших в темницу, аки бы обрели епископа от тех тяжких оков избавлена, на псальмопениях божественных воздевша руки стояща; а оковы все кроме лежаща. Видевше ж сие, посланные сингклитове плачюще, рыдающе и припадающе х коленом его; возвратившижеся скоро к[b] жестокой и непокоривой оной прегордой власти, паче же ко прелютому и ненасытному кровоядцу оному зверю, вся по ряду ему возвеща. Его же абие возопивша глаголют: ''Чары, рече, чары он сотворил, неприятель мой и изменник!'' Тех же советников, видевше умилившихся о сем, начат им претити и грозити различными муками и смертьми. Потом медведя лютаго, заморивши гладом, повелел ко епископу оному в темницу пустити и затворити — сие воистинну слышах от достовернаго самовидца, на то зрящаго — потом на утрие сам прииде и повелел отомкнути темницу, уповающе сьеденна его быти от зверя епископа, и паки обретоша его, благодати ради Божия, цела, а ни мало чем врежденна, тако же, яко и прежде, на молитве стояща; зверя же в кротость овчю преложившась, во едином угле темничном лежаща. Оле чюдо! Зверие, естеством люте бывше, чрез естество в кротость прелагаются;[c] человецы же, по естеству от Бога кротцы сотворенны, от кротости в лютость и безчеловечие само-

[a] Т. веком: Ar., Patr., Pog.   [b] Pog. к omitted in Ar., Patr.
[c] Яко святый Герасим аргументует или свидетельствует о святой первомученице Фекле тому подобно, иж зверие люти медведи (Т. иж to медведи omitted in Ar.) устыдешася и почиташе ее чрез естество в кротость приложишася, и прочее: in margin of Ar., Pog., T. In text of Patr.

and was not satisfied with the unheard-of humiliation of the venerable bishop; and he ordered him, tormented, stricken in years, weighed down with many afflictions and already infirm of body, to be bound by his arms and legs and loins with exceedingly heavy chains and to be cast into a narrow gloomy dungeon. And he ordered that dungeon to be locked with heavy bolts and locks, and he placed his partners in evil on the prison guard. Then about a day or two later he sent certain of his advisers to the prison to see if he was already dead. And some of them who went into the prison say that they found the bishop freed from his heavy bonds and standing with his hands raised, singing divine psalms; and all his fetters lay on one side. And when they saw this, the counsellors who had been sent wept, sobbed and fell down before his knees. And they quickly returned to that cruel, inflexible proud tyrant, or rather to that fierce insatiable blood-drinking beast, and told him all about it. And they say that he straightway cried out: "Spells, spells has he cast, my enemy and traitor!" And when he saw that those counsellors of his were moved to pity for the metropolitan, he began to upbraid them and threaten them with various forms of torture and death. Then he ordered a wild, half-starved bear to be let into the bishop's cell and locked in—this I have verily heard from a reliable witness who saw it—and on the following morning came himself and had the cell unlocked, hoping to find the bishop eaten by the beast, and again he was found whole, thanks to the grace of God, and in no way damaged by anything, and standing in prayer as before; and the beast, whose ferocity had been turned into lamb-like gentleness, was found lying in a corner of the dungeon. O miracle! Beasts, fierce by nature, are turned into gentle animals contrary to nature![1] And men, created gentle by God according to nature, change of their own accord from gentleness

[1] A marginal note reads as follows: "In like manner, the holy Gerasimus argues, or bears witness, concerning Saint Thekla the protomartyr, that fierce wild bears were put to shame and respected her, becoming gentle contrary to nature, and so forth."

властно волею изменяются! Его же глаголют абие отходяща, глаголюща: "Чары, рече, творит епископ!" Воистинну некогда тое ж мучители древнии о творящих чюдеса мученицех глаголали.

Потом глаголют епископа от мучителя заведенна во един монастырь, глаголемый Отрочь, во Тверской земле лежащий,[a] и там глаголют его нецыи пребывша мало не год целый, и аки бы посылал до него и просил благословения его, да простит его, тако же и о возвращению его на престол его; он же, яко слышахом, отвещал ему: "Аще, рече, обещаешися покаятися о своих гресех и отгнати от себя оный полк сатанинский, собранный тобою на пагубу християнскую, сиречь кромешников, або апришнинцов[b] нарицаемых, аз, рече, благословлю тя и прощу, и на престол мой, послушав тебе, возвращуся. Аще ли же ни, да будеши проклят в сем веце и в будущем и с кромешники твоими кровоядными, и со всеми согласующими тебе в злостях!" И овыи глаголют его в том монастыре удавленна быти, за повелением его, от единаго прелютаго и безчеловечнаго кромешника; а друзии поведают, аки бы во оном любимом его граду, глаголем Слободе, еже кровьми християнскими исполнен, созжена быти[c] на горящем углию. Ащели же сице или сице, всяко священномученическим от Христа венцем венчан, егоже измлада возлюбил, за негож и на старость пострадал.

По убиении же митрополита, не токмо много кририков,[d] но и нехиротонисанных мужей благородных околько сот помучено различными муками и погублено; бо там есть, в той земле, мнози мужие благородные светлых родов имения мают, во время мирное архиепископом служат, а егда брань належит от супостатов окрестных, тогда и в войску християнском бывают, которые не хиротонисанны.

[a] Patr., T. лежащие: Ar. [b] Ar. опришинцов: T. [c] Pog., T. бысть: Ar., Patr. [d] Patr., Pog., T. криков: Ar.

---

[1] The headquarters of the *Oprichnina*.

to ferocity and inhumanity! They say that he left immediately, saying: "The bishop casts spells!" Indeed, formerly the torturers of old used to say the same thing about the martyrs who worked miracles.

Then, they say, the bishop was taken by the tormentor to a monastery named Otroch' in the land of Tver'; and some people say that he remained there for nearly a whole year, and that the tsar sent to him asking for his blessing, and asking him to forgive him and return to the metropolitanate. But he, so I have heard, answered him, saying: "If you promise to repent of your sins and to dismiss that satanic host which you have gathered together to destroy Christianity, that is to say your children of darkness or those who are called your *oprichniki*, then I will bless you and forgive you and hearken to you and return to my throne. But if not, then may you be cursed in this life and in the life to come, both with your bloodthirsty children of darkness and with all those who acquiesce in your wicked deeds!" And some say that he was strangled in that monastery at the tsar's command by a certain ferocious and inhuman child of darkness, while others say that he was burned on blazing coals in that favourite town of the tsar, called [Aleksandrova] Sloboda,[1] which is filled with the blood of Christians. Whatever was the case, he was crowned with a holy martyr's crown by Christ, whom he had loved since his childhood and for whom he had suffered in his old age.[2]

Now after the killing of the metropolitan, not only were many clerics[3] subjected to various forms of tortures and put to death, but so also were several hundred noble men who had not been ordained. For in that land of theirs there are many noble men of distinguished families who own estates and who in peacetime serve the archbishops; but when war comes owing to the enemies that are round about, those of them who are not ordained fight in the Christian army.

[2] According to the Life of St Philipp, Malyuta Skuratov (Malyuta-Grigory Luk'yanovich Skuratov-Bel'sky) smothered the metropolitan in the Tver' Otroch' monastery on 23 December 1569. The various accounts of his conflict with Ivan, his imprisonment and murder differ considerably in detail from Kurbsky's.

[3] кририков in error for клириков.

И прежде, даже оному Филиппу на митрополию еще не возведенну, умолен был от князя великого епископ Казанский, именем Герман, да будет архиепископом Руские митрополии: он же аще и много возбраняшесь от тое вещи, так от него, яко и соборне, принужден к сему. И уже аки два дни в полатах церковных на митрополичье дворе бывша его глаголют, но обаче еще воспрещающася от оныя тяготы великого пресвитерства, ноипаче же под так лютым и неразсудным царем быти в том сану не хотяще. И вдался с ним, глаголют, в беседование, тихими и кроткими словесы его наказующе, воспоминающе ему он страшный суд Божий и истязания нелицеприятное кождаго человека о делех, так царей, яко и простых. По беседовании же оном, отоиде царь от него во свои полаты, и абие совет той духовный любимым своим ласкателем изъявил: уже бо слеташася к нему отовсюду, вместо оныя добрыя избранныя рады,[a] не токмо наветники презлыя и поразиты прелукавыя и блазни, но и татие,[b] воистинну, и разбойницы и всяких скверн нечистых исполненные[c] человецы. Они же, боящеся, аще бы епископа послушал совета, абие бы паки были отогнани от лица его и изчезли в свои пропасти и норы, егда услышавше сие от царя, отвещали яко едиными усты: "Боже, рече, сохрани тебя от таковаго совета! Паки ли хощеши, о царю, быти в неволе у того епископа, еще горшей, нежели у Алексея и у Селивестра был еси пред тем много лет?" И моляше его со слезами, х коленам его припадающе,[d] паче же един от них, глаголемый Алексей Басманов, с сыном своим. Он же послушав их, абие епископа с полат церковных изгнати повелел,[e] глаголюще: "Еще, рече, и на митрополию не возведен еси, а уже мя неволею обвязуешь!" И по дву днех обретен во дворе своем мертв епископ он Казанский: овыи глаголют удушенна его тайне, за повелением его, овы же ядом смертоносным уморенна. А был той Герман светла рода человек, яже Полевы нарицаются та шляхта по

[a] Т. ради: Ar.   [b] Т. такие: Ar., Patr., Pog.   [c] Т. исполненных: Ar., Pog.   [d] Patr., Pog., Т. припадающим: Ar.
[e] Т. послал от церковных изгнати повелел: Ar.

And even before Philipp had been elevated to the dignity of metropolitan, the [arch]bishop of Kazan', German by name, was begged by the grand prince to become archbishop of the Russian metropolitanate. And although he strongly resisted such an offer, he was forced to it both by the tsar and by a council [of the clergy]. And they say that he spent about two days in the ecclesiastical chambers of the metropolitan's court, but that he still refused to accept the burden of that great office, especially as he had no desire for that office under so fierce and insensate a tsar. And they say that he engaged in conversation with the tsar, instructing him with quiet and meek words, reminding him of the dreadful judgement of God and of the impartial questioning of all men, tsars and simple folk alike, concerning their deeds. And after that conversation the tsar went away to his palace and forthwith told his favourite flatterers of that spiritual advice, for they had all run to meet him from all sides—instead of that good Chosen Council there were not only wicked slanderers and most cunning parasites and buffoons, but thieves, indeed, and bandits and men filled with all kinds of foul impurities. And when they heard this from the tsar, they were afraid lest he should listen to the advice of the bishop and lest they should be driven away again from his presence and disappear into their holes and warrens. And they answered as it were with one mouth, saying: "May God protect you from such advice! Do you wish, O tsar, again to be a captive of that bishop to a still worse degree than you were the captive of Aleksey [Adashev] and Sil'vestr many years ago?" And they entreated him with tears, falling before his knees, especially one of them named Aleksey Basmanov and his son. And he listened to them and immediately he ordered the bishop to be driven out of the ecclesiastical palace, saying: "You have not yet been elevated to the metropolitanate and already you are binding me in captivity!" And two days later the bishop of Kazan' was found dead in his court. Some say that he was secretly strangled at the command of the tsar, others that he was killed by deadly poison. And German was a man of distinguished stock—that branch of the nobility was called Polev after their patrimony; and he was a man of great physical

отчине; и бе он яко тела великого муж, так и разума многаго, и муж чистаго и воистинну святаго жительства, и священных писаней последователь, и ревнитель по Бозе, и в трудех духовных мног; к тому и Максима Философа мало нечто отчасти учения причастен был; аще же и от Осифлянских мнихов четы произыде, но отнють обычая лукаваго и обыкновенного их лицемерия непричастен был, но человек простый, истинный и непоколебим в разуме, и велик помошник был в напастех и в бедах обьятым, тако же и ко убогим милостив зело.

Потом убил архиепископа Великого Новаграда, Пимина. Тот-то был Пимин чистаго и зело жестокаго жительства, но в дивных был обычаех, бо глаголют его похлебовати мучителю, и гонитель был вкупе на Филиппа митрополита, а мало последи и сам смертную чашу испил от него: бо приехав сам в Новград Великий, в реце его утопити повелел.

И тогда же таковое гонение воздвиг во оном месте великом, иже, глаголют, единого дня посещи, и потопити, и пожещи, и другими различными муками помучити больши пятинадесяти тысящ мужей единых, кроме жен и детей, повелел.

В[a] том же тогда прелютом пожаре убиен от него Андрей, глаголемый Тулупов, с роду княжат Стародубских, мужь кроток и благонравен, в довольных летех был; и другий мужь Цыплетев, нареченный Неудача, с роду княжат Белозерских, со женою и со детками погублен, тако ж

---

[a] Patr., Pog., T.   в omitted in Ar.

---

[1] German Polev was archbishop of Kazan' from 12 March 1564 to 6 November 1567 when he died in Moscow. There is no other evidence to show that he was metropolitan-elect after Afanasy retired to the Chudov monastery in May 1566, or that he was found dead two days after being driven out of the metropolitan's court in Moscow—indeed, he was present at Metropolitan Philipp's enthronement in July 1566.

[2] Again Kurbsky's information is inaccurate. Archbishop Pimen was indeed one of the bitter enemies of Philipp and probably had a hand in his dismissal (November 1568). In early 1570, when Ivan IV came to Novgorod with his bloody punitive campaign, he accused Pimen of plotting to

stature and of much intellect, a man of pure and, indeed, holy life, versed in the holy scriptures, zealous towards God and great in spiritual activity; furthermore, to a certain extent he even shared in the teaching of Maksim the Philosopher [Maksim the Greek]; even though he came from that band of Josephian monks, he had no share at all in their cunning habits or their usual hypocrisy, but was a simple man, true and unshakable in wisdom and a great helper of those in trouble and distress; and he was also very merciful to the poor.[1]

Then he put to death the archbishop of Novgorod the Great, Pimen. Now this Pimen was a man of pure and exceedingly strict life, but he was also a man of strange ways, for they say that he flattered the torturer and that he persecuted Metropolitan Philipp together with the tsar, and shortly afterwards he himself drank the cup of death at his hands: for when the tsar came to Novgorod the Great, he ordered him to be drowned in the river.[2]

And at that same time he raised such persecution in that great city, which, they say, he visited for one day, and he ordered more than fifteen thousand men alone—to say nothing of their wives and children—to be drowned, burned and tormented with other forms of torture.[3]

And in that same ferocious conflagration Andrey Tulupov, of the family of the princes of Starodub, was put to death by him; he was gentle and virtuous and of ripe years.[4] And another man, by the name of Neudacha Tsyplyatev, of the family of the princes of Beloozero, was killed with his wife and little children;

betray the city to Poland, arrested him and sent him to Moscow. He died in September 1571 in a monastery in the Tula district.

[3] The "campaign" against Novgorod and Pskov lasted some six weeks and was caused, ostensibly, by the "treachery" of the Novgorodians and Pskovites. Ivan came to Novgorod "between Christmas and Epiphany", i.e. between 25 December 1569 and 6 January 1570 (*PL* II, p. 261). The estimates of the total number of those executed in Novgorod range from 1500 to 60,000.

[4] Prince Andrey Vasil'evich Tulupov-Starodubsky was evidently executed (together with his wife, son and three daughters) in Novgorod in 1570. In 1550 he had been given a *pomest'e* in the district of Novgorod (Veselovsky, *Sinodik*, pp. 349–50). Another Tulupov, Boris Davidovich, was a member of the *Oprichnina* and was executed some time after 1574 (Kobrin, *Sostav oprichnogo dvora*, p. 79).

был благонравен и искусен и богат зело; а были тые даны[a] на послужение великия церкви Софии, сиречь Премудрости Божия. И другие с ними благородные шляхетные мужи и юноши различные помучени и побиени.

И слышахом, иже великие, проклятые, кровавые богатства тогда приобрел; бо[b] в том великом в старожительном месте, в Новеграде, род живет куплелюбен;[c] бо мают от самого места порт к морю, сего ради и богати зело бывают; подобне,[d] яко мню, великих ради богатств губил их.

Потом поставлено[e] другаго архиепископа в того место, мужа, яко слышахом, нарочита и кротка; но, аки по дву летех, и того повелел убити со двема опаты, сиречь игумены великими, або архимандриты.

К тому же в то время множество презвитеров и мнихов различне помученно и погубленно.

Тогда[f] же убиен от него Корнилий, игумен, Печерскаго монастыря начальник, муж свят и во преподобию мног и славен: бо от младости своей во мнишеских трудех провозсиял, и монастырь он предреченный воздвиже и его многими труды и молитвами к Богу, идеже и бесчисленные чудеса прежде истекали благодатию Христа Бога нашего и пречистыя Его Матере молитвами, поколь было именей ко монастырю тому не взято, и нестяжательно мниси пребы-

---

[a] Patr., Pog., T. дани: Ar.　　　[b] Patr., Pog., T. о: Ar.
[c] Patr., Pog., T. куплелюбил: Ar.　　　[d] Patr. подобен: Ar., Pog.
[e] T. отом поставлена: Ar.　　　[f] Patr., Pog., T. огда: Ar.

---

[1] The Tsyplyatevs were a branch of the Monastyrev family, which before 1485 was in the service of the princes of Vereya and Beloozero. They were *pomest'e* holders in the area of Novgorod and had close service links with the archiepiscopal palace ("the church of Sofia") (Veselovsky, *Sinodik*, pp. 311–12).

[2] For порт, see above, pp. 114–15.

[3] Pimen's successor was Leonid. According to the Pskov Chronicle he was disgraced by Ivan, taken to Moscow and subjected to a singularly humiliating punishment. The date given is 7083 (1574–5) (*PL* ii, p. 262). The Novgorod chronicles disagree about the date of his execution: the *Letopisets novgorodsky tserkvam Bozhiim* says that he was appointed in 1571 and that after two years he went to Moscow where he was eventually executed

and he too was virtuous, skilled and very rich. And they [Tulupov and Tsyplyatev] were in the service of the great church of Sofia, that is to say the church of the Wisdom of God. And various other well-born noblemen and youths were tortured and slain with them.[1]

And we have heard that at that time he acquired great, accursed, bloody wealth. For in that great, long-inhabited city of Novgorod there lives a trade-loving people, for from the city itself to the sea the river is navigable,[2] and for this reason the inhabitants are extremely rich. It seems likely to me that he destroyed them because of their great wealth.

Then another archbishop was appointed in the place of that one, a man who was distinguished and gentle, so we have heard. But after about two years he had him too put to death together with two abbots, that is to say great igumens or archimandrites.[3]

Furthermore at that time a large number of priests and monks were subjected to various forms of torture and were destroyed.

And at that time the abbot Kornily was put to death by him. He was the head of the Pechersky [Caves] monastery, a holy man, great and glorious in his piety, for from his youth he had shone forth in monastic exploits; and he raised up that monastery, which I have mentioned, both by means of his many exploits and by his prayers to God, and in that monastery countless miracles took place because of the grace of Christ our God and the prayers of His most pure Mother, so long as estates were not added to the monastery and the monks lived

---

(*NL*, p. 345). The *Kratky letopisets novgorodskykh vladyk* says that he was appointed archbishop on 6 December 1571 and that he arrived in Novgorod on 23 December 1571. He was archbishop "for four years less a month and a half", after which he was taken to Moscow in disgrace (*v gosudar'skoy opale*) "and there he died on 20 October" (*NL*, p. 148).

From the above it would seem that Leonid was probably removed in 1575. His successor, Aleksandr, was not appointed until September 1576 (*NL*, p. 148).

If Kurbsky in fact finished his *History* in 1573 (see Zimin, *Kogda Kurbsky napisal*), then either his information on Leonid is wrong, or this paragraph was added at a later date.

вали; егда же мниси стяжания почали любити, паче же недвижимыя вещи, сиречь села и веси, тогда угасоша божественная чюдеса.

Тогда[a] вкупе убиен с ним другий мних, ученик того Корнилия, Васьян имянем, по наречению Муромцов; муж был ученый и искусный и во священных писаниях последователь. И глаголют их вкупе во един день орудием мучительским некаким раздавленных; вкупе и телеса их преподобно-мученическия погребены.

Потом[b] место великое Иваняграда, иже близу моря стоит на реце Нарви, выграбив все, сожещи повелел. Такоже и во Пскове великом[c] и во иных многих градех многие безчисленные беды, и тщеты, и кровопролития тогда быша, ихъже по ряду исписати невозможно. А всем тем служители быша ласкатели его, со оным прелютым варваров полком,[d] нарицаемых кромешников, яко и пред тем уже многожды о них рехом: вместо нарочитых, доброю совестию украшенных мужей, собрал себе со всея тамошния Руския земли человеков скверных и всякими злостьми исполненных, и к тому еще обвязал их клятвами страшными, и принудил окаянных не знатись не токмо со друзи и братиями, а ни с самыми родители, но точию во всем ему угождати и скверное его и кровоядное[e] повеление исполняти, и на таковых и паче тех прелютых, ко крестному целованию принуждаще окаянных и безумных.

О вселукаваго супостата человеческого умышление! о неслыханные презлости и беды, паче всех преступлений человеков в пропасть поревающе! Кто слыхал от века таковые, иже Христовым знамением кленущесь на том,

---

[a] Patr., Pog., T. огда: Ar.   [b] Patr., Pog., T. о том: Ar.
[c] T. великому: Ar.   [d] Patr. полков: Ar.   [e] Patr., Pog., T. скверно его и кроядное: Ar.

---

[1] Kornily, abbot of the Pskov monastery of the Caves (Pskov-Pechery monastery), was executed by Ivan probably in February 1570, that is, after the Novgorod expedition. From the evidence of the Novgorod Chronicle it

as non-possessors. But when the monks began to love possessions—especially immovable things, that is to say villages and hamlets,—then the divine miracles expired.[1]

And at that time another monk, Vassian Muromtsev by name, a pupil of Kornily, was put to death together with him. He was a learned and skilled man and versed in the holy scriptures. And they say that they were both crushed together on the same day by some kind of instrument of torture; and their holy martyred corpses were buried together.[2]

Then he utterly plundered the great city of Ivangorod, which stands on the Narova river near the sea, and ordered it to be burned down. And likewise in great Pskov and in many other towns there were at that time countless disasters and losses and bloodshed, all of which it is impossible to enumerate. And all these things were brought about by his flatterers[3] together with that ferocious horde of barbarians called his children of darkness, as we have many a time said before. Instead of distinguished men adorned with good conscience, he gathered around him from all the land of Russia foul men, filled with every kind of evil, and, furthermore, he bound them with terrible oaths and forced the accursed ones to have no dealings not only with their friends and brethren but also with their very parents, and to please him in everything and to carry out his foul bloodthirsty orders. And on such terms, and on terms still fiercer than these, he forced the accursed and insane men to kiss the cross.

O device of the most cunning enemy of man! O unheard-of wickedness and misfortune, which, more than all crimes, hurl men into the gulf! Who has ever heard of such men who give an oath with the sign of Christ, that Christ be persecuted and

would appear that Kornily, who met Ivan IV on his arrival in Pskov, was instrumental in persuading the tsar not to carry out mass executions in the city, as he had done in Novgorod. (N. E. Andreyev, *Kurbsky's letters to Vas'yan Muromtsev*, p. 436.)

[2] Vassian Muromtsev, a monk of the Pskov monastery of the Caves, was evidently a close friend of Kurbsky, who addressed three letters to him (*RIB*, vol. 39, cols. 377–410). For details of Vassian Muromtsev and his death, see Andreyev, *Kurbsky's letters to Vas'yan Muromtsev*, pp. 433–6.

[3] Lit. "his flatterers were the servants of all these...".

да Христос гоним будет и мучим?[a] и на том крестное знамение целовати, да церковь Христова растерзается различными муками? и клятись клятвами странными на том, да любовь естественная, от Сотворителя нашего в нас всажденная, к родителем и ближним и другом, расторгнетца? Зде ми зри беды неслыханные! Зде заслепление человеков оных, яко диявол навел их хитролесне Христа отверщись! Первие прельстив царя, потом уже вкупе со царем тех окаянных в якую пропасть оповергл[b] и навел от оных обетов священных, яже бывают самому Христу на святом крещению, отоврещись сице: еже Христовым именем кленущись, евангельских заповедей отрицатись! А что глаголю евангельских? и естественных, яко рех, которые в поганских языцех соблюдаеми и сохраняеми, и сохранитись будут и соблюдатись по впоенному в нас прирождению от Бога.[c] Во евангели учит врагов любити и гонящих благословляти, и протчие; а[d] естественные внутрь всех человеков без гласа вопиют и без языка учат к родителем покорение, а ко сродным и другом любовь имети; а диявол с клевретом своим полк кромешников сопротив всех тех вооружил, и клятвами очаровал: и воистинну чары, всех чаров проклятие и сквернейшее, над человеческим бедным родом стались от чаров зачатого царя. Господь заповедует, не

[a] Како Христа седяща одесную Отца зде мучима быти глаголеш? Тако воистинну: егда церковь от мучителей гонима бывает, тогда Христос, приемлюще на ся церковное лице, сам терпети исповедуется: "Савле, рече, Савле, почто мя гониши?": in margin of Ar., Pog., T. In text of Patr.   [b] Разсмотряй зде прилежнее и читай златыми усты толкованы Павловы словеса к Коринфом, в первом послании о том беседует, во нравоучении 33-м беседы пространнейше о вложенном в нас от Бога естественнаго закона любви соблюдении, як к родителем и ближним сродником и ко южиком простиратися сродною любовию подобает. И тамо узришь, читателнику, и веру имешь не туне мя плачуща и рыдающа и нарекающа о сем: in margin of Ar., Pog., T. In text of Patr.   [c] В яковый ров человеческий род диавол вверже по (sic) своим таинником, зри зде. Се маньяков или (Patr., Pog. их: Ar.) похлебников плоды полезны таковы: in margin of Ar., Pog. In text of Patr.   [d] T. a omitted in Ar.

---

[1] A marginal note reads as follows: "How can you say that Christ, who sits at the right hand of the Father, is tormented here? In this way, verily:

250

tormented?¹ And kiss the cross, that the Church of Christ be torn asunder with various torments? And swear strange oaths, that the natural love for parents, relatives and friends, implanted in us by our Creator, be shattered? Behold, I tell you of unheard-of woes, of the blinding of those men—for the devil cunningly led them to reject Christ! First of all he deceived the tsar; then, together with the tsar, he cast those accursed men into the pit² and led them away from those sacred vows which are made to Christ Himself at holy baptism, and [taught them] to reject them thus: to deny the commandments of the Gospel, though vowing in the name of Christ! But why do I say "commandments of the Gospel"? As I have said, they also deny the commandments of nature, which are observed and kept amongst the pagan peoples and which should be observed and kept according to the instinct inspired in us by God.³ In the Gospel we are taught to love our enemies and to bless them that persecute us,⁴ and so forth; while the commandments of nature within all men cry out without voice and teach without tongue that we must submit to our parents and love our relatives and friends. But the devil and his accomplice have armed the host of the children of darkness against all such people and bound them with vows as with spells—indeed spells more accursed and fouler than all other spells have been cast upon the wretched human race as a result of the spells which brought about the conception of the tsar.⁵ The Lord commands us not

when the Church is persecuted by tormentors, Christ, taking upon Himself the face of the Church, Himself admits that He suffers, saying: "Saul, Saul, why persecutest thou Me?"

² A marginal note reads as follows: "Here consider diligently and read the commentary of Paul's words to the Corinthians by the Golden Mouth [St John Chrysostom]; in his morally instructive 33rd homily on the first epistle he discourses at great length on the preservation of the natural law of love instilled in us by God, [showing] that it is right for such love to be spread to parents and close relatives and kinsmen. And there, o reader, you will see and believe that I do not weep and sob in vain when talking of this." (See Migne, *PG*, vol. 61, cols. 275 *sq.*)

³ A marginal note reads as follows: "See here into what pit the devil and his accomplice cast mankind. Such are the good fruits of his maniacs or toadies."   ⁴ Matt. v. 44.

⁵ Lit. "the spells of the conceived tsar". For Vasily III's use of spells and charms to induce fertility, see above, pp. 200 *sq.*

приимати имени своего туне, а ни малейшими отнюдь клятвами обязатись свободному естеству сущему, сиречь а ни небом, ни землею, ни главою своею, и прочими не клятись;[1] а те предреченные кромешники, аки забывши, отрекше всех тех, сопротивные пострадаша.[a]

Но что дивитеся, зде живущие издавна под свободами христианских кролей, аки вере не подобны беды наши, оные предреченные, мняще? Воистинну, паче вере не подобны бы обрелися, аще бы все по ряду исписал. А сие писал, к сокращению трагедии тое жалостные зряще, понеже и так едва от великие жалости сердце ми не росторглося.

О преподобном Феодорите священномученике

В тех же летех мужа погубил славнаго во преподобии, и воистинну святаго и премудраго, архимандрита саном, Феодорита именем, о немъже и о жительстве его священном вкратце достоит воспомянути. Был он муж родом от места Ростова славнаго, отнюду же и святый Сергий провозрасте, и исшел тот Феодорит в третеенадесять лето возрасту своего, от дому родителей своих и поиде аж на Соловецкий остров, в монастырь, иже лежит на Ледовом море, и там пребыл аки лето едино; в четвертоеже-надесять лета возраста своего, приял на ся мнишеский образ и вдался во святое послушание, яко есть обычай мнихом[b] юным, единому презвитеру святу и премудру и многолетну сущу, Зосиме именем, тезоименитому ученику самого святаго Зосимы Соловецкаго. И послужив ему в послушанию духовному[c] неотступно пятьнадесят лет; там же навыче всякой духовной премудрости, и взыде ко преподобию по степенем добродетелей; потом хиротонисан был от архиепископа Новгородцкого дьяконом, и потом, пребывше аки лето едино у старца

[a] T. пострадаше: Ar., Patr., Pog.   [b] Pog. мнихов: Ar., Patr.
[c] *sic*.

---

[1] Matt. v. 34–5.   [2] Lit. "have suffered opposite things".

to take His name in vain and bids free nature not to swear by any oath at all, that is to say neither by heaven, nor by earth, nor by one's head, nor by anything else.[1] But those children of darkness, whom I have been talking about, have done the opposite,[2] forgetting, as it were, or renouncing all these commandments.

But why are you amazed, you who have lived here for so long under the freedom of Christian kings, thinking that these misfortunes of ours which I have described are unbelievable? Indeed, were I to enumerate them all, these misfortunes would be found to be still more unbelievable. But I have written about these things with a view to curtailing this piteous tragedy, for as it is my heart has nearly burst from great pity.

Concerning the venerable priest-martyr Feodorit

In those years he put to death a man glorious in his holiness and indeed saintly and wise, an archimandrite by rank, Feodorit by name. It is fitting briefly to mention him and his holy life. He was a man whose family came from the glorious town of Rostov, from where St Sergy came too.[3] Now Feodorit left his parents' house in his thirteenth year and went as far as the island of Solovki, to the monastery which is situated on the Frozen Sea, and there he spent about a year. And in his fourteenth year he accepted the monastic habit and devoted himself to the holy novitiate, as is the custom of young monks, under a holy wise priest of venerable years called Zosima, the pupil and namesake of St Zosima of Solovki himself.[4] And he served him unflaggingly for fifteen years in spiritual obedience. And during that time he became accustomed to all kinds of spiritual wisdom and he mounted the steps of virtue to holiness. Then he was ordained deacon by the archbishop of Novgorod,[5] and, after that, having spent one more year with his Elder, he

[3] St Sergy of Radonezh was born on the estate of his parents in the vicinity of Rostov.
[4] St Zosima (d. 1478) was one of the founders of the monastery of Solovki.
[5] Presumably in or before 1509; from 1509 to 1526 there was no archbishop of Novgorod.

своего, изыде ис того монастыря, за благословением его, на созерцание ко славному и великому мужу, чюдотворцу сущу, Александру Свирскому. И пребыв у него яко чистый у чистаго и непорочный у непорочнаго; он же прия́л его со провидением, вне монастыря, во стретение его изшедше; ибо никогда же знаяше его, а ни слышав о нем, рече ему: "Сын Авраамль прииде к нам, Феодорит диякон." И зело любяше его, поколь поживе в манастыре оном. Потом от Александра иде аж за Волгу реку, в тамо сущие великие монастыри, ищуще храбрых воинов Христовых, яже воюют сопротив начал властей темных, миродержцов века сего. И обходит те все обители; вселился в Кирилов великий монастырь, понеже обрел там духовных мнихов, Сергия, глаголемаго Климина, и других святых мужей; и тамо пребыв аки два лета, ревнующи их жестокому и святому жительству, умучая и покоряя плоть свою в порабощение и в послушание духа. И оттуду изыде в пустыни тамошние и обрете тамо божественнаго Порфирия, исповедника и первомученика, бывша уже игумена Сергиевы обители, много страдавша мученьми и тяжкими оковами от князя великого, отца того. А что тому страданию святаго Порфирия за вина была, достоит вкратце воспомянути.

Был той Порфирий привлечен от пустыни насилием, за повелением князя великого Московского Василия, на игуменство Сергиева монастыря, и случилась вещь в то время такова: сродника своего ближняго той-то прелютый князь Василий — яко обычай есть Московским князем издавна желати братей своих крови и губити их, убогих ради и окаянных отчизн, несытства ради своего — изымал того брата своего, во крови ближняго, княжа Северского[a] Василия, нареченного Шамятича, мужа славнаго и зело храбраго и искусного в богатырских вещах, и поистинне рещи, пагубу бусурманов, яже не токмо отчину свою

---

[a] Patr., Pog., T. князя Верейского: Ar.

---

[1] St Aleksandr Svirsky (d. 1533) founded his monastery on the river Svir', between Lakes Ladoga and Onega.

left the monastery with his blessing and went to be supervised by the great and glorious Aleksandr Svirsky, who was a miracle-worker.[1] And he stayed with him—pure with the pure, unsullied with the unsullied. And Aleksandr received him with foresight, going outside the monastery to meet him, for he had never known him, nor had he heard of him; and he said: "The son of Abraham, the deacon Feodorit, has come to us." And he loved him greatly as long as he lived in that monastery. Then from Aleksandr he went as far as the district beyond the river Volga, to the great monasteries situated there, seeking the brave warriors of Christ who fight against the rule of the powers of darkness, against the mighty rulers of this world. And he went around all those monasteries; and he settled in the great monastery of St Kirill, for he found spiritual monks there—Sergy Klimin and other holy men. And he stayed there for about two years, zealously imitating their austere and holy way of life, mortifying and subduing his flesh so that it became subject and obedient to the spirit. And from there he went to the local hermitages[2] and found there the divine Porfiry, confessor and martyr,[3] who had already been abbot of the monastery of St Sergy and who had suffered many torments and heavy bonds at the hands of the grand prince, the father of the tsar. Now it is worth briefly recalling what the cause of the saintly Porfiry's suffering was.

Porfiry was forcibly dragged from his hermitage at the command of Grand Prince Vasily of Moscow to the abbacy of the monastery of St Sergy, and the following incident occurred at this time: that ferocious prince, Vasily, seized his close relative —for it has long been the custom of the grand princes of Moscow, as a result of their insatiable greed, to desire the blood of their brothers and to destroy them for the sake of their wretched, miserable patrimonies. And so at that time he seized his cousin, who was close to him in blood-relationship, Vasily Shemyachich, prince of Seversk, a glorious and exceedingly brave man, skilled in deeds of valour, and, truly speaking, the destroyer of the Mussulmans; for not only did he defend

---

[2] The word пустынь, пустыня means literally "desert" or "wilderness". It is also used to designate a hermitage, or *skit*, in a remote district.

[3] Lit. "first martyr", an appellation usually reserved for St Stephen.

Северу от частого нахождения безбожных Измаильтян оборонял, порожающе их многажды зело часто, но и на дикое поле под самую орду Перекопскую ходяще многажды, и тамо пресветлыя одоления над ординскими цари поставляюще. Се толь преславнаго мужа, воистинну победоносца, той-то князь Василей предреченный, от чародейцы Греческия рожден, заточил в темницу и тяжкими оковами вскоре уморити повелел.

В то время случилося ему во оный Сергиев монастырь приехати, на свято великого Пянтикостия — яко там есть обычай Московским князем на кождое лето того праздника в том монастыре торжествовати, аки бы то духовне. Святый же игумен Порфирий, яко муж обычаев простых и во пустыне воспитан, начал просити его и молити о предреченном же Шемятиче, да свободит брата от темницы и от так тяжких оков. Мучитель же начал, дыхающе аки огнем, претити ему; старец же тихо отвешававше и моляше: ''Аще, рече, приехал еси ко храму безначальные Троицы, от трисиянного Божества милости грехов своих просити, сам буди милосерд над гонимыми от тебя без правды; аще ли, як глаголеши, срамотяще нас, аки бы повинны были тобе и согрешили пред тобою, остави им долги малых динарий, по Христову словеси, яко же и сам от него желаеш прощения многих талантов.'' Мучитель же абие изгнати его из монастыря повелел; о немже молил его, удавити вскоре. Старец же, абие с радостию совлекшеся со одежд игуменских и отрясши прах от ног своих, во свидетельство Божие на него, и приявши свои пустынные одежды худые и раздранные, пеш, аж во оную пустыню потече, от младости ему вожделенную.[a] Мучитель же, не престая потом на святаго яростию неистовася, за оклеветанием[b] нскоторых любостяжательных и

[a] T. возжеленные: Ar.   [b] Patr., T. оклеветание: Ar.

---

[1] Prince Vasily Ivanovich Shemyachich was the grandson of Vasily II's enemy, Dmitry Shemyaka. In 1500, together with Prince Semen Ivanovich of Mozhaysk, he transferred his allegiance and his large estates east of the Dnepr from Aleksandr of Lithuania to Ivan III. As appanage prince of

his patrimony of Seversk against the frequent incursions of the godless Ishmaelites, defeating them very many times, but also he himself often marched to the steppe-land against the Crimean horde itself and there won brilliant victories over the khans of the horde. This was the glorious man, a victor indeed, who was imprisoned and soon ordered to be killed in heavy fetters by the Prince Vasily I have mentioned, who was born of a Greek sorceress.[1]

At this time he [Vasily III] happened to come to the monastery of St Sergy at the great festival of Pentecost—for in that land it is the custom of the Russian princes each year to celebrate this festival in the monastery of St Sergy, performing, as it were, a spiritual duty. Now the holy abbot Porfiry, as a man of simple ways and as one who had been brought up in a hermitage, began to beg and beseech him to free his cousin Shemyachich, whom I have just mentioned, from prison and from such heavy fetters. But the tormentor began to threaten him, breathing fire, as it were. The Elder, however, answered him quietly and besought him, saying: "If you have come to the temple of the everlasting Trinity to ask the threefold Divinity for mercy for your sins, then be yourself merciful to those persecuted by you without justice; and if, as you say shaming us, they are guilty towards you or have sinned before you, then forgive them their debts of a few pence, following the word of Christ, as you yourself wish to be forgiven by Him the debt of many talents."[2] But the tormentor immediately ordered Porfiry to be driven out of the monastery and ordered him, on whose behalf Porfiry had entreated him, to be strangled forthwith. And the Elder straightway took off his abbot's garments with joy and shook off the dust from his feet as a divine testimony against him, and took his mean tattered hermit's garments and hastened on foot as far as that hermitage, which he had longed for since his youth. But the tormentor ceased not to rage with fury against the holy man owing to the accusations made by certain possession-loving and most cunning monks,

Novgorod-Seversky, he served Ivan III and Vasily III faithfully. In 1523 he was summoned to Moscow by Metropolitan Daniil and was arrested.

[2] Matt. xviii. 23 *sq.*

вселукавых мнихов, сущих человекоугодников прескверных, паки святаго мужа ис так дальние пустыни, аж до Москвы, привлещи повелел и, катом предавши, различными муками мучити.

Аз же, беды его и мучения все оставя, вкратце едино воспомяну, к концу истории тоей поспешающи, яже дивного сего мужа равноапостольское незлобие в память ми приходит. Егда же уже тогда святый зело был муками удручен, едва жив отдан под стражю Пашку некоему, по их истопнику или отдвернику, еже мучителю был верной кат или спекулатар над полачи; его же оковал он веригами тяжкими и к тому змученного мужа гладом удручиша, угождающи и верен показующися мучителю, хотящему вскоре смерть навести. Христос же, наш царь премилосердый, не оставляше раба своего в бедах, женою оного спекулатаря посещаше,[a] яже к нему немалое человеколюбие показывала,[b] тайне питаше и раны исцелеваше, и но немалых днех сохранила его на едином месте, хотяще его от уз свободити, яко да избегнути возможет от мучительских рук юзник Христов. И пришедша тогда глаголют мужа ея, и вопросил жены своей о узнику, порученному[c] ему под стражу от мучителя; она же отвещала: "Избегнул, рече, вчера еще, и не вем о нем."[d] Муж же ея, убоявся князя прелютого, яже поручил ему под стражу, извлече нож и хотяше сам себя абие заклати; святый же из сокровенного места, яко Павел апостол древле стражу темничному, велегласно возопил: "Не убивай себя, о господине Павле! (тако бо оному спекулатару имя было). Зде бо есмь цел, и твори со мною, еже хощешь!" Егда же прииде сия повесть к мучителю во уши, и устыдевся преподобномученика, разрешив от уз, и отпустити его повеле. Святый же паки с радостию, яко Христов победоносец, раны мученические, яко язвы

[a] T. посещаже: Ar.   [b] Patr., T. показывало: Ar.   [c] sic.
[d] T. о нем omitted in Ar.

---

[1] One of the meanings hazarded by Sreznevsky for истобъка–истопка is "prison" (Sreznevsky, *Materialy*, vol. i, col. 1147).

foul men-pleasers, and again ordered the holy man to be dragged from his distant hermitage as far as Moscow, to be handed over to the executioners and to be tortured with various kinds of torture.

Leaving aside all his misfortunes and torments, I will recall one thing briefly as I hasten towards the end of this my long story, for the gentleness of this wonderful man which is like unto that of the apostles comes to my memory. When the holy man was exhausted by torture, he was handed over, barely alive, to the custodianship of a certain Pashka, a gaoler[1] or doorkeeper in their language, who was the tormentor's faithful executioner, or chief of the hangmen.[2] And he bound him with heavy fetters and he exhausted the already tortured man with hunger, thus showing himself to be pleasing and true to the tormentor, who wanted to bring about his death with dispatch. But Christ, our most merciful tsar, did not leave His servant in trouble, but visited the executioner's wife, who showed Porfiry no little kindness, secretly feeding him and healing his wounds. And after several days she hid him in a certain place intending to free him from his bonds, so that the prisoner of Christ might be able to escape from the hands of the tormentor. And they say that her husband came and questioned his wife about the prisoner who had been entrusted to his care by the tormentor. And she answered, saying: "He ran away yesterday and I do not know where he is." And her husband, fearing the ferocious [grand] prince, who had entrusted Porfiry to his care, took out his knife and was about to kill himself, when the holy man cried out in a loud voice from his place of hiding (just as of old the apostle Paul cried out to the keeper of the prison):[3] "Do not kill yourself, master Paul (for such was the name of the executioner), for I am here, alive. Do with me what you wish!" Now when this tale came to the ears of the tormentor, he was filled with reverence for the holy martyr and loosed him from his bonds and ordered him to be set free. And the holy man, like a victor in Christ, bore with joy his martyr's wounds, like

[2] Lit. "executioner over the hangman". The word спекулатор in Old Church Slavonic is synonymous with палач (cf. Greek: σπεκουλάτωρ).
[3] Acts xvi. 27–8.

17-2

Христовы, вместо цветов прекрасных, на телеси святем носяще, паки в пустыню свою отиде и тамо водворяяся, по пророку Давыду глаголющему: удаляясь от мирских мятежей, ждуще Бога спасающаго его. Яко рех, оставя другия страдания его тамо живущим о житии его и о преставлении писати, а мы, яко зде страннии и пришельцы, ко предреченной кроткой повести о преподобном Феодорите возвратимся.

И в той же пустыне живщу ему с Порфирием, обрел Артемия, премудраго Иоасафа, глаголемаго Белобаева, и других немало пустынников, мужей святых, некоторых и престаревшихся во днех; и там с ними во трудех духовных подвизающеся вкупе, поживе аки четыре лета. Тогда же старец его, провидев свое отшествие к Богу, шлет к нему епистолию, просяще, да возвратится к нему; он же с радостию, яко елень,[a] потече пеш, шествуя так должайший путь, вящей нежели от триста миль, по великим и непроходимым пустыням. И прииде болезненными ногами с таковым тщанием и с охотою: ни во что же вменяше многих трудов и жестокого и долгого пути сопротив умышленному усердъному желанию; и возвращается, творя послушание, яко Тимофей к Павлу, и объемлет многолетного святаго старца, и лобызающе и целующе пречестнейшие седины презвитерские, и пребывает при нем, служаще ему в немощах и в недузех его, аж до смерти старца, аки лето едино или мнее. По разлучению же от тела святые души его, тело презвитера погребает.

И вкусил и напился оные сладости пустынные, яко же глаголет премудрый Метофраст, пишучи историю о[b] святом Николаю. Понеже пустыня покоя и ума почивания, наилутчая родительница и воспитательница, а клеврет и тишина мысли, и Божественного зрения плодовитый корень, истинная содружебница з Богом сопряжения духовного, а сего ради разжегся желанием пустынного безмолвного

ª Patr., Pog. елен: Ar.   ᵇ Т. и о: Ar.

---

¹ Ps. lv. 7–8.

the wounds of Christ, upon his holy body, instead of fair flowers; and he set off once more to his hermitage and settled there, as the prophet David said, escaping from the storms of the world and waiting for God who saves him.[1] But as I have already said, let us leave it to those who live in Russia to describe his other sufferings when writing about his life and death, while we, as strangers and newcomers in this land, return to the short tale of the venerable Feodorit which we were narrating before.[2]

While he dwelt in that hermitage with Porfiry, he met Artemy, the wise Ioasaf Belobaev and several other hermits, holy men, some of them men of ripe old age. And together with them he toiled in spiritual exploits and lived there for about four years. At that time his Elder,[3] foreseeing his own departure to God, sent him a letter asking him to return to him. And he hastened with joy on foot, like a deer, making the very long journey, more than three hundred miles, through great and impassable wildernesses. And with such dispatch and eagerness he arrived, his legs ailing, for he set at nought against his premeditated fervent desire the many toils and the harsh long journey. And he returned as an act of obedience, like Timothy to Paul, and embraced the ancient holy Elder, kissing and caressing his most holy priestly grey hairs, and he dwelt with him, serving him in his infirmities and ailments right up to his death, which took place a year later or less. And when his holy spirit departed from his body, he buried the body of the priest.

And he tasted and drank his fill of the sweetness of a hermit's life, as the wise Metaphrastes writes in the story of St Nicholas: "For the hermitage is the peace and calm of the mind, the best parent and tutor and servant, and the quietness of thought, and the fruitful root of divine vision, the true helper in the spiritual union with God."[4] For this reason he became enflamed with the desire for the silent life of the hermit and went away to the

[2] Porfiry was abbot of the Trinity monastery of St Sergy from 1521 until 1524 (A. V. Gorsky, *Istoricheskoe opisanie*, pp. 70–2). Little more is known of his abbacy than the information given here by Kurbsky. Stroev gives the dates of his abbacy as 2 February 1521–September 1525 (Stroev, *Spiski*, col. 138).

[3] I.e. Zosima of the Solovetsky monastery.

[4] *PG*, vol. 116, col. 328.

жительства, отходит в далечайшую пустыню, в язык глубоких варваров, Лопарей диких, пловуще великою Колою рекою, яже впадает своим устьем в Ледоватое море; и тамо исходит ис кораблеца и восходит на горы высокие, ихже наречет святое писание ребра северовы, и вселяется в тех лесех пустых, оных непроходимых. По колицих же месяцех, обретает тамо единого старца, пустынника — памятамися, Митрофан бе имя ему — пришедшаго во оную пустыню пред ним аки за пять лет, и пребывают вкупе в прегорчайшей пустыне, Богом храними, питающесь от жестоких зелей и корение, ихже тамо производит пустыня оная. И пребыв тамо со оным предреченным старцом аки двадесят лет, во святом и непорочном жительстве, потом оба возвращаютца во вселенную[2] и приходят до великого места Новаграда, и поставляется от Макария архиепископа Феодорит презвитером[3]. Потом бывает и самому архиепископу духовником, и приводит тамо немало светлых и богатых граждан к пути спасеному, и, не бывше епископом, воистину светлого епископа дела исправляет. И вкратце рекше: целит недужных, очищает прокаженных, не телесы, но душами, возвращает заблуждших, подъемлюще на рамяна и приводяща ко Христу, первому пастырю, уловивши воистинну от сетей диявольских, и исчистив[a] покаянием, усвояет и приводит чистых к церкви Бога живаго.

Паки по дву летех потом, приемлет от богатых некоторых немало сребра в возложение Господеви, и возвращается ко оной пустыне, уже с некоторыми другими, и тамо на устию предреченные Колы реки созидает монастырь и в нем поставляет церковь, во имя пребезначальные Троицы.

[a] Т. источив: Ar.

---

[1] Ps. xlviii. 2.   [2] Lit. "the universe".

[3] When exactly Feodorit was ordained priest by Makary (archbishop of Novgorod from 1526 to 1542) is hard to say. It seems likely that Kurbsky's chronology is at fault here and that Feodorit spent a total of twenty years among the Lapps, i.e. before and after his visit to Novgorod. As we know that Feodorit quit the north and became archimandrite of the Spaso-Evfim'ev monastery in 1551/2, he evidently began his missionary work in

most distant hermitage, to the land of the remote barbarians, the wild Lapps, sailing along the great Kola river, which flows into the Frozen Sea; and there he disembarked and ascended the high hills which the holy scriptures call "the sides of the north",[1] and he settled in those barren and impenetrable forests. And after several months he found an Elder there, a hermit—his name was Mitrofan, I remember,—who had come to this wilderness about five years before him. And the two dwelt together in this most desolate wilderness, protected by God and feeding from the coarse herbs and roots which that wilderness produces. And he stayed there with that Elder for about twenty years, leading a holy unsullied life. Then both of them returned to the world[2] and came to the great city of Novgorod, and Feodorit was ordained priest by Archbishop Makary.[3] After this he became the spiritual father of the archbishop himself, and he led several distinguished rich citizens to the path of salvation, and, although he was not a bishop, he performed the works of a truly distinguished bishop. In short, he healed the sick, cleansed those who were afflicted not in body but in soul, returned the stray [sheep], lifting them on to his shoulders and bringing them to Christ, the first shepherd, saving them, indeed, from the snares of the devil, and purifying sinners with repentance he won them over and brought them pure to the Church of the living God.

Then after two years he accepted a considerable amount of silver from certain rich men as an offering to God and returned to that wilderness, this time with several others. There, at the mouth of the river Kola, which I mentioned above, he founded a monastery and in it built a church named after the everlasting

Lapland c. 1530. According to the chronicle, in 1526, in answer to a request from the Lapps, Makary chose a priest and deacon from his diocese who went to Lapland, built a church (the Nativity of St John the Baptist) and converted many Lapps (*PSRL* xx, p. 404). Seven years later Makary sent another priest and deacon to the Kola peninsula where they founded the churches of the Annunciation and St Nicholas (*ibid.* p. 415).

Who Mitrofan was is not known. Klyuchevsky, in his work on the Lives of the saints, considers that he should not be confused with yet another missionary to the Lapps, Trifon (V. O. Klyuchevsky, *Drevnerusskie zhitiya svyatykh*, pp. 337–40).

Собирает там среду мнишескую, и правило им священное им уставляет, заповедающе им обще и отнюдь нестяжательно жительствовати, сиречь безъименно, своими руками пищу набывающе, яко рече великий апостол: аще кто не делает, да не яст; и паки: руце мои послужиша ми и сущим со мною.¹ Потом приходящих к нему оных глубоких варваров наказует помалу и нудит на веру Христову, понеже искусен уже был языку их; произволивших же некоторых оглашает к пути спасенному и потом присвещает святым крещением, яко сам он поведал ми, иже той язык Лопский, которые просветеся с святым крещением, людие зело просты и кротцы и отнюдь всякаго лукавства неискусны, ко спасеному же пути тщаливи и охочи зело, яко последи множества от них мнишеское житие возлюбили, за благодатию Христа нашего и за того священными учении, понеже, науча их писанию, и молитвы некоторые привел им от Словенска в их язык.

Потом же по летех немалех, егда распространяшесь в том языце проповедь евангельская, и явленны бысть чюдеса и знамения некоторыя, яко глаголет божественный Павел: знамение, рече, не верующим, но безверников ради. Тогда наученных от него и оглашенных Лопян единого дня крестишася яко две тысящи со женами и детьми. Сице он блаженный, апостолом подобный муж, исправил во глубоких варварех, за благодатию Христовою, труды своими!

Что же по сих начинается? Не терпит древний супостат человеческого рода, очима завистными᷍ᵃ зряще, благочестие возрастаемо, разседашеся ненавистию, и что же творит? Подущает на него новособранных монастыря мнихов, шепчюще невидимо во уши и глаголюще им во сердце: "Тяжек, рече, вам и неподъем. И никто же может от человеков претерпети уставом, вам преданным от него: како можете без имений жити, своими руками хлеба добывающе?" Понеже другую заповедь отец был Феодорит предал им из

ᵃ Patr., Pog., T. завитными: Ar.

¹ 2 Thes. iii. 10.　　　² Acts xx. 34.

Trinity. And he collected there a group of monks and he drew up a sacred rule for them, enjoining them to live in common and with no property whatsoever, that is to say without possessions, getting their food with their own hands, as the great apostle said: "If anyone would not work neither should he eat";[1] and again: "My hands have ministered unto me, and to them that are with me."[2] Then, little by little, he instructed those remote barbarians who came to him and he urged them towards the belief in Christ, for he was already skilled in their tongue. Some of them who wished it he prepared for the path of salvation and then he sanctified them with holy baptism, for he himself told me that the Lapp people, who were illumined with holy baptism, are a very simple and meek folk and they are quite unused to any form of cunning; but they are very zealous and keen to tread the path of salvation; indeed, later on many of them grew to love the monastic life thanks to the grace of our Christ and the holy teachings of Feodorit, for he taught them writing and he translated some prayers from Slavonic to their tongue.

Then, after several years, when the preaching of the Gospel had been spread amongst the people, and when certain miracles and signs had been manifested (as the divine Paul says: "signs not to them that believe but to them that believe not"[3]), about two thousand of the Lapps who had been taught and prepared by him were baptized in one day together with their wives and children. Such were the achievements amongst the remote barbarians wrought with God's grace by the deeds of that blessed man, who is like unto the apostles!

Now what occurred after this? The ancient enemy of mankind, watching with envious eyes, did not suffer piety to increase and was devoured by hatred. And what did he do? He incited the newly-gathered monks of his monastery against him, whispering invisibly in their ears and saying to their hearts: "He is severe towards you and hard to tolerate.[4] And no one amongst men can suffer the rules which he has laid down for you. How can you live without possessions, getting your bread with your own hands?" For their father Feodorit had given them another commandment from the Rule of Zosima and

---

[3] I Cor. xiv. 22.   [4] Or, perhaps, "intolerant".

уставу Соловецких Зосимы и Саватея: "К тому не токмо женам,[a] а ни скота единого отнюдь и женского полу не имети тамо!" Сего ради сложившеся со дияволом, мниси оные взнеистовишеся: имают старца святаго и бьют нещадно, и не токмо из монастыря извлачают, но и от страны тоя изгоняют, аки врага некоего. Он же поиде от тех пустынь по неволе во вселенную, и бывает игуменом во едином малом монастыре, в Новогородцкой земле лежащим, и тамо аки два лета пребыл. Потом возвестил о нем Артемий премудрый цареви, ибо тогда был игуменом великим Сергиева монастыря; царь же абие призывает к себе его, и поставляется от архиепископа архимандритом Еуфимиеву монастырю, яже близу великого места Суздаля лежит. Там оное достоинство того великого монастыря управляет лет четыре, або пять. Понеже и тамо обрел зело необнузданных мнихов и своевольно, не по уставам и святым правилом, живущих,[b] ихже уздает и востязает страхом Божиим, наказующи по великому Василиеву уставу жительствовати; к тому не токмо мнихов, но и самого епископа Суждальского, за сребролюбие и пиянство, напоминает и обличает, понеже был муж не токмо в разуме и премудрости мног, но и от рождения своего чист и непорочен; к тому и трезвость во вся дни живота своего храняще. И сих ради, яко глаголет Златоустый, сопротився правда неправде, милосердию лютость, воздержанию невоздержание, трезвости пиянство, и прочие; того ради, ненавидяще его яко мниси, так епископ градцкий.

В тех же тогда летех возрастоша[c] плевелы между чистою пшеницею спания ради, и опильства[d] многаго пастырей наших, сиречь отроды ересей Люторских; явишася лясфиму[e] на церковныя догматы; митрополит же Российский, за повелением царевым, повелел оных ругателей везде имати,

[a] Т. к тому не может нам: Ar., Patr., Pog.   [b] Patr., Pog., T. живущим: Ar.   [c] Patr., Pog., T. возрастша: Ar.   [d] Ar. и от пияства: Patr.; и поивства: T.   [e] *sic.*

[1] Cf. above, p. 262, n. 2.

Savvaty of Solovki: "Not only shall there be no women there, but no female cattle either!" As a result of this those monks, in concord with the devil, were filled with fury: they seized the holy Elder and mercilessly beat him and not only dragged him out of the monastery but drove him out of the land like an enemy. And against his will he went from those wildernesses back into the world,[1] and he became abbot of a small monastery in the land of Novgorod and spent about two years there. Then the wise Artemy told the tsar about him, for at that time Artemy was the great abbot of St Sergy's monastery.[2] And the tsar straightway summoned him, and the archbishop [i.e. metropolitan] appointed him archimandrite of the Evfim'ev monastery, which is situated near the great town of Suzdal'. And there he maintained the dignity of[3] that great monastery for about four or five years. And there too he found exceedingly unbridled monks, who lived according to their will and not according to the rules and the holy canons; and he bridled them and curbed them with the fear of God, instructing them to live according to the great Rule of St Basil. And, what is more, he admonished and chid not only the monks but also the bishop of Suzdal' himself[4] for love of money and drunkenness, for Feodorit was not only a man of great understanding and wisdom but also pure and unsullied from his birth. Furthermore, he maintained sobriety during all the days of his life. And so, as Chrysostom says, injustice came up against justice, ferocity—mercy, lack of restraint—restraint, drunkenness—sobriety, and so forth. For this reason both the monks and the bishop of the town hated him.

Now during those years tares had grown up among the pure wheat because men slept[5] and because of the great drunkenness of our pastors—that is to say offshoots of Lutheran heresies: there appeared blasphemies against the teachings of the Church. And so the metropolitan of Russia, at the command of the tsar, ordered those blasphemers to be seized throughout the country,

---

[2] Artemy was appointed abbot in 1551. He remained abbot for only six and a half months. See Zimin, *Peresvetov*, p. 155, n. 99.

[3] Or, perhaps, "managed", "administered".

[4] Afanasy, bishop of Suzdal' from 1551 to 1564.   [5] Matt. xiii. 24 *sq.*

хотяще истязати их о расколех их, имиже церковь возмущали, и где елико аще обретено их, везде имано и провожено до места главного Московского, паче же от пустынь Заволских, бо и там прозябоша оная ругания. И началось было сие дело исперва[a] добре, но в конец злый проиде, сего ради, иже восторгающе плевелы исторгали с ними и чистую пшеницу, по Господню словеси; к тому и тех раскольников, иже были достойни исправлению пастырскому, сотвориша над ними немилосердие и прелютое мучение сице, яко мало напреди нами слово изъявит.

Егда видевше любостяжательные и[b] всякого лукавства исполненныя мнихи приводимых от Заволских предреченных пустынь и от-инуды раскольников, тогда оклеветают преподобнаго и премудраго Артемия, бывшаго игумена Сергиева монастыря, иже бо он отшел в пустыню, и царя не послушав — от того великого монастыря, многаго ради мятежу и любостяжательных, издавна законопреступъных мнихов — аки бы он причастен и согласник был в некоторых Люторских росколех. Тако же и на других мнихов, по Великого Василия уставу живущих нестяжательно, неповинне лжеклевещут. Тогда абие царь наш и с преуродивыми епископы, отнюдь неискусными, уверил[c] им и собрал соборище, отовсюду совлече духовного чину тамошних, и повелел привесть из пустыни, оковавше, преподобного мужа Артемия, так честного и премудрости исполненного, не поставя очевистя,[d] и ни на суде еще бывша, и другаго старца нарочита, в жительстве нестяжательном провозсиявша и писанием священным искусного, Саву именем, по наречению Шах. Егда же собрано соборище оно и поставлены

[a] Т. и перва: Ar., Patr., Pog.   [b] Т. любостяжательно: Ar.
[c] Т. уверит: Ar.   [d] Ar. очевистне: Т.

---

1 At the end of 1553 a Church Council was summoned to deal with Matfey Bashkin, a member of the service nobility at the court of Ivan IV, who had admitted to Sil'vestr that he held certain heretical views. At the council Bashkin gave evidence which compromised Artemy, who since quitting the Trinity monastery in late 1551 or early 1552 had been living in the hermitage founded by Porfiry, and certain other "trans-Volga Elders". For details, see Zimin, *Peresvetov*, ch. iv, sections 2 and 3.

intending to question them about their heresies, by means of which they were stirring up the Church.[1] And wherever any of them was found they were seized and brought to the capital city, Moscow, especially from the trans-Volga hermitages, for in those places these blasphemies flourished. At first the matter was conducted in good manner, but finally it ended badly because those who plucked the tares rooted up also the good wheat with them, according to the word of the Lord. Furthermore, they dealt unmercifully with those heretics who were worthy of pastoral correction and inflicted the fiercest torture on them, as we shall shortly narrate.

When the monks, who loved possessions and who were filled with all kinds of cunning, saw the heretics being brought from the above-mentioned hermitages from beyond the Volga and from elsewhere, they accused the venerable and wise Artemy who had formerly been abbot of the monastery of St Sergy (for, without listening to the tsar, he had gone off to a hermitage from that great monastery because of the rebelliousness of the brethren and because of the monks who loved possessions and had long transgressed the law) of being involved in, and in agreement with, certain Lutheran heresies. And they also falsely accused other innocent monks, who lived as non-possessors according to the Rule of Basil the Great. Then our tsar and the foolish, utterly unskilled bishops believed them, and he summoned a council, gathering together from all sides men of spiritual calling, and, without allowing him to confront him,[2] he ordered the venerable Artemy, who was so holy and so full of wisdom and who had never been on trial before, to be brought in chains from his hermitage together with another distinguished Elder, Savva Shakh by name, who had shone forth in his life of non-possession and who was versed in the holy scriptures.[3] Now when the council had assembled and

[2] I have taken очевистя (variant: очевистне) as an adverb meaning "face to face". See above, p. 156 (да очевисте на них клеветы будут), where this is clearly Kurbsky's meaning.

[3] After giving evidence at Bashkin's trial, Artemy returned to Porfiry's hermitage. Accused of flight by his enemies, he was brought back to Moscow to face a new council.

и истязаны раскольницы о руганию их на церковные дохматы, тогда между ими Артемия истязанно и вопрошенно; он же, яко неповинный, со всякою кротостию отвещаваше о своем правоверию; лжеклеветников же, паче же реку сикованцов, вопрошено о доводе: они же подали свидетелей мужей скверных и презлых. Старец же Артемий отвещал, иже не суть достойны свидетельствовати; они же паки подали Федорита Соловецкого, архимандрита суща Суздалского, и другаго старца славнаго во преподобию, Иоасафа Белобаева, аки бы те слыхали хульные словеса от Артемия. Егда же те нарочитые мужие на свидетельство поставлены, тогда обличили наветника главнаго, Нектария, мниха, ложне клевещущаго; Артемия же оправдавше, яко отнюдь неповинного, паче же во всяком преподобию провозсиявшаго. Тогда епископ Суздальский он, пияный и сребролюбный, по ненависти первой, глагола: "Феодорит, рече, давный согласник и товарыщ Артемиев; негли и сам еретик есть, понеже с ним во единой пустыни немало лет пребыл." Царь же наш, напамятуючи, иже Артемий зело похваляет Феодорита пред ним, абие уверив, яко пияный пияному и вредоумный вредоумному, понеже к тому и ненависть на него имел, иже не послушал его и не хотел больши быти на игуменстве в монастыре Сергиеве. Нецыи же епископи оправдавше его, ведуще его быти мужа нарочита. Тогда же царь с митрополитом своим, угождающе ему во всем, и со другими, яко рех, неискусными и пияными епископы, вместо исправления и духа кротости, аки оных раскольников не наказуют любезно, но со всякою яростию и лютостию зверскою, в заточение, в[a] дальные[b] грады, ускте и темные

---

¹ For this use of the word "sycophant", see *Correspondence*, p. 201, n. 10.

² Ex-abbot of the Ferapontov monastery (near the White Lake monastery of St Kirill). He accused Artemy, *inter alia*, of criticizing Joseph of Volokolamsk's utterances on the Trinity and of "praising the Latins". (Zimin, *Peresvetov*, p. 159.)

when the heretics had been called and interrogated on their abuse of the teachings of the Church, Artemy was interrogated and questioned in their midst. And he, guiltless as he was, answered with all meekness concerning his orthodoxy; and the false accusers, or rather should I say sycophants,[1] were questioned about their charge. And they produced as witnesses foul and most evil men. But the Elder Artemy answered, saying that they were not worthy to give evidence; and so they called as witnesses Feodorit of Solovki, who was archimandrite of the Suzdal' [Evfim'ev monastery] and another Elder, glorious for his piety, Ioasaf Belobaev, alleging that they had heard Artemy utter blasphemous words. But when those distinguished men were called to give evidence, they accused the chief prosecutor, Nektary,[2] a monk, of making false accusations. And they exculpated Artemy, saying that he was entirely innocent and was indeed distinguished in every kind of piety. Then the bishop of Suzdal', that drunkard and lover of money, who had hated him previously,[3] said: "Feodorit is an old friend of Artemy and has long been in agreement with him; perhaps he himself is a heretic, for he stayed several years in the same hermitage with him." And our tsar, remembering how Artemy had highly praised Feodorit in his presence, straightway believed the bishop, as a drunkard believes a drunkard and a madman a madman, for he bore hatred against Artemy, as he had not listened to him and had not wanted to remain any longer abbot of the monastery of St Sergy.[4] And certain bishops found him innocent, for they knew him to be a distinguished man.[5] Then the tsar and his metropolitan, whom he sought to please in all things, and other bishops, who were, as I have said, inexperienced men and drunkards, instead of reforming them and showing meekness of spirit, not only refused to instruct the heretics with love, but treated them with every possible ferocity and bestial cruelty, sending them in fetters to

[3] Because Feodorit had "admonished and chid him...for love of money and drunkenness". See above, p. 267.

[4] See above, pp. 268–9.

[5] Who the bishops were is not known. Zimin thinks that one of them was Kassian of Ryazan', who later interceded for Ioasaf Belobaev when he was accused of heresy (Zimin, *Peresvetov*, p. 161).

271

темницы отсылают окованных; такожде и преподобного, оковавши веригами желсэными, биют неповинного святаго мужа, и отсылают аж на Соловецкий остров, в вечное заточение, аж до смерти; и того предреченнаго мниха Саву тако же в заточение на смерть отсылают к Ростовскому владыце Никандру, в пиянстве погруженному. И, запроводивши Артемия на Соловъки, вмещут зело в ускую келью, не повелевающе ему дати ни малого утешения отнюдь: гонящего на того епископы богатые и миролюбивые, так и оные вселукавые и любостяжательные[a] мниси, а иже бы не токмо не был в Руской земле он муж, но иже бы и имя его не именовалось. А то сего ради: прежде бо его царь зело любяше и многажды беседовавше, поучаяся от него; они же боящеся, да не паки в любовь ко царю приидет и укажет цареви, иже яко епископи, так и мниси с начальники своими законопреступно и любостяжательно, не по правилом апостольским и святых отец, живут. Сего ради всякие творяху, дерзающе и исполняюще так презлые дела свои на святых, да покроют злость свою и законопреступления; понеже тогда и других неповинных мужей помучиша различными муками, научающе на Артемия клеветати, иже добровольне не возмогоша навести их: негли мук не претерпевши, нечто произнесут. Таков в нынешнем веце, паче же во оной земле, презлый и любостяжательный, лукавства исполнен, мнишеский род! Воистинну всяких катов горши, понеже к лютости вселукав зело. Но ко предреченной повести о Феодорите возвратимся.

Тогда же он блаженный муж неповинне пострадал от лжесшивателей, наипаче же от того-то епископа Суздальского, пьяного и сребролюбиваго, иже клеветаше вкупе нань[b] со мнихи монастыря Евфимьева, яко имуще нань ненависти, предреченныя ради вины. Но аще и многия

[a] T. любытяжательные: Ar.   [b] Patr., Pog., T. нам: Ar.

---

[1] The sentences were carried out in the end of January 1554 (*ibid.* p. 161).

be imprisoned in distant towns, in narrow dark dungeons. And also they bound the venerable and holy man, innocent though he was, with iron chains and beat him and sent him as far as the island of Solovki to everlasting imprisonment, even until his death. And as for the above-mentioned monk Savva, he was also sent for life imprisonment to Archbishop Nikandr of Rostov, who was immersed in drunkenness.[1] And having escorted Artemy to Solovki, they put him in a very narrow cell and forbade him to be given the slightest comfort whatsoever; for the rich worldly bishops as well as those cunning monks who loved possessions persecuted him,[2] so that not only was the man banished from the Russian land, but even his name was not mentioned. And it was for the following reason: earlier the tsar had loved him dearly and had many times conversed with him and received instruction from him; and they were afraid lest he should return to the tsar's affections and show the tsar that the bishops and the monks and their leaders were living as transgressors and lovers of possessions, and not according to the rules of the apostles and the holy fathers. Therefore they did all these things, boldly carrying out their evil deeds against the holy men in order to cover their wickedness and transgressions; for at that time they tormented other guiltless men as well with various forms of torture, instructing them to give evidence against Artemy; and if they could not get them to do this of their own free will, they [the witnesses] would say something simply because they were unable to bear the tortures. Such is the monkish race in the present age, especially in the land of Russia—most evil, possession-loving, full of cunning! Indeed they are worse than all executioners, for in their ferocity they are all-cunning. But let us return to the tale of Feodorit, which we were telling before.

At that time the blessed man suffered in his innocence from false accusers,[3] especially from the bishop of Suzdal', the drunkard and money-lover, who accused him, as did the monks of the Evfim'ev monastery, who hated him for the reasons I have given above. But even though many people devised false

---

[2] гонящего presumably in error for гоняше бо.
[3] Lit. "fabricators of lies".

замышляху[a] нань сикованцыи, но не можаху ни единаго приткнути; но обаче, яко они вселукавые мниси искусны тому, в неволю отослаша его в монастырь Кирилов, в немъже той епископ Суздальский прежде игуменом был, да тем и ученицы его отомстят ему прежнюю ненависть епископа. Он же егда там завезен был, и видяще его тамо живущии мниси, нарочитыя и доброжительныя мужие, яже не суть ведомы о лукавом совете и о презлом деле их, вседушне ради ему бывше, видяще бо его мужа издавна в преподобию и святыни многа. И о сем паче лукавыя мнихи завистию разседаеми были, видевше мужа от налепших и святых мнихов почитаема, и вяще прилагаху ему ругание и бесчестие. И пребыл святый у них аки полтора лета, в таковых бедах претерпевающе.

Потом пишет к нам, сыновом своим духовным, изъявляющи нам от тех вселукавых мнихов нестерпимую скорбь свою. Мы же, колико нас собравшеся, сингклитским саном почтенных, приходим с тем ко архиепископу Макарию, сказующе ему сие по ряду. Он же, услышав и устыдевся яко нашего сана, так и мужа[b] святости,[c] понеже и ему был он духовник, и дает скоро епистолии свои во он монастырь, повелевающе отпустити мужа и жительствовати ему свободне, идеже хощет. Он же, из Кирилова изшед, вселися в месте в Ярославле, в монастыре великом, идеже лежит во своем месте князь Феодор Ростиславич Смоленский, и тамо пребыл аки лето едино или два.

И призывает его царь к себе, яко мужа искуснаго и мудраго, посылающи его послом ко патриарху Констянтинопольскому, просяще благословения о коронацию и о таковом благословению и о величанию, имже и яковым чином цесари[d] Римские сущие христианские от папы и патриархов венчаеми были; он же, повеления царева послушав, уже во

---

[a] Т. замыкаяху: Ar.   [b] Patr., Pog. так тако: Ar.   [c] Patr., T. святостми: Ar.   [d] Patr., Pog. цеса: Ar

---

[1] Lit. "sycophancies". Cf. *Correspondence*, p. 201, n. 10.

accusations[1] against him, they could not prove one of them.[2] However—these most cunning monks are skilled in this—they sent him off to be imprisoned in the monastery of St Kirill, of which the bishop of Suzdal' had once been abbot, so that his [the bishop's] pupils might repay him for the hatred which the bishop formerly bore him. And when he was brought there and when the monks of the monastery—excellent men of good life—who were not informed of the cunning counsel and of the evil monks' wicked deed, saw him, they were glad with all their heart, for they saw that he was a man who had long been great in holiness and sanctity. And therefore the cunning monks were all the more devoured with envy when they saw him revered by the best and holy monks, and they added still more insult and dishonour. And the holy men stayed with them for about one and a half years, enduring such distress.

After that he wrote to us, his spiritual children, telling us of the intolerable distress inflicted upon him by those most cunning monks. And several of us who were honoured with the rank of counsellor went to Archbishop Makary and related everything to him. And when he heard this, he was filled with respect both for our rank and for the holy man, for Feodorit had been his confessor, and he quickly sent an epistle to that monastery, ordering him to be released and to be allowed to live in freedom, wherever he wanted. And Feodorit left the monastery of St Kirill and settled in the town of Yaroslavl', in the great monastery in which Prince Fedor Rostislavich of Smolensk rests in his own town, and there he stayed for about one or two years.[3]

And the tsar summoned him, as being a skilled and wise man, and sent him as ambassador to the patriarch of Constantinople, asking for a blessing for his coronation and his glorification, by which ceremony the Christian Roman emperors were crowned by pope and patriarchs. And Feodorit obeyed the order of the tsar, and although he was already old in years and infirm in

[2] Acts xxv. 7. For this use of притꙑнꙋти, see Sreznevsky, *Materialy*, vol. iii, col. 1481.

[3] Fedor Rostislavich, Kurbsky's ancestor, was prince of Yaroslavl' and Smolensk. He was buried in the Spassky monastery in Yaroslavl', where his relics were found in 1463. (*PSRL* viii, p. 150.)

старости и в немощном теле, обаче поиде с радостию на таковое посольство. И ходил тамо и семо вящей нежели год, многи на пути беды и труды подъял, тамо же и огненным недугом в Констянтинополю аки два месяца объят был; но и ото всех сих благодатию Божиею избавлен, возвратився здрав и принесе со благословением соборным послание от патриарха ко царскаго сана возведению великому князю нашему; а потом и книгу вскоре царского величества всю патриарх послал к нему со своими послы до Москвы, с митрополитом единым и со мнихом презвитером проти-псалом, яже ныне митрополитом Андреянопольским есть. Но и к тому глаголют: святому мужу оному сам патриарх удивлялся, яко преслухался речения и беседования его премудрого, так и жительства его умиренного и священ-нолепного.

Князь же великий, обрадовавшеся патриаршеского послания благословению, дарит Феодорита тремяста сребренники великими и кожухом драгих соболей под аксамитом, и к тому якою властию духовною, аще бы он хотел. Он же, мало усмехнувся рече: ''Аз, царю, повеления твоего послушах и исполних,[a] еже заповедал ми еси, не вменяя ни мало во старости моей трудов о сем; но довольство ми и се за мздовоздаяние, иже апостольского наместника, великого архиепископа, сиречь патриарха вселенского,[b] благословение приях. А яко даров, так и власти не потребую[c] от твоего величества: даруй[d] их тем, яже просит от тебе и потребует; аз яко серебреник, так и драгоценными одеждами не обыкох наслаждатися, а ни ими украшатися, паче же отрекохся всех таковых в начале пострижения[e] власов моих; но доброту душевную, благодати духа внутрь украшати тщуся. Но точию сего прошу, да с покоем и со безмолвием в келье до изшествия моего да пребуду.'' Царь же

[a] Patr., Т. исполнив: Ar. [b] Patr. вселенско: Ar. [c] Patr., Pog., Т. не потребу юх: Ar. [d] Pog., Т. дару: Ar. [e] Т. постражения: Ar.

[1] A rank in the Byzantine church hierarchy—the equivalent of choir-master.

body, he nevertheless went on this embassy with joy. And he took more than a year to go there and back, and suffered many hardships and afflictions on the journey. And there in Constantinople he was taken ill with a fever for about two months. But by the grace of God he was delivered from all these things, and he returned safe. And together with a conciliar blessing he brought an epistle from the patriarch concerning the elevation of our grand prince to the rank of tsar. Then soon afterwards the patriarch sent his ambassadors—a metropolitan and a *protopsaltis*[1] priest-monk, who is now metropolitan of Adrianople—to Moscow with the whole text of the coronation service.[2] And they say, furthermore, that the patriarch himself was so astonished at that holy man [i.e. Feodorit] that he listened attentively to his wise speech and conversation as well as to the story of his humble and holy life.[3]

Now the grand prince was glad that the patriarch had sent his blessing and he gave Feodorit three hundred large silver pieces and a valuable sable-fur coat lined with velvet, and, what is more, he offered him whatever spiritual authority he wanted. But Feodorit smiled a little and said "I hearkened to your command, O tsar, and carried out your instructions without taking into account the labours involved and in spite of my old age. But this is sufficient reward for me, namely that I have received the blessing of the apostolic vicar, the great archbishop, that is to say the oecumenical patriarch. And I require neither gifts nor authority from your majesty. Give them to those who ask you for them and have need of them; I am not wont to enjoy either silver coins or valuable clothes, nor to bedeck myself with them; but rather did I renounce all such things at my tonsure; and I try to bedeck [myself with] goodness of soul and the grace of the spirit within. I only ask this of you, that I may stay in my cell, in calm and silence, until my departure from this life." And the tsar began to beseech him

[2] Lit. "the book of the royal majesty".
[3] In early 1557 Feodorit was sent to Constantinople to obtain a decree confirming Ivan IV in his title of tsar (he had been crowned tsar in 1547 by Metropolitan Makary). His mission was successful, as in 1561 Patriarch Ioasaf II sent his decree of confirmation to the tsar.

нача молити его, да не обесчестит сану царского и да возмет сие; он же, повинувся мало, взял от трех-сот сребреник точию двадесять и пять, и поклонився по обычаю, и изыде от лица царева. Царь же повелел и кожух он послати за ним и положити во храмине, идеже он обитал тогда; Феодорит же кожух той продав, яко и пенези нищим абие разда; потом полюби жити в монастыре, яже близу великого града Вологды, егоже создал святый Димитрий[a] Прилуцкий. А то место Вологда от Москвы лежит сто миль, на пути едучи ко Ледовому морю, на порту.

И забывши ненависть оных нечеловеколюбных мнихов, с Вологды, так дальний путь, не ленився посещати их в монастырю, от него созданном, аж до дикие Лопи два крот ездяши при мне, от Вологды до Колмогор реками плавающе а двесте миль, а от Колмогор Двиною рекою великою до моря, а морем до Печенги другую двести миль, яже нарицается[b] Мурманская земля, идеже живет Лопский язык; тамо же и Кола,[c] река великая, в море впадает, на еяже устье монастырь он создан от него. Воистинну сие удивлению достойно: в такой старости и такие неудобные и жестокие пути претерпел, летом плавающу ему[d] по морю, зимою же на пруткошественных еленех ездяще по непроходным пустыням, посещающе детей своих духовных, яко мнихов

---

[a] той святый Димитрий, яже князю Констянтину острожскому (Patr. Островскому: Ar.) явил в видению (Т. явил в видению omitted in Ar., Patr., Pog.) от многолетных его вериг свободил, имиже был связан по рукам и по ногам, яко иссохшие уже ему руце прикосновением своим исцелил, яко и зде уж князь выехал во свое отечество зело святаго о сем прославлял и почесть и любовь к нему велию имел (Patr. им: Ar.) даже до преставления своего. In margin of Ar., Pog., T. In text of Patr.   [b] Т. нарицаются: Ar.   [c] Pog. Коло: Ar.   [d] Pog. плавающему: Ar.

---

[1] A marginal note reads as follows: "This St Dmitry, who appeared to Prince Konstantin Ostrozhsky in a vision, freed him from the chains by which he had been bound hand and foot for many years, and by his touch healed his hands, which had already become withered, so that the prince left for his estates, greatly glorifying the saint for this and entertaining great honour and love for him until his death." The Ostrozhsky mentioned here

not to dishonour the tsar's rank and to accept these things; and Feodorit obeyed him partially and took only twenty-five of the three hundred silver coins, and, having bowed according to custom, departed from the presence of the tsar. And the tsar ordered the fur coat too to be sent after him and to be placed in the room where he was dwelling at the time. But Feodorit sold the fur coat and immediately distributed the money amongst the poor. Then he conceived a desire to live in the monastery which is near the great town of Vologda and which St Dmitry Prilutsky founded.[1] Now the town of Vologda lies one hundred miles from Moscow on the route to the Frozen Sea which is navigable.[2]

And having forgotten the hatred of those inhuman monks, he did not shrink through laziness from making the long journey from Vologda and visiting them in the monastery which had been founded by him; and twice, when I knew him,[3] he travelled as far as the wild Lapps, sailing the two hundred miles from Vologda to Kholmogory by river and from Kholmogory by the great Dvina river to the sea, and another two hundred miles by sea to the Pechenga district, which is called the land of Murmansk, where the Lapp people lives. And there the great Kola river flows into the sea, and at its mouth is the monastery which he founded. It is indeed astonishing that in such advanced years he suffered such discomforts and such hardship of travel: in the summer he travelled by sea, in the winter, on swift-running reindeer, through impenetrable wildernesses, visiting his spiritual children, both the monks

was Prince Konstantin Ivanovich, commander-in-chief of the Polish–Lithuanian army at the end of the fifteenth century. In 1500 he was taken prisoner by the Muscovites at the battle on the Vedrosha. He was confined in the Spaso-Prilutsky monastery (founded *c.* 1375 by St Dmitry Prilutsky a few miles from Vologda). In 1506 he was persuaded to join the service of the grand prince and was given his freedom. But he managed to escape to Lithuania where he took part in many campaigns against the Muscovites.

[2] I.e. the Sukhona and Dvina rivers. For this use of порт, see above, p. 114, n. 3.

[3] Lit. "in my presence". Presumably this refers to the time between 1558 and 1564, when Kurbsky was his spiritual son. It is not known, however, when Kurbsky was in the district of Vologda during these years.

оных, так и Лопянов, наученных и крещенных от него, пекущися о спасению душ их, в неверных сеюще проповедь евангельскую и размножающе благочестие, врученный ему от Христа Бога талант, во языце оном глубоких и грубых варваров, не щадяще ни старости и немощнаго тела, сокрушеннаго многими леты и великими труды. Зде ми зри, полуверне, лицемерный христианине, умягченный, раздроченный различными наслажденьми, яко храбри еще обретаются старцы в православной християнской земле, во правоверных дохматех воспитанныя: чем престареются и изнемогут телом, тем храбше[a] ревностию по благочестию полагают и острозрительнейшие и приятнейшие ко Богу бывают.

И яковое было бы о том предреченном святом Феодорите удивление, аще бы вся по ряду исписал добродетельныя его дела и предивные, ихже аз един елико могу памятати! Что возглаголю о том, яковые он имел дарования от Бога, сиречь дары духа: силы исцеления, дар пророчествия, дар мудрости, яко грешники уловляти от презлых дел дияволих и наводити на путь покаяния и приводити от нечестия и многолетнаго древняго неверия в веру Христову поганские народы? А что бы рекл и яко бы изглаголал о восхищению его в самые обители небесныя, и о видениях его неизреченных, имъже Бог посетил его? Понеже аще в телеси тленном суща, бестелесными и невещественными почтен достоинствы и аероплаветельными хождении. А яковую той муж тихость и кротость многую имел, и яковыя наказания премудрыя, и в гощениях[b] предивные и насладчайшие беседования и пользовательные апостолоподобныя вещания, егда случилось ему беседовати к сыновом духовным, ихже некогда и аз недостойный многажды причастен был тех священных учений! Еще к тому немало ко удивлению: яко умел[c] он и искусен был целити согнившия и состаревшия неисцельныя раны,[d] сиречь презлыя дела в человецех обыкновенныя многими леты! Яко все мудрыя глаголют,

---

[a] Patr. храбрство: Ar.
[b] Patr., Pog. гещениях: Ar.
[c] Patr., Pog., Т. имел: Ar.
[d] Patr., Pog., Т. ради: Ar.

whom I mentioned and the Lapps who had been instructed and baptized by him, caring for the salvation of their souls and sowing the preaching of the Gospel amongst the unbelievers and increasing piety, the talent entrusted to him by Christ our God, amongst that tribe of remote and coarse barbarians; nor did he spare his age or his infirm body broken by many years and by great toil. See, half-believing, hypocritical Christian, softened and worn out by various delights, see how brave are the Elders who can still be found in the Orthodox Christian land and who have been brought up on the true teachings! The older they grow and the more exhausted in body, the bolder becomes their zeal for piety and the more sharp-sighted and pleasing to God they become.

And what astonishment there would be concerning this holy Feodorit, about whom I have been talking, were I to relate all his virtues and wondrous deeds, as many as I alone can recall! What shall I say about the gifts he had from God, that is to say the gifts of the spirit: the strength of healing, the gift of prophecy, the gift of wisdom, the gift of saving sinners from the evil works of the devil and leading them to the path of penitence and bringing the pagan peoples from impiety and from the ancient unbelief of many years to belief in Christ? And what should I say about, and how should I describe, his assumption into the very dwellings of heaven and his unspeakable visions with which God visited him? For although his body was corruptible, he was honoured for his bodiless and immaterial virtues and for his walking on air. And what great calm and meekness did he possess, and what wise instructions did he give, and what wondrous sweet converse and what useful apostle-like talk did he treat us to when he happened to discourse with his spiritual children, amongst whom I too, unworthy though I am, many a time shared in his sacred teachings! And furthermore this too is not a little astonishing: he was an able and skilled healer of incurable wounds which had festered with age—that is to say of wicked deeds which become habitual in men after many

иже многолетныя обыкновения, от младости утвердившися во человеческих душах, во естество обращаются ине, плохо или неудобь заглажаеми бывают; таковыя он умел[a] ветхия гнусности и нечистыя злости расторгати и искореняти от душ человеческих, и нечистых и скверных сущих очищати и просвещати, и ко Господу усвояти многим покаянием и слезами, и самым дияволом запрещати силою Святаго Духа, по данной ему от Бога власти презвитерской, да к тому ни наступит, а ни дерзнет паки и осквернит покаявшихся душ человеческих. Сие воистинно не токмо от достоверных мужей слышах, но очима видех и над самим собою искусив бывшее и приключившеся мне благодеяние многое от его святыни, понеже исповедник мне был и премногу зело любовь ко мне имел; тако же и аз к нему многогрешный, по силе моей, любовию и службою простирался. О мужу налепший и накрепчайший, мне превозлюбленнейший и пренадсладчайший, отче мой и родителю духовный! Коль ми люто и скорбно от зрения наичестнейших седин твоих разлученну бывшу!

Что же таковый превосходный муж получил во отечестве своем неблагодарном, от того лютого и безчеловечного царя? То: нецыи глаголют, аки бы воспомянул нечто о мне ему; он же, глаголют, восклехтал, яко дивий вепрь, и воскрежетал неистово зубами своими и абие повелел таковаго святаго мужа в реце утопити. И сице приял мученичества венец и получил второе крещение, егоже и Господь наш Исус Христос по крещению Иоаннове возжелел, яко сам рече: "Коль, рече, желаю чашу сию пити и крещением сим креститись!" А нецыи глаголют о скончанию его, приходящие ото оные земли, аки бы тихою и спокойною смертию о[b] Господе почил он святый муж. Аз же истинне не мог достаточнее выведатися о смерти его, аще и со прилежанием о том выведавахся;[c] яко слышал от некоторых, так и написах,

[a] Т. имел: Ar., Patr., Pog.   [b] Patr., Pog., Т. от: Ar.   [c] Т. выведахся: Ar.

---

[1] An unexpected use of the instrumental, probably in error for the dative.

years. As all wise men say, habits of many years standing, which have hardened in men's souls from childhood, become part of men's nature and are bad or difficult to blot out. Such long-standing abominations and impure evils he knew how to tear asunder and uproot from the souls of men, and he knew how to purify and illumine those who are impure and foul and to bring them close to the Lord with much penitence and many tears and to forbid the devil himself,[1] by the power of the Holy Spirit and by the priestly authority given him by God, to assail men and to dare to befoul penitent human souls. These things, in truth, I have not only heard from reliable men, but have seen them with my own eyes, and I have personally experienced what happened, and I have experienced the great benefits which accrued to me from his holiness, for he was my confessor, and his love for me was exceedingly great; and likewise I too, great sinner though I am, strove towards him as best I could, with love and service. O most excellent and firmest of men, most beloved by me and sweetest, my father and spiritual parent! How bitter and grievous it is for me to have been separated from seeing your venerable grey hair!

And what did such an excellent man receive in his thankless fatherland from that fierce inhuman tsar? The following: some people say that he mentioned something about me to the tsar; and the tsar, they say, let out a shriek[2] like a wild boar and fiercely gnashed his teeth and immediately ordered the holy man to be drowned in the river. And thus he received a martyr's crown and the second baptism, which Our Lord Jesus Christ desired after the baptism by John, as He Himself said: "How I wish to drink of this cup and be baptized with this baptism!"[3] And certain people who came from that land say, concerning his death, that the holy man died a quiet and calm death in the Lord. I could not find out sufficient about his death, although I made diligent enquiries. As I have heard from certain people, so I have written, while in my wanderings,[4]

---

[2] The verb клектати usually describes the sound made by birds, particularly eagles.

[3] Mark x. 38–9.

[4] I.e. abroad. Cf. *Correspondence*, p. 181, n. 6.

в странстве будучи, и долгим ростоянием отлученный и туне отогнан ото оные земли любимаго отечества моего.

А еже всех[a] по ряду не написах о нем, яко выше рекох, ово ко краткости истории зряще, ово зде живущих в грубых и в духовных отнюдь неискусных, к тому и маловерных ради человеков. И аще Бог поможет, и обрящем некоторых духовных мужей, желающих сего, тогда мало нечто воспомянем о предивных видениях его и о пророчествиях и о чюдесех некоторых, яко духовные духовным на пользу поведающе. Телесные бо, яко рече апостол, не приемлют еже от духа, понеже не вмещают, затворяюще волею утробы свои, и глупство видится им, еже о духовных глаголемое, понеже в телесных вещах со прилежанием обращаются, а о духовных не радят, паче же а ни разумети хотят.

[a] Patr., T.   а еже в тех: Ar.

---

[1] Rom. viii. 5.

separated by a long distance and driven out without guilt from my beloved fatherland.

And if I have not narrated everything about him, then this, as I have said above, is both because I am concerned with the brevity of this story, and for the sake of those living in this country who are ignorant and completely unacquainted with things of the spirit and, furthermore, for the sake of men of little faith. Should God help us and should we find some spiritual men who desire this, then we will recall a little about his wondrous visions and prophecies and certain of his miracles, narrating things of the spirit for the benefit of men of the spirit. For those that are of the flesh, as the apostle said, do not receive that which comes from the spirit,[1] for they cannot contain it, wilfully closing their bellies, and their folly—what they say about things of the spirit—is visible to them, for they diligently deal with things of the flesh and have no care for things of the spirit, and, furthermore, they have no desire to understand.

IX

И ныне, скончавающе и историю новоизбиенных мучеников, да похвалим по силе нашей, елико можем. И кто бы, ум здрав имеюще, возбранял их похвалити? Развие бы кто гнусного, и ленивого, и лютаго, и неистового ума был. Речет кто негли: "Мученики царей нечестивых не послушав и идолом не послужили, и пред лютыми мучители единого Бога исповедали, и сего ради различные муки претерпели и смерти срогие подъяли, радующесь, за Христа Бога." Сие воистинну и аз вем; но и те новоизбиенные от лютого и безчеловечного царя. Аще он Богу мнится и веровати и служити в Троице славим, и крещением просвещен был, но Бога единого и дияволи ведят, в Троице же слави-маго и икономахи и другие мучители и исповедали, — но тако же и те множество мучеников и исповедников пре-лютыми мученьми помучители¹ за Христа: бо был крещен и Фока мучитель и цесарем Римским и Грецким, но обаче, безчеловечия его ради, мучитель наречен есть. Аз же реку нечто поистинне дерзостнейше: положил бы некто два драконы ядовитых и видел их единого вне, а другаго внутрь; которого же бы удобнее было устрещися, внешняго или внутренняго? Кто бы прел, иже внешняго! Тако царие быша прежнии мучители нечестивыя идолослужители, болваном глухим и немым жертву приносящие и бо-ящиеся[a] тех богов новых, ихже не подобаше боятися, по реченному: убояшеся страха, идеже не бе страха, и быша оные церкви Христовы явственныя и внешние неприятели. Но новый наш, не внешной, но воистину внутренный дракон, не болваном служити повелел, а ни[b] жертвы приносити им, но первие[c] сам самого диявола волю исполнил, возненавидел[d] уский и прискорбный путь, покаянием ко спасению

---

[a] Т. боящесь: Ar.   [b] Patr., Pog., Т. аки: Ar.   [c] Patr., Pog., Т. перви: Ar.   [d] Patr., Pog., Т. вонененавидел: Ar.

---

¹ помучители in error for помучили.

IX

And now, to conclude our story of the recently-slain martyrs, let us praise them according to our strength and as best we can. Who indeed, having a sound mind, would forbid us to praise them? Only if he were a man of foul, lazy, savage and ferocious mind. Someone may say: "The martyrs did not obey impious tsars and did not serve idols, and they confessed one God in the presence of fierce torturers, and for this reason they suffered various torments and rejoicingly underwent harsh deaths for Christ their God." This indeed I know; so too do those who have recently been slain by the fierce, inhuman tsar. He may think he believes in and serves God, who is glorified in the Trinity, and he may have been enlightened by baptism, but so too do the devils know one God, who is glorified in the Trinity, and so too did the iconoclasts and other torturers confess Him—yet they also tortured[1] a number of martyrs and confessors in Christ with exceedingly fierce torturers: indeed, even Phocas[2] the Tormentor was baptized, and he was Greek and Roman emperor, but still, because of his inhumanity, he was called the Tormentor. But I shall say something bolder still: supposing someone were to take[3] two poisonous dragons and were to see one of them within and one of them without—which would he be more likely to be afraid of, the internal or the external dragon? Who would argue that it was the external dragon! Thus the former tormentor-tsars were impious idolaters, bringing sacrifices to deaf and dumb idols and fearing those new gods whom they should not have feared, according to the word [of the prophet]: "they feared fear where no fear was",[4] and they were the visible, external enemies of the Church of Christ. But our new dragon—not an external dragon, but indeed an internal dragon—ordered men not to serve idols or to bring sacrifices to them, but himself was the first to carry out the will of the very devil, hating the narrow,

[2] East Roman emperor 602-10.   [3] Or, perhaps, "to imagine".
[4] Ps. xiv. 5 (LXX version).

приводящ, и потек с радостию по широкому и пространному пути, водящиму[a] в погибель; яко и самым нам многожды слышащим ото уст его: егда же уже был развратился, тогда во слух всем глаголал: "Едино, рече, пред себя взяти, или здешное или тамошное!"[b] сиречь или Христов прискорбный путь,[c] или сатанин широкий.

О безумный и окаянный! забыл еси прежде тебя царей царствовавших, и в Новом и в Ветхом завете, паче же прародителей твоих, княжат Руских святых, ходящих по Христову ускому пути, сиречь мирне и воздержне живущих; но обаче царствующих блаженне, яко и ты сам в покаянию был немало лет и добре царствовал. Ныне, егда развратился еси и прельстился от ласкателей, тогда таковые словеса отрыгнул еси, избравши себе пространный Антихристов путь, и отринул от себя всех предобрых и разумных мужей, и собравше войско дияволе, сиречь похлебников и отовсюду злодеев, во всем согласующим злостем своим, нарицающесь церковником, погнал церковь Божию. И яко погнал! и коль страшно и прелюто, иже рещи и выписати не возможно!

— Яко напреди мало рехом, но обаче мало нечто и отчасти о том гонению в предреченных изъявлено. — Не нудил жертвы приносити болваном, но дияволом вкупе с собою согласовати повелевал, трезвым во пиянстве погружатися нудил,[d] от негоже все злые возрастают; не Крону жрети и дети закалати, но отрекшись естества, сиречь отца и матери и братии, резати человеков по составом повелел, яко и Басманова Феодора принудил отца убити, и Никиту безумнаго Прозоровского — Василия, брата своего, и других многих; не пред Афродитовым[e] болваном блудотворения и нечистоты плодити, но на явственнейших своих скверных пированиях прескexternal глаголы со восклицанием и со вопиянием

[a] Patr. водящим: Ar., Pog.   [b] Patr., Pog. тамошно: Ar.
[c] T. путь omitted in Ar., Patr., Pog.   [d] Patr., Pog., T. нудим:
Ar.   [e] T. Анродитовым: Ar.

[1] Matt. vii. 13–14.   [2] Cf. *Correspondence*, pp. 8–9.
[3] Kurbsky's *History* is the only source to mention F. Basmanov's parricide

grievous way which leads to salvation through repentance, and
running with joy along the broad, wide way which leads to
destruction;[1] for we ourselves many a time heard from his lips
(he used to say this in the hearing of all when he had already
become depraved): "I must choose one thing—either that
which is here or that which is there!"; in other words either
the grievous path of Christ, or the broad path of Satan.

O mad, accursed man! You have forgotten the tsars who
ruled before you, both in the Old Testament and in the New
Testament; especially you have forgotten your ancestors, the
holy Russian princes who trod the narrow way of Christ, that
is to say who lived with moderation and restraint, and yet
ruled blessedly, just as you yourself ruled well for several years
when you were in a state of penitence. Now that you have
become depraved and seduced by your flatterers, you have
belched forth such words, choosing for yourself the broad way
of the Antichrist, and you have cast aside all good wise men
and you have collected a devilish army, that is to say flatterers
and evil-doers from all sides, who in all things approve of your
wickednesses; and, calling yourself a churchman, you have
persecuted the Church of God. And how you persecuted it! It
is not possible to say or to describe how fearfully and how
ferociously!—as I have said shortly before, a small part of this
persecution has been described in what has been written above.
He did not force people to bring sacrifices to idols, but ordered
them together with himself to be in concord with devils and
forced sober men to drown in drunkenness, from which spring
up all evil things. He did not order men to sacrifice to Cronus[2]
and to slay their children, but ordered them to renounce nature,
that is to say to renounce father and mother and brothers, and
to cut men up in pieces—for instance, he forced Fedor Basmanov to kill his father and the mad Nikita Prozorovsky to kill
his brother Vasily, and many others as well.[3] He forced men
not to multiply their fornications and impurities before the idol
of Aphrodite, but at his most manifest foul feasts to belch forth
exceedingly filthy words with exclamations and shrieks—as for

and N. Prozorovsky's fratricide. For the Prozorovskys, see above, p. 191,
n. 4.

отрыгати — а что потом последовали, делы исполняемые скверности и нечистоты, сие совести их пущаю лучше ведати — не[a] в Бахусову звезду[1] поставленому болвану пиянствующе и безчинствующе, ни праздник его во едино время и в год сие творя, но весь целый век свой, егда возненавидел воздержательное житие, тысящу крат горщи, нежели оные поганы, Бахуса почитающе, пиянствующе и безчинствующе, крови христианские на проклятых пированиях проливающе не хотящих согласовати ему в таковых; яко един муж храбрый посреди пиру обличил его предо всеми, емуж было наречение Молчан Митков.[3] Егда нудим был от него предреченными оными великими, дияволу обещанными, чашами пити, тогда велегласно возопивша глаголют его и рекша: "Царю! воистинну яко сам пиешь, так и нас принуждаешь, окаянный, мед кровию смешанный братий наших, правоверных християн, пити!" Он же абие возгоревся гневом великим, копьем, яже во проклятом жезле своем носяще, абие рукою своею пробил его и вне храмины лютым кромешником повелел извлещи его, едва дышуща, и добити. И сице исполнил помост полаты кровии посреди проклятого пиру. Едали сей муж не мученик воистинну, светлый и знаменитый победоносец?

Християнский, речешь, царь? И еще православный, отвещаю ти: християнов губил и от православных человеков рожденных и ссущих младенцов не пощадил! Обещал, рече, Христу на крещение, отрекшися диавола и всех дел и всех ангел его? Реку[b] ти паки: поправши заповеди Христа своего и отвергшеся законоположения евангельского, егда не явственно обещался дияволу и ангелом его, собравши воинство полков диявольских и учинивши над ними стратилаты окаянных своих ласкателей, и ведый и волю Царя Небесного, произвел делом всю волю сатанинъскую, по-

[a] Т. но: Ar.　　　　　[b] Т. рек: Ar.

---

[1] Lit. "to the star of Bacchus".

[2] For this expression, see above, pp. 162–3.

[3] Little is known about Molchan Semenovich Mitkov except that he was

290

the things that followed after this, things full of filth and impurity, I can only permit my conscience to know of such things; he did not indulge in drunkenness and impropriety before an idol set up to Bacchus,[1] nor did he celebrate his festival at one time only or in one year only, but throughout all his life after he had conceived a hatred for restrained behaviour; and his worship of Bacchus and his drunkenness and impropriety were a thousand times worse than those of the pagans, for at his accursed feasts he shed the Christian blood of those who did not wish to concur with him in such deeds. Indeed, one brave man, in the middle of a feast, reproved him before all, and his name was Molchan Mitkov. When he was forced by him to drink those great beakers, pledged to the devil,[2] then, they say, he cried out in a loud voice and said: "O tsar, not only do you yourself drink, but, accursed one, you force us too to drink mead mixed with the blood of our brothers, the Orthodox Christians!" And the tsar straightway blazed up with a great anger and with his own hand transfixed him with a spear, which he used to carry within his accursed staff, and ordered his fierce children of darkness to drag him out of the chamber still barely breathing and to finish him off. And thus did he cover the floor of the room with blood in the middle of that accursed feast. Was not this man in truth a martyr, a glorious and distinguished conqueror?[3]

You are a Christian tsar, you say? And, furthermore, Orthodox? My answer to you is: you have destroyed Christians and you have not spared men born of Orthodox parents and babes at the breast! You made a promise, you said, to Christ at your baptism, you renounced the devil and all his works and all his angels? I say to you again: you trampled upon the commandments of your Christ and rejected the legislation of the Gospel when you secretly gave your promise to the devil and his angels, gathering together an army of devilish troops and placing over them as generals your accursed flatterers; and although you knew the will of the heavenly Tsar, you carried out in deed the whole will of Satan, by manifesting unheard-of

one of those who stood surety for Prince Ivan Bel'sky in 1562. See Veselovsky, *Sinodik*, p. 310.

казующе лютость неслыханную, никогда же бывшую в Русии, над церковью[a] живаго Бога! Не боится, а ни ужасаетъся новых богов? Глаголю ти: аще не боится новых, но боится чаров, сиречь стараго и древняго Велиара, научившися и ведуще, иже знамением честнаго креста всеужасие попираются[b] и изгоняется. К тому, не яко ли у мучителей древних различные[c] орудия мученей, тако же и у нашего новаго? не скаврады ли и пещи? не бичевания ли жестокое и ногти остр-острые? не клеща ли рожденные,[d] торгания ради телес человеческих? не игол ли за нохти биени и резание по составом? не претрения[e] ли вервми наполы не токмо муж, но и жен благородных, и другие безчисленные и неслыханные роды мук, на[f] неповинных, произведенные от него? Еще ли не мучитель прелютый!

О окаянныи и вселукавые пагубники отечества, и телесоядцы, и кровопийцы сродник своих и единоязычных! поколь маете безстудствовати и оправдати такова человека разстерзателя? О преблаженныи и достохвальные святые мученики, новоизбиенные от внутренного змия! за добрую совесть вашу пострадасте, и мало зде претерпевше и очистившеся прехвальным сим крещением, чисти к пречистейшему Христу отоидосте мзды трудов восприяти! Едали те много не потрудишася? едали те не доброе страдаша? Не токмо христиан убогих от варваров в земле своей обороняюще, но и царьства кровопийственные бусурманские целые мужеством храбрости своея разориша и с самими цари их безверными, и пределы разширяша царьства христианского аж до Каспинского[g] моря и окрест, и грады тамо христианские поставиша, и святые олтари воздвигоша и многих неверных к вере приведоша. И что возглаголю о разпространению границ и на другие страны, служаще цареви своему и общей вещи христианской верне?

И яковую мзду зде получиша от того лютого и безчеловеч-

[a] Patr., Pog. церковь: Ar.   [b] T. попирающе: Ar.   [c] T. различного: Ar., Patr., Pog.   [d] Ar. раждеженные: Patr., Pog. [e] Patr., T. потрения: Ar.   [f] Patr., Pog., T. но: Ar.   [g] T. ксапийскаго: Ar.

ferocity, unprecedented in Russia, against the Church of the living God! Is he not afraid of, is he not terrified of new gods? I say to you: he may not fear new gods, but he fears charms, that is to say the old and ancient Belial, although he has been instructed and knows that by the sign of the holy cross terror is vanquished and dispelled. Furthermore, are not the various instruments of torture of the ancient torturers the same as those used by our new torturer? Pans and stoves? Cruel flogging and extremely sharp iron claws? Red-hot[1] pincers for lacerating human bodies? Needles to drive under the finger-nails? Dismemberment of bodies?[2] Cutting people in half with cords—not only men but noble women—and other countless unheard-of kinds of torture inflicted by him on guiltless people? Is he not indeed a fierce torturer?

O accursed and cunning destroyers of your fatherland, eaters of the flesh and drinkers of the blood of your kinsmen and fellow-countrymen! How long will you act shamelessly and exonerate such a tormentor? O most blessed and praiseworthy of holy martyrs, newly-massacred by the inner serpent! You suffered for your good conscience, and, having endured a little in this life and having purified yourselves in this most laudible baptism, you have departed, pure to the most pure Christ, to receive the reward for your toils! Did they not toil much? Was not their suffering for the good? Not only did they defend poor Christians in their land from the barbarians, but by their heroic bravery they destroyed whole tsardoms of blood-drinking Mussulmans together with their infidel khans, and they extended the limits of the Christian tsardom as far as the Caspian Sea and round about, and they founded Christian cities there and erected holy altars and brought many unbelievers to the faith. And what shall I say about the extension of the frontiers in other directions too, as they faithfully served their tsar and the Christian commonwealth?

And what reward did they receive in this life from that fierce

---

[1] рожденные (var. раждеженные) clearly in error for разженные. See *Correspondence*, pp. 6–7.
[2] Lit. "cutting by joints".

ного царя! Едали Христос не воздаст им и не украсит венцы мученическими таковых, иже обещал и за чашу студеные воды отдати мзду?¹ А сего ради, воистину, будут ездити или пловати на облацех во стретение Господне в первом воскресению, яко рече Богослов во Апокалипсисе: "блажен, рече, иже получит часть в первом воскресению"², и Павел: "яко бо о Адаме все умирают, тако и о Христе все оживут; кождо во своем чину: начаток Христос", сиречь пострадавший Христос воскресеᵃ первый в нетленном телеси, начальник воскресению за него пострадавших; "потом Христу веровавшие во пришествие Его", сиречь во второе, егда со ангелы явится; "потом кончина", сиречь Антихристово убиение и общее всех воскресение. "Тогда, рече Соломон, станет во дерзновение мнозе праведник пред лицем мучителя" рекше, очевисте с мучившим его, або со обидевшим; тогда, глаголю, и те последние мученики, со древними страстотерпцы и победоносцы, встретят Христа своего, посреди аера от превыспренних небес грядущаго со всеми ангелы своими, на избавление их: они же от земли многими и великими полки, яко небопарный Павелᵇ глаголет, "восхищенныи будут на облацех во сретение Господне на воздусех, и тако всегда з Господем будут". Их же и нас да сподобит, по премногой благодати своей, а не по нашим делам, Господь наш Исус Христос, истинный Бог, Емуже слава со безначальным Отцем и со пресвятым и благим и животворящим Святым Духом, ныне и присно и во веки веков. Аминь.

ᵃ Т. сиречь пострадавшим воскресе: Ar.   ᵇ Patr., Pog. павелел: Ar.

---

¹ Matt. x. 42.   ² Rev. xx. 6.   ³ 1 Cor. xv. 22–3.

and inhuman tsar! Surely Christ will repay and will adorn with martyr's crowns those whom He promised to reward for a cup of cold water![1] For this reason, indeed, they will ride or sail upon the clouds to meet the Lord in the first resurrection, as [St John] the Theologian said in the Apocalypse: "Blessed is he that shall have part in the first resurrection",[2] and Paul: "For as in Adam all die, even so in Christ shall all be made alive. But every man in his own order: Christ the firstfruits",[3] that is to say Christ, having suffered, was the first to arise in His incorruptible body, the leader of the resurrection of those who suffered for Him; "afterward they that believe in Christ at His coming",[4] that is to say at His second coming, when He shall appear with His angels; "then the end",[5] that is to say the slaying of the Antichrist and the general resurrection of all men. "Then," said Solomon, "shall the righteous man stand in great boldness before the face of the tormentor",[6] that is to say, face to face with him that tortured him or afflicted him; then, I say, shall these last martyrs together with the ancient martyrs[7] and conquerors meet their Christ, who shall come through the air from the very high heavens with all His angels to deliver them. And from the earth, in many great hosts, as the heavenly-soaring Paul says, "they shall be caught up in the clouds to meet the Lord in the air, and so shall they ever be with the Lord".[8] May they and we be deemed worthy [of salvation], according to His great grace and not according to our deeds, by our Lord Jesus Christ, the true God, to whom glory [is due] together with the eternal Father and the most holy and good and life-giving Holy Spirit, now and for ever and unto the ages of ages. Amen.

[4] 1 Cor. xv. 23.   [5] 1 Cor. xv. 24.   [6] Wisdom of Solomon v. 1.
[7] Lit. "sufferers of passion".   [8] 1 Thess. iv. 17.

WORDS BORROWED FROM
OTHER LANGUAGES

або (Pol. *albo*) or

аер (Lat. *aer*) air

акафист (Gk. ἀκάθιστος ὕμνος) acathistus, hymn of praise to
the Mother of God

ани (Pol. *ani*) neither/nor

антипат (Gk. ἀνθύπατος) governor

аспр (Lat. *asperiolus, asperialis*) squirrel skin

блазенство (Pol. *błazeństwo*) buffoonery

важить (Pol. *ważyć*) to weigh up, consider

вальный гуф (Pol. *walny huf*) main force

вежа (Pol. *wieża*) tower

вуй (Pol. *wuj*) (maternal) uncle

выспа (Pol. *wyspa*) island

вытекать (Pol. *wyciekać*) to make a sortie

вытечка (Pol. *wycieczka*) sortie

вязень (Pol. *więzień*) prisoner

гаковница (Pol. *hakownica*) musket, arquebus

галия (Pol. *galeon*) galley

герцовать (Pol. *harcować*) to fight, skirmish

гетман (Pol. *hetman*) commander

година (Pol. *godzina*) hour

град, город (Pol. *gród*) fortified place, citadel

гуф, гуфец (Pol. *huf, hufiec*) detachment

дело (Pol. *działo*) gun

желнер (Pol. *żołnierz*) soldier

живиться (Pol. *żywić się*) to be fed, to feed onself

запомнить (Pol. *zapomnieć*) to forget
заточить (Pol. *zatoczyć*) to put, place or train (of guns)
зацный (Pol. *zacny*) distinguished, worthy
збройка, зброя, збруйка (Pol. *zbroja*) armour
землянин (Pol. *ziemianin*) landowner

кат (Pol. *kat*) executioner
кгалия, *see* галия
кнегт (Gmn. *knecht*) soldier
княжа, pl. княжата (Pol. *książę*, pl. *książęta*) prince
колико (Pol. *kilka*) several
колько десять (Pol. *kilkadziesiąt*) several tens of
кортун (Pol. *kartan*) siege gun
куль (Pol. *kula*) cannon-ball
кунтур, кунтор (Gmn. *Komtur*) commander (of the Order)
кроника (Pol. *kronika*) chronicle

ложничий (Pol. *łożniczy*) gentleman of the bedchamber

маньяк (Pol. *maniak*) maniac
марцыпан (Pol. *marcepan*) almond cake
машкара (Pol. *maszkara*) mask
место (Pol. *miasto*) town
мурованный (Pol. *murowany*) stone, built of stone

неякий (Pol. *niejaki*) (a) certain
неяко (Pol. *niejako*) somewhat

обоз (Pol. *obóz*) camp

памятать (Pol. *pamiętać*) to remember
парозит (Lat. *parasitus*) parasite
пахолик (Pol. *pacholik*) boy, servant
пащека (Pol. *paszczęka*) jaw
певне (Pol. *pewnie*) certainly

пенег, pl. пенези (Pol. *pieniądz*) money
печенег (Pol. *pieczenarz*) hanger-on
плювия (Lat. *pluvia*) rain
повет (Pol. *powiat*) district
поветренный (Pol. *powietrzny*) pestilential, infectious
подскарбий (Pol. *podskarbi*) treasurer
позычать (Pol. *pożyczać*) to borrow
польный (Pol. *polny*) field (*adj.*)
помятамися (Pol. *pamięta mi się*) I remember
постинать (Pol. *pościnać*) to behead
посядать (Pol. *posiadać*) to possess
потаемный (Pol. *potajemny*) secret
потварь (Pol. *potwarz*) slander
похлебник (Pol. *pochlebca*) toady, flatterer
почта (Pol. *poczet*) detachment
привилей (Pol. *przywilej*) charter
прикрый (Pol. *przykry*) unpleasant, hard, difficult
пришанцоваться (Pol. *przyszańcować się*) to dig in close to
пруткий (Pol. *prędki*) quick

рада (Pol. *rada*) council
раздроченный (from Pol. *dręczyć*) wearied, exhausted
райтор (Pol. *rajtar*) knight, cavalryman
расховаться (Pol. *schować się*) to hide
роковать (Pol. *rokować*) to parley
ротмистр (Pol. *rotmistrz*) cavalry captain, cavalry commander
ручничный (Pol. *ruszniczny*) musket (*adj.*)

сенат (Pol. *senat*) council
сигклит (Gk. σύγκλητος) counsellor
скарб, скорб (Pol. *skarb*) treasure, possessions
справа (Pol. *sprawa*) affair, business
стаинник (Pol. *stajennik*) servant (*lit.* stable-lad)
стайня (Pol. *stajnia*) stable
статечный (Pol. *stateczny*) reliable, solid
сточить битву (Pol. *stoczyć bitwę*) to fight a battle
стрый (Pol. *stryj*) uncle (paternal)

таней (Pol. *taniej*) cheaper
трвать (Pol. *trwać*) to last
тыждень (Pol. *tydzień*) week

ублагать (Pol. *ubłagać*) to entreat, propitiate, make peace with
уробить (Pol. *urobić*) to build, fashion, mould

чело (Pol. *czoło*) front line
чюйный (Pol. *czujny*) watchful

шанец (Pol. *szaniec*) trench (with rampart)
шкота (Pol. *szkoda*) loss
шляхетный (Pol. *szlachetny*) noble
шляхта (Pol. *szlachta*) nobility
штурм (Pol. *szturm*) assault

FOREIGN WORDS MENTIONED IN THE TRANSLATION OR FOOTNOTES

altyn: coin, value of 3 copecks
archimandrite: head of a monastery, abbot
ataman: leader, commander (*lit.* Cossack chief)

Blizhnyaya duma: privy council.
boyar: nobleman, or, as rank, member of Boyar Council

den'ga: coin, value of half a copeck
duma: council
dvoretsky: steward
d'yak: secretary, civil servant

hafiz: adept in the Koran
hetman: commander, leader

igumen: head of monastery, abbot

karach: Tatar dignitary
kaznachey: chancellor, treasurer

mirza: prince, Tatar dignitary
molla: priest, judge

namestnik: governor

okol'nichy: rank in the hierarchy, below boyar
opala: disgrace
oprichnina: Ivan IV's special court, or bodyguard, established 1565

pan: lord (Polish, West Russian)
pomest'e: grant of land to service man in reward for service

posluzhny spisok: list of serving boyars
postel'nichy: gentleman of the bedchamber
povalusha: building, or room
pud: measure of weight (16·3 kilograms)
pyatina: one of the five districts of Novgorod

razryady: list of military appointments

sazhen': measure of distance (2·134 metres)
seunch: message, messenger
seyyid: descendant of the prophet
sinodik: list of dead for whose souls monastery or church is asked
    to pray
skit: hermitage
skomorokhi: strolling players, buffoons, actors
spal'nik: gentleman of the bedchamber

tsarevich: khan's son

ulus: nation, tribe, people

verst: measure of distance (3500 feet—about two-thirds of a
    mile)
voevoda: general, commander

yartaul: advance guard
yasak: tribute, order, command, or signal
yurt: independent Tatar horde

LIST OF WORKS CITED

Adrianova-Peretts, V. P. See *Poslaniya Ivana Groznogo*

Andreyev, N. Kurbsky's letters to Vas'yan Muromtsev. *SEER*, vol. XXXIII, no. 81, 1955.

Aufzeichnungen über den Moskauer Staat. See Staden.

Bazilevich, K. V. *Vneshnyaya politika Russkogo tsentralizovannogo gosudarstva. Vtoraya polovina XV veka.* Moscow, 1952.

Belokurov, S. A. Nadgrobnye plity XVI v. v sele Obraztsove Moskovskoy gubernii. *Chteniya*, 1911, III.

Chteniya v imperatorskom obshchestve istorii i drevnosti. Moscow.

Dal', V. *Tolkovy Slovar'.*

Drevneyshaya Razryadnaya Kniga. Chteniya, 1902, I.

Drevnyaya rossiyskaya vivliofika. SPb, 1773–5.

Epstein, F. See Staden.

Fennell, J. L. I. *Ivan the Great of Moscow.* London, 1961.

—— *The Correspondence between Prince A. M. Kurbsky and Tsar Ivan IV of Russia 1564–1579.* Cambridge, 1955.

Golubinsky, E. *Istoriya russkoy tserkvi.* Moscow, 1900–4.

Gorsky, A. V. Istoricheskoe opisanie Svyato-Troitskoy Sergievy Lavry. *Chteniya*, 1878, IV.

Herberstein, Baron Sigismund von. *Rerum Moscoviticarum Commentarii.* Translated into English by E. H. Major. London, Hakluyt Society, 1851.

Istoricheskie zapiski. Moscow.

Klyuchevsky, V. O. *Drevnerusskie zhitiya svyatykh kak istorichesky istochnik.* Moscow, 1871.

Kobrin, V. B., Sostav oprichnogo dvora Ivana Groznogo. *Arkheografichesky ezhegodnik za 1959 g.* Moscow, 1960.

Likhachev, D. S. See *Poslaniya Ivana Groznogo.*

Lur'e, Ya. S. See *Poslaniya Ivana Groznogo.*

Migne, J. P. *Patrologiae cursus completus. Series graeco-latina.* Paris, 1857–66.

Novgorodskie letopisi. Ed. Arkheograficheskaya Kommissiya. SPb, 1879.

Polnoe sobranie russkikh letopisey.

Poslanie Taube i Kruze. Ed. M. G. Roginksy, *Russky istorichesky zhurnal,* vol. 8. Petrograd, 1922.

Poslaniya Ivana Groznogo. Eds. D. S. Likhachev, Ya. S. Lur'e, V. P. Adrianova-Peretts. Akademiya Nauk SSSR, 1951.

Pskovskie Letopisi. Ed. Nasonov, vols. 1–2. Akademiya Nauk SSSR, 1947–55.

Roginsky, M. G. See *Poslanie Taube i Kruze.*

Russkaya istoricheskaya biblioteka. SPb, 1872–1927.

Sadikov, P. A. *Ocherki po istorii oprichniny.* Akademiya Nauk SSSR, 1950.

Semenov, P. *Geografichesko-statistichesky slovar' Rossiyskoy Imperii.* SPb, 1862.

Skrynnikov, R. G. Kurbsky i ego pis'ma v Pskovo-Pechersky monastyr'. *TODRL,* vol. xviii, 1962.

—— Oprichnaya zemel'naya reforma Groznogo. *IZ,* vol. 70, 1961.

Slavonic and East European Review. University of London.

Smirnov, I. I. *Ocherki politicheskoy istorii Russkogo gosudarstva 30–50-x godov XVI v.* Akademiya Nauk SSSR, 1958.

Solov'ev, S. M. *Istoriya Rossii s drevneyshikh vremen.* Ed. 'Obshchestvennaya Pol'za', SPb.

Sreznevsky, I. I. *Materialy dlya slovarya drevne-russkogo yazyka.* SPb, 1893–1903.

Staden, Heinrich von. *Aufzeichnungen über den Moskauer Staat.* Ed. F. Epstein. Hamburg, 1930.

Stroev, P. *Spiski ierarkhov i nastoyateley monastyrey Rossiyskoy tserkvi.* SPb, 1877.

Tikhomirov, M. N. Maloizvestnye letopisnye pamyatniki XVI v. *IZ,* vol. 10, 1941.

—— *Rossiya v XVI stoletii.* Akademiya Nauk SSSR, 1962.

—— Zapis' o regenstve Eleny Glinskoy i Boyarskom pravlenii 1533–47. *IZ,* vol. 46, 1954.

Trudy otdela drevnerusskoy literatury. Akademiya Nauk SSSR, Institut Russkoy literatury.

Ustryalov, N. G. *Skazaniya Knyazya Kurbskogo.* SPb, 1868.

Veselovsky, S. B. *Feodal'noe zemlevladenie v severovostochnoy Rusi.* Akademiya Nauk SSSR, 1947.

—— Sinodik opal'nykh tsarya Ivana. *Problemy istochnikovedeniya,* vol. III. Akademiya Nauk SSSR, 1940.

Zhmakin, V. *Mitropolit Daniil i ego sochineniya.* Moscow, 1881.

Zimin, A. A. *I. S. Peresvetov i ego sovremenniki.* Akademiya Nauk SSSR, 1958.

—— Kogda Kurbsky napisal "Istoriyu o velikom knyaze Moskovskom"? *TODRL,* vol. XVIII, 1962.

—— O sostave dvortsovykh uchrezhdeniy Russkogo gosudarstva kontsa XV i XVI v. *IZ,* vol. 63.

—— *Reformy Ivana Groznogo.* Moscow, 1960.

—— Sostav Boyarskoy dumy v XV–XVI vekakh. *Arkheografichesky ezhegodnik za 1957 g.* Moscow, 1958.

—— Zemsky Sobor 1566. *IZ,* vol. 71. Moscow, 1961.

INDEX

Portugal, 142–3
Postel'nichy, 80 n., 122–3
Povalusha, 214–15
Pronsk, 39 n., 222 n., 226 n.
Pronsky-Rybin, Vasily Fedorovich, Prince, 192–3
Pronsky-Shemyakin, Yury Ivanovich, Prince, 36–7, 120–3
Pronsky-Turuntay, Ivan Ivanovich, Prince, 28 n., 188 n., 192–3
Protopsaltist, 276–7
Prozorovsky family, 190–1
Prozorovsky, Aleksandr Ivanovich, Prince, 190–1
Prozorovsky, Mikhail Fedorovich, Prince, 190–1
Prozorovsky, Nikita Ivanovich, Prince, 191 n., 288–9
Prozorovsky, Vasily Ivanovich, Prince, 190–1, 288–9
Prussians, 144–5
Pskov, town and district, 11 n., 106–7, 114–15, 118–19, 146 n., 245 n., 248–9
Pskov-Pechery Monastery, 246–9
Pskovskoe, Lake, *see* Chudskoe
Pushkin family, 219 n.
Pushkin, Dmitry, 218–19
Pushkin-Kurchev, Tret'yak-Dmitry Ivanovich, 219 n.
Pyatina, 108–9

Radogoshch, 213 n.
Raguel, 86–7
Razladin, Vasily Prokof'evich, 218 n.
Razladin-Kvashnin, Feodosia, 218–19
Razladin-Kvashnin, Ivan Vasil'evich, 218–19
Razladin-Kvashnin, Nikifor Vasil'evich, 218–19
Razladin-Kvashnin, Vasily Vasil'evich, 216–20
Rededya, Kasogian chieftain, 211 n.
Reheboam, 84–5
Repnin(-Obolensky), Mikhail Petrovich, Prince, 180–1
Revel', 110–11, 120 n., 134–5, 144–5
Rhodes, 144–5
Riga, 118–19, 120 n., 134 n., 144–5, 148–9
Ringen, 118–19, 214 n.
Rome, 2 n.
Rõngu, *see* Ringen
Rostislavl', 28 n.

Rostov, town and district, 252–3
Rostovsky, Vasily Volk, Prince, 186–9
Rostovsky-Katyrev, Andrey Ivanovich, Prince, 186–9
Rostovsky-Lobanov, *see* Lobanov-Rostovsky
Rostovsky-Temkin, *see* Temkin-Rostovsky
Rozhdestvensky Convent, 4 n.
Rugodiv, *see* Narva
Ryapolovsky, Dmitry Ivanovich, Prince, 186–7
Ryapolovsky, Semen Ivanovich, Prince, 5 n., 170–1
Ryazan', princes of, 192–3
Ryazan', town and district, 14–15, 30–1, 120 n., 224–5
Rybin, *see* Pronsky-Rybin
Ryndekh, *see* Ringen
Ryurik, 220–1

Saburov, Ivan Yur'evich, 222–3
Saburov, Solomonia Yur'evna, Grand Princess, first wife of Vasily III, 4–5, 6 n., 222–3
Saburov, Timofey-Zamyatnya Ivanovich, 222–3
Sadikov, P. A., 187 n., 188 n., 192 n., 193 n., 196 n., 210 n., 211 n., 221 n., 223 n.
St Sofia (Novgorod), 246–7
Saltykov, *see* Morozov-Saltykov
Saracens, 142–5
Sarmatians, 162–3
Sarykhozin family, 228–9
Sarykhozin, Mark, 229 n.
Satin, Aleksey, 178–9
Satin, Andrey, 178–9
Satin, Fedor, 178–9
Saul, *see* Paul, St
Savva Shakh, hermit, 268–9, 272–3
Savvaty of Solovki, St, 264–5
Schlichting, Albert, viii
Scythians, 162–3
Selivan, 82–3
Semen Yakovlevich, 210–11
Semenov, P., 112 n.
Semigallia, *see* Courland
Septuagint, 173 n., 174 n.
Serebryany, *see* Obolensky-Serebryany
Sergy of Radonezh, St, 76 n., 81 n., 252–3

Printed in the United States
139542LV00002BA/19/P